ZIKH RASNA

𐌀𐌍𐌔𐌀𐌐 𐌋𐌉𐌉
ZIKH RASNA

A Manual of the Etruscan Language and Inscriptions

Rex E. Wallace

Beech Stave Press

Ann Arbor • New York

Typeset with X∃TEX using the Gentium typeface designed by Victor Gualt-ney and Etrusco by James Patterson

Library of Congress Cataloging-in-Publication Data

Wallace, Rex.
  Zikh Rasna: a manual of the Etruscan language and inscriptions / Rex E.
  Wallace.
      p. cm.
  Includes bibliographical references and index.
  ISBN 978-0-9747927-4-3 (alk. paper)
1. Etruscan language–Grammar. 2. Inscriptions, Etruscan. I. Title.
P945.W35 2008
499′.94–dc22

                                                              2008028165

Printed in the United States of America

12 11 10 09 08   6 5 4 3 2 1

CONTENTS

    Introduction 43 • Roots and Stems 44 • Word Classes 45
    • Nouns and Noun Stems 45 • Cases 46 • Plurals 49 • Gram-
    matical Gender 51 • Noun-forming Suffixes 51 • Adjec-
    tives 52 • Adjective-forming Suffixes 53 • Numbers 54

5. Pronouns and the Article 57

    Introduction 57 • Personal Pronouns 58 • Demonstra-
    tives 59 • The Article 63 • Other Pronominal Forms 64

6. Verbs and Participles 67

    Introduction 67 • Verbs 67 • Participles 72 • Verb-forming
    Suffixes 76

7. Nomenclature 77

    Introduction 77 • Origins and Development 79 • Nomen 80
    • Praenomen 81 • Cognomen 82 • Patronymic, Metronym-
    ic, and Gamonymic 83 • Other Familial Relationships 85
    • Slaves and Ex-slaves 85 • Inflectional Features 88 • Ono-
    mastic Phrases 89 • Origin and Formation of Names 92

8. Syntax 95

    Introduction 95 • Functions of Cases 95 • Postpositions 102
    • Absolute Construction 104 • Noun Phrases with *avil*
    'year' 105 • Syntax of the Article 106 • Demonstrative
    Pronouns 107 • Relative Pronouns 109 • Agreement 110
    • Sentence Types 111 • Mood 112 • Coordination and Sub-
    ordination 114 • Order of Constituents 119

9. Vocabulary 123

    Introduction 123 • Native Vocabulary 123 • Borrowings
    from Greek 127 • Borrowings from Sabellic Languages 128
    • Borrowings from Latin and Faliscan 128 • Etruscan Words
    in Latin 129 • An Etruscan Word in Faliscan 131 • Theo-
    nyms 131 • Place-names 133

PREFACE AND ACKNOWLEDGMENTS

Zikh Rasna was written to provide those interested in Etruscan language studies with an up-to-date grammatical overview of the language as well as an introduction to the interpretation of inscriptions and the analysis of word-forms. The primary focus is linguistic, but I have attempted to accommodate the needs of non-specialists by keeping the technical terminology to a reasonable minimum and by being as explicit as I could possibly be about the analysis of Etruscan word-forms in inscriptions. Every inscription cited in the book is accompanied by a translation and a word-by-word analysis.

The Etruscan language as it was written covers a chronological span of approximately 750 years (ca. 700 BCE–50 CE). As a result there is a substantial diachronic element present in the discussion of both the writing system and the grammatical system. Inscriptions that are discussed in the text and that are cited as examples are drawn from the entire chronological span of the language.

The book is organized into twelve chapters. Chapter 1 is an introduction to Etruscan and to the methods that linguists employ to analyze the language. Chapter 2 is an overview of the alphabet and writing system. Chapters 3 through 8 cover grammatical material (3: Phonology; 4: Morphology of Nouns and Adjectives; 5: Pronouns and Article; 6: Verbs and Participles; 7: Nomenclature; 8: Syntax). Chapter 7 belongs to the grammatical section because it tackles the morphology of Etruscan names and their syntactic relationships within the onomastic phrase. Chapter 9 is a survey of vocabulary. Chapters 10 and 11 are concerned with the analysis of Etruscan texts. Chapter 10 is a survey of inscriptions that are short and in most instances formulaic in terms of their syntactic structure. Chapter 11 focuses on the *Tabula Cortonensis*, a longer and syntactically more sophisticated inscription and therefore much more difficult to analyze and interpret. Chapter 12 is an examination of the possible relationship of Etruscan to other languages.

Almost every page of the text reveals my indebtedness to the work of other scholars in the field of Etruscan language studies. I take this opportunity to mention Luciano Agostiniani, Mauro Cristofani, Giovanni Colonna, Carlo de Simone, Karl Olzscha, Massimo Pallottino, and the late Helmut Rix. Since the book is introductory in nature, I have not attempted to cite the source of every idea or claim presented here. References to important articles and books are provided in every chapter following the relevant paragraphs or sections. This serves as a comprehensive acknowledgement of the debt that I owe those who work in this field. It also serves as a guide for readers wishing to explore topics that are of special interest.

Etruscan language studies have moved forward dramatically in the last fifty years. A much larger body of grammatical knowledge now exists about which all scholars working on the language agree. Nevertheless, it is safe to say that disagreement about fundamental features of the grammatical system and the lexicon remains. As a result, an introduction such as this one, even though aiming at the target of *communis opinio*, must necessarily include personal views on controversial aspects of the analysis of the language. The reader is urged to keep this critical point in mind at all times.

Acknowledgments

I would like to thank those colleagues who were instrumental in helping me complete this project: first and foremost, my good friend Bill Regier (University of Illinois), who discussed the minutiae of every chapter with me and who saved me from many errors and infelicities; Miles Beckwith (Iona College) and Michael Weiss (Cornell University), who offered very thoughtful notes on the chapters dealing with the description of phonology, morphology, and syntax; Don Ringe (University of Pennsylvania), who shared his ideas on Etruscan and linguistic relationships; Larissa Bonfante (New York University), who provided numerous bibliographic references and notices for Etruscan inscriptions; and Benjamin Fortson (University of Michigan), who edited the manuscript and helped me rewrite passages that were not very clearly worded. I appreciate the care with which he and his co-editor, Steve Peter, prepared the book for publication. Errors that remain are my responsibility.

James Patterson, a graduate student at the University of Texas, Austin, developed the Etruscan fonts used in the text to represent Etruscan letter-forms. I am grateful to him for letting me put them to the test. It is also my pleasure to acknowledge the assistance of my students: Andreas Breuing, Dustin Brownell, Konstantina Choros, and Jesse Sawyer, who helped with the construction of the index; and Daeil Kim, who converted the drawings of inscriptions into digital files.

The drawings of inscriptions printed in the text were copied from those originally published in *Studi Etruschi*. I thank the editor of the journal, Giovannangelo Camporeale, for giving me permission to publish copies.

This book is dedicated to Maureen Ryan. She enthusiastically supports my interest in Etruscan language studies and she cheerfully accompanies me on my quests to inspect inscriptions at museums, exhibitions, and archaeological sites. I cannot imagine a more patient and understanding partner. *Zikh mlakh mlakasi.*

Rex E. Wallace
University of Massachusetts Amherst
August 2007

ABBREVIATIONS AND CONVENTIONS

Abbreviations of Etruscan Cities and Regions

1. The following abbreviations of Etruscan cities and regions are used in this text: AS = Ager Saenensis; AT = Ager Tarquiniensis; AV = Ager Vulcentanus; Cl = Clusium; Cm = Campania; Co = Cortona; Cr = Caere; Fa = Falerii et Ager Faliscus; Fs = Faesulae; La = Latium; Li = Liguria; Pe = Perusia; Po = Populonia; Ru = Rusellae; Sp = Spina; Ta = Tarquinia; Um = Umbria; Vc = Vulci; Ve = Veii; Vn = Vetulonia; Vs = Volsinii; Vt = Volaterrae.

Grammatical Abbreviations

2. The following abbreviations are used in the description of grammatical features and word classes: NOM = nominative; ACC = accusative; GEN = genitive; PERT = pertinentive; LOC = locative; ABL = ablative; ANIM = animate; INANIM = inanimate; FEM = feminine; MASC = masc; SG = singular; PL = plural; PRES = present; ACT = active; PASS = passive; IMPV = imperative; ART = article; DEM = demonstrative; DEF = definite; INDEF = indefinite; PERS = person; PRO = pronoun; PART = particle; POST = postposition; SUBORD = subordinator.

Onomastic Abbreviations

3. The following abbreviations are used to describe onomastic phrases: PRAE = praenomen (personal name); COGN = cognomen (personal or familial name); FEM = feminine; MASC = masculine. Divinities, heroes, and mythological figures are identified by means of the abbreviation THEO = theonym.

Bibliographic Abbreviations

4. The following abbreviations are used in the citation of bibliographic references:

AGI = Archivio glottologico italiano
AION = Annali dell' Istituto Universitario Orientale di Napoli, Sezione linguistica

AMAP = Atti e Memorie dell'Accademia Petrarca di Lettere, Arti, e Scienze
AnnMuseoFaina = Annali della Fondazione per il Museo "Claudio Faina"
ANRW = Temporini, Hildegard, ed. 1972. *Aufstieg und Niedergang der römischen Welt: Geschichte und Kultur Roms im Spiegel der neueren Forschung. Part I: Von den Anfängen Roms bis zum Ausgang der Republik.* Berlin: de Gruyter.
ANSP = Annali della Scuola Normale Superiore di Pisa, Classe di lettere e filosofia
AÖAW = Anzeiger der Österreichischen Akademie der Wissenschaften in Wien
ArchClass = Archeologia Classica
BdA = Bolletino d'Arte del Ministro per i Beni Culturali e Ambientali
BNF = Beiträge zur Namenforschung
CRAI = Comptes Rendus de l'Académie des Inscriptions et Belles-Lettres
ENews = Etruscan News: Newsletter of the American Section of the Institute for Etruscan and Italic Studies
HS = Historische Sprachforschung
JIES = Journal of Indo-European Studies
InL = Incontri Linguistici
MDAI(R) = Mitteilungen des Deutschen Archäologischen Instituts, Römische Abteilung
MH = Museum Helveticum: Revue suisse pour l'étude de l'antiquité classique
MSS = Münchener Studien zur Sprachwissenschaft
PBSR = Papers of the British School at Rome
PP = La Parola del Passato: Rivista di Studi Antichi
REE = Rivista di Epigrafia Etrusca
REL = Revue des Études Latines
RFIC = Rivista di Filologia e di Istruzione Classica
S&C = Scrittura e Civiltà
SCO = Studi Classici e Orientali
SE = Studi Etruschi
SciAnt = Scienze dell'Antichità: Storia, Archeologia, Antropologia
ZPE = Zeitschrift für Papyrologie und Epigraphik

Citation of Inscriptions and Words

5. Etruscan inscriptions published before 1989 are cited from *Etruskische Texte*, the corpus of Etruscan inscriptions edited by Helmut Rix et al. I follow the readings for inscriptions given in *Etruskische Texte* unless otherwise noted. I also employ Rix's conventions for citing and formatting inscriptions, except that I use a pipe (see below) to indicate line divisions. Inscriptions published after 1989 are cited from *Etruscan Texts Project* (abbreviated ETP), an on-line supplement to *Etruskische Texte*. Inscriptions cited from this source are prefixed with the abbreviation ETP. (For information about ETP on-line, the reader is directed to the project's Web site: etp.classics.umass.edu.)

The following abbreviations are employed in the citation of inscriptions:

EG = Guarducci, *Epigrafia Greca I*
ET = Rix et al., *Etruskische Texte*
ETP = Wallace, Shamgochian, and Patterson, *Etruscan Texts Project* on-line
FID = Hartmann, *Die frühlateinischen Inschriften und ihre Datierung*
LF = Giacomelli, *La Lingua falisca*
RI = Schumacher, *Die rätischen Inschriften*
ST = Rix, *Sabellische Texte*

6. Inscriptions written in native Italic alphabets (Etruscan, Faliscan, Oscan) are transcribed in **boldface** type; Lemnian and Raetic inscriptions are also transcribed in boldface. Latin inscriptions are transcribed in SMALL CAPITALS. Greek words are printed in a Greek font. Words cited from non-epigraphic sources are printed in *italics*.

7. The following epigraphic symbols are employed in the presentation of inscriptions in transcription:

Round brackets **(abc)** indicate characters omitted by the engraver, generally for the purpose of abbreviation.

Curly brackets **{abc}** indicate extra characters erroneously incised by the engraver.

Square brackets **[abc]** indicate characters which have been restored or which can no longer be read.

Angled brackets **<abc>** indicate characters omitted by the engraver and supplied by the editor; angled brackets are also used to indicate characters that have been supplied by the editor in place of characters erroneously incised by a scribe.

The underdot **a̞** indicates characters that are damaged and/or are no longer clearly legible.

The pipe **|** indicates a line-break.

8. The format for the citation of inscriptions varies depending on the purpose of the citation. When citing an inscription for the purpose of analysis and interpretation, I include the following information: (1) reference number, findspot, date; (2) the text of the inscription; (3) a translation of the inscription; and (4) a grammatical analysis of the word-forms in the inscription. An example is cited below.

AT 1.35, Ager Tarquiniensis (Tuscania), ca. 200 BCE
sarcophagus (tufa)

eca mutna velus | statlanes lari|sal
'This (is) the sarcophagus of Vel Statlanes, (son) of Laris.'

eca 'this', DEM PRO, NOM; **mutna** 'sarcophagus', NOM/ACC; **velus** 'Vel',
MASC PRAE, 1ST GEN; **statlanes** 'Statlanes', MASC NOMEN, 1ST GEN;
larisal 'Laris', MASC PRAE, 2ND GEN

When citing inscriptions for the purposes of illustrating information
about features of morphology or syntax, I use a pared-down version of
the citation form: inscription, reference number, translation, and word-
by-word analysis.

eca mutna velθurus | veluóla (AT 1.38)
'This (is) the sarcophagus of Velthur, the (son) of Vel.'

eca 'this', DEM PRO, NOM; **mutna** 'sarcophagus', NOM/ACC; **velθurus**
'Velthur', MASC PRAE, 1ST GEN; **veluóla** = velus 'Vel', MASC PRAE, 1ST GEN
+ -óla 'the', DEF ART, 2ND GEN

9. Hypothetically reconstructed Etruscan words are preceded by an
asterisk, e.g. *rat^h-i-t^hi*. If the meanings of Etruscan words are highly conjectural, then the meaning is followed by a question mark within parentheses, e.g. **fratuce** 'incised (?)'.

Citation of Sounds

10. The sounds of Etruscan are transcribed using symbols from the
International Phonetic Alphabet. When a distinctive sound is cited in pho-
nemic representation, it is placed within oblique lines, e.g., /m/. Vowel
length is indicated by a colon-like symbol after the vowel sign in question;
thus, /a:/ represents a long *a*-sound. When a more detailed representation of a sound is required, that is to say, when there is need of a phonetic
representation, the sound is placed within square brackets, thus [p].

Names of Letters of the Alphabet

11. The names of the letters of the alphabet are: a (𐌀) = *alpha*; b (𐌁) =
beta; c (𐌂) = *gamma*; d (𐌃) = *delta*; e (𐌄) = *epsilon*; v (𐌅) = *wau (digamma)*; z (𐌆)
= *zeta*; h (𐌇) = *heta*; (⊗) = *theta*; i (𐌉) = *iota*; k (𐌊) = *kappa*; l (𐌋) = *lambda*; m
(𐌌) = *mu*; n (𐌍) = *nu*; ṡ (𐌎) = *samek*; o (O) = *omicron*; p (𐌐) = *pi*; σ (𐌑) = *sade*;
q (𐌘) = *qoppa*; r (𐌓) = *rho*; s (𐌔) = three-bar *sigma*; ç (ϟ, ϟ) = four-bar and

multi-bar *sigmas*; t (T) = *tau*; u (V, Y) = *upsilon*; š (X) = *ksi*; φ (Φ) = *phi*; χ (Y) = *khi*.

Transcription of Etruscan Letters

12. The letters in the following list are those found on the *Tavola d'Al-begna di Marsiliana*. This abecedarium lists the full panoply of letters in-herited from the Euboean Greek alphabet. Some of the letters in this inventory, e.g. ⩍, ⩌, O, ⊞, were never used to write Etruscan inscriptions, others, e.g. X, were used sporadically or only for a short period of time. By the fifth century BCE these five letters were eliminated from the Etruscan alphabet.

Etruscan letter	transcription	sound
Ａ	a	/a/, as in English *pop*
⩍	b	
)	c	/k/, as in English *lack*
⩌	d	
⨅	e/ê	/e/, as in English *get*
⅂	v	/w/, as in English *win*
I	z	/tˢ/, as in English *cents*
⊟	h	/h/, as in English *hot*
⊕	θ	/tʰ/, as in English *top*
⅄	k	/k/, as in English *lack*
⅃	l	/l/, as in English *leaf*
Ｍ	m	/m/, as in English *man*
Ⅿ	n	/n/, as in English *nerd*
⊞	ṡ	
O	o	
Ｍ	σ/ό	/s/, as in English *sin*; /ʃ/, as in English *shin*
⼀	p	/p/, as in English *map*
⼼	q	/k/, as in English *lack*
⼌	r	/r/, as in Italian *roba*
⼌	s/ś	/s/, as in English *sin*; /ʃ/, as in English *shin*
⼌ ⼌	ç/ζ	/s/, as in English *sin*; /ʃ/, as in English *shin*
T	t	/t/, as in English *mat*
V	u	/u/, as in English *good*
X	š	/s/, as in English *sin*
Φ	φ	/pʰ/, as in English *pat*
Y	χ	/kʰ/, as in English *cat*
8	f	/f/, as in English *fat*

13. The letters representing the sibilant sounds /s/ and /ʃ/ are transcribed in the following way:

s = three-bar *sigma*
ς = *sigma* with four bars or more
σ = *sade*
ṡ = *samek*
ś = *ksi* (the sign of the cross).

The palatal sibilant /ʃ/ is always marked by a diacritic in the form of an acute stroke placed above the letter, regardless of its form. When the palatal sibilant /ʃ/ is spelled by means of three-bar *sigma* it is written as ś. When it is spelled by means of **sade**, it is written as ό. The dental sibilant is never spelled with the diacritic. Thus, when the dental sibilant /s/ is spelled by three-bar *sigma* it is written as s, and when it is spelled by *sade* it is written as σ. At Caere the palatal sibilant is written as a four-bar *sigma*. This is transcribed as ς. The Etruscan word meaning 'tomb' has the phonological representation /ʃutʰi/. The word-initial sibilant in /ʃutʰi/ is found with three spellings during the Neo-Etruscan period. These are cited below.

(a) όuθi at Tarquinia
(b) ςuθi at Caere
(c) śuθi at Clusium

The letter *ksi* (X) is transcribed as ś. This letter was also used to spell the dental sibilant /s/, but primarily at Veii and Caere and then only for a short period of time spanning the end of the seventh and the beginning of the sixth centuries BCE. The letter *samek* was a 'dead' letter in the Etruscan alphabet; that is to say, it was not employed to represent sounds in Etruscan inscriptions. This letter appears only in *abecedaria* incised during the Archaic period.

14. In the orthographic system employed by scribes at Cortona, the letter *epsilon* stood for two sounds. If the letter was written in retrograde direction, it spelled a vowel that was distinct, probably in quality (see Chapter 3), from the *epsilon* that was written in the direction of writing. We transcribe retrograde *epsilon* at Cortona by means of *e* with a circumflex over it, namely, ê.

15. Letters that are pointed with syllabic puncts are transcribed by means of periods that are placed on both sides of the letter in question in the following manner, .s. Etruscan words are sometimes separated by word-dividers, e.g. **mi · veneluσ**. A word-divider may take the form of a single point set at mid-line level as in the example cited above, or it may be two, three, or even four points lined up vertically as in **mi : karkuσ** or

vel **:** matunas. Word-dividers with one, two and three points are reproduced in this text. Word-dividers with more than three points are transcribed by **:** .

Transliteration in Translations of Etruscan

16. When Etruscan inscriptions are translated into English, I use the
digraphs *ph*, *th*, *kh* to render the Etruscan letters φ (**Φ**), θ (**⊕**), χ (**Υ**). I use
sh to spell the palatal sibilant and *ts* to spell *zeta*.

MAPS

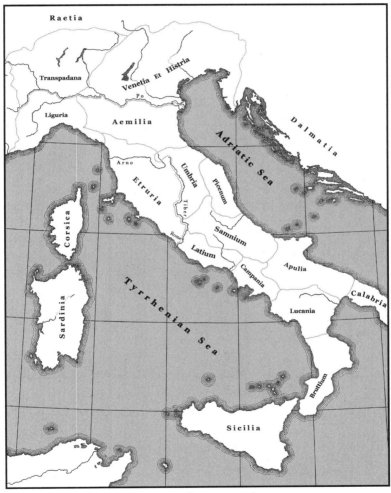

Regions of Ancient Italy

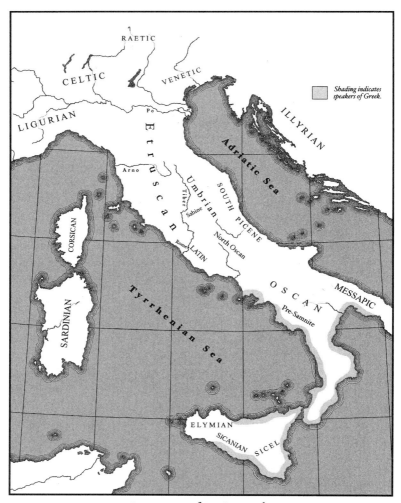

Languages of Ancient Italy

LIST OF FIGURES

1 OVERVIEW OF THE STUDY OF ETRUSCAN

Introduction

1.1 In the words of the ancient Greek historian Dionysius of Halicarnassus, the Etruscan people were like no other because of their language (*Roman Antiquities* I, 30). Modern investigation bears this out. The Etruscan language stands apart from others spoken in ancient Italy with respect to its linguistic structure and its non-Indo-European pedigree.

1.2 The historical homeland of the Etruscans was Etruria. This territory was situated to the north of Rome; it was bounded on the south and the east by the Tiber River, on the north by the Tuscan Apennines, and on the west by the Tyrrhenian Sea (maps 1 and 2). Etruscan was also spoken beyond the confines of Etruria as a result of colonial expansion, commercial ventures, and piracy.

1.3 The Etruscan language has no modern descendants. The spread of Latin was ultimately responsible for its demise. Southern Etruria came under the control of Rome at the beginning of the fourth century BCE. By the end of the third century most of Etruria was, if not officially, effectively subject to Roman authority. The installation of Roman colonies in Etruria during the third and second centuries had a great impact on the vitality of the Etruscan language. As a result of contact with Latin speakers, and the social, political, and economic advantages of speaking Latin, the number of monolingual speakers of Etruscan steadily declined. During the course of the first century BCE, Latin replaced Etruscan as the dominant language in Etruria. Etruscan may have been learned as a first language as late as the middle of the first century CE, but there is no evidence to suggest that it survived as a native tongue much beyond that. Ancient literary sources record that Etruscan priests who specialized in haruspicy and in other forms of divination continued to conduct ceremonies throughout the imperial period and into the Middle Ages, and it is possible that priests recited prayers in Etruscan on these occasions. If so,

Etruscan may have survived as a liturgical language long after it ceased to be used as a language of everyday communication.

Etruscan Inscriptions

1.4 Etruscan is known almost exclusively from inscriptions (including painted texts [*dipinti*] and seals for stamping texts), of which more than 10,000 have been recovered. If pieces of ceramic with potters' marks and inscribed pan and cover tiles are added to this number, the total is closer to 12,000. The only surviving text that is not an inscription is the *Liber Linteus Zagrebiensis*, which was written in ink on linen.

1.5 The Etruscan language had a tradition of writing that spanned approximately 750 years. The earliest inscription dates to ca. 700 BCE; the latest inscriptions can be assigned to the period of the early Roman emperors.

Etruscan inscriptions are generally divided into two chronological layers: Archaic Etruscan and Neo-Etruscan. The linguistic feature that serves as the boundary marker for the chronological division is vowel syncope, a phonological change by which vowels in medial syllables were lost, e.g. Archaic Etruscan **zamaθi** 'gold (fibula)' vs. Neo-Etruscan **zamθi** (see §3.20). This change began to be recorded in Etruscan inscriptions around 470 BCE give or take a decade. The highest percentage of surviving inscriptions belongs to the Neo-Etruscan period. The number of Archaic Etruscan inscriptions is around 700 or a few more.

1.6 Evidence for the Etruscan language has been recovered principally from the major inhabited areas of Etruria. The following Etruscan cities are significant from the point of view of Etruscan epigraphy (the Latin and Etruscan names, where they are known, are cited in parentheses): Arezzo (*Arretium*, Etruscan *Aritim-*), Chiusi (*Clusium*, Etruscan *Cleusi-* [?]), Cortona (Etruscan *Curtun-* [?]), Cerveteri (*Caere*, Etruscan *Kaiseri-*), Fiesole (*Faesulae*), Orvieto (*Volsinii*, Etruscan *Velzna-*), Perugia (*Perusia*, Etruscan *Pershia-*), Pisa (*Pisae*), Populonia (Etruscan *Pupluna*, *Pufluna*), Roselle (*Rusellae*), Tarquinia (*Tarquinii*, Etruscan *Tarχna-*), Veio (*Veii*), Vetulonia (*Vetulonia*), Volterra (*Volaterrae*, Etruscan *Velaθri*), and Vulci (Etruscan *Velca-*).

Etruscans also inhabited urban centers beyond the borders of Etruria proper. Etruscan inscriptions have been recovered from northern Italy in Aemilia (Bologna, Ravenna, Rubiera, Adria, Spina) and Liguria (Genova), and from southern Italy in Campania (Capua, Etruscan *Capua-*, Nola, Pompeii, Pontecagnano). For several centuries, Etruscan speakers inhabited important settlements in Latium (Rome, Praeneste).

Evidence for the Etruscan language outside of the Italian peninsula is much less abundant, but there are tantalizing signs of the mobility of Etruscan speakers. Excavation at Aleria on the island of Corsica has yielded pottery with Etruscan inscriptions. An Etruscan inscription has been discovered in southern France (*Gallia Narbonensis*) at Pech Maho. It can be attributed to Etruscans who were engaged in a commercial enterprise. A series of boundary stones discovered at Smindja in Tunisia suggest that a contingent of Etruscans settled in this area in the second or first century BCE, perhaps as a result of increasing pressure from Roman colonization in northern Etruria. One of the most important Etruscan documents in our possession, the *Liber Linteus Zagrebiensis*, was discovered in Egypt. It is likely—though we do not know for certain—that the linen book was produced in Etruria and carried abroad.

1.7 Etruscan inscriptions belong in large part to epigraphic categories that are familiar to those who study ancient Greek and Latin inscriptions: epitaphs, proprietary inscriptions, inscribed gifts, votive dedications, inscriptions on private buildings (including tombs), prohibitions, artisans' signatures, curse tablets, and manufacturers' names. Mirrors, vases, the walls of tombs, and sarcophagi were occasionally incised or painted with captions, that is, with the name of the figure that was portrayed (by painting or through engraving) on the object or fabric in question. Inscriptions belonging to the categories listed above make up approximately 90% of the epigraphic corpus. Most of these texts are very short; many, particularly epitaphs, bear only names.

Examples of Etruscan inscriptions belonging to the major epigraphic categories are cited in (1). For details about presentation, transcription, and epigraphic notation the reader is referred to *Abbreviations and Conventions* on pages iii–iv.

(1) Etruscan inscriptions by epigraphic category

(a) funerary inscription
ETP 192, Ager Tarquiniensis (Tuscania), 275–250 BCE
sarcophagus (stone)

cleusinas : laris : larisal : clan
'Laris Cleusinas, son of Laris'

cleusinas 'Cleusinas', MASC NOMEN, 1ST GEN; laris 'Laris' MASC PRAE, NOM/ACC; larisal 'Laris', MASC PRAE, 2ND GEN; clan 'son', NOM/ACC

(b) proprietary inscription
Cr 2.20, Caere, 675–650 BCE container (ceramic)

mi karkanas θahvna
'I (am) the container of Karkana'

mi 'I', 1ST PERS PRO, NOM; **karkanas** 'Karkana', MASC PRAE, 1ST GEN;
θahvna 'container', NOM/ACC

(c) prohibition
Cm 2.46, Campania (Suessula), 500–450 BCE bowl (ceramic)

mi e.i. mi.n.pi capi mi nunar
θevru.c.l.na.s.
qupe.s. fulu.ó.la
'Don't take me. I (am) *nunar*. (I am the property) of Qupe
Thevruclnas, the (son) of Fulu.'

mi 'I', 1ST PERS PRO, NOM; e.i. 'not', NEG; **mi.n.pi** = mi.n. 'me', 1ST PERS
PRO, ACC + -pi '?', ENCLITIC PART (?); **capi** 'take', IMPV; **mi** 'I', 1ST PERS PRO,
NOM; **nunar** '?'; θevru.c.l.na.s. 'Thevruclnas', MASC NOMEN, 1ST GEN;
qupe.s. 'Qupe', MASC PRAE, 1ST GEN; **fulu.ó.la** = fulus 'Fulu', MASC PRAE,
1ST GEN + -ó.la 'the', DEF ART, 2ND GEN

(d) inscribed gift
ETP 269, origin unknown, 625–600 BCE kantharos (bucchero)

mini muluvanice tetana ve.l.ka.s.na.s. veleliiasi
'Tetana Velkasnas gave me to/for Veleliia.'

mini 'me', 1ST PERS PRO, ACC; **muluvanice** 'gave', PAST ACT; **tetana**,
'Tetana', MASC PRAE, NOM/ACC; ve.l.ka.s.na.s. 'Velkasnas', MASC NOMEN,
1ST GEN; **veleliiasi** 'Velelia', FEM PRAE, 1ST PERT

(e) votive dedication
Ta 3.2, Tarquinia, ca. 580 BCE Attic vase (ceramic)

itun turuce vene.l a.telinas. tinas cliniiaras
'Venel Atelinas dedicated this (vase) to the sons of Tinia.'

itun 'this', DEM PRO, ACC; **turuce** 'dedicated', PAST ACT; **vene.l** 'Venel',
MASC PRAE, NOM/ACC; a.telinas. 'Atelinas', MASC NOMEN, 1ST GEN; **tinas**
'Tinia', THEO, 1ST GEN; **cliniiaras** 'son', ANIM PL, GEN

(f) text of religious nature
ETP 251, Pyrgi, 500–450 BCE fragment of skyphos (ceramic)

mi menervas
'I (was dedicated) to Menerva'

mi 'I', 1ST PERS PRO, NOM; menervas 'Menerva', THEO, 1ST GEN

(g) tomb construction
Ru 5.1, Rusellae, 300–200 BCE stone (tufa)

vl · afuna · vl · pes
naliśa · cn · śuθi
ceriχunce
'Vel Afuna, (son) of Vel and Pesnei, built this tomb.'

vl, abbrev. for vel 'Vel', MASC PRAE, NOM/ACC; afuna 'Afuna', MASC NOMEN,
NOM/ACC; vl, abbrev. for velus 'Vel', MASC PRAE, 1ST GEN; pesnaliśa =
pesnal 'Pesnei', FEM NOMEN, 2ND GEN + -iśa 'the', DEF ART, NOM; cn 'this',
DEM PRO, ACC; śuθi 'tomb', NOM/ACC; ceriχunce 'built', PAST ACT

(h) artisan's inscription
Ve 6.2, Veii, 650–625 BCE vase (bucchero)

mi<ni> mamarce zinace
'Mamarce made me.'

mi<ni> 'me', 1ST PERS PRO, ACC; mamarce 'Mamarce', MASC PRAE, NOM/
ACC; zinace 'made', PAST ACT

(i) *tessera hospitalis*
ETP 362, Ager Saenensis (Poggio Civitate, Murlo), ca. 600 BCE
fragment of tessera (ivory)

[mi veleli]as vheisalna[ia]
'I (belong to) Velelia Feysalnai'

[mi] 1ST PERS PRO, NOM; [veleli]as FEM PRAE, 1ST GEN; vheisalna[ia]
'Feysalnai', FEM NOMEN, 2ND GEN

(j) caption
Ta 7.3, Tarquinia, ca. 525 BCE painted on wall of tomb next to
figure

θanaχvil
'Thanakhvil'

θanaχvil 'Thanakhvil', FEM PRAE, NOM/ACC

(k) alphabet (abecedarium)
     Cr 9.1, Caere, 675–650 BCE vase (bucchero)

a b c d e v z h θ k l m n š o p σ q r ç t u š φ χ

1.7.1 The standard edition of Etruscan inscriptions is Helmut Rix *et al., Etruskische Texte* (1991),
which includes those inscriptions published up to 1990, the point at which the text was delivered
for publication. Inscriptions are collected and published on an annual basis in *Rivista epigrafia
etrusca* (REE), which is the epigraphic section of the journal *Studi Etruschi* (SE). *Etruscan Texts Project*,
an on-line edition of Etruscan inscriptions that have been recovered since 1990, is available at
etp.classics.umass.edu. The texts are accompanied by a database that permits investigators to
search the corpus by epigraphic type, region, date, find-spot, and so forth. After a hiatus of over 35
years, publication of the *Corpus Inscriptionum Etruscarum*, the *editio major* of Etruscan inscriptions,
resumed in 1970 under the direction of the late Mauro Cristofani. Cristofani completed the final
fascicle of volume II and oversaw the publication of the first two fascicles of volume III (CIE III, 1
[*Tarquinii cum agro*] in 1982; III, 2 [*Volsinii cum agro*] in 1987), and the final fascicle of volume II, CIE
II, 2 (*Latium et Campania*) in 1996. Volume III, 4 was published in 2004 and work is now under way
on the fascicle containing *instrumenta* from Caere and environs.

1.8 Several texts do not fit into the categories described in §1.7. These
are the longest and most famous texts. Short descriptions are provided
below.

(a) The *Liber Linteus Zagrebiensis* stands apart from all other Etruscan
documents. First, it is not an inscription; it was written in black ink on
linen. Second, it is by far the longest text in the corpus. Approximately
half of the linen book is preserved; we possess almost 200 lines of text,
which yield about 1300 word-forms. The *Liber Linteus* was written in a
variety of Etruscan that can be attributed to a northern Etruscan prov-
enance, possibly Volaterrae or Clusium. Etruscans who immigrated to
Egypt during the late Ptolemaic period carried the document with them.
At some point the book lost its religious significance and it was ripped
into strips in order to bind the remains of a young woman. The Etruscan
writing on the linen that covered the mummy was not discovered until
scientists at the archaeological museum in Zagreb began their analysis of
the body.
    The text was a calendar that listed the dates for the celebration of re-
ligious festivals, gave the names of the deities to be honored at them, and
described the types of ritual actions to be performed and prayers to be
recited.

(b) The *Tabula Capuana* is a *tegola* or tile made of terracotta. The upper
portion of the tile is damaged and the middle section is in poor condition.
Sixty lines of text have survived; approximately 300 words can be read.
Horizontal lines divided the text into sections or "chapters". The content

of the *Tabula* seems to be similar to that of the *Liber Linteus*. It consists of a description of the ritual acts to be completed by priests in honor of certain divinities. The *Tabula* dates to the middle of the fifth century BCE.

(c) The so-called *Piombo di Magliano*, the leaden disk of Magliano, was also inscribed with religious prescriptions. They were written in a spiral on both sides of the disk. The disk dates to ca. 400 BCE.

(d) The *Cippus Perusinus* is a contract or an agreement between two important Etruscan families, the Afuna and the Velthina, about access to water. The inscription was incised on two sides of a travertine cippus of rectangular shape. The inscription is set out in 45 lines and includes 130 words. The date of cippus and inscription is the second century BCE.

(e) The recently discovered *Tabula Cortonensis* is also a legal document (for analysis and interpretation see Chapter 11). It refers to the acquisition of property from a certain Petru Shceva on the part of two brothers who belonged to the Cushu family. The inscription was incised on two faces of a bronze tablet that was broken into eight pieces in antiquity. Seven pieces were recovered. The bronze holds 40 lines of text and approximately 200 words. A likely date for the inscription is the end of the third century BCE.

(f) One of the most famous Etruscan artifacts is a bronze model of a liver that was recovered from Piacenza. The surface of the liver was divided into compartments within which were inscribed the names of Etruscan divinities. Models such as these may have been used to train junior members of the organization of diviners in the art of haruspicy. The bronze cannot be dated more precisely than to the final centuries of the Neo-Etruscan period.

(g) The *elogium* of Laris Pulenas was incised on a stone sarcophagus that dates to the first half of the second century BCE. The figure of the deceased was sculpted on the lid of the sarcophagus in the act of presenting a scroll on which can be read his illustrious lineage as well as important details about his role in the political and religious life of the community.

(h) In 1964 the world of Etruscan studies was astounded by the announcement of the recovery of three gold tablets from excavations of a cult sanctuary at Pyrgi, the port city of Caere. Two of the tablets were composed in Etruscan and a third in Punic. The longest Etruscan inscription (tablet A) and the Punic inscription referred to the same event,

namely, the dedication of the sanctuary to Uni/Astarte by the king of
Caere, Thefarie Velianas. This discovery was hailed as the long-sought
breakthrough in Etruscan language studies. Unfortunately, as was soon
determined, even though the Etruscan and Punic texts described the same
event, they did so in such linguistically diverse ways that it was difficult
to compare the syntactic structures of the two languages and extract information about Etruscan. The interpretation of many parts of the inscription remains controversial today. The third tablet (Etruscan tablet
B), on which was incised an Etruscan inscription of 16 words, also has as
its subject Thefarie Velianas. The content of this text is not particularly
clear, though it appears to refer in some way to the king's hopes for the
longevity of the sanctuary.

1.8.1 References to these inscriptions are legion. Here we cite a few of the most important
resources, all of which supply additional bibliography. *Liber Linteus:* For discussion of the difficulties involved in "reconstructing" the text see Roncalli (1985). For analysis and interpretation,
the best places to start are Olzscha (1939) and Steinbauer (1999:315–55). Rix (1991a) and (1997)
are excellent introductions to those sections of the *Liber* that are thought to be prayers. *Tabula
Capuana:* The most up-to-date resource is Cristofani (1995); a selection of photographs appears
at the end of the text. *Piombo di Magliano:* See entry no. 5237 in CIE II, 1, 2. *Cippus Perusinus:* The
latest full-length treatment is Facchetti (2000a). For discussion of the text and its organization
and arrangement on the stone, see Roncalli (1987) and (1990). *Tabula Cortonensis:* Agostiniani and
Nicosia (2000) are responsible for the *editio princeps*; the photographs at the end of the text are
spectacular. For additional references bearing on the interpretation of this important inscription
and for section-by-section commentary, see Chapter 11. *Liver of Piacenza:* For a sensible introduction see Maggiani (1982:53–88). *Elogium of Laris Pulenas:* Heurgon (1957) is a good introduction.
References to earlier work are provided in footnote 1. *Pyrgi Tablets:* See the contributions in *Die
Göttin von Pyrgi* (1981). Steinbauer (1999:196–209) has summary treatments of the Etruscan texts
as well as the Punic.
        For photographs of the *Piombo di Magliano*, the *Cippus Perusinus*, the elogium of Laris Pulenas,
as well as the Pyrgi Tablets, see Borelli and Targia (2004:80–3 [English version]).

1.9 Although the number of Etruscan inscriptions that have survived
is rather high, it would be a mistake to consider this material represen-
tative of all of Etruscan writing. No doubt Etruscan texts were written on
perishable materials such as papyri, parchment, and wax tablets; these
have not survived. Thus it is not necessarily the case that Etruscans did
not compose poetry or record and comment on historical events; envi-
ronmental conditions in Etruria were such that all such materials, if they
once existed, have been lost.

Glossae

1.10 In addition to Etruscan inscriptions, 58 vocabulary items have
come down to us in the form of citations from Greek and Roman writers.
The citations, or *glossae* (glosses) as they are called, are found to a great

extent in the works of later Latin commentators on classical authors, such as Servius who provided notes on the *Aeneid* of Virgil, or in the works of lexicographers and antiquarians, such as Verrius Flaccus, Festus, Hesychius, and Isidore of Seville. A few glosses are embedded in the texts of major authors such as Livy, Suetonius, and Dionysius of Halicarnassus.

The glosses cited in (2) are typical of those in the corpus.

(2)   Glossae

(a)   κάπρα· αἴξ. Τυρρηνοί (Hesychius)
       'kapra "goat". Tyrrhenians'

(b)   *aclus Tuscorum lingua Iunius mensis dicitur* (*Liber Glossarium* m. 1)
       'the month of June is called *aclus* in the language of the Etruscans'

(c)   *atrium appellatum ab Atriatibus Tuscis* (Varro, *Lingua Latina* V, 161)
       '*atrium* gets its name from the Etruscans of Atria'

(d)   αἰσοί· θεοί, ὑπὸ Τυρρηνῶν (Hesychius)
       '*aisoi* "gods", among the Tyrrhenians'

(e)   *quod aesar Etrusca lingua deus uocaretur* (Suetonius, *Augustus* 97)
       'because the word for 'god' in the Etruscan language is *aesar*'

(f)   τὸ λοιπὸν πᾶν ὄνομα θεὸν παρὰ τοῖς Τυρσηνοῖς νοεῖ
       (Dio Cassius, LVI, 29, 4)
       'all the rest of the name [i.e. *aisar*, the end of *Kaisar*] means 'god' in Tyrrhenian'

The vocabulary compiled from historical and literary sources is potentially significant because it covers semantic areas that are not represented in the epigraphic sources, e.g. the names of plants (μούτοθκα 'anagallis'), birds (*capys* 'falcon'), and animals (ἄριμος 'monkey'). Unfortunately, taken as a whole, the glosses are not reliable as a source of information about Etruscan vocabulary. Several glosses are not Etruscan words. For example, gloss (2a) is Latin. Almost all *glossae* are cited in forms that reveal strong Latin and Greek influences. As a result they provide little information about the forms of Etruscan words and their phonological and morphological composition. Nevertheless, a few glosses stand out, such as the names of the months (2b) or the word for 'god' (2d–f), because these words appear in and have contributed to our understanding of Etruscan texts.

1.10.1 Etruscan glosses were published in Pallottino (1968, nos. 801–60) and in Bonfante and Bonfante (2002:186–91). The latter provide English translations for the Greek and Latin. Briquel (2006b) is a concise version of a substantially longer article (2006c) on Etruscan glosses.

Investigative Methods

1.11 The procedures employed to investigate the meanings of Etruscan words and texts are traditionally organized under three headings: the
combinatory method, the bilingual method, and the etymological method.
Descriptions typically treat the methods as independent investigative
techniques. In reality, successful interpretation of texts demands that the
researcher draw on a variety of analytical strategies.

All investigative methods presuppose the division of Etruscan texts
into word-forms. For Neo-Etruscan inscriptions, identifying word-forms
is rarely an issue because punctuation in the form of word-dividers separates the texts into constituents. For Archaic Etruscan inscriptions, which
were often written without any punctuation, identification of word-forms
is made by reference to vocabulary compiled from texts in which words
were separated from one another. It is also possible to isolate word-forms
by identifying suffixes commonly found at the ends of Etruscan words.
Even so, a few inscriptions defy constituent analysis, e.g. Cr 0.1, 0.4, and
Fa 0.4.

Investigative methods also presuppose the grouping of inflectionally
distinct word-forms under the heading of a single word or lexeme. Most
researchers assume that word-forms that are spelled the same—inflectional distinctions aside—belong to the same lexical item. For example,
the word-forms **rasnal**, **rasnas**, **rasna** are classified as a single lexeme,
which we may cite in stem form as **rasna-**. For the interpretation of Etruscan texts this is a reasonable practice because of the difficulties determining the meanings of words. However, homonyms are common cross-
linguistically, so it is necessary to recognize that they may appear also in
Etruscan.

1.11.1 The most accessible discussions of investigative methods are to be found in Agostiniani (1992:59–66), de Simone (1985) and (1989a), Pallottino (1986:312–18) and Rix (1971). For reac-
tions to the methodological issues discussed in Rix (1971), see Cristofani (1972a) and Pfiffig (1974).
De Simone's review (2004b) of Facchetti (2002a) focuses on methodological issues. Facchetti (2005)
is an essay on the methodological problems faced by scholars who interpret Etruscan texts.

1.12 The combinatory method refers to the identification of the meanings of words based exclusively on their distribution within texts. This
method of analysis is indispensable in identifying and describing the syntactic contexts in which words appear, but there are also drawbacks. By itself this method cannot provide much insight into the meanings of words
beyond a very general specification. In actual practice this type of analysis relies on extra-linguistic information such as the archaeological context in which an inscription was found and the type of object on which

an inscription was incised in order to provide a basis for delimiting the semantic area of the words in the text.

1.13 The most productive investigative technique for Etruscan is a form of bilingual comparison or, described more accurately, comparison of parallel inscriptions. This method compares inscriptions in Etruscan with those in other languages of ancient Italy (including Ancient Greek) that are assumed to have the same linguistic content and similar syntactic structures, e.g. epitaphs, votive texts, proprietary texts, and so forth. The basic assumption behind this method is that the peoples of late Iron Age Italy participated in a cultural *koiné* and that this was reflected linguistically in roughly identical syntactic structures across languages for certain categories of inscriptions.

As an example of this method of comparison, we examine the proprietary inscriptions given in (3). The idea here is that the Etruscan inscriptions on ceramic correspond in content and in syntactic structure to those found in Latin and in Faliscan, a language closely related to Latin (3a). One form of this type of inscription has the following syntactic structure: 'I', 1st singular pronoun, nominative + name of type of ceramic, nominative + name of proprietor, genitive.

The Faliscan and Latin pronominal forms below, **eqo** and **eco** /ego:/ respectively, correspond to Etruscan **mi**. The words for the pieces of ceramic correspond, if not in name, at least in structural position. Thus Faliscan **quton{e}**, Latin **urna**, and Etruscan **qutum** and **spanti** all refer to particular styles of ceramic. The remaining words are personal names: Faliscan **uo<l>tenosio**, Latin **tita<s> uendias**, and Etruscan **karkanas** and **larices**. In Latin and Faliscan the names are inflected for genitive case. If Etruscan **karkanas** and **larices** are compared with other members of their paradigms, e.g. **karkana** (Cr 6.1) and **larice** (Ve 3.3), then we hypothesize that the suffix -s in **karkanas** and **larices** had possessive function in Etruscan. More importantly, we conclude that proprietary inscriptions in Etruscan, Latin, and Faliscan were structurally the same: 1st singular pronoun + name of ceramic + name of proprietor inflected in the genitive.

(3)   Proprietary inscriptions

   (a)   Latino-Faliscan proprietary inscriptions

   eqo quton{e} uo<l>tenosio (Faliscan, LF 2, ca. 600 BCE)
   'I (am) the wine pitcher of Voltenos.'

   eqo 'I', 1ST SG PRO, NOM; quton{e} 'wine pitcher', NOM SG; uo<l>tenosio
   'Voltenos', MASC PRAE, NOM SG

eco urna tita<s> uendias (Latin, FID 2.1.11, ca. 600 BCE)
'I (am) the urn of Tita Vendia.'

eco 'I', 1ST SG PRO, NOM SG; urna 'urn', NOM; tita<s> 'Tita', FEM PRAE,
GEN SG; uendias 'Vendia', FEM NOMEN, GEN SG

(b) Etruscan proprietary inscriptions

mi qutum karkanas (Cr 2.18)
'I (am) the wine pitcher of Karkana.'

mi 'I', 1ST SG PRO, NOM; qutum 'wine pitcher', NOM/ACC; karkanas
'Karkana', MASC PRAE, 1ST GEN

mi spanti larices (Cr 2.2)
'I (am) the plate of Larice'

mi 'I', 1ST SG PRO, NOM; spanti 'plate', NOM/ACC; larices 'Larice', MASC
PRAE, 1ST GEN

This method of comparison has been very fruitful when examining inscriptions that are short and formulaic in their structures, but even in these cases difficulties arise because different languages need not convey the same content in linguistically parallel ways. For example, proprietary inscriptions in Oscan, a language of the Sabellic branch of Italic, and in Ancient Greek sometimes exhibit the following syntactic structure: 1st singular verb 'be' + name of ceramic + name of proprietor inflected in genitive case (4).

(4) Oscan and Ancient Greek proprietary inscriptions

(a) vipiieis veliieis culchna sim (Oscan, ST Cm 22)
'I am the drinking cup of Vibis Veliis.'

vipiieis 'Vibis', MASC PRAE, GEN SG; veliieis 'Veliis', MASC NOMEN, GEN SG;
culchna 'drinking cup', NOM SG; sim 'I am', 1ST SG PRES ACT

(b) θαριο ειμι ποτεριον (Greek, EG I, Attica 2)
'I am the drinking cup of Tharios.'

θαριο 'Tharios', MASC NAME, GEN SG; ειμι 'I am', 1ST SG PRES ACT;
ποτεριον 'drinking cup', NOM SG

Comparison of these inscriptions with the Etruscan proprietary inscriptions cited in (4b) might lead an investigator to interpret Etruscan mi as a first singular verb. Fortunately we know this analysis is out of bounds because we have additional information about the syntactic behavior of this pronoun from other inscriptions.

Bilingual comparison has borne fruit also in the case of longer Etruscan texts. Sentences or sections of the Etruscan *Liber Linteus* and the *Tabula Capuana*, which are collections of ritual pronouncements, have been analyzed by means of what are considered to be roughly parallel passages in the Umbrian *Iguvine Tablets*.

1.13.1 See Rix (1985). This article builds on the work of Karl Olszcha. The most important background items are Olszcha (1954), (1955), and (1959).

1.14 The phrase 'picture bilingual' is used to describe the writing that accompanies paintings or engravings on mirrors, vases, and the walls of tombs. For the most part, these texts are captions. They are the names of the deceased, e.g. **araθ vinacna** 'Ara(n)th Vinacna' (Ta 7.17), or the names of mythological or heroic figures, e.g. **caóntra** 'Cassandra' (Vc 7.9), **nestur** 'Nestor' (Vc 7.11), that are depicted in the paintings or engravings. Occasionally, however, inscriptions serve as commentary on or descriptions of the scene itself. In some cases, the scenes that are depicted may provide a general framework for the interpretation of the inscription, and yet it is often difficult, if not impossible, to determine the meanings of nouns and verbs.

A famous example is the *dipinto* on an Attic red-figure vase recovered from Vulci (Vc 7.38). The scene on the vase shows Admetos and Alkestis embracing. They are flanked by two Etruscan demons of the underworld, one of which is securely identified as Charun. Admetos and Alkestis are identified by the captions **atmite** and **alcsti**. The scene is described by sentence (5).

(5)   eca : ersce : nac : aχrum : flerθrce (Vc 7.38)

> eca 'this', DEM PRO, NOM; ersce '?', PAST ACT; nac '?', SUBORD; aχrum 'Acheron', NOM/ACC; flerθrce '?', PAST ACT

The general sense of the scene depicted on the vase is that Alkestis, who has agreed to take her husband's place in Hades, is taking leave of him. Nevertheless, despite the picture, it is impossible to be certain of the meaning of the two most important words in the text, the verbs **ersce** and **flerθrce**, and thus the text's overall meaning.

1.15 The etymological method of investigation seeks to find vocabulary correspondences between languages that the researcher hypothesizes to be related to one another. For Etruscan this has not yielded reliable results because no one has succeeded in establishing vocabulary correspondences between Etruscan and other languages, apart from a few forms in Lemnian and Raetic, that cannot reasonably be attributed to borrowing (see Chapter 12). Nor has anyone shown that regular sound correspondences can be set up between Etruscan and another language, which is the *sine qua non* for securing linguistic relationships. So far the etymological method is of limited value for Etruscan studies. This is not to say that vocabulary matches do not exist between Etruscan and other languages of ancient Italy, e.g. Etruscan **zatlaθ** 'guard' and Latin *satelles*, Etruscan **qutum** 'drinking vessel' and Faliscan **quton**, Etruscan **vinum** 'wine' and Umbrian **vinum**, and Etruscan **aska** 'wine vessel' and Ancient Greek ἀσκός 'wine bag'. Such matches do exist, but they are the result of borrowing (see §§9.11–14).

The temptation to identify Etruscan words based on words that are similar in form in other languages of ancient Italy, particularly in Latin and Ancient Greek, is strong. However, the identification of loanwords in Etruscan based on form alone is risky business when there is no way of independently verifying their meaning.

1.15.1 The etymological method of investigation was practiced in the 19th century and in the early part of the 20th century by scholars and amateur sleuths who were convinced that Etruscan was a member of the Indo-European language family. Wilhelm Deecke discredited this idea in 1875 in his review of Corssen (1874–75), but articles claiming an Indo-European ancestry for Etruscan continue to be written and published, even in reputable journals (see §12.5.1).

1.16 Another investigative method, which may be referred to as the typological method, brings to bear studies in language typology on aspects of the Etruscan grammatical system. Although this type of investigative procedure is not concerned with determining the meanings of words or interpreting texts, it is useful as a means of checking the validity of the grammatical structures that have been posited for Etruscan. By examining the sound systems of the languages of the world it is possible to determine what sets of sounds and what combinations of sounds are commonplace. For example, it is common for languages to have a set of stop consonants that are voiceless and unaspirated, e.g. /p, t, k/, and also a set of stop consonants that are voiceless and aspirated, e.g. /p^h, t^h, k^h/. Indeed, this is the very system of stop consonants that is generally proposed for Etruscan.

1.16.1 Agostiniani (1993) demonstrates the use of typological investigation in Etruscan language studies. Devine (1974) and Boisson (1991) investigate the Etruscan system of stop consonants with reference to typological considerations.

1.17 Our review of investigative methods suggests that the only viable analytical approach to the interpretation of Etruscan inscriptions is one that covers all methodological angles, one in which the investigator examines the archaeological context in which an inscribed object was found, seeks syntactic comparanda among the other languages of ancient Italy, and examines the syntactic contexts in which the words were found. These approaches to the acquisition of the meaning of words must go hand-in-hand with morphological and morphosyntactic analysis, as was demonstrated in our discussion of proprietary inscriptions in §1.13.

1.18 The fact that comparative linguistic methods cannot be used to investigate Etruscan grammar, and the fact that the meanings of words can be won only by methods involving informed guesswork, have great consequences for the nature and general reliability of the information presented in descriptions of the Etruscan grammatical system. For many Etruscan words, it is possible to make informed guesses about the general semantic area to which they belong, but it is not possible to attribute a particularly specific meaning (see, for example, **alice**, which is one of several verbs assigned the meaning 'give'). Despite the obstacles, our understanding of the Etruscan language and of Etruscan inscriptions has improved dramatically in the past half-century. Important advances have been made in our knowledge of the alphabet and the writing systems, the components of grammar, and the interpretation of texts. Although a general consensus is developing concerning the major features of the nouns and adjectives, pronouns, and verbs, it is probably safe to say that no two Etruscologists agree on all of the details of the grammatical system. The fact that much about the Etruscan language remains uncertain makes it a fascinating area of study. This manual makes every effort to point out where disagreements and controversies exist.

2 THE WRITING SYSTEM

Introduction

2.1 The Etruscans borrowed the alphabet from Euboean Greeks who established settlements on the island of Pithekoussai off the coast of Campania in the first half of the eighth century BCE. The precise date of borrowing cannot be determined, but evidence suggests that Etruscans were in contact with Greek colonists by 750 BCE if not earlier, so it is reasonable to think that the alphabet was taken at about that time or shortly thereafter. This idea is supported by the fact that the earliest Etruscan inscription is dated to ca. 700 BCE (Ta 3.1; see Fig. 2.1, p. 23).

2.1.1 The most informative articles on the origins of the Etruscan alphabet are Cristofani 1972b and 1978a. Colonna (1976) focuses on the development of the alphabet within the Archaic period. Cristofani (1978b) addresses the question of the spread of the alphabet to neighboring populations.

2.2 The earliest Etruscan *abecedarium*—a list of the letters of the alphabet arranged in canonical order—had twenty-six letters. It was incised on a miniature ivory writing tablet recovered from the tomb of the Circle of the Ivories at Marsiliana d'Albegna (AV 9.1). Many of the letterforms on the tablet are the ancestors of letters that appear in alphabets in use today throughout much of world, and are therefore recognizable even though written in sinistroverse direction (from right to left) as was usual in Etruscan inscriptions (see further §2.19).

(1) Archaic Etruscan alphabet

𐌙 𐌘 𐌗 𐌖 𐌕 𐌔 𐌓 𐌒 𐌑 𐌐 𐌏 𐌎 𐌍 𐌌 𐌋 𐌊 𐌉 𐌈 𐌇 𐌆 𐌅 𐌄 𐌃 𐌂 𐌁 𐌀 (AV 9.1)
a b c d e v z h θ i k l m n ṡ o p ό q r s t u s̽ φ χ

2.2.1 For a catalogue of Etruscan alphabets see Pandolfini and Prosdocimi 1990:19–94.

2.3 The alphabet borrowed from Euboean Greeks included letterforms that were superfluous from an Etruscan point of view. The Etruscan phonological system had fewer consonantal and vocalic sounds than the Ancient Greek system. As a result, some letters, namely, *beta* (𐌁), *delta* (𐌃), *omicron* (𐌏), and *samek* (𐌎), were not used to represent sounds in the Etruscan phonological system. These letters remained in the alphabet for almost 200 years (700–500 BCE). When Etruscans recited their abc's they were no doubt named in their proper position, but they were never used to write inscriptions. From a functional point of view, they were "dead" letters.

Alphabetic Reforms

2.4 Etruscan abecedaria are preserved in surprisingly large numbers. They were often incised on ceramic objects that were placed in tomb chambers as part of the funereal deposit of the deceased. By examining these alphabets it is possible to follow the changes in the number, forms, and order of letters of the Etruscan alphabet. In (2) we cite four abecedaria that date from the sixth to the third centuries BCE. They were recovered from different areas of Etruria. (2a) and (2c) were recovered from northern Etruria, from the sites of Perusia and Vetulonia respectively. (2b) and (2d) were recovered from sites of Rusellae and of Bomarzo (the *Ager Hortanus*) in central Etruria.

(2) "Reformed" Etruscan alphabets

    (a) V Ⓞ V Τ ₹ ۹ M ٦ ٦ Ψ J ٦ I Θ ⊟ I ₹ ₹ A (Pe 9.1; sixth c. BCE)
        a e v z h θ i k l m n p σ r ś t u φ χ

    (b) 8 Υ Φ V Τ ₹ ٩ Ρ M ٦ ٦ Ψ J ٦ I ⊗ ⊟ I ₹ ₹) A (Ru 9.1;
        sixth c. BCE)
        a c e v z h θ i k l m n p ó q r s t u φ χ f

    (c) [8 V] Ρ V Τ ₹ ٩ M ٦ H Ħ J) I Ο ⊟ Ɛ ₹ ∃ A (Vn 9.1;
        fourth/third c. BCE)
        a e v z h θ i c l m n p σ r ś t u φ [χ f]

    (d) 8 Υ Φ V Τ ₹ ٩ M ٦ ٦ Ψ J I ⊗ ⊟ I ₹ ₹) A (AH 9.2;
        third c. BCE)
        a c e v z h θ i l m n p ó r s t u φ χ f

2.5 The most important alphabetic reforms, as attested by abecedaria, are listed in (3).

(3) Alphabetic reforms

    (a) elimination of 8, ◁, ⊞, Ο, and Χ from the series of letters
    (b) addition of 8 to the end of the series of letters
    (c) elimination of ٦ and ۹ in southern Etruria
    (d) elimination of) and ۹ in northern Etruria
    (e) replacement of ٦ by) in northern Etruria

The most noteworthy observation is the fact that the alphabetic reforms were not implemented at the same time throughout Etruria. For
example, abecedarium (2a) does not yet have reform (b), but it does have
(a) and (d). Abecedarium (2b) has reforms (a) and (b), but does not have
(c). (2c) and (2d) have reforms (a) through (c/d). In addition, alphabet
(3c) has reform (e). This abecedarium is worthy of note for another reason. When the letter Ɔ replaced the letter ᛉ, Ɔ was not retained in its usual
position following *alpha* in the series of letters, but was placed instead in
the position of ᛉ between *iota* and *lambda*.

2.5.1 For an overview of the different phases of development of the alphabet see Pandolfini
and Prosdocimi 1990:11–5.

2.6 By the beginning of the Neo-Etruscan period, regional Etruscan alphabets had settled on twenty letters (abecedaria (2c) and (2d)), but the
letters and the letter-forms that were used differed in form from region
to region within Etruria, sometimes dramatically so. For example, at Asciano in northern Etruria the letter *heta* (= /h/) was written as a circle
with a single cross bar (⊘ ⊖ ⊘) and thus in a form that resembled *theta*
in standard Greek font. *Theta* in turn took the form of a circle O, its medial cross bar being eliminated. Also in the north, *zeta* was written with
oblique bars that did not dissect its vertical stroke; this gave the letter
the shape ⊾ or its retrograde counterpart. In some styles of writing the
letters *epsilon* and *wau* were written so that they tilted in the direction of
writing, e.g. ⋏, ⋏.

2.6.1 For discussion of regional variation in styles of writing during the Neo-Etruscan period
see especially Maggiani 1983, 1984, and 1988.

Letters, Sounds, and Transcription

2.7 Throughout the history of Etruscan writing, only twenty-three
letter-forms were used to represent sounds in the Etruscan phonological inventory. As described in §2.3 and §2.4, some letter-forms survived
only for a short period of time; one letter (**8**) was added to the alphabet.
The letters *sigma* (ʕ/ʃ) and *sade* (**M**) were used with different sound values
in different regions of Etruria. In one particularly important case, which
involved the spelling of /s/ and /ʃ/ at Caere and Veii, variant shapes of
sigma (ʕ/ʃ) were exploited for different phonological purposes.

2.8 Below is a list of all of the letters of the Etruscan alphabet in canonical order. They are cited in the form that they had during the Archaic

period. To the right of each letter is the transcription used in this book and the sound or sounds that the letter represented. In our discussion, we employ the ancient Greek letter names for the letters of the alphabet because we do not know by what names the Etruscans referred to them.

(4) Letters, transcriptions, sounds

Letter	Transcription	Sound(s)	Letter	Transcription	Sound(s)
𐌀	a	/a/	𐌞	ś	—
𐌁	b	—	O	o	—
)	c	/k/	M	σ, ó	/s/, /ʃ/
𐌃	d	—	1	p	/p/
𐌄	e	/e/	٩	q	/k/
𐌅	v	/w/	٩	r	/r/
I	z	/tˢ/	⟨/ϟ ϟ	s, ś / ς, ς́	/s/, /ʃ/
𐌇	h	/h/	T	t	/t/
⊕	θ	/tʰ/	V	u	/u/
I	i	/i/, /y/	X	š	/s/
𐌊	k	/k/	Φ	φ	/pʰ/
𐌋	l	/l/	Y	χ	/kʰ/
M	m	/m/	8	f	/f/
𐌍	n	/n/			

2.8.1 The basic ideas behind the transcription of Etruscan texts are discussed by Rix (1991b: 20–3).

2.9 Etruscologists disagree about the transcription of the sibilant sounds /s/ and /ʃ/. In this text we adopt a system of transcription that is different—and we would argue more user-friendly—than the systems employed in other texts. Ours has the advantage of marking both sound and letter-form (*sade, sigma, ksi*) in a manner that is easy to recognize.

The sibilant letters are transcribed as follows: *sade* = σ (M); three-bar *sigma* = s (⟨); four-bar and multi-bar *sigma* = ς (ϟ ϟ); *ksi* = š (X).

The letter *ksi* (X) was used primarily at Caere and Veii and then only for a short period of time, perhaps a generation, to represent the dental sibilant /s/. This sign is not phonologically ambiguous; it never represents the palatal sibilant /ʃ/. The letter *sade* (M) and the letter *sigma*, in all of its variant forms (⟨ ϟ ϟ), could represent either /s/ or /ʃ/ depending on the chronological period of the inscription and the region of Etruria in which the inscription was incised. As a result, we use a diacritic sign in the form of an acute over the letter to indicate the palatal point of articulation, e.g. ś = /ʃ/, ó = /ʃ/, ς́ = /ʃ/. The letters s, σ, ς, when they are written without a diacritic, represent the dental sibilant /s/.

2.9.1 Wallace (1991) gives a synopsis of the problems with the competing "systems" for transcribing Etruscan sibilants.

Regional Differences in Writing

2.10 The Etruscan or Etruscans who adopted and adapted the Euboean Greek alphabet to the Etruscan sound system encountered two difficulties. The first was the spelling of the fricatives. This difficulty stemmed from the fact that Etruscan had four fricative sounds—a dental /s/, a palatal /ʃ/, a labiodental fricative /f/, and a glottal /h/—while Ancient Greek had only a dental /s/ and a glottal /h/. The second difficulty was the spelling of the voiceless unaspirated velar stop /k/. Ancient Greek had both voiced and voiceless velar stops and used three letters (*gamma*, *kappa*, and *qoppa*) to represent them. Etruscan on the other hand had only a single velar stop. Different ways of representing this sound account for much of the geographical diversity found in Etruscan writing.

2.11 For the fricative /f/ Etruscan scribes at first resorted to a combination of letters, either **vh** or **hv**, e.g. **tihvaries** 'Tifaries'. Scribes in some locations favored the sequence **hv**, e.g. at Caere and Veii, while scribes in other locations preferred **vh**. During the sixth century BCE this graphic combination was replaced by a new letter that had a form similar to our number 8, namely, **8**. The letter may have been borrowed from an archaic Italic alphabet, possibly Umbrian.

2.12 The spelling of the sibilants /s/ and /ʃ/ was complicated. There was considerable diversity, both geographical and chronological. The writing of these sounds may be divided into three geographical areas.

(a) The city of Caere and the city of Veii: In these two settlements variant forms of the letter *sigma*, three-bar *sigma* and four-bar *sigma*, were assigned to stand for different sounds. The following system was in place by the end of the sixth century BCE. (For the Archaic system, see §2.13.)
     ‌ₓ = /s/   ⅀ = /ʃ/

(b) Central Etruria: In this area three-bar *sigma* and *sade* were used to represent the sibilants. The system was as follows:
     ‌ₓ = /s/   M = /ʃ/

(c) Northern Etruria: In the inscriptions recovered from this region, the system for representing the sibilant sounds was the opposite of the system used in the central Etruria.
     M = /s/   ‌ₓ = /ʃ/

The upshot of these regional differences was that by the beginning of the Neo-Etruscan period, ca. 480–460 BCE, the same word could have three different spellings. For example, the word for 'tomb', which had the same phonological shape /ʃutʰi/ throughout Etruscan-speaking territory, was spelled in the following ways (Etruscan writing was in sinistroverse direction):

(a) IOVϿ, ṣuθi at Caere
(b) IOVM, óuθi at Tarquinia
(c) IOVꝛ, śuθi at Clusium

2.13 The earliest inscriptions from the city of Caere did not indicate graphically the phonological distinction between the two sibilants. Both sounds were represented either by three-bar *sigma* or by four-bar/multi-bar *sigma*, depending on the inscription. Presumably, lack of an orthographic distinction reflected an earlier state of affairs in which a single letter spelled both of the sibilant sounds. For example, in inscription Cr 3.1 the palatal sibilant in the name uśile, phonologically /uʃile/, was spelled by means of three-bar *sigma*, whereas in Cr 2.3 the word çpanti, which was phonologically /spanti/, was represented by a multi-bar *sigma*.

In the Archaic period at Caere the underrepresentation of sibilants was resolved by different strategies. Some writers employed the letter *sade* to represent the palatal sibilant, while others assigned a functional distinction to the two forms of *sigma*: three-bar *sigma* was used for the dental sound /s/, and four-bar *sigma* for the palatal /ʃ/. By the end of the sixth century BCE the convention of representing the two sibilants by means of different forms of *sigma* became standard practice.

2.14 In the Neo-Etruscan period the spelling of the dental sibilant in northern areas of Etruria was complicated by influence from Latin. Some writers replaced the letter *sade* with the letter *sigma* in order to spell the sound /s/, which was the sound that *sigma* spelled in the Latin orthographic system. As a result, there was a return of sorts to a system in which the sibilants were underrepresented graphically.

2.15 Etruscan did not have voiced stop sounds. This is the reason why the letters *beta* and *delta*, which represented the sounds /b/ and /d/ in archaic Greek, were not employed in Etruscan orthography. In this regard it is most interesting to note that during the seventh century BCE, and even into the sixth century in some areas, the spelling of the voiceless velar sound /k/ was subject to a spelling convention that violated the general principle in Etruscan orthography that one sign represent one sound. During the Archaic period some scribes, particularly in southern Etruria, used the letters c, k, and q to represent the velar stop /k/. *Gamma* was used before *epsilon* and *iota*; *kappa* before *alpha*, and *qoppa* before *upsilon*. For example, the word /kakriku/, which was incised on one of the earliest Etruscan ceramic objects known to have writing (Fig. 2.1, Ta 3.1), was spelled in the following manner: VꟼIꟼƆꟇꟁ (kacriqu).

Fig. 2.1. Earliest Etruscan inscription. Inscription on kotyle from Tarquinia (Ta 3.1), *SE* 37 (1969):503.

Etruscan scribes simplified this early orthographic rule in two ways. Those who worked in the central and southern areas of Etruria selected the sign *gamma* c to represent /k/; scribes in northern areas selected *kappa*. *Qoppa* eventually disappeared from the writing system and was eliminated from all abecedaria.

2.16 As early as the end of the fourth century BCE and no later than the third century, scribes in northern Etruscan cities began to replace *kappa* with *gamma* to represent the sound /k/. This change in orthographic habit is usually attributed to Latin influence, and that could very well be part of the reason. However, the fact that this change in spelling begins relatively early means that the impetus may have come from central or southern Etruscan sources rather than Latin ones. In this case one might assign to Latin orthography the role of support or reinforcement for such an orthographic rule change.

2.17 The regional writing traditions described above are summarized in (5):

(5) Neo-Etruscan writing traditions

	/s/	/ʃ/	/k/
Caere, Veii	ꟊ	ꟊ	Ɔ
central	ꟊ	M	Ɔ
northern	M	ꟊ	Ꟁ (later Ɔ)

2.17.1 The most informative overview of the regional differences in spelling Etruscan sounds is found in Cristofani 1972b and 1978a. For variation in the spelling of /k/ and /s/, see Rix 1983.

2.18 The orthographic system employed by scribes at Cortona deviated in one significant respect from all others. In this system the letter *epsilon* stood for two sounds. When *epsilon* was written in retrograde (dextroverse) direction, it spelled a vowel that was distinct in quality, perhaps also in quantity (see Chapter 3), from the *epsilon* that was written in sinistroverse direction, the standard direction of writing. Retrograde *epsilon* at Cortona is transcribed by means of **e** with a circumflex over it, namely, ê, e.g. **pêtru ścêvaσ**.

2.18.1 Agostiniani and Nicosia (2000:47–52) discuss retrograde *epsilon* in the *Tabula Cortonensis* and in other inscriptions from Cortona.

Direction of Writing

2.19 Most Etruscan inscriptions were written in sinistroverse direction (Fig. 2.2). This is true for all periods of writing with the exception of a short period of time at the end of the seventh and the beginning of the sixth centuries BCE in the southern Etruscan cities of Caere and Veii. Inscriptions from these two cities were written in dextroverse direction (Fig. 2.3). This style of writing lasted a generation or so, and then writing from right-to-left re-established itself as the standard. In the second and first centuries BCE Etruscan inscriptions were sometimes written in dextroverse direction; this was due to Latin influence.

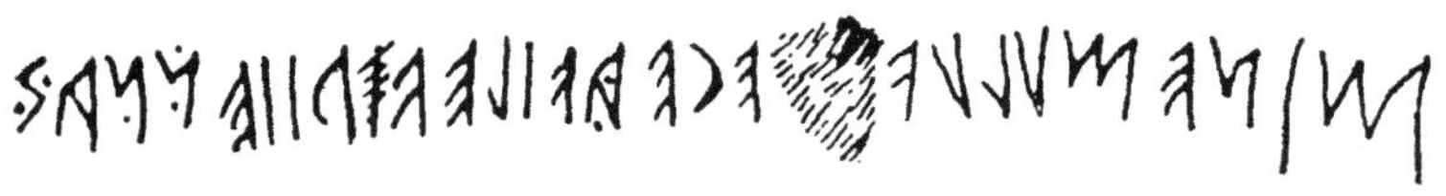

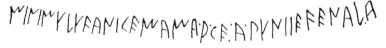

Fig. 2.2. Sinistroverse direction of writing. Inscription on bucchero vase from Veii (Ve 3.11), *SE* 13 (1942):456.

Fig. 2.3. Dextroverse direction of writing. Inscription on handle of bucchero vase from Veii (Ve 3.5), *SE* 13 (1942):455.

Etruscan inscriptions were rarely written in boustrophedon style (as the ox plows). The inscription from Magliano, which was incised on a sheet of lead (recall §1.8), was written in a spiral, beginning at the outermost boundary of the sheet and working toward the inside (Fig. 2.4).

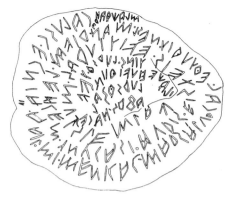

Fig. 2.4. Inscription written in spiraliform. Inscription from Magliano (AV 4.1), *SE* 65–68 (2002):182.

Punctuation

2.20 Etruscan inscriptions had very little in the way of punctuation. Archaic Etruscan inscriptions for the most part did not separate words. Inscriptions were often written as a single orthographic unit in a style known as *scriptio continua* (Fig. 2.5). However, even in the oldest chronological layer of Etruscan inscriptions, words were occasionally separated by punctuation, which typically had the form of three dots arranged vertically, ⋮ (Fa 2.3, 6.1). It was common for inscriptions of later periods to be divided into words by means of punctuation. This type of punctuation customarily took the form of a colon (Fig. 2.6) or a single dot set at mid-line level (Fig. 2.7), a form that was particularly common during the Neo-Etruscan period.

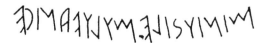

Fig. 2.5. Inscription without punctuation (scriptio continua). Inscription on bucchero amphora from Caere (Cr 3.1), *SE* 40 (1972):422, REE 30.

Fig. 2.6. Inscription with punctuation in the form of a colon (:). Inscription on cover of sarcophagus from Ferento, *Ager Hortanus* (AH 1.52), *SE* 51 (1985):168, REE 28.

Fig. 2.7. Inscription with punctuation in the form a dot (·). Inscription on stone block from Rusellae (Ru 5.1), *SE* 39 (1971):324, REE 14.

2.21 About 600 BCE a distinctive orthographic feature developed in the Etruscan settlement of Veii. The final letter of a syllable that was closed (a syllable ending in a consonant) and the first letter of a word that began with a vowel were marked by means of dots or points (Fig. 2.8). This feature is known as syllabic punctuation. Most commonly this orthographic feature took the form of a single point or a dot placed on both sides of a letter, as in the word **mama.r.ce** (Fig. 2.3). However, other forms of syllabic punctuation were possible. In the inscription cited in Fig. 2.3 the word **:a.puniie** was punctuated with two dots positioned in front of the *alpha* and with one dot behind.

Syllabic punctuation seems to have developed in a school of writing at the Portonaccio sanctuary in Veii, where scribes associated with the sanctuary were employed by worshipers to compose votive inscriptions on their behalf. How syllabic punctuation originated and why it developed here and nowhere else in Etruria are different questions entirely. Some Etruscologists suspect that the origin of syllabic punctuation was connected to the teaching of writing. Students learned to punctuate syllables that did not have CV structure, which in Archaic Etruscan was by far the most common type of syllable. Perhaps this reflected a pedagogical principle: students were first taught to write syllables and words that had CV structure, and then syllables and words with other more complex structures.

2.21.1 The best works on the topic of syllabic punctuation in Etruscan are Lejeune 1966, Rix 1968b, and Wachter 1986. Discussion of syllabic punctuation in Etruscan is generally coupled with discussion of punctuation in Venetic, an Italic language of northern Italy. The Veneti borrowed the principle of syllabic punctuation from the Etruscans of Veii.

2.22 It was quite rare for the texts to be divided into larger units such as the sentence or the paragraph, but evidence for such divisions does

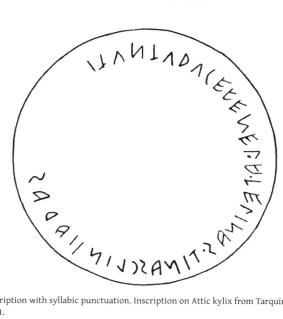

Fig. 2.8. Inscription with syllabic punctuation. Inscription on Attic kylix from Tarquinia (Ta 3.2), *SE* 13 (1942):301.

exist. For example, the *Tabula Capuana* was divided into sections or paragraphs by long horizontal lines. The *Tabula Cortonensis* used a sign having the form of a Z to segment the text into units. The *Cippus Perusinus* was divided into three chunks of text by leaving space between the end of one section and the beginning of another.

The Demise of Etruscan Writing

2.23 The end of Etruscan writing is tied to the demise of Etruscan as a spoken language. The date at which Etruscan documents ceased to be written at the various cities within Etruria depended on the political relationship of that city with Rome. Cities with very close ties to Rome, particularly those located in southern Etruria, switched to the Latin language and Latin writing system earlier than those cities in the north. It also seems reasonable to think that the highest social classes learned to speak Latin earlier than other classes because it was beneficial to their social, economic, and political survival.

At Caere and Vulci the earliest Latin inscriptions belong to the second century BCE. In contrast, at Volaterrae Latin inscriptions do not appear until the age of Caesar and Etruscan inscriptions were produced during the reign of Augustus. Latin was used at Perusia for funerary inscriptions in the last decades of first century BCE. At Pisae, which was situated at the northernmost boundary of Etruria just across the river Arno, Latin inscriptions are not attested until the first half of the first century CE. Of course the switch to Latin, both in speech and in writing, did not happen overnight. It is possible to recognize an intermediate period in which both Latin and Etruscan were spoken and written side by side. This is especially apparent in Etruscan/Latin bilingual funerary inscriptions (for examples, see Chapter 10, §9.3, nos. 23–5).

2.23.1 See the discussion in Kaimo 1975. This material is updated in Adams 2003:166–84.

3 PHONOLOGY

Introduction

3.1 The most reliable source of information about the Etruscan sound system is the alphabet. The basic assumption is that the phonological value of the sound represented by each letter in the Etruscan alphabet was similar to the value it had in ancient Greek unless there is good reason to believe otherwise. So, for example, in Ancient Greek the signs ૧, Τ, Ϫ represented voiceless unaspirated stops (/p, t, k/); presumably the Etruscans borrowed these signs to represent sounds of the same or similar quality. The second source of information about pronunciation comes from borrowings. Languages generally adapt foreign words to fit their own phonological systems by substituting sounds that are similar to the sounds in the donor language. We assume this observation to be valid for words borrowed by Etruscans.

3.2 The chronology of Etruscan inscriptions encompasses approximately 750 years. During that span of time some Etruscan sounds changed their quality, new sounds were introduced, and the distribution of sounds within words changed. Thus, a description of Etruscan phonology must include both a synchronic and a diachronic component. An additional complicating factor is dialect differences. A description of these differences makes up another component of Etruscan phonology.

3.3 In its earliest attested stage, the Etruscan sound system had twenty-one distinctive sounds or phonemes: four vowels and seventeen consonants. In addition, Etruscan had a small number of diphthongs. The phonemes in the system remained relatively stable over time, but their distribution within words sometimes changed dramatically.

3.3.1 Overviews of the Etruscan phonological system are to be found in Rix 1984b:214–22; 2004:946–50 and Steinbauer 1999:69–90. Both authors include discussion of diachronic features. Agostiniani (1992) provides a useful synopsis of the most important features of the system.

Consonants

3.4 The sound system of Etruscan included seventeen consonantal phonemes. They break down into the following phonological categories: six stop consonants, four fricatives, one affricate, two nasals, one lateral, one rhotic, and two semivowels. In chart (1) they are displayed according to their articulatory features. There were two sets of voiceless stop consonants with three distinctive points of articulation: labial, dental, and velar. At each point of articulation the stop consonants were distinguished by the presence or absence of the feature aspiration. The system also had four fricatives and one affricate. All these consonants were voiceless. Two nasals, a lateral liquid, a rhotic, and two semivowels—one palatal, the other labiovelar—rounded out the system. These sounds, which are referred to collectively as resonants or sonorants, were voiced.

(1) Etruscan consonants

	labial	dental	palatal	velar	glottal
stops	p	t		k	
	p^h	t^h		k^h	
affricate		t^s			
fricatives	f	s	ʃ		h
nasals	m	n			
lateral		l			
rhotic		r			
semivowels			y	w	

Most Etruscologists agree about the number of consonantal sounds as well as their articulatory features. Nevertheless, a few areas of disagreement and uncertainty remain. These are discussed below.

3.5 The most radical proposal regarding the system of consonants involves the phonological interpretation of the letters traditionally identified as voiceless aspirated stops, namely, φ θ χ /p^h t^h k^h/. According to this proposal, the letters φ and θ represented palatalized stops /p^y t^y/, and the letter χ represented a velar fricative /x/.

Little evidence can be marshaled in support of this interpretation. The claim that φ and θ represented palatalized stops is based in large part on spelling alternations of the type larθial vs. larθal, arnθial vs. aranθal, and amφiare vs. amφare, in which the *iota* that sometimes follows θ and φ is taken to be a mark of palatalization. The problem is that the spellings θi and φi were restricted almost exclusively to the words cited above. Other Etruscan words, such as θanaχvil (θanχvil) and ramuθa (ramθa),

which are attested hundreds of times, were never spelled as *θianaχvil
or *ramuθia. Whatever the reason for the variation in spelling in larθial,
arnθial, and amφiare, it is confined to these words and so cannot be used
to make generalizations about the pronunciation of the letters φ and θ
across the entire lexicon. Evidence for the claim that the letter χ represented a velar fricative comes primarily from Latin spellings of the Etruscan name aχunia, which was written as *Achonia* and *Ahonea*. The name
aχói was also spelled occasionally as ahói. These spellings are found in funerary inscriptions from Perusia that date to the end of the Etruscan period. They may indicate the assimilation of /kʰ/ to the following fricative,
but even if this were so, it would represent a late and regionally circum-
scribed change. These spellings do not support a revision of the phonological features of the stop system. Indeed, the customary transcription
of Etruscan aspirates in Latin employs the same digraphs used to spell
the ancient Greek aspirates, namely *ph* (*Phisius*), *th* (*Thana*), and *ch* (*An-
charius*). These spellings support the interpretation of φ θ χ as aspirated
stops in Etruscan.

The proposal described above does not have enough support to su-
persede the view that the letters φ θ χ stood for aspirated stop sounds.
Moreover, from a typological point of view it does not yield a system of
stop consonants as satisfying as the traditionally proposed system.

3.5.1 Rix was the main proponent of the view that the stops traditionally interpreted as aspirated were palatalized. See Rix 1984b:219–20 and 2004:947 for details. Steinbauer (1999:57–60)
offers a variant of this view. Boisson (1991) and Agostiniani (1992:49–50) discuss the problems
with Rix's proposal from a typological perspective.

3.6 It is universally agreed that Etruscan had two sibilant sounds. One
sibilant, which was spelled by three-bar *sigma* in the south and by *sade*
in the north, had dental or alveolar articulation, /s/. The second sibilant,
which was spelled by three-bar *sigma* in the north and by *sade* or four-bar
sigma in the south (see §2.12), is generally considered to have had palatal
articulation, /ʃ/. A minority view claims a long and intense articulation
/ss/ for the second sibilant. This idea does not have much to recommend
it. Consonant length is not found as a phonologically distinctive feature
anywhere else in the Etruscan phonological system.

3.6.1 Zavaroni (2002) resurrects the issue of the phonetic realization of the second sibilant,
though there seems to be little reason to do so. For the evidence in favor of a palatal articulation
see Rix (1984b:220–1).

3.7 The Etruscan letter z, which is generally assumed to be a dental affricate /tˢ/, has recently been reinterpreted as a palatal affricate /tʃ/. This
interpretation is supported by typological studies of the sound systems

of the world's languages. Such studies have shown that if a language has a single affricate consonant in its inventory then that consonant is typically a palatal /tʃ/, rather than a dental /tˢ/.

Interestingly, the evidence bearing on the pronunciation of this letter, which is cited in (2), supports the standard phonological interpretation. Typological data represent tendencies, and are by definition not exceptionless. As it happens, although languages with a single affricate tend to have a palatal /tʃ/, there are languages that have /tˢ/ as the only affricate in their inventory. Etruscan appears to be one of these languages.

(2)   Evidence for **z** = /tˢ/

   (a)   The Greek letter **z** on which the Etruscan was modeled stood for a voiced affricate /dᶻ/.
   (b)   Orthographic variation, **tz** for **z**, e.g. **citz** for **ciz** /kitˢ/ 'three times'.
   (c)   Spelling of word-final **-ns** by **-nz**, e.g. **fuflunz** for **fufluns** 'Fufluns' THEO. (The spelling **fuflunz** may indicate the development of an epenthetic /t/ between /n/ and /s/, cf. modern English *sense* /sents/.)
   (d)   Oscans borrowed Etruscan **z** to spell the consonant cluster /ts/, e.g. Oscan **húrz** /horts/ 'enclosure'.
   (e)   Umbrians did not borrow Etruscan **z** to spell the voiceless palatal affricate in their system. They invented a new letter.

3.7.1 Agostiniani (1992:51–2; 1993:30–2) argues in favor of the idea that the letter *zeta* represents the palatal affricate sound /tʃ/.

Vowels

3.8 The Etruscan vowel system had four members, two high vowels and two non-high vowels. A diagram of the system is given in (3).

(3)   Etruscan vowels

	front	back
high	i	u
mid	e	
low	a	

As was the case with consonants, the quality of Etruscan vowels is assumed to be similar to the quality of the vowels that *iota*, *epsilon*, *alpha* and *upsilon* represented in ancient Euboean Greek. In other words, we assume that **i** was a high front vowel /i/, that **u** was high, back, and rounded /u/, that **e** was a mid front vowel /e/, and that the vowel **a** was low, back, and unrounded.

3.8.1 De Simone (1970a:48–50) investigates the phonological parameters of the Etruscan vowel system.

3.9 Some scholars have argued that the low vowel **a** may have been rounded originally and that the Archaic vowel system can be represented more accurately as a quadrangle in terms of distinctive features (4).

(4) Archaic Etruscan vowels

	front/unround	back/round
high	i	u
non-high	e	a [ɒ]

The claim that the vowel **a** was rounded helps make sense of the spelling of some early loanwords from Italic. Etruscan scribes choose to spell the Italic diphthong /ow/ in the name *loucios* as **au**, e.g. Etruscan **lavcie**. During the sixth century BCE the vowel was unrounded and the spelling of this loanword in later inscriptions changed to **luvcie** in response to the new phonetic status of the vowel **a**.

Near the end of the Neo-Etruscan period Latin transcriptions of Etruscan words sometimes replaced Etruscan **u** with the Latin letter *o*, e.g. Etruscan **crepu** = Latin *grebo*, Etruscan **fulni** = Latin *folnius*. On the basis of these Latin transcriptions, some scholars have assumed that the Etruscan vowel /u/ may have developed a more open articulation during the second and first centuries BCE.

3.9.1 See Agostiniani 1992:48 for the configuration of the vowel system and for the claim that the phonetic realization of **a** was different in the Archaic period from that found in Neo-Etruscan. For the interpretation of Latin transcriptions of Etruscan **u** see Rix 1984b:215.

3.10 In Archaic Etruscan vowels were not distinguished by vowel length. However, this feature may have become a distinctive part of the vocalic system during the Neo-Etruscan period thanks to sound changes in which diphthongs were converted to simple vowels, e.g. **cnaive** 'Gnaeus' > **cneve** /knewe/, possibly /kneːwe/, and the contraction of contiguous vowels of similar quality, e.g. **cehen** 'this' > **cen** /ken/, possibly /keːn/. The great influx of Greek loanwords, many of which had long vowels, may also have contributed to the addition of vowel length to the language. Even so, it is impossible to know exactly how these changes and borrowings affected the system because there was no way to distinguish long from short vowels in the Etruscan writing system and none was ever devised (but see the following paragraph).

Etruscans employed four vowel signs and they were used, at least originally, to designate vowels of different quality, not quantity. The only
exception may have been the use of *epsilon* in the orthographic system
employed at Cortona. When *epsilon* was written facing in the direction of
writing, it spelled the regular mid vowel in the system (transcribed **e**).
However, when *epsilon* was written in retrograde direction (opposite the
direction of writing), it spelled a different vowel, possibly one that was
distinctively long (transcribed **ê**). Retrograde *epsilon* was used to spell the
product of the monophthongization of diphthongs, e.g. **sparzê(te)** 'on the
tablet' < *sparzay(-te)*, the product of the contraction of vowels of similar
quality, e.g. **cên** 'this' < *keen* < *kehen*, and the vowel in the first syllable
of a word, e.g. **vêtnal**, which could indicate lengthening under expira-
tory accentuation (for accent, see §3.17). At the very least, this spelling
convention indicates a vowel whose quality was distinct from that of the
'regular' *epsilon*.

3.10.1 See Agostiniani and Nicosia 2000:46–52 and Eichner 2006.

Change of i to e

3.11 Toward the end of the Archaic period, about 500 BCE, the high
front vowel **i** /i/ was lowered to a mid vowel **e** /e/ if the vowel in the
following syllable was **a** /a/ or **e** /e/, that is to say, was a non-high vowel.
Examples of this change were restricted to the initial syllables of words.

(5)   Vowel lowering

	Archaic Etruscan	Neo-Etruscan
(a)	ika 'this' NOM	eca
(b)	itan 'this' ACC	etan
(c)	piθe MASC PRAE	peθe
(d)	licene MASC PRAE	lecne
(e)	θihvarie MASC PRAE	θefarie

The vowel **i** /i/ remained unchanged if the initial syllable of a word
began with the sound /tˢ/, for example, **zilaθ** 'governor', **zilac** 'governorship', **zinace** 'fashioned', and **ziχvanace** 'designed'. Some words, such as
θina 'vessel for water', copied the *i*-vocalism of the bases from which they
were built (in this case **θi** 'water').

3.12 The change described in §3.11 is not to be confused with an apparent change of **i** to **e** in words such as **muluveneke** from earlier **muluvanice** /muluwanike/. The changes in the medial syllables of this word,

including the spelling of original i as **e**, were the result of vowel weakening, a change discussed in §3.15. The change of i to e in the accusative singular of the 1st person pronoun (**mine, mene**, both from earlier **mini** /mini/) remains a case apart, and has yet to be satisfactorily explained (see also §5.3).

Diphthongs

3.13 In addition to the four simple vowels cited in (3), Etruscan had diphthongs that were combinations of vowels followed by the semivowels /y/ or /w/. In the Archaic period the evidence for these sounds comes almost exclusively from names, e.g. **paiθinie-** /paytʰin(i)ye/, **teiθurna-** /teytʰurna/, **aukana-** /awkana/, and **clevsu[** /klewsu-/. In Neo-Etruscan, diphthongs were added to the inventory as a result of sound changes and borrowing, e.g. /ew/ **teurat** < **tevaraθ** 'judge' NOM/ACC; /aw/ **cavθa** < **cavaθa** 'Cautha' THEO, NOM/ACC; and /uw/ **luvcies** 'Lucius' MASC PRAE, 1ST GEN (borrowed from Sabellic or Latin).

3.14 In the fourth century BCE the diphthong /ay/ (spelled **ai**) was subject to two developments. The first and more general change of /ay/ to /ey/ is exemplified by the name **kaikna** /kaykna/, which came to be pronounced as **ceicna** /keykna/, and by the name **apunai**, which came to be pronounced as /apuney/ **apunei**. This change is generally believed to have spread throughout Etruria, but there may be exceptions. For example, at Caere the uninflected stem of feminine family names was spelled as **-ai** throughout the Neo-Etruscan period, e.g. **matunai, velχai**, etc. Either this change did not encompass the area of Caere or the original feminine ending **-ai** was analogically regenerated. It is also possible that the spelling of the nominative/accusative of feminine nomina was simply fixed as **-ai** by convention.

The second change was more restrictive. It occurred when the diphthong /ay/ stood before the sound /w/, as in the name **laive** /laywe/. In this case original /ay/ developed to a single vowel sound /e/, perhaps a long /e:/, e.g. **leve** /lewe/ (perhaps /le:we/). In just this way the Archaic personal name **cnaive** developed to **cneve** in Neo-Etruscan. The entire series of changes, /ay/ > /ey/ > /e/ or /e:/, is documented by forms of the Greek loanword Αἴϝας 'Ajax': **aivas, eivas**, and **evas**.

3.15 Original /ey/ at the end of a word changed to a simple vowel /i/, possibly a long /i:/, e.g. **hustilei** > **hustli**. This change happened to a whole host of feminine family names that were built by adding the suffix **-i** to masculine names ending in **-e**, e.g. masculine **hustile** →

feminine **hustilei**. This development is to be contrasted with that found in feminine names that originally ended in -**ai**. The word-final diphthong in these words changed to -**ei**, e.g. **nuzarnai** > **nuzrnei**. Archaic Etruscan names and their Neo-Etruscan descendents are presented in (6). It is important to note that, despite the changes, the two types remained distinct in Neo-Etruscan. It may be that the suffix -**i** was re-added to the stem as a form of morphological renewal, that is to say, in order to generate a form that had the appearance of being feminine, i.e. **nuzarnai** > *nuzarne* → **nuzrnei**.

(6)   Feminine names ending in -**ai** and -**ei**

	Archaic Etruscan	Neo-Etruscan
(a)	nuzarnai	nuzrnei
(b)	hustilei	hustli

3.16 Exactly how the developments of the locative endings -**ai** and -**ei** (see §4.14) fit into the framework of changes described in §3.14 and §3.15 is not easy to say. Evidence suggests that the locative endings -**ai** /ay/ and -**ei** /ey/ developed to /e/, possibly a long /e:/, in word-final position, e.g. **spure** 'in the community' < *spura-i*. If this is the case, then the developments described above for feminine names ending in -**ai** cannot be by regular sound change.

3.17 In northern Etruria, in the environs of Perusia and Clusium, names borrowed from Sabellic languages, such as **raufi**, **aufle**, and **plauti**, could be pronounced (and spelled) in diverse ways. For example, at Perusia the name **raufi** had three pronunciations: **raufi** /rawfɪ/, **rufi** /rufɪ/, and **rafi** /rafɪ/. Some scholars have suggested that these differences in spelling reflect a change whereby /aw/ turned into a vowel articulated somewhere between /a/ and /u/, hence the fluctuation in spelling, **a** vs. **u**. Interestingly, however, this change did not affect the Etruscan name **aule**, and the nouns **lautni** 'freedman' and **lautniθa** 'freedwoman' were very rarely spelled with simple **u** or **a**, e.g. **latni**. It seems reasonable to suppose, then, particularly since words such as **raufi** were borrowed from a Sabellic language, that the spellings with **u** and **a** are due rather to the pronunciation found in the donor language, Umbrian, in which the original diphthong *au* developed to a long open /o:/ sound.

3.17.1 Meiser (1996:192–6) discusses the phonology of Sabellic loanwords in Etruscan.

3.18 By the Neo-Etruscan period the number of diphthongs in the phonological inventory, their distribution within words, and their quality differed from region to region. As we saw in §§3.14–15, the diphthong /ay/ disappeared except in feminine family names in the south, and /ey/, though historically having a wider distribution (since it came from both *ey and *ay), became /i/ or /i:/ word-finally. Other diphthongs in the system were restricted to words borrowed from Greek and Italic languages.

Vowel Weakening, Syncope, and Accent

3.19 Toward the end of the seventh century BCE Etruscan scribes began to vary the spelling of the medial vowels of words. For example, the penultimate vowel in the name **avile**, which was originally /i/, was sometimes spelled as **i**, sometimes as **u**, **e**, or **a**. Examples of this fluctuation in spelling are given in (7). This feature of spelling indicated that distinctions in vowel quality were being effaced in medial position. The pronunciation of the medial vowels in the words cited below was probably /ə/, the so-called *schwa* vowel.

(7) Examples of spelling of medial vowels

	spelling	pronunciation
(a)	avile, avule, avale, avele	/awəle/
(b)	aχile, aχale, aχele, aχule	/akʰəle/
(c)	ramuθa, ramaθa, rameθa	/ramətʰa/
(d)	θanaχvil, θaneχvil, θanucvil	/tʰanəkʰwil/
(e)	menerva, menarva	/menərwa/

3.20 In the first half of the fifth century BCE, more precisely between ca. 480 and 460 BCE, the words cited above came to be spelled without medial vowels at all, reflecting syncope (loss) of the vowels in pronunciation.

(8) Vowel syncope

	Archaic Etruscan	Neo-Etruscan
(a)	avile	avle, aule
(b)	aχile	aχle
(c)	ramuθa	ramθa
(d)	θanaχvil	θanχvil
(e)	menerva	menrva

Syncope did not only affect trisyllables, but also deleted all the medial vowels of words of four syllables or more, as in (9). The wholesale loss of vowels in medial syllables resulted in the appearance of clusters of consonants heretofore unattested in the language (see §3.23).

(9) Vowel syncope

	Archaic Etruscan	Neo-Etruscan
(a)	laricena	larcna /larkna/
(b)	vestiricina	vestrcna /westr̥kna/
(c)	elacsantre	elcsntre /elksn̥tre/

Given the loss of vowels in the medial syllables of words such as **lari-cena** (9a), we might have expected **spuriena** to develop to *spurna*. However, this form is not attested. The Neo-Etruscan descendent of **spuriena** is **spurina**, a form in which medial -ie- changed to -i-. Two explanations are possible, each one depending upon a different phonological interpretation of the spelling -ie-: (1) Medial -ie- stood for /ye/. Following this interpretation, the consonant /y/ vocalized after the medial vowel -e- was lost, i.e. /spuryena/ > /spuryna/ > /spurina/. (2) Medial -ie- represented two vowels /ie/ in hiatus. Following this interpretation /ie/ developed to /i/, possibly long /i:/, by means of a sound change in which /e/ assimilated to and ultimately contracted with the preceding /i/, i.e. /spuriena/ > /spuriina/ > /spuri(:)na/.

The fact that the vowel -i- in recent Etruscan **spurina** was not subject to medial vowel syncope suggests that the vowel that developed from earlier -ie- could have been phonetically longer than medial vowels that were subject to syncope. Examples of the development of medial -ie- are given below.

(10) Development of medial -ie-

	Archaic Etruscan	Neo-Etruscan
(a)	vipiienna	vipina
(b)	spuriena	spurina
(c)	aniena	anina

3.20.1 The historical development of Etruscan vowels in medial syllables is discussed in considerable detail in de Simone 1970a:50–91. Rix 1976:180–1 is a thoughtful appraisal of de Simone's proposal concerning changes in the medial vowel sequence -ie-.

3.21 Evidence also suggests that vowels in word-final closed syllables were syncopated. Unfortunately, the phonological environments in which this change occurred are less clear. Vowels appear to have been lost before word-final -nθ (11a) and word-final -ns (11b, 11c), and between -s and word-final -l (11d), but beyond that it is difficult to say. Since a vowel before word-final -n was not syncopated, e.g. **laran**, **cepen**, the loss of the syllable-final vowel in the pronominal accusative forms, e.g. **ecn** and **cn** below, should probably be tied to their status as unaccented clitics.

(11) Syncope in final syllables

	Archaic Etruscan	Neo-Etruscan
(a)	aranθ	arnθ NOM/ACC
(b)	turans	turns 1ST GEN
(c)	laruns	larns 1ST GEN
(d)	selvansel	selvansl 2ND GEN
(e)	ikan	ecn, cn ACC

3.22 Direct evidence for word accent in Etruscan does not exist, nor is there any orthographic indication of the syllable or syllables on which word accent was positioned. However, the developments described above in sections 3.19–21 strongly suggest that there was a stress accent on initial syllables.

3.22.1 See the short discussion in de Simone 1970a:91–2.

Syllabic Consonants

3.23 One of the most peculiar features of Neo-Etruscan, at least from the point of view of spelling, is the exotic-looking combination of consonants that some words have in medial syllables due to the loss of vowels. Examples of these clusters of consonants are given in (12) in the left-hand column. Despite the appearance, the clusters were pronounceable and a straightforward phonological explanation can be offered.

(12) Vocalization of liquids, rhotics, and nasals

(a)	ravnθu	[ravn̥tʰu]
(b)	raθmsnal	[ratʰm̥snal]
(c)	herclna	[herkl̥na]
(d)	nuzrni	[nutˢr̥ni]

The sound in the middle of these clusters is a liquid, rhotic, or nasal consonant and in this phonetic context these sounds vocalized. In other words, when found between two less sonorant consonants, the liquid, rhotic, and nasal consonants acquired syllabic function. The spellings in the left-hand column correspond then to the phonetic representations on the right-hand side.

A similar explanation may be offered for liquids and nasals that form the nucleus of a word-final syllable. For example, we assume that **selvansl** was pronounced as [selwans̥l] with vocalization of the final liquid. Similarly, **turns, larns,** and **arnθ** may have had two syllables, in each instance the nasal forming the nucleus of the final syllable. Vocalization of liquids, rhotics, and nasals is not unusual from a phonetic point of view. Compare modern English dialects in which the nasals, rhotic, and liquid vocalize in word-final position after apical (tongue tip) consonants, e.g. *writer, little, button, bottom.*

In Neo-Etruscan, then, the liquid, rhotic, and nasal sounds had different pronunciations depending on their position within words. If they stood between two less sonorant consonants, they vocalized and formed the nucleus of the syllable. When they were adjacent to more sonorant sounds, namely vowels, they were pronounced as nonsyllabics.

Loss of Penultimate e

3.24 A special case of vowel loss—the loss of -e- in penultimate syllables—must be distinguished from vowel syncope. Vowel syncope affected Etruscan words beginning in the first half of the fifth century BCE. Loss of penultimate -e- was a prehistoric change. Whereas vowel syncope affected all medial vowels, the change described here affected only -e- in penultimate position standing between a liquid or rhotic and a dental nasal. The change is found most commonly in family names that were formed by adding the suffix *-na* to the stem of a personal name, e.g. **uśele-na-* > **uśel-na-**, **hapire-na-* > **hapir-na-**, **rutile-na-* > **rutel-na-**.

Anaptyxis

3.25 Anaptyxis refers to the insertion of a vowel between two consonants. For example, some Neo-Etruscan speakers at Perusia pronounced the family name **marcna** /markna/ as **markana** /markana/, as in **markanal** 2ND GEN. In this instance, the vowel -a- broke up the cluster -rkn- /rkn/. As the word **markanal** illustrates, anaptyxis can be ordered in chronological sequence after syncope. Consider the historical derivation of this name, shown in (13).

(13) Chronological developments of **marke-na-*

(a)	**marke-na-*	original stem, cf. praenomen **marce**
(b)	**marc-na-**	medial vowel syncope
(c)	**mark-a-na-**	anaptyxis

Anaptyxis cannot be described by a single phonological rule. First of all, to judge by the spellings that have survived, the same consonant cluster was sometimes susceptible to anaptyxis and sometimes not. At Volsinii, for example, the family name **hescnas** /hesknas/ spelled without anaptyxis is more common than the same name spelled with anaptyxis, hescanas /heskanas/. Secondly, the anaptyctic vowel did not always appear in the same position in the same consonant cluster, even for speakers of the same region. In (14d), there are two different treatments for the same word, both attested at Clusium. It is worth noting that the second example, θacutura /tʰacutura/, was written with two anaptyctic vowels! Finally, it is not always possible to predict the quality of the anaptyctic vowel. In southern and central Etruria it tended to be a; in northern Etruria it could be a, e, or u, as (14c) and (14d) show. The various spellings point to a mid-central vowel /ə/ as in the vowel-weakening cases.

(14) Anaptyxis

	without anaptyxis	with anaptyxis	
(a)	aleθnei	aleθanei	Tarquinia
(b)	hescnas	hescanas	Volsinii
(c)	hepni	hepani, hepeni	Asciano
(d)	θactra	θacatra, θacutura	Clusium

Anaptyxis, it should be noted, is distinct from the phonological process described in §3.23. In words such as **herclna**, the liquid positioned between two consonants was vocalized and treated as the nucleus of a syllable. In contrast, in a word such as **hescnas**, the medial sound of the cluster -scn- was a stop consonant and could not vocalize. A vowel was inserted to break up the cluster.

Etruscan Dialects

3.26 The territory of Etruria was divided into two dialect areas, a northern area and a southern area. The boundary-line between the two ran eastward from Rusellae through territory just south of Clusium and Arretium. The boundary-line is drawn primarily on the basis of phonological features. The major piece of evidence for northern and southern dialect areas was the distribution of the palatal sibilant /ʃ/.

In northern Etruscan dialects the dental sibilant /s/ was palatalized to /ʃ/ before stop consonants, thus falling together with original /ʃ/. The personal name **spurie** was pronounced as /spurie/ in the south, but as /ʃpurie/ in the north, both pronunciations deriving from prehistoric Etruscan *spurie. Another important phonological difference between the north and the south, again involving the palatal sibilant, was the change of /ʃ/ to /s/ (depalatalization) in word-final position, a change that was restricted to southern areas of Etruria. The most important example of this change is the personal name **laris**, which ended in a palatal sibilant in prehistoric Etruscan, */lariʃ/.

What is most interesting about this situation is that in the southern dialect the dental sound at the end of **laris** was subsequently generalized throughout all forms of the personal name, the result of which was a paradigm that was distinct from the one found in northern dialects. The name **laris** was spelled in the same way throughout Etruscan territory, as ⵣ𐌉𐌖𐌋, despite the fact that the spelling represented two distinct pronunciations.

(15) Paradigms of the personal name **laris**

	South Etruscan	North Etruscan
NOM/ACC	laris /laris/	laris /lariʃ/
2ND GEN	larisal /larisal/	larisal /lariʃal/
2ND PERT	larisale /larisale/	larisale /lariʃale/

3.27 Within these two large dialect areas, northern and southern Etruria, it is possible to recognize a handful of features, again mostly phonological, that point to more localized dialect differences. In some northern Etruscan dialects, in particular those spoken at Siena and environs, aspirated stop consonants became unaspirated in absolute word-final position and also when standing between two consonants. Compare the forms in (16).

(16) Aspirated stops at Siena and environs

	original		Siena and environs
(a)	arnθ	>	arnt PRAE, NOM/ACC
(b)	arnθni	>	arntni NOMEN, NOM/ACC
(c)	larθ	>	lart PRAE, NOM/ACC
(d)	larθli	>	lartli NOMEN, NOM/ACC

Another such feature, namely the change of word-initial f- to h-, served to set off the dialect of Clusium from other north Etruscan dialects in the third and second centuries BCE. Compare, for example, the names **fasti, faltu**, and **felusni** with the corresponding forms **hasti, haltu**, and **helusni**. Yet another feature distinguished the dialect spoken at Clusium. The name **salvi** owes its origins ultimately to Latin *Salvius* /salwius/. The name was consistently spelled **sali** at Clusium, thus pointing to a simplification of the medial cluster -lv- /lw/ to -l- /l/ by loss of -v- /w/.

3.27.1 The following articles discuss regional phonological developments in Etruscan: Agostiniani 1983 and 1986, and Rix 1962 and 1989a.

4 NOUNS, ADJECTIVES, AND NUMBERS

Introduction

4.1 The languages of the world may be classified according to their morphological characteristics. Latin and Ancient Greek were inflectional languages of the fusional type. In these languages the features of case and number were fused together into a single suffix. Thus the Latin nominal suffix *-um* specified both genitive and plural, as in *principum* 'of leading men'. Etruscan, in contrast to Latin and Ancient Greek, had features that are associated with agglutinating languages. In the Etruscan noun system, where the agglutinating arrangement seems most clear, distinct suffixes expressed each grammatical function. Etruscan nouns had one set of suffixes for number and another set for case. Number suffixes preceded case suffixes, so that a fully inflected Etruscan noun had the structure stem + number suffix + case suffix.

4.2 The uninflected stems (on this concept, see §4.4) of the Etruscan word for 'god' were **ais** and **aise-**. The plural was formed by adding the suffix **-r** (**-ra-** before other case endings) to the stem **aise-**, thus **aise-r** 'gods'. The genitive plural was formed by adding the genitive suffix, in this case the so-called 1st or *s*-genitive suffix, directly to the plural suffix, **aise-** + **-ra-** + **-s** → **aiseras** 'of the gods'. Similarly, the uninflected forms of the word 'son' were **clan** and **clen** (on which see §4.17). To form the pertinentive case in the singular the suffix **-si** was added directly to the stem, **clen** + **-si** → **clensi** 'to/for the son'. The pertinentive plural was formed by attaching **-si** to the plural suffix **-r(a)-**, thus **clena** + **-ra-** + **-si** → **clenarasi** 'to/for the sons'.

4.3 The stems and endings of most Etruscan nouns, adjectives, and verbs can be readily separated from one another, as in the examples cited above. However, for some words this was not the case in the Neo-Etruscan period. The best example of the fusion of stem and case ending is the locative case of nominal stems ending in a vowel. For example, the noun **spura** 'community' has as its locative **spure** 'in the community', which comes from a prehistoric form **spura-i*. In the locative case the stem and

the ending fused together due to a sound change whereby word-final *-*ai*
/ay/ developed to a simple vowel /e/ (possibly /e:/, as discussed in §3.14).
Thus, even though Etruscan words were predominantly agglutinative in
their structure, there were exceptions.

4.3.1 Rix (1984b:222–9; 2004:951–4) and Steinbauer (1999:69–90) describe the nominal system. Facchetti (2002a:9–52) tackles many thorny problems in Etruscan nominal morphology from
both synchronic and diachronic points of view, but in many cases his analyses do not convince
for methodological reasons (see the review of de Simone 2004b).

Roots and Stems

4.4 The uninflected form of an Etruscan word is the stem. For example, the stem of the word 'son' is **clan**. This stem is morphologically simple; it is not divisible, at least as far as we can tell, into smaller constituents. Other stems are morphologically complex. The nominal stem θina
'of/for water' is made up of a stem θi- 'water' and an adjective-forming
suffix -na. Similarly, the verbal stem ziχun- 'incise' has two constituents,
a verb stem ziχ- 'to incise, scratch' and a factitive or causative suffix -un.
Morphologically simple stems, such as θi- 'water' or **clan** 'son', can also
be referred to as roots.

4.5 Identifying the constituents of complex stems in Etruscan is difficult business. In the case of θina- and ziχun- the suffixes are well known
and the roots to which the suffixes were added are also found as independent words, θi 'water' and ziχ 'writing, document'. In many cases, however, we may suspect that a word is morphologically complex, though we
cannot prove that it is so. In other cases, we can show by morphological
analysis that a stem is complex, though we cannot determine the meaning of the suffix or the meaning of the root.

4.6 The fact that the Etruscan language changed over time compli-
cates the description of words.
As a simple example, we offer the Archaic Etruscan verb **turuce** 'gave'
and its Neo-Etruscan descendant **turce**. The morphological analysis of the
Archaic word is the following: stem turu- + past active suffix -c- + indicative mood suffix -e. In Neo-Etruscan this verb developed to **turce** by loss
of its medial vowel; the Neo-Etruscan verb must be analyzed as **tur-** + -c-
+ -e.
The Neo-Etruscan word for 'god' had two stems, **ais** and **aise-**. The stem
ais was the uninflected form; it was used for nominative/accusative functions. The stem **aise-** was used to build other forms of the paradigm of
this word, e.g. **aise-r** PL, NOM/ACC, **aise-ra-s** PL, GEN. The fact that words
such as **ais** had multiple stems can be attributed to a prehistoric sound

change that eliminated word-final vowels, thus *aise* > **ais**. This prehistoric change left **ais** and many other Etruscan words with multiple stem-forms. As a result, noun inflection became more complicated: the final vowel that appeared in the stem that took inflection (as in **aise-**) could no longer be predicted from the uninflected stem (**ais**).

Word Classes

4.7 In Etruscan, identification of the syntactic class to which a word belonged is not always possible, particularly if the word in question is an uninflected form, is a *hapax*, or is found in a syntactic context that is ambiguous with respect to function. For some forms, such as the root **ziχ**, word class depended on function in a sentence. The root **ziχ** could have nominal function ('written document') or verbal function ('to incise') depending on its usage. Similarly, some words could transgress word class boundaries. Words that were formally adjectives could function as nouns. The adjective **θina** 'of, for water' was also used as a substantive to refer to a type of storage vessel for water or other liquids.

4.8 Etruscan words can be divided into two large groups based on whether or not the stem permitted inflection. Inflected words included verbs, nouns, adjectives, pronouns, and numbers. Subordinators, conjunctions, negators, postpositions, and particles were uninflected.

Nouns and Noun Stems

4.9 Much of the complexity surrounding the inflection of Etruscan nouns can be attributed to the loss of word-final vowels in prehistoric times (see §4.6). Another complicating factor has to do with the fact that the distribution of stems within paradigms sometimes changed over the course of time. For example, the noun meaning 'city' had two stems in Neo-Etruscan, namely **meθlum-** and **meθlume-**. The stem **meθlum-** was the nominative/accusative form; the stem **meθlume-** was the one upon which other cases were formed, e.g. the *s*-genitive **meθlume-s** 'of the city' and the locative **meθlume** 'in the city' (from earlier *meθlume-i*). But a second locative was formed on the stem **meθlum-**, namely **meθlumθ**. In this instance the postposition -θ 'in' was attached directly to the nominative/accusative stem without the addition of the regular locative ending -i. This 'new' locative was probably formed by analogy to consonant stem formations, e.g. **raχθ** 'altar; fire (?)' < *raχ-i-θi*, in which the medial vowel was syncopated, thus giving the appearance of a postpositional form built directly to the nominative/accusative stem.

4.10 Etruscan nouns can be divided into three main types based on the final sound of the stem: (1) vocalic stems, e.g. θina 'water container'; (2) consonant stems, e.g. cilθ 'citadel (?)'; and (3) vocalic/consonant stems, a class that covers nouns with two stem-forms, e.g. meθlum-/meθlume-. Vocalic stems can be grouped into sub-types according to the final vowel of the stem; thus, -a (e.g. θina 'water container'), -e (flere- 'divinity'), -i (6uθi 'tomb'), and -u (kraikalu- 'Kraikalu' MASC NOMEN). Consonant stems can be divided into sub-types depending on whether or not there were multiple stem-forms. For example, the noun clan 'son' had several stems, clan-, clin-, clen-. These formal distinctions are only marginally useful because the inflectional distinctions that existed for nouns do not seem to be tied strictly to the form of the noun stem, but concern the semantic classification of the noun, as will be discussed below.

Cases

4.11 Etruscan nouns were inflected for five cases. The uninflected stem functioned as the case that we label nominative/accusative, e.g. meθlum 'city', zilaχ 'governorship'. The four oblique cases were the genitive (GEN), the pertinentive (PERT), the ablative (ABL), and the locative (LOC) (for paradigms, see §4.16). The genitive, pertinentive, and ablative cases had two formally distinct sets of suffixes, one based on the sound /s/ and another based on the sound /l/, e.g. genitive meθlume-s 'of the city', genitive zilac-al 'of the governorship'.

4.11.1 Some Etruscologists use the term absolutive to refer to the uninflected stem. This is unfortunate because it may give the impression that Etruscan has ergative/absolutive morphology. It does not.

4.12 The genitive case had two sets of endings, a so-called 1st genitive which ended in -s and a 2nd genitive which ended in -l. During the Neo-Etruscan period, the 2nd genitive had two forms, -al, e.g. ati-al 'of (the) mother', and, less commonly, -l, e.g. klaninσ-l 'of Klanins' THEO. In the Archaic period the ancestor of the 2nd genitive appeared simply as -a, without the suffix-final -l. So, for example, the Archaic 2nd genitive of the feminine family name hirminai had the form hirminai-a. Two common personal names, aranθ and larθ, formed their genitives in the same manner: larθi-a and aranθi-a. (A stem-final -i appears before the genitive ending in these two forms.) The Archaic feminine personal name corresponding to masculine larθ was larθai; its genitive was larθai-a, revealing a stem distinct from that found in the genitive of its masculine counterpart larθi-a.

4.13 The pertinentive case and the ablative case also had two sets of endings, one set built with an -s and another built with -l. The 1st pertinentive case had the form -si, e.g. alóaiana-si 'Alshaiana' MASC PRAE, clensi 'son', apa-si 'father'. The 2nd pertinentive case had the forms -ale, e.g. araθi-ale 'Aranth' MASC PRAE, and -(a)la, e.g. vestiricina-la 'Vestiricinai' FEM NOMEN. The ending -(a)la was restricted, as far as can be determined, to feminine family names.

The 1st ablative had a form similar to the 1st genitive in that it too ended with an s-suffix. The difference between the 1st ablative and the 1st genitive was linked to changes in the quality of the stem vowel in the ablative. The changes were as follows: a → e, e → ei (sometimes written e, i), u → ui. The 1st ablative of the stem rasna- was rasnes; the ablative of the stem tute was tuteis; and the ablative of the stem velu- was veluis. The 2nd ablative had the form -als in Neo-Etruscan and the form -(a)las in the Archaic period, e.g. arnθ-als 'Arnth' MASC PRAE, veleθna-las 'Velethnai' FEM NOMEN.

4.14 The ending for the locative case, regardless of stem type, was -i. In Neo-Etruscan this ending appeared most clearly in nominal stems ending in consonants, e.g. zilc-i 'in the governorship' and caper-i 'with a garment (?)'. For nominal stems ending in the vowels -a and -e, the locative ending -i coalesced with the stem-vowel to become -e, e.g. rasne 'among the people' < *rasna-i. If the nominal stem ended in -i, then the vowels of the stem and the ending contracted and the result was -i. For i-stem nouns the locative generally had the same form as the nominative/accusative, e.g. zamθi + -c 'and with a gold fibula' < *zamθi-i + -c 'and' ENCLITIC CONJ, although there is at least one instance, namely θii 'by means of water' LOC, in which the locative was marked by double spelling of the vowel -i.

The locative case was regularly characterized by means of a postpositional element -θ(i) 'in', e.g. spure-θi 'in the community' LOC + POST < *spura-i-θi. This postpositional element was so common that by the end of the Neo-Etruscan period some Etruscan speakers perceived it as the regular case suffix of the locative. The Neo-Etruscan word zilc 'governorship' had as its regular locative zilci. But there was an alternative form zilcθi, in which the postposition was added directly to the stem, which itself was unmarked by the locative case suffix -i.

4.15 Even though the inflectional endings came in two sets for the genitive, pertinentive, and ablative cases, it is not always possible to predict which set of endings a particular noun favored. For example, the noun flere 'divinity' was inflected with a 1st genitive, flere-s, but the noun spura 'community' was inflected with a 2nd genitive spura-l.

Some Etruscologists claim that a few nouns were inflected with both the *l*-genitive and the *s*-genitive, but it is not at all clear that these two inflectional forms were functionally the same. In fact it may well be—though the evidence is scanty—that some nouns had a 'mixed' inflection, employing the ending of the *l*-type for the genitive case but the ending of the *s*-type for the ablative (see the paradigm of **cilθ** in (1) below). On the other hand, for Etruscan names the distribution of the two sets of suffixes is clearer, as the type of suffix was governed by the final sound of the stem form. Names ending in vowels took *s*-inflection, e.g. **marce-s** 'Marce', **ramuθa-s** 'Ramutha'; those ending in consonants (-**s**, -**ś**, -**θ**) followed *l*-inflection, e.g. **laris-al** 'of Laris'. Feminine family names, regardless of the shape of the formative suffix, always inflected with endings of the *l*-type, e.g. **vipina-l** 'Vipinei'.

4.16 Partial paradigms of Etruscan nouns from the Neo-Etruscan period are cited below according to stem type.

(1) Singular paradigms, consonant stems

NOM/ACC	zilc 'governorship'	tiur 'month'	laris 'Laris'	cilθ 'citadel'
1ST GEN		tivrs		
2ND GEN	zilacal		larisal	cilθl
1ST PERT				
2ND PERT			larisale	
1ST ABL				cilθσ
2ND ABL				
LOC	zilci	tiuri-m[1]		

(2) Singular paradigms, vowel stems

NOM/ACC	mutna 'sarcophagus'	rasna 'people, public'	θi 'water'
1ST GEN			θis
2ND GEN	mutnal-θi[2]	rasnal	
1ST PERT			
2ND PERT			
1ST ABL	mutnes	rasnes	
2ND ABL			
LOC	mutne	rasne	θii

---

[1] **tiuri-m**: **-m** is an enclitic conjunction 'and'.
[2] **mutnal-θi**: **-θi** is the postposition 'in'.

(3) Paradigms, consonant/vowel stems

NOM/ACC	meθlum 'city'		vel 'Vel'	larθ 'Larth'
1ST GEN	meθlumes		velus	
2ND GEN				larθial
1ST PERT			velusi	
2ND PERT				larθiale
1ST ABL			veluis	larθals
2ND ABL				
LOC	meθlume/meθlum-θ[3]			

4.17 The noun **clan** 'son' had irregular inflection. The stem-vowel was modified in the oblique cases of the singular and in all cases of the plural, as seen in the following paradigm:

(4) Paradigm of **clan**

	singular	plural
	singular	plural
NOM/ACC	clan	clenar
1ST GEN	cles, clens	cliniiaras
1ST PERT	clinsi, clensi	clenaraσi
ABL	clen	

Exactly how the stems with *e*-vocalism and *i*-vocalism are to be explained is not clear. In at least one form, **cliniiaras**, the -i- may have arisen by vowel raising or umlaut before the sequence **-nii-** (phonetically /ny/ or /niy/). Scholars who take this view argue that the resultant high vowel then spread from **cliniiaras** to other forms of the paradigm. Unfortunately, no other Etruscan nominal form behaves in precisely the same way this one does.

Plurals

4.18 Etruscan nouns were inflected for two numbers, singular and plural. The plural was formed by means of two suffixes, one ending in **-r(a)-** and another ending in **-χva** (plus variants **-cva** and **-va**, on which see below), **aise-r** 'gods' vs. **avil-χva** 'years'. The two inflectional types are to be distinguished in terms of a feature such as animacy *vel sim*. The class of animate nouns, encompassing those referring to humans and the noun **ais** 'god', inflected by means of an *r*-plural, while inanimate nouns inflected by means of **-χva**.

---

[3] **meθlum-θ**: -θ is the postposition 'in'.

4.19 The plural suffix for inanimate nouns had three forms, -χva, -cva, and -va. The distribution of these endings was determined by the quality of the final sound of the stem to which they were added. Stems ending in dental consonants took the suffix -cva, e.g. cilθ : cilθ-cva 'citadels (?)', culσ : culσ-cva 'gates'. Stems in palatal vowels (/i, e/) and consonants (/ʃ/) had the suffix -va or -ua, e.g. hupni : hupni-va 'burial niches', zusle : zusle-va 'offerings', murσ́ : murz-ua 'ossuaries'. The remaining stem-types inflected with -χva, e.g. fler : fler-χva 'sacrifices'.

(5) Plural forms

	singular (NOM/ACC)	plural (NOM/ACC)
ANIMATE	clan 'son'	clenar
	ais 'god'	aiser
	papals 'nephew'	papalser
	huσ́ 'child'	huσ́ur
	atrs 'parent'	atrser
INANIMATE	singular (NOM/ACC)	plural (NOM/ACC)
	avil 'year'	avilχva
	fler 'sacrifice'	flerχva
	pulum 'star'	pulumχva
	culs 'gate'	culscva
	cilθ 'citadel (?)'	cilθcva
	hupni 'burial niche'	hupniva
	zusle 'offering'	zusleva
	murσ́ 'ossuary'	murzua

4.20 Some Etruscologists analyze the nouns **tular** 'boundary', **naper** 'unit (of measurement)', and **hilar** '?' as animate plurals. The first two forms are probably singular noun stems ending in -r, of the type exemplified by **caper** 'garment (?)', **caperχva** INANIM PL. The fact that an adjective **tularia** 'of the boundary' is derived from the stem **tular** supports this analysis, as there are no examples of derivational suffixes added to inflectional endings. **Hilar** is a member of a triad of forms associated with the root hil-, namely, **hil**, **hilar**, and **hilχvetra**. The view that **hilar** is an animate plural is troublesome because **hilχvetra** is best analyzed as an inanimate plural locative plus the postposition -**tra** 'on behalf of', i.e. hil-χva-i- + -tra. It seems more reasonable then to assume that the plural of **hil** is hilχva and that **hilar** is the same type of derivative formation as **tular**.

4.21 The inflection of plural noun forms follows, insofar as can be determined, a regular pattern of inflection. Inanimate nouns took the 2nd genitive ending -l; animate nouns took the 1st genitive ending -s. Partial plural paradigms are cited below. Animate nouns are listed first; inanimate nouns follow.

(6) Plural paradigms

> *animate plural inflection*
> NOM/ACC   **clenar** 'sons'   **aiser** 'gods'
> 1ST GEN   cliniiaras   aiseras
> 1ST PERT   clenarasi
>
> *inanimate plural inflection*
> NOM/ACC   cilθcva 'citadels (?)'   flerχva 'sacrifices'
> 2ND GEN   cilθcval   avilχval 'years'
> LOC   cilθcve-ti[4]   órenχve '?'

Grammatical Gender

4.22 Etruscan nominal forms were generally not inflected for grammatical gender, but the following exceptions are to be noted. The suffixes -i and -(i)a, which were borrowed from one of the Italic languages, were used to derive the names of women from those of men, e.g. Neo-Etruscan larθ → fem. larθ-i, óeθre → fem. óeθr-a. The suffix -θa was added to the noun **lautni** 'family servant/dependent' to form the corresponding feminine form, i.e. **lautniθa**. This suffix may be the same as that used to form feminine names such as **ramuθa**.

Noun-forming Suffixes

4.23 The formation of Etruscan noun stems is poorly understood. Many suffixes can be and indeed have been postulated, but few have been identified to the degree that their derivational behavior can be considered secure. That being said, a few suffixes deserve to be mentioned.

The suffix -(u)za is perhaps the best known. It was added to nouns to build diminutives. This formation is particularly common in designations for types of pottery, e.g. **qutumuza** 'a small drinking-vessel', **leχtumuza** 'a small oil-flask', and **çunθeruza** 'a small pyxis', all of which belong to the Archaic Etruscan period. Neo-Etruscan formations of this type such as **θapnza** 'small bowl' and **spanza** 'small plate' reflect medial vowel syncope; the bases to which they were added, **θapna** and **spanti**, ended in a vowel (in the case of the latter, */spanti-tsa/ > /spanttsa/ or perhaps

---

[4] cilθcve-ti: -ti is the postposition 'in'.

/spantsa/, written **spanza**). At least two other nouns are securely identified as diminutive formations, namely, **alza** 'small gift', which was derived from the root noun **al-** 'give', and **turza** 'votive gift', which was built
to the root **tur-** 'dedicate'. This suffix was also used to form names of endearment. In the *Tabula Cortonensis* the son of Larth was called **larza**, that
is to say, 'Larth junior'.

The suffix -**θura** was added to names to form collectives referring to
members of a family or to the extended family itself. Members of the
Clavtie family were designated by the term **clavtieθura-**, those of *Velthina*
family by **velθinaθura-**. The suffix -**θura** was also added to the name of the
god **paχa-** (Bacchus) to form a noun referring to his followers, namely,
paχaθura- 'Bacchants'. It seems likely that in origin -**θura** was made up
of two morphemes, a derivational suffix -**θu** and the plural suffix -**r(a)**.
Following this analysis **clavtieθurasi** is to be parsed as a pertinentive plural formation; the function of the suffix -**θu** must have been to indicate
possession or relationship, thus, 'of/for/to the Clavtie family'.

A small set of words ended in the suffix -**(a)θ**. Most can be interpreted
as agent nouns, e.g. **zilaθ** 'one who governs', **tevaraθ** 'one who judges',
snenaθ 'attendant', and **trutnuθ/trutnvt** 'one who interprets (lightning)
(?)'. Other possible members of this group include **leinθ** and the name
of the underworld divinity **vanθ** 'Vanth', but their meanings cannot be
determined.

A scene involving the giant Atlas was carved on a bronze mirror from
Vulci (Vc S.2). The caption **aril** accompanies the figure of the giant. The
root of this word is **ar-**, whose meaning belonged to the semantic sphere
of making, building, constructing, working, etc. As a result, **aril** is sometimes analyzed as **ar-** + **-il**, and the suffix is interpreted as an agent noun
suffix. However, other nouns belonging to this category of formation,
namely, **acil** 'work', **θil** 'water rights (?)', **avil** 'year', and **óuθil** 'deposition
(?)', permit an action noun reading and it may be best to interpret **aril**
also in this manner, thus 'labor'.

4.23.1 Several interesting articles focusing on nominal morphology have appeared in the last
few years. Agostiniani 2003 is a detailed examination of the diminutive suffix -**za**. For an interpretation of the morpheme -**(a)θ** see Wylin 2002b. Wylin (2004) argues that -**ó** /ʃ/ is an agentive
suffix.

Adjectives

4.24 Etruscan adjectives appear to have had form classes similar to
those of nouns. For this reason, it is often difficult to distinguish formally between adjectives and nouns. The difficulty is exacerbated by the

fact that adjectives could function syntactically as substantivized nouns, e.g. θina 'of/for water' → 'container for water'. For all intents and purposes, Etruscan adjectives can be identified only by means of syntactic context, and then in many cases only because the evidence suggests that the canonical order was noun + adjective. For example, in inscription Cr 4.4, one of the gold tablets from Pyrgi, the word θuta, which appears in the phrase meχ θuta 'sacred place (?)', is interpreted as an adjective based on its position in the phrase, not on its formal characteristics. Compare the phrase ati θuta 'revered (?) mother' in AT 1.193.

4.25 As far as can be determined, Etruscan adjectives inflected for case in a manner similar to nouns. The adjective mlaχ 'good, beautiful' is found in agreement with the heads of phrases marked for genitive case, e.g. çpuriaç mlakaç 'of the good Spuria', and for pertinentive case, e.g. ave[lesi] mlakaçi 'for/to the good Avile'. The adjective mlaχ was also used as a substantive in the noun phrase mlacasi 'for/to the good (man)'. At this point we find no evidence to indicate that Etruscan adjectives inflected for number.

Adjective-forming Suffixes

4.26 The most common adjective-forming suffix was -na, which was used to build possessive adjectives from noun stems. For example, the adjective paχana 'belonging to Pakha [Bacchus]' was derived from the nominal stem paχa-, and the adjective eleivana 'containing oil' was derived from the stem eleiva- 'oil'. The suffix -na was also used to form family names from personal names, e.g. spurie → spurie-na. In the prehistoric period this suffix formed patronymics. When the Etruscans adopted the system of family names from Italic peoples, many patronymic formations in -na were reanalyzed as family names (see §7.4).

The primary function of the suffix -χ was to form adjectives from place names, e.g. rumaχ 'of/from Rome', velznaχ 'from Volsinii', and sveamaχ 'from Sovana (?)'. It is possible that this suffix, in unaspirated form -c, was also used to form adjectives such as neθśrac, if this word is correctly interpreted as a modifier meaning 'of the haruspex'. The morphological composition of this word is not clear; nor is it certain that aspirated stops in word-final position changed to the corresponding plain stops in southern Etruria.

The word tularias, which is a derivative of the stem tular- 'boundary' and may be parsed as stem tular- + adjective-forming suffix -ia- + 1st genitive ending -s, can safely be interpreted as modifying the name

selvansl 'Silvans' (divinity) in Ta 1.17. Presumably, then, -ia- is a suffix
that forms adjectives and that has a meaning something along the lines
of 'associated with'.

Numbers

4.27 The inner workings of the Etruscan system of numbers are reasonably well understood even if we do not know the words for the higher
numbers such as 100 or 1,000.

The numbers 1–10 are listed in (5). Numbers '1' through '6' are secure
thanks in large part to the existence of dice with the names for the numbers incised on them. Stems of the numbers '7', '8', and '9' are known
through derivative formations, but it is not entirely clear what stem cor-
responds to what numerical value. The customary assignment of values
is: **cezp-** '7', **semφ-** '8', and **nurφ-** '9'. The number '10' is **σar** /sar/. Inflected
forms appear in the phrases **ciσ σariσ** '13' (= **ci-σ** '3' 1ST GEN + **σari-σ** '10' 1ST
GEN) and **huθzars** '16' (= **huθ-s** '6' 1ST GEN + **sar-s** '10' 1ST GEN).

(7) Cardinal numbers 1–10

1	θu, θun-	6	huθ
2	zal, zel-, esl-, esal-	7	cezp-
3	ci, ce-	8	semφ-
4	σa, σe-	9	nurφ-
5	maχ, muv-	10	σar, σari-

In those cases where variant forms for a number exist, the free form is
cited first. Forms followed by dashes are those attested in inflected forms
and/or in derivatives. The variant forms of the numbers are in most cases
without convincing explanation. However, the *e*-vocalism of the number
'3' **ce-** can be gotten from **ci** by vowel lowering.

4.27.1 The most cogent discussion of Etruscan numbers is that provided by Agostiniani (1995).
Agostiniani (1997b) settles the question of whether **huθ** was '6' or '4' in favor of the former.

4.28 Recently it has been argued that **snuiaφ/snuiuφ**, which is found
in the final clause of Pyrgi tablet Cr 4.4, stood for the number '12'. The
arguments for this interpretation are interesting, but not entirely convincing.

4.28.1 See Giannecchini 1997 for arguments that **snuiaφ** may have meant '12'.

4.29 The number '20' is attested by multiple stem-forms. The free form
is **zaθrum**; the stems **zaθrm-** and **zaθrmi-** appear in inflection. The suf-

fix -alχ was employed to form the decades greater than '20'. For example cealχ '30' was formed by joining ci '3' and -alχ (-e- here by vowel lowering). Similarly, '70' was formed from the number '7' cezp- and the suffix -alχ, cezpalχ. The number '50' had an idiosyncratic formation, muvalχ. Here the stem for '5' is muv- rather than maχ.

When a decade was inflected the stem was either -alχl- or -alχu-, e.g. cealχls 1ST GEN, cialχus 1ST GEN. The distribution of the two stems reflects regional phonological developments. The stem -alχl- appears in inscriptions from Volci; -alχu- is the form in the *Liber Linteus*, which exhibits northern dialect features.

4.29.1 Rix (1989b) has a substantial section on the prehistory of the forms for the decades and their regional developments, including comparative data from Lemnian (see §§12.6–9).

4.30 Numbers other than the decades were formed by additive phrases (for numbers ending in 1–6) or subtractive phrases (for numbers ending in 7–9). The Etruscan phrase maχ cezpalχ, '75', stood for '5 (and) 70'. The number '19', θunem zaθrum, was literally '20 minus 1'. The Etruscan phrase is to be parsed as θun-em '1 + minus' + zaθrum '20'.

Phrases such as ci cealχ '3 + 30' were considered two words for the purposes of inflection. The 1st genitive of the phrase cited above was cis cealχ<l>s. In contrast, subtractive phrases were marked inflectionally as single units, e.g. ciem zaθrms '20 minus 3' 1ST GEN, where the number '20', zaθrms, was inflected for case.

4.31 Numbers appear to have been inflected in the same manner as nouns, though there are no undisputed examples of numbers inflected for case outside the 1st genitive.

4.31.1 Cristofani (1995:49) suggests that ciiei is the locative of the number '3', but the identification is far from certain.

4.32 Funerary inscriptions often indicated the age of the deceased by ciphers. The Etruscan symbols for numbers were the following: one = I, five = Λ, ten = X, fifty = Λ, and one hundred = X. The Etruscan symbols for 500 and 1,000 are unknown, although some have hypothesized that these numbers were represented by Q and ⊕ and thus similar to those found in Latin.

4.32.1 Rix (1969) discusses the forms of the ciphers as well as the origin of the Etruscan letter Λ = /m/.

4.33 Ordinal numbers were derived by means of the suffix -śna, which was added to the stem of a number, e.g. zaθrum-śne 'on the 20th' LOC.

Numbers could be turned into adverbs by adding the suffix -z (also -zi),
e.g. θunz 'once', eslz '2 times', ciz '3 times', nurφzi '9 times'. The distribution of the variant forms of the suffix is unclear.

Two participles were derived from numerical bases. Both forms appear in contexts referring to the expansion of the size of tomb chambers.
Zelarvenas is a -**nas** participle derived from the number two. It appears in
a funerary inscription in which it governs the noun **tamera** 'tomb chamber'. This suggests a meaning along the lines of 'having doubled (the size
of)'. The participle **óarvenas**, which also governs the noun **tamera** as object, seems to mean 'having quadrupled (the size of)'. Both participles
were derived from numerical stems ending in the suffix -**(a)r**, which is
best interpreted as a formative for multiplicative adjectives, e.g. **zelar**
'double', **óar** 'quadruple'. The verb stems were formed by the suffix -**ve**.

4.33.1 For the interpretation of the participles **zelarvenas** and **óarvenas** see Agostiniani 1997b.

5 PRONOUNS AND THE ARTICLE

Introduction

5.1 Etruscan pronouns had several distinctive features when compared with nouns and adjectives. Pronouns had a distinct case-form for the direct object of a transitive verb, e.g. **mini** 'me' accusative (direct object) vs. **mi** 'I' nominative (subject). As we have seen, nouns and adjectives did not formally distinguish subject and direct object cases. The pronominal genitive was different from nominal genitive forms, e.g. pronominal genitive -**la** in **cla** 'of this' vs. nominal genitives -**(a)l** (**atial** 'of the mother') and -**s** (**marces** 'of Marce'). (One suspects, though, that pronominal -**la** and nominal -**(a)l** come ultimately from the same prehistoric form.) Demonstrative pronouns had two sets of forms in Neo-Etruscan, one with an initial vowel, e.g. **eta** 'this', and one without, e.g. **ta**. Finally, demonstratives could stand either as free words, e.g. **etan** 'this', or they could be affixed to a word, e.g. -**cle** LOC (**hanipaluscle** 'in (for/by?) the (army) of Hannibal').

The Etruscan article -**ða** 'the', whose inflection follows that of the enclitic demonstrative pronouns, is discussed in this chapter because it appears to have begun its existence as a demonstrative and was later re-analyzed as an article. (This type of functional shift is common; the definite articles in Ancient Greek and English were also originally demonstrative pronouns.)

5.2 The identification of nominative and accusative pronominal forms is in most instances absolutely secure. However, the identification of other case forms of pronouns is less so, in part because they are often attached as enclitics to the preceding word and in part because they are found in syntactic contexts that are difficult to interpret.

5.2.1 Facchetti 2002a:27–37, 53–73 is the most expansive discussion of the Etruscan pronominal system in print, but his treatment must be regarded with caution because of its speculative nature. Rix (1984b:229–31; 2004:954–6) and Steinbauer (1999:91–5) provide shorter, more accessible synopses. The most conservative assessment is Cristofani 1991a:71–4.

Personal Pronouns

5.3 The Etruscan 1st person pronoun 'I, me' is well attested in nominative and accusative case forms, almost all belonging to the Archaic period or to the earliest decades of the fifth century BCE. The nominative was the bare pronominal stem **mi**. The accusative ended in the suffix -**ni**, which was added directly to the pronominal stem, **mini** = **mi**- + -**ni**.

(1) Etruscan 1st person pronoun

NOM   **mi**
ACC   **mini, mine, mene, min(pi), men(pe)**

The accusative had multiple spellings in Archaic Etruscan inscriptions. The oldest and most common spelling was **mini**. Other spellings are best taken to be chronological developments from this original form. **Mine** and **mene** are attested in inscriptions that date to ca. 600 BCE or later. **Mene** appears in three inscriptions from Veii. **Mine** appears in ten inscriptions, five of which were recovered from Veii. The accusatives **min**- and **men**- are attested once each and always in combination with the enclitic particle -**pi**/-**pe**. Both forms are from inscriptions that date to the fifth century BCE; they arose as the result of vowel syncope, **minpi** < *mini-pi*. The *e*-vocalism in the pronominal forms (and in the particle -**pe**) has not been satisfactorily explained, but it is difficult to connect the change of -**i** to -**e** in these forms to the change described in §3.10.

5.4 Recently, an old idea that **un** and **une** were 2nd person pronouns has been resurrected. This identification rests crucially on the interpretation of passages in the *Liber Linteus* as prayers, for example the *neθuns*-ritual (LL VIII, 3ff. and IX, 1ff.), an interpretation for which there is as yet no consensus. As a result, other interpretations for **un** and **une** are possible, e.g. as a 3rd person pronoun. Compare the competing interpretations for LL VIII, 11–12 cited in (2).

(2) trin · flere · neθunsl · une I mlaχ · puθs θaclθ θartei zivaσ fler
(LL VIII, 11–12)

(a) 'say: O spirit of Neptune, to/for you (?), O good (god), the living victim, an unblemished one (?), is placed (?) on the θarte of the θac-'

trin 'say', IMPV; **flere** 'spirit', VOC = NOM/ACC; **neθunsl** 'Neptune', THEO, 2ND GEN; **une** 'for you (?)', PERT; **mlaχ** 'good', VOC = NOM/ACC; **puθs** 'place (?)', IMPV; **θaclθ** = **θacl** '?', 2ND GEN + -θ 'in', POST; **θartei** '?', LOC; **zivaσ** 'living', NOM/ACC; **fler** 'victim', NOM/ACC

(b) 'Invoke the spirit of Neptune. For him (?) the living victim, an unblemished one (?), is placed (?) on the θarte of the θac-.'

> trin 'invoke', IMPV; flere 'spirit', NOM/ACC; neθunsl 'Neptune', THEO, 2ND GEN; une 'for him (?)', 3RD SG PRO, PERT; mlaχ 'unblemished (?)', NOM/ACC; puθs 'place (?)', IMPV; θaclθ = θacl '?', 2ND GEN + -θ 'in', POST; θartei '?', LOC; zivaσ 'living', NOM/ACC; fler 'victim', NOM/ACC

In interpretation (2a), the imperative trin 'say' introduces the prayer; the phrases flere · neθunsl and mlaχ are vocatives. Une refers to the addressee, namely, the spirit or godhead of Nethuns (Neptune). In interpretation (2b), the imperative trin 'invoke' governs the noun phrase flere neθunsl. Une has anaphoric function; it refers back to flere neθunsl. Zivaσ fler is the subject of the verb puθs and the adjective mlaχ is in apposition to the subject phrase.

Both interpretations have good points and bad points. Both accept, however tentatively, an interpretation of the word puθs as a passive. This is a speculative interpretation.

A short inscription from Volsinii (Vs 2.40) is also offered as support for the idea that une is the 2nd pronoun. In this inscription une is parsed as a pertinentive form that derives from an earlier *un-ale by syncope (*un-le), regressive assimilation (*un-ne), and simplification (une). However, as is often the case, other interpretations are possible, so one cannot rule definitively in favor of the view that un/une means 'you'.

(3) ţuris : mi : une : ame (Vs 2.40)
     'Doris, I am for you (?).'

> ţuris 'Doris', NOM/ACC = VOC; mi 'I', 1ST SG PRO, NOM; une 'for you', 2ND SG PRO, PERT; ame 'am', NON-PAST ACT

5.4.1 For background and presentation of the evidence see Rix 1991a. See Wylin 2000:223–8 for critique and a counterproposal.

Demonstratives

5.5 Two demonstrative pronouns were well attested in Etruscan. The Archaic Etruscan forms were ika and ita. The Neo-Etruscan descendants were eca and eta. The e-vocalism in the initial syllables of eta and eca was the outcome of vowel lowering, ika > eca.

The Neo-Etruscan demonstratives had two sets of forms, one with an initial vowel and one without: eca/ca and eta/ta. The forms without an initial vowel probably arose from contexts in which they were employed as enclitics, the initial vowel being lost due to vowel syncope or perhaps via metanalysis in forms where the stems to which the demonstrative was affixed ended in a vowel.

At this point in time, the demonstratives **eca** (**ika**) and **eta** (**ita**) cannot be distinguished from one another in meaning or function (for usage, see Chapter 8). Both mean 'this' when they have deictic function. The claim that the two demonstratives were distributed along geographic lines, one south and the other north, finds no support in the epigraphic evidence. Nor does the suggestion that their usage was determined by whether the noun they referred to was animate or inanimate. The idea that **eca** was expanding its sphere of usage at the expense of **eta** during the final centuries of the Neo-Etruscan period may have something to recommend it, though we cannot say why this should be the case.

Neo-Etruscan demonstrative paradigms are given in (4) and discussed below; Archaic Etruscan paradigms are deferred until (5). We list here only the forms that are considered secure, beginning with the forms that stand as free words. A dash following a pronoun indicates that a postposition was affixed to it; a dash in front of a pronoun indicates that it was affixed to a noun as an enclitic.

(4)   Neo-Etruscan demonstrative paradigms

NOM	eca, ca	-ca	eta, ta	-ta
ACC	ecn, cn		etan, tn	-tn[1]
2ND GEN		-cla		-tla
1ST ABL			teiσ	-tiσ[2]
LOC	cei		tei[3]	
	ecl-θi, cl-θi	-cle[4]		

The Neo-Etruscan locative form -cle appears to be built on the genitive stem of the demonstrative **eca/ca**: *cla- + -i > **cle**. The locative forms that were followed by postpositions were built on the same genitive stem, though one deprived of its final vowel, **ecl-/cl-**. These locative formations stand in contrast to the locatives **cei** and **tei**, which were built to the stems **ca-** and **ta-** by addition of the locative suffix -i (for the change of *ai to ei and e, see §3.14). Interestingly, there may have been a functional difference between the two locative formations. The locatives **ecl-θi**, **cl-θi**, and -cle have prototypical locative function, while the locative of **eta/ta**, **tei**,

---

[1] -tn was affixed to the stem **ċacni-**.

[2] -tiσ was attached to the ablative noun **śparzêσ-tiσ** to form a phrase, 'from this tablet'.

[3] Tei is found in the *Liber Linteus* as a modifier of the word **faσei**, which seems to mean 'libation' or 'drink offering'. The phrase may be translated 'by means of this libation'.

[4] -cle was affixed to a genitive to form a phrase, **hanipalus-cle** 'in (by/for) the (army) of Hannibal'.

has instrumental function, which is also a possible, though ultimately unverifiable, interpretation for the function of **cei**. Unfortunately, we cannot be sure that this functional distribution is not just an accident of attestation.

Three forms that are not listed in (4), namely **ecs**, **ceσ**, and **cσ**, are generally classified as 1st genitive forms but they appear in contexts that are difficult to analyze. As far as can be determined, an ablative function is just as likely as a genitive. For **ceσ**, an interpretation as an ablative makes more sense from a formal point of view because *e*-vocalism is what would be expected in a 1st ablative form of the pronoun **ca**.

(5)   Archaic Etruscan demonstrative paradigms

NOM	ika	ita	-ita[5]
ACC	ikan	itan, itun, itane	
2ND GEN			-itala,[6] -itula[7]
LOC			-itale,[8] -itule[9]

Some texts list -itas and -icas as genitive forms, but there is nothing particularly attractive about these analyses, particularly since the genitive case of demonstratives ended in **-la**.

The nominative and accusative cases of the demonstratives were distinct in form. The accusative ending was **-n**. At some point in Etruscan prehistory this ending may have been the same as the accusative form found in the 1st person pronoun, **mini = mi + -ni**, so Archaic Etruscan **ikan** < *ikani*. In fact, the Archaic accusative form **itane** may reflect this prehistoric form even though, once again, we cannot explain the change of word-final *-i* to **-e** (cf. **mine**). Accusative **itun** shows the effects of vowel weakening in word-final syllables before nasals. For **ecn** we assume the loss of the vowel in the final syllable and vocalization of the nasal (see §3.23).

One of the most controversial aspects associated with demonstratives concerns the interpretation of the forms **-cle**, **-itale**, and **-itule**, which are classed here as locatives. In terms of form, they appear to be pertinentives and as such stand in contrast to the locative formations **tei** and **cei**.

---

[5]-ita was affixed to the stem riθna-, i.e. riθnaita.

[6]-itala was affixed to the stem sele-, i.e. seleitala. This word may modify the noun **zilacal**, which is inflected for genitive case.

[7]-itula was affixed to the stem riθna-, i.e. riθnaitula. This form may modify the following genitive **senaziula.s.tra**, if we are correct in segmenting that form as **senaziulas** GEN + **-tra** POST. Compare -itula in the form **smucinθiunaitula**, which modifies the genitive **selvansel** 'Selvans' THEO.

[8]-itale is affixed to teçiame-, i.e. teçiameitale. This word may modify the following noun **ilucve**, which was inflected for locative case.

[9]-itule was affixed to a stem ióve-, i.e. ióveitule. The phrase may be translated as 'on the Ides'.

In terms of function, however, they modify nouns inflected for locative case. Exactly how this discrepancy between form and function is to be explained is not clear.

5.6 The notes appended to paradigms (4) and (5) reveal that the demonstrative when used as an enclitic had two distinct modes of behavior. First, it could be affixed to an inflected nominal form as part of a noun phrase, e.g. **hanipalus-cle** 'in (for/by) the (army) of Hannibal', often with the head of the phrase suppressed. Second, it could be affixed to uninflected nominal stems to form nouns. So, for example, the form **lurmicla** is to be parsed as **lurmi-cla**. **Lurmi** is an uninflected nominal stem; **-cla** is an enclitic demonstrative with genitive inflection. This form translates as 'to/for the *lurmi* (one)'; it refers to a divinity of undetermined type.

5.7 The Neo-Etruscan demonstrative **eca/ca** also served as the base for a pronominal form extended by an *l*-suffix. The identification of **cnl** as an accusative form is secure, as is shown by (6), but the interpretation of the other members of the paradigm, namely **cal**, **clal-**, and **clel**, is much less so.

(6)   cnl · nuθe · malec · lart · cêlatina ... (ETP 74, 23A)
      'Lart Celatina listens to (?) and watches over this (legal proceeding?).'

      cnl = cn 'this', DEM PRO, ACC + -l '?', DEICTIC PARTICLE; nuθe 'listen to (?)', NON-PAST ACT; malec = male 'watch over', NON-PAST ACT + -c 'and', ENCLITIC CONJ; lart 'Lart', MASC PRAE, NOM/ACC; cêlatina 'Celatina', MASC NOMEN, NOM/ACC

The affix -l may be a deictic particle, cf. Latin -c in the demonstratives *hic, haec, hoc*. The claim that -l was a plural marker, which has been offered as an interpretation for these forms, cannot be proved or disproved based on the evidence at hand.

(7)   Neo-Etruscan demonstratives + -l

NOM	ca-l
ACC	cn-l
2ND GEN	cla-l-um[10]
LOC	cle-l

5.7.1 For the interpretation of cn-l as a plural see Pfiffig 1969:109–10. See also Facchetti 2002a: 28–34, 54.

---

[10]-um is an enclitic conjunction.

5.8 Another demonstrative pronoun may be attested in the form **sa-** /sa/. The syntactic contexts in which this word is found favor the identification as a pronominal form, but they do not guarantee the interpretation as a demonstrative. A meaning similar to Latin *idem*, 'the same', is also a possibility.

(8) óeθre curunas · | ̣veluṣ [· r]amθa[s ·] avenalc | saṃ ṃaṇ · óu̯θ[i]θ · arce | ... (Ta 1.35)
'Shethre Curunas (was) (son) of Vel and Ramtha Avenei; and this (man) (or 'the same fellow') constructed the monument (?) in the tomb ...'

óeθre 'Shethre', MASC PRAE, NOM/ACC; **curunas** 'Curunas', MASC NOMEN, 1ST GEN; ̣veluṣ 'of Vel', MASC PRAE, 1ST GEN; **[r]amθa[s]** 'Ramtha', FEM PRAE, 1ST GEN; **avenalc** = avenal 'Avenai', FEM NOMEN, 2ND GEN + -c 'and', ENCLITIC CONJ; saṃ = sa- 'he, the same', 3RD PRO, NOM + -m 'and', ENCLITIC CONJ; ṃaṇ 'monument (?)', NOM/ACC; óu̯θ[i]θ = óu̯θ[i] 'tomb', LOC + -θ 'in', POST; **arce** 'constructed', PAST ACT

5.8.1 Wylin (2005) reviews the epigraphic material bearing on the interpretation of sa- as a demonstrative pronoun.

The Article

5.9 Etruscan **-(i)óa** had the function of a definite article. The article was an enclitic, e.g. **velθuruóa** = velθurus + -óa 'the (son) of Velthur'. The collocation of morphemes in these so-called articulated phrases often effected changes in the form of the final sound of the stem to which the enclitic article was affixed. The most important changes took place when the article was added to genitive forms ending in -s. In these cases the final -s of the inflectional ending was assimilated to the palatal sibilant of the enclitic, e.g. velus + -óa /welus-ʃa/ → /weluʃʃa/. The resulting cluster was then simplified, yielding a single palatal sibilant, veluóa = /weluʃa/. When the article was added to the 2nd genitive suffix, which ended in the liquid -l, a transition vowel appeared between the noun and the article, e.g. larθal-i-óa 'the (son) of Larth'.

5.9.1 For the identification of -óa as an article, one must begin with the description in Rix 1963:54–66.

5.10 We possess no secure examples showing the inflection of personal pronouns or demonstratives for number, but there are convincing examples of plural inflection for the article. The paradigm is given in (9).

(9) Paradigm of the article

	singular	plural
NOM	-óa	-óva
ACC	-ón	
GEN	-óla	-óula
PERT	-óle	-óvle
LOC	-óe	-óve

The function of the articular forms -óva, etc., as plurals is guaranteed by a passage from the recently recovered *Tabula Cortonensis* (10). The article -iśvla, which was affixed to larisal (lariśaliśvla), refers to the Cushu brothers who were engaged in the transaction described in the *Tabula*. The article agrees in case and number with the plural genitive cuśuθu-raσ.

(10) ... cuśuθuraσ · lariśaliśvla · pêtruσc · ścêvaσ ... (ETP 74, 21–22A)
     '... of the Cushu brothers, the (sons) of Laris, and of Petru Shceva ...'

   cuśuθuraσ 'Cushu brothers', PL, 1ST GEN; lariśaliśvla = lariśal 'Laris', MASC
   PRAE, 2ND GEN + -iśvla 'the', DEF ART PL, 2ND GEN; pêtruσc = pêtruσ 'Petru',
   MASC PRAE, 1ST GEN + -c 'and', ENCLITIC CONJ; ścêvaσ 'Shceva', MASC NOMEN,
   1ST GEN

   5.10.1 See Eichner 2002 and Adiego 2006 for the evidence that the affix -óva is the plural of
   the article.

Other Pronominal Forms

5.11 The Etruscan words **an** and **in** served as relative or anaphoric pronouns of the third person. The pronoun **an** was selected if the antecedent was a person and thus presumably a member of the animate class of nouns. The pronoun **in** was the inanimate counterpart to **an**. It is not clear whether these two forms inflected for case or number. It has been suggested that a form attested in the *Liber Linteus*, **ananc**, may be the accusative of **an** followed by the enclitic conjunction -c, but the context in which it appears is not particularly clear. Inanimate **inni**, which is attested in the *Tabula Cortonensis*, is generally taken to be an accusative form (in- + -ni), but it does not clearly function as a relative or an anaphoric pronoun in the context in which it appears (see §11.6, Section I.1).

Etruscan had other, less well-attested, and therefore less well-understood, pronominal forms. A brief survey follows.

Cehen 'this' and its Neo-Etruscan descendant **cên** were almost certainly demonstratives of some type. Sentence (11), extracted from the *Tabula Cortonensis*, supports this interpretation.

(11) cên · zic · ziχuχe ... (ETP 74, 18A)
   'This document was written ...'

> cên 'this', DEM PRO, NOM; zic 'document', NOM/ACC; ziχuχe 'was written',
> PAST PASS

To judge by the form of other demonstratives, **cehen** must be a complex form, made up perhaps of a pronominal stem **ce-** plus a deictic particle **-hen**. Neo-Etruscan **cên** developed from **cehen** by loss of medial -h- followed by vowel contraction, i.e. **cehen** > *ceen* > **cên**.

Enan may be an indefinite pronoun. It is found in a prohibition incised on the wall of a tomb.

(12) **ein θui ara enan** (ETP 285)
   '(One) shall not make (set up?) anything here.'

> ein NEG; θui 'here', ADV; ara 'put, place', JUSSIVE; enan 'anything', INDEF PRO,
> ACC

This pronoun is sometimes connected with the genitive **enaσ**, which is attested in the *Liber Linteus*, but it is not clear that these two forms belong to the same pronominal paradigm.

Some Etruscologists claim that **ipa-** was an interrogative/relative pronoun. Possible members of the paradigm are, in addition to nominative **ipa**, the oblique case forms **ipaς** 1ST GEN, **ipal** 2ND GEN, and **ipei** LOC. The form **inpa** is generally parsed as **in-pa** and analyzed as an accusative, but this is not guaranteed. The evidence for interrogative/relative function is, however, far from conclusive.

Finally, the word **heva** may have had pronominal inflection. Alongside a 2nd genitive **hevl** there is a pronominal accusative **hevn**. As far as meaning is concerned, a reasonable guess is 'all, every'.

5.11.1 For the interpretation of **ipa** as an interrogative/relative see Rix 1984b:231 and Facchetti 2002a:67–8. For a different proposal see Wylin 2002a:219 and fn. 13, who translates **ipa** as 'other, another'.

6 VERBS AND PARTICIPLES

Introduction

6.1 Details about the Etruscan verbal system are less secure than details about the nominal and pronominal systems. In large part this is due to the type of inscriptions that are attested. Epitaphs, proprietary inscriptions, signatures of artisans, captions, and so forth make up a very high percentage of Etruscan texts. Many inscriptions belonging to these categories, particularly epitaphs (the most abundant category), do not have verb forms. The verbs in inscribed gifts, dedications, and votive inscriptions, epigraphic categories with numerous examples from the Archaic period, are restricted in large part to lexical items from the same semantic sphere, e.g. **turuce** 'dedicated (as an offering)', **muluvanice** 'gave (as a gift to)' and **alice** 'offered, presented'. Other verbs that are attested in inscriptions of this type have the same formal characteristics as the verbs mentioned above, e.g. **zinace** 'fashioned, fabricated', **ziχvanace** 'inscribed, painted'. As a result, lack of evidence is a serious impediment to a comprehensive overview of the verbal system. Another source of difficulty is the fact that the Etruscan verb is not as clearly characterized as nominal forms. As a result, it is not always easy to identify verb forms, even within the context of a sentence. Finally, the best sources for Etruscan verbs are the texts with the most complicated syntactic structures, namely the *Liber Linteus*, the *Tabula Capuana*, and the *Cippus Perusinus*, which are texts that we do not understand very well.

6.1.1 Wylin 2000 is the most comprehensive analysis of the Etruscan verb in print. Belfiore (2001) subjects Wylin's analysis of the verb system to a critical evaluation. Shorter, but nonetheless useful, synopses of the verb may be found in Rix 1984b:231–5 and 2004:956–61 and in Steinbauer 1999:101–6.

Verbs

6.2 The synopsis of Etruscan verb forms in (1) is a conservative presentation and reflects only those verbal categories that are virtually certain. It is possible that other formal categories existed and that they should be added to those presented here. Some of these categories and some of the verbs that are posited for them are discussed below.

We recognize three formal categories for mood: imperatives, jussives, and indicatives. Tense is represented by two categories: past and non-past. Whether the label 'non-past' is appropriate deserves some attention because there are inscriptions in which verb forms that are unmarked for past tense seem to refer to events in the past. It is possible that the major distinction here is aspectual and that our 'past indicative' forms are to be interpreted as perfective in aspect. The category of voice has two formally distinct representatives: active and passive. This distinction is securely attested only for past tense forms (but see §6.8).

(1)   Etruscan verbs

Imperative		tur 'give'		
Non-past Indicative	ame 'is'			
Past Indicative	amce 'was'	turuce 'gave'	menece 'made'	
Past Passive			menaχe 'was made'	
Jussive		tura 'shall give'		

6.3 The uninflected root or stem of the verb had imperative function, e.g. **tur** 'give', **trin** 'utter, invoke', **óin** 'take'. The verb **capi** 'take, seize, steal', which appears in the prohibition **ei minipi capi** 'don't steal me', ends in a vowel. This vowel may be part of the verb stem or it may be a suffix characterizing imperatives in prohibitions. The Etruscan word *capys* 'falcon' = 'one who seizes (?)' points in the direction of the first hypothesis.

6.4 Inflectional suffixes were added to the verb root or stem in order to signify past tense, and to signify indicative and jussive mood. The past active was marked by the suffix -c, and the non-past active was signaled by the absence of this suffix, e.g. **amce** 'was' vs. **ame** 'is'. Indicative mood was marked by the suffix -e, e.g. **am-e, amc-e**. The suffix of the jussive mood was -a, e.g. **ar-a** 'one should make'. The position of the suffixes in the verbal complex was root/stem + tense + mood, e.g. **turu-c-e**.

6.4.1 Some Etruscologists treat the suffix -e in opposition to -ce as indicating present tense (Colonna 1982) or as marking injunctive mood (Rix 1984b:233), that is to say, as signaling a category that covers activities unmarked for tense.

6.5 The verbs **tenve** and **zilaχnve**, both attested in the funerary inscription describing the political offices held by a certain Vel Lathites (Vs 1.179), make sense only if taken as referring to events in the past (**mar<u>nuχ spurana: eprθnevc : tenve** 'he held the office of *marunukh* of the city and the office of *eprthnev*'). These verbs appear to be built directly from the stem of *u*-participles, e.g. **tenu-** + **-e**. Functionally, they appear to be no different from past tense verbs formed with the suffix -c. In fact, the verbs zilaχnve 'held the office of governor' and zilaχnce/zilaχnuce are found in syntactic contexts that are virtually the same.

6.6 The verb **akarai**, which is found in the clause **ikan ziχ : akarai** 'X composed (?) this document/text' at the end of an otherwise incomprehensible text from the Archaic period (Cr 0.4), can also be interpreted as a past active form. The verb seems to have been built from the root **ak-**, which is attested in other Etruscan verbs and participles with meanings having to do with 'making, building, producing, bearing', e.g. **acasce, acasri, acnanas**, but it is not clear how the remaining portion of the verb is to be parsed because there are no comparable forms attested (see §12.8).

6.7 Etruscan verbs were inflected for voice. Past-tense verbs had the suffix -c for active voice, as seen above, while in the passive they had the suffix -χ (for possible present passive forms see §6.8). Compare the past passive **menaχe** '(it) was made/fashioned' (**mena-χ-e**) with the corresponding past active form **mene-c-e** '(he) made/fashioned' (**menece**). Thus, in the past tense at least, voice and tense were fused together in a single suffix, namely -c for the active and -χ for the passive.

6.7.1 For the past-tense suffixes, both active and passive, see de Simone 1970b:115–39 and Cristofani 1973a:181–92.

6.8 Two verbs, namely **cerine** and **tenine**, are analyzed by some Etruscologists as passive forms. Following this analysis, the verbs are segmented as **ceri-n-e** and **teni-n-e** and -n is identified as a passive suffix. This analysis stands or falls on the interpretation of two inscriptions, namely Vc 1.87 and Pe 3.3.

Vc 1.87, cited in (2), is a funerary inscription incised on a monument known as the *Ara Guglielmi*. If **cerine** is interpreted as a passive, the inscription may be translated as follows: 'This (monument) and tomb (or: This funerary (monument)) (belong(s) to) Vel Etspu. They (It) are (is) constructed by (his) son.' The argument is that **cerine** cannot easily be interpreted as active in voice because it is most likely that the son of Vel Etspu constructed the monument and tomb for his father.

(2)   Etruscan **cerine**

eca : óuθic : velus : ezpus | clensi : cerine (Vc 1.87)

eca 'this', DEM PRO, NOM; óuθic (a) óuθi 'tomb', NOM/ACC + -c 'and', ENCLITIC CONJ; (b) óuθic 'funerary', NOM/ACC; velus 'of Vel', MASC PRAE, 1ST GEN; ezpus 'Etspu', MASC NOMEN, 1ST GEN; clensi 'son', 1ST PERT; cerine 'construct (?)', PRES PASS (?)

Pe 3.3, cited in (3), is the famous Arringatore inscription; it was incised on the border of the toga of a life-size bronze statue of an orator.
The inscription is a dedication on behalf of Aule Meteli. According to the
view that **tenine** is passive voice, the inscription requires that the phrase
tece śanσl 'Sans in Tece' refer to the divinity to whom the statue was dedicated: 'This (statue) is erected (?) for the divinity *Tece Sans* by the city
ward (?) *Khishuli* (?) in honor of Aule (Meteli), son of Vel Meteli and Veshi.'

(3) Etruscan **tenine**

auleσi : meteliσ : ve : veśial : clenσi | cen : flereσ : tece : śanσl : tenine
| tuθineσ : χiśulicσ (Pe 3.3)

auleσi 'Aule', MASC PRAE, 1ST PERT; meteliσ 'Meteli', MASC NOMEN, 1ST GEN;
ve, abbrev. of velus 'Vel', MASC PRAE, 1ST GEN; veśial 'of Veshi', FEM NOMEN,
2ND GEN; clenσi 'son', 1ST PERT; cen 'this', DEM PRO, NOM; flereσ 'divinity',
1ST GEN; tece śanσl 'Tece Shans' THEO, 2ND GEN; tenine 'is offered (?)', PRES
PASS (?); tuθineσ 'city ward (?)', 1ST ABL; χiśulicσ 'Khishuli', 1ST ABL

The analysis of the verbs **cerine** and **tenine** as passives and the interpretation of the inscriptions cited above, while plausible, are not universally accepted, and other interpretations are possible.

For (2) one may imagine that the son of Vel Etspu died unexpectedly
and a grieving father constructed the monument and tomb in his mem-
ory: 'This is the tomb of Vel Etspu; he constructed (it) for his son'. This interpretation avoids a potential problem with the passive analysis, namely
the attribution of agentive function to the pertinentive form **clensi**. We
might rather expect an ablative form in a Neo-Etruscan inscription (see
§8.7).

For (3) we offer the following interpretation: 'For Aule Meteli, son of
Vel and Veshi. This (statue) belongs to the divinity Shans in Tec. He (Aule
Meteli) receives it from the city ward (?) *Khishuli* (?)'. The meaning of the
verb form **tenine** is a problem under either analysis. The verb root **ten-** is
customarily found in construction with the titles of political or religious
offices and is usually interpreted as meaning 'held (the office of X)'. The
meanings offered for this verb in (3) do not easily jibe with that extracted
from other syntactic contexts.

If these verbs are passives there is the further problem that they are
unmarked for past tense. Virtually all commentators interpret them as
referring to events in the past.

6.8.1 Colonna (1985) argues that the suffix **-n** must have passive value. Wylin (2000:111–8)
offers a spirited defense of this proposal.

6.9 As noted above Etruscan verbs did not inflect for number. In the sentences cited below, (4a) and (4b), the subject noun phrase changes from singular (4a) to plural (4b), but the inflection of the verb **ceriχunce**, past tense and active voice, does not change to reflect the difference in the number of the subject.

(4) Lack of inflection for number

    (a)   **vel ⫶ matunas ⫶ larisaliça ⫶ | an ⫶ cn ⫶ çuθi ⫶ ceriχunce** (Cr 5.3)
         'Vel Matunas, (son) of Laris, he/who had this tomb constructed.'

         vel 'Vel', MASC PRAE, NOM/ACC; matunas 'Matunas', MASC NOMEN, 1ST GEN; larisaliça = larisal 'Laris', MASC PRAE, 2ND GEN + -iça 'the', DEF ART, NOM; an 'he/who', ANA/REL PRO, NOM; cn 'this', DEM PRO, ACC; çuθi 'tomb', NOM/ACC; ceriχunce '(had) constructed', PAST ACT

    (b)   **laris · av | le · laris | al · clenar | sval · cn · çuθi | ceriχunce ...**
         (Cr 5.2)
         'Laris (and) Aule, sons of Laris, (while) living had this tomb constructed.'

         laris 'Laris', MASC PRAE, NOM/ACC; avle 'Aule', MASC PRAE, NOM/ACC; larisal 'Laris', MASC PRAE, 2ND GEN; clenar 'sons', ANIM PL, NOM/ACC; sval 'living', NOM/ACC; cn 'this', DEM PRO, ACC; çuθi 'tomb', NOM/ACC; ceriχunce '(had) constructed', PAST ACT

6.10 Etruscan verbs did not inflect for person. In the sentences cited in (5), the subjects are 1st person (5a) and 3rd person (5b) respectively and yet the verb form does not change.

(5) Lack of inflection for person

    (a)   **mi araθiale ziχuχe** (Fa 6.3)
         'I was designed/painted by/for Ara(n)th.'

         mi 'I', 1ST PERS PRO, NOM; araθiale 'Ara(n)th', MASC PRAE, 2ND PERT; ziχuχe 'was designed, painted', PAST PASS

    (b)   **iχ · ca | ceχa · ziχuχe** (Pe 8.4, 20–21)
         'as (?) this (contract) was written above'

         iχ 'as', SUBORD; ca 'this', DEM PRO, NOM; ceχa 'above', ADV; ziχuχe 'was written', PAST PASS

6.11 In addition to verbs belonging to the mood categories imperative, indicative, and jussive, Etruscan had a special verb formation that
marked activities as being obligatory, called the necessitative. This formation was made by addition of the suffix -ri to verb roots/stems, e.g.
nunθeri 'must be offered (?)'. If the verb root/stem was transitive, then
this formation was semantically passive. Most of the forms ending in -ri
were derived from the uncharacterized verb root, sometimes with and
sometimes without a vowel mediating between the root and the ending,
e.g. nunθ-e-ri, θez-e-ri 'must be immolated'. Sentence (6), cited from the
Liber Linteus, illustrates the function of the necessitative in Etruscan.

(6)   The necessitative

   zaθrumsne · lusaσ · fler · hamφisca · θezeri (LL VI, 9)
   'On the 20th (day) for (the divinity) Lusha the victim, the one from
   the left (?), must be immolated.'

   zaθrumsne '20th', LOC; lusaσ 'Lusha', THEO, 1ST GEN; fler 'sacrificial victim',
   NOM/ACC; hamφisca 'left (?)', 1ST ABL + 'the', DEM PRO, NOM; θezeri 'must be
   immolated', NECESS

Participles

6.12 In addition to finite verb forms, Etruscan had uninflected formations that may be described as participles, all of which were built from
verb roots or verb stems by means of suffixes. The precise function of
these participle formations is not always clear, although it has been suggested, perhaps reasonably so, that the formations specified different
temporal or aspectual relationships with respect to the action of the main
verb.

   6.12.1 For the form and the syntax of participles see the references in §6.1.1.

6.13 Participles ending in -u are found in a two types of formations. In
the first, the suffix was added directly to the verb root, as in, for example,
mul-u 'given' and ces-u 'buried'. In the second, it was affixed to a verb
stem that was characterized by another suffix, as in zina-k-u 'fashioned'
and ali-q-u 'presented', both of which were built by adding the *u*-suffix to
the stem of the past active. The difference in meaning between the two
formations, at least as far as can be determined at this point, seems to
have been minimal, e.g. mul-u 'given' vs. zinak-u 'fashioned [out of clay]'.
   Syntactically *u*-participles often served as the only verbal element in
an Etruscan verb phrase. In (7a) **mulu** is the main verbal element in the

sentence. A tensed form of the verb 'to be' is to be understood. In (7b), **aliqu** serves as the verbal term.

(7) *U*-participles

(a) **mi liceneši mulu hirsunaieši** (Cr 3.18)
'I (am/was/have been) given to/for/by Licene Hirsunaie.'

mi 'I', 1ST PERS PRO, NOM; **liceneši** 'Licene', MASC PRAE, 1ST PERT; **mulu** 'given', U-PART; **hirsunaieši** 'Hirsunaie', MASC NOMEN, 1ST PERT

(b) **mi aliqu ׃ auvilesi** (Fa 3.1)
'I (am/was/have been) presented to/for/by Avile.'

mi 'I', 1ST PERS PRO, NOM; **aliqu** 'presented', U-PART; **auvilesi** 'Avile', MASC PRAE, 1ST PERT

Some scholars have suggested that what are generally labeled *u*-participles were truly finite forms. However, *u*-participles appear to stand outside of the regular system of verb inflection in the sense that they were not marked, at least as far as can be determined, for voice or mood. Moreover, they appear to serve as input for the creation of indicative mood forms, e.g. **tenve**, which was built from the *u*-participle **tenu**- plus the indicative mood marker. Since this is the case, it seems best to treat *u*-participles as non-finite forms.

U-participles are generally translated as passive in voice, particularly if the roots/stems from which they were built were transitive. For example, **aliqu** was built to the active voice, past tense stem /alik-/ and yet in (7b) it was used in a syntactic construction that demands a passive reading. Even so, *u*-participles were not obligatorily passive. The participle **tenu** in inscription (8) must be treated as active in voice.

(8) **arnθ ׃ χurlces ׃ ... zilc ׃ parχis ׃ amce | marunuχ ׃ spurana ׃ cepen ׃ tenu ׃ avils ׃ maχs semφalχls lupu** (AT 1.171)
'Arnth Khurkles ... was governor of the *parkh* (?). Having held the office of *marunuc* of the city (as) priest, (he) died at age seventy-five.'

arnθ 'Arnth', MASC PRAE, NOM/ACC; **χurlces** 'Khurlkes', MASC NOMEN, 1ST GEN; **zilc** 'governor', NOM/ACC; **parχis** '?', 1ST GEN; **amce** 'was', PAST ACT; **marunuχ** '?', NOM/ACC; **spurana** 'of the community', NOM/ACC; **cepen** 'priest', NOM/ACC; **tenu** 'having held', U-PART; **avils** 'year', 1ST GEN; **maχs** 'five', 1ST GEN; **semφalχls** 'seventy-five', 1ST GEN; **lupu** 'dead', U-PART

6.14 Participles ending in -**as** or, less commonly, -**asa** also admitted
two types of formations. These suffixes could be added to the bare verbal
root, as in **sval-as** and **ac-as**, or to a stem that had already been characterized by a suffix, as in **sval-θ-as, trin-θ-aσa,** and **acna-n-as.** The functions of
the suffixes -**θ** and -**n** are by no means certain, and there is much disagreement among Etruscologists as to their meaning. Likewise, the function of
the final -**a** in the participle ending -**as-a** cannot be determined, though
it is tempting to think that it is an enclitic particle of some sort. As far as
can be determined, participles ending in -**as** and in -**asa** functioned in the
same manner.

(9)   Participles

-as	-θ-as/a	-n-as/a
sval-as	sval-θ-as	acna-n-as
ac-as	trin-θ-aσa	acna-n-asa

Participles in -**as** referred to activities that took place contemporane-
ously with the main verb. The clearest example is the following:

(10) Participle in -**as**

> av[le · al]eθnas · ... zilaχṇ[ce] | spureθi · apasi · svalas ... (AT 1.108)
> 'Aule Alethnas ... served as governor (while) living in the community
> of his father'
>
> av[le] 'Aule', MASC PRAE, NOM/ACC; [al]eθnas 'Alethnas', MASC NOMEN, 1ST GEN;
> zilaχṇ[ce] 'served as governor', PAST ACT; spureθi 'in the community' =
> spure- 'community', LOC + -θi 'in' POST; apasi 'father', 1ST PERT (see §8.6);
> svalas 'living', AS-PART

The participles ending in -**θas** and in -**nas(a)** referred to activities that
occurred before the action of the main verb.

(11) Participles in -**θas** and -**nas(a)**

> (a) velθur : partunus : larisaliśa : clan : ramθas : cuclnial : zilχ :
> ceχaneri : tenθas : avil | svalθas : LXXXII (Ta 1.9)
> 'Velthur Partunus, the son of Laris and of Ramtha Cuclni,
> having held the presidency on behalf of the *Cekhana*, having
> lived for eighty-two years, (died).'
>
> velθur 'Velthur', MASC PRAE, NOM/ACC; partunus 'Partunus', MASC
> NOMEN, 1ST GEN; larisaliśa = larisal 'Laris', MASC PRAE, 2ND GEN + -iśa
> 'the', DEF ART, NOM; clan 'son', NOM/ACC; ramθas 'Ramtha', FEM PRAE, 1ST
> GEN; cuclnial 'Culcni', FEM NOMEN, 2ND GEN; zilχ 'governorship', NOM/

ACC; ceχaneri = ceχane- '?', LOC + -ri 'for', POST; tenθas 'having held', θAS-PART; avil 'year', NOM/ACC; svalθas 'having lived', θAS-PART

(b) larθ : arnθal : plecus : clan : ramθasc : apatrual : eslz : |
zilaχnθas : avils : θunem : muvalχls : lupu : (Ta 1.183)
'Larth, son of Arnth Plecus and Ramtha Apatrui, having held
the governorship twice died at fifty-one years.'

larθ 'Larth', MASC PRAE, NOM/ACC; arnθal 'Arnth', MASC PRAE, 2ND GEN;
plecus 'Plecus', MASC NOMEN, 1ST GEN; clan 'son', NOM/ACC; ramθasc =
ramθas 'Ramtha', FEM PRAE, 1ST GEN + -c 'and', ENCLITIC CONJ; apatrual
'Apartrui', FEM NOMEN, 2ND GEN; eslz 'twice', ADV; zilaχnθas 'having
held the office of governor', AS-PART; avils 'year', 1ST GEN; θunem =
θun- 'one', NUM + -em 'from'; muvalχls 'fifty', 1ST GEN; lupu 'dead',
U-PART

(c) aleθnas · v · v ... papalser · acnanasa · VI · manim · arce (AT 1.105)
'Vel Alethnas, son of Vel, ... having produced six descendants
constructed this tomb monument.'

aleθnas 'Alethnas', MASC NOMEN, 1ST GEN; v, abbrev. for vel 'Vel', MASC
PRAE, NOM/ACC; v, abbrev. for velus 'Vel', MASC PRAE, 1ST GEN; papalser
'grandchildren', ANIM PL, NOM/ACC; acnanasa 'having produced', NASA-
PART; manim 'tomb monument', NOM/ACC; arce 'constructed', PAST ACT

6.15 In the *Liber Linteus* verbal forms ending in -θ appear beside imperative verb forms in clauses describing activities to be performed by
the priest or the official of the ceremonies. These forms may also be analyzed as participles, although other interpretations, possibly as imperative forms, may be worth considering (12). It is possible that there is a
formal connection between these forms and those participles discussed
above that were formally marked by the suffix -θ, e.g. sval-θ-as. At this
point, however, the relationship is not clear.

(12) Verbal forms in -θ

(a) śacnicleri · cilθl · śpureri | meθlumeric · enaσ · raχθ · tur · heχσθ |
vinum (LL IX, 5–6)
'On behalf of the sanctuary (?) of the citadel (?), on behalf of the
community, and on behalf of the city of Ena (?) place (it) on
the *rakh* (after/while) pouring (?) the wine (or: (and) pour (?)
the wine).'

sanicleri = sanicle- 'sanctuary (?)', LOC + -ri 'on behalf of', POST; cilθl
'citadel (?)', 2ND GEN; spureri = spure- 'community', LOC + -ri 'on behalf
of', POST; meθlumeric = meθlume- 'city', LOC + -ri 'on behalf of', POST

+ -c 'and', ENCLITIC CONJ; enas 'Ena (?)', 1ST GEN; raχθ = raχ '?', LOC + -θ 'on', POST; tur 'put', IMPV; heχσθ 'pour (?)', θ-PART or θ-IMPV; vinum 'wine', NOM/ACC

(b) raχθ · tura · nunθenθ · clitram · σrenχve | tei · faσei (LL II, 10–11) '(One) shall place (it) on the *rakh* (after/while) anointing (?) the litter with *σrenχvas* (and) with this libation (or: (One) shall place (it) on the *rakh*. (Then) anoint (?) the litter with *σrenχvas* (and) with this libation).'

raχθ = raχ '?', LOC + -θ 'on', POST; tura 'put', JUSS; nunθenθ 'by anointing (?)', θ-PART or θ-IMPV; clitram 'litter', NOM/ACC; σrenχve '?', INANIM PL, LOC; tei 'this', DEM PRO, LOC; faσei 'libation', LOC

6.15.1 For the claim that verbs forms ending -θ are to be understood as imperatives with durative aspect, see Wylin 2000:154–7 and 2002b:91. Participles built to these stems, e.g. svalθas, would, following this approach, have a durative value.

Verb-forming Suffixes

6.16 Precious little is known about suffixes used to form Etruscan verbs. In fact, one of the few suffixes that can be securely identified is that found in **mul(u)vanice**, one of the most common verbs in Archaic Etruscan inscriptions. This verb appears to have been built from the participle stem **mulu-** by means of a suffix **-vani-**, which probably had, in origin at least, causative function, e.g. **muluvanice** 'had X given as a gift in honor of Y', **ceriχunce** 'had X built' < *ceriχvanice*, **ziχ(v)anace** 'had X inscribed'.

Other Etruscan verbs with the nasal suffix **-nu-/-n-** do not belong to the group described in the preceding paragraph in terms of meaning. The verb **zilaχnuce**, **zilaχnce**, which seems to be built on a stem **zilaχnu-** (with -u subject to syncope), itself derived form the noun stem **zilaχ-**, is intransitive in meaning, 'to serve as governor'. It is possible that these suffixes were distinct historically, and that changes such as syncope conspired to give them the same appearance in Neo-Etruscan.

7 NOMENCLATURE

Introduction

7.1 The epitaph cited in (1) was incised on the lid of a sarcophagus recovered from a cemetery near Tarquinia. The inscription gives the name of the deceased followed by a phrase referring to an official or religious office held by the same.

(1) **lartiu cucḷnies · larθal · clan | larθialc einanal | camθi eterau** (Ta 1.96)
'Lartiu Cuclnies, son of Larth and Larthi Einanei, *camthi eterau.*'

> **lartiu** 'Lartiu', MASC PRAE, NOM/ACC; **cucḷnies** 'Cuclnies', MASC NOMEN, 1ST GEN; **larθal** 'Larth', MASC PRAE, 2ND GEN; **clan** 'son', NOM/ACC; **larθialc** = **larθial** 'Larthi', FEM NOMEN, 2ND GEN + -c 'and', ENCLITIC CONJ; **einanal** 'Einanei', FEM NOMEN, 2ND GEN; **camθi** '?', NOM/ACC; **eterau** '?', NOM/ACC

The epitaph records the four components characteristic of the system of personal nomenclature during the Neo-Etruscan period: the praenomen or personal name (**lartiu**), the nomen or family name (**cucḷnies**), the patronymic (praenomen of the father, **larθal clan** 'son of Larth'), and the metronymic (praenomen and nomen of the mother, **larθial einanal**). The praenomen and the nomen were the core constituents of the name of a freeborn Etruscan. We have every reason to assume that the official name included these two constituents and perhaps also the patronymic.

7.1.1 Rix 1995a is a concise overview of the main features of the Etruscan system of nomenclature.

7.2 During the third and second centuries BCE a fifth constituent, the cognomen, was commonly included in funerary inscriptions at Clusium and Perusia.

(2) **lθ : peθna : aθ : titial : ścirẹ** (Cl 1.147)
'Larth Pethna Shcire, (son) of Arnth and Titi'

> **lθ**, abbrev. of **larθ** 'Larth', MASC PRAE, NOM/ACC; **peθna** 'Pethna', MASC NOMEN, NOM/ACC; **aθ**, abbrev. of **arnθal** 'Arnth', MASC PRAE, 2ND GEN; **titial** 'Titi', FEM NOMEN, 2ND GEN; **ścirẹ** 'Shcire', MASC COGN, NOM/ACC

77

Funerary inscriptions of Etruscan women could include a sixth constituent, the gamonymic. This was the name of the deceased's husband.
In actual practice, epitaphs in which all six components were written are
not very common, but (3) is an example.

(3)   velia : šeianti : aθ : unatn | cumerunia raθum|naśa (Cl 1.324)
      'Velia Sheianti Cumerunia, (daughter) of Arnth (and) Unatnei, the
      (wife) of Rathumna'

      velia 'Velia', FEM PRAE, NOM/ACC; šeianti 'Sheianti', FEM NOMEN, NOM/ACC; aθ,
      abbrev. of arnθal 'Arnth', MASC PRAE, 2ND GEN; unatn, abbrev. of unatnal
      'Unatnei', FEM NOMEN, 2ND GEN; cumerunia 'Cumerunia', FEM COGN, NOM/ACC;
      raθumnaśa = raθumnaσ 'Rathumna', MASC NOMEN, 1ST GEN + -śa 'the', DEF
      ART, NOM

7.3   The number of constituents employed to indicate the name of the
deceased in funerary inscriptions varied considerably, even within the
same area. The only constant was the praenomen and nomen. For example, at Caere, during the Neo-Etruscan period, we find funerary inscriptions with the following constituents: praenomen and nomen (4), with
patronymic (5), with metronymic (6), with patronymic and metronymic
(7), and with cognomen (8). The structures exemplified by (4) and (5) were
common at Caere, while (6), (7), and (8) were rare in this zone.

(4)   marce · maclae (Cr 1.60)
      'Marce Maclae'

      marce 'Marce', MASC PRAE, NOM/ACC; maclae 'Maclae', MASC NOMEN, NOM/ACC

(5)   avle · tarχnas · larθal · clan (Cr 1.10)
      'Aule Tarkhnas, son of Larth'

      avle 'Aule', MASC PRAE, NOM/ACC; tarχnas 'Tarkhnas', MASC NOMEN, 1ST GEN;
      larθal 'Larth', MASC PRAE, 2ND GEN; clan 'son', NOM/ACC

(6)   ḷi · tarχnas · crucrials (Cr 1.6)
      'Laris Tarkhnas, (born) from Crucri'

      ḷi, abbrev. of laris 'Laris', MASC PRAE, NOM/ACC; tarχnas 'Tarkhnas', MASC
      NOMEN, 1ST GEN; crucrials 'Crucri', FEM NOMEN, 2ND ABL

(7)   av · tarχnas · av · c · | crucrials · (Cr 1.5)
      'Aule Tarkhnas, son of Aule, (born) from Crucri'

      av, abbrev. of avle 'Aule', MASC PRAE, NOM/ACC; tarχnas 'Tarkhnas', MASC

NOMEN, 1ST GEN; **av**, abbrev. of **avles** 'Aule', MASC PRAE, 1ST GEN; **c**, abbrev. of **clan** 'son', NOM/ACC; **crucrials** 'Crucri', FEM NOMEN, 2ND ABL

(8) r · matunai | çaṇatnei (Cr 1.138)
    'Ramtha Matunai Canatnei'

   r, abbrev. of **ramθa** 'Ramtha', FEM PRAE, NOM/ACC; **matunai** 'Mathunai', FEM NOMEN, NOM/ACC; **çaṇatnei** 'Canatnei', FEM COGN, NOM/ACC

Origins and Development

7.4 The complex system of nomenclature attested during the Neo-Etruscan period grew out of a prehistoric system in which a person had a single, personal name. The origin of the historically attested system, in which a freeborn Etruscan had both a personal name and a family name, is to be tied to the development of urban centers in central Italy during the eighth century BCE. In conjunction with the rise of larger, more socially cohesive, communities, a more complex social network grew up around the head of the extended family unit in which it was important to designate membership. The nomen developed from the adjectival patronymic of the titular head of the family. When the patronymic adjective ceased to refer to an individual's father, but was used instead to refer to the family unit, the patronymic adjective, reinterpreted as a name for the family, became part of the nomenclature of those born into that family, e.g. **laris larecena** 'Laris, (son) of Larece' → 'Laris, (member of) the Larecena (family)'.

This change in the function of the patronymic adjective must have happened shortly before 700 BCE, perhaps among the Faliscans, a people who inhabited the territory of the *Ager Faliscus* in southeastern Etruria. Regardless of the locus of origin, however, this system of nomenclature spread rapidly in all directions and was ultimately adopted by Etruscans, Umbrians, Romans and other Latin-speaking peoples, South Picenes, and Oscans. Examples of names in the languages of ancient Italy are presented in (9). Each name has two constituents, a praenomen and a nomen.

(9) Names with praenomen and nomen

   (a) Etruscan **laris velkasnas**
   (b) Faliscan **velos ofetios**
   (c) Latin *Ancus Marcius*
   (d) South Picene **petroh púpúnis**
   (e) Umbrian **vuvçis teteies**
   (f) Oscan **pakis heleviis**

At the beginning of the third quarter of the seventh century, a "new" form of the patronymic makes its appearance. It was expressed by the genitive of the praenomen of the father and, as an optional element, the word **clan** 'son' in apposition to the name. One of the earliest examples is cited in (10). In this inscription, **cles** 'son', which is the irregular genitive singular of **clan**, is in agreement with the name of the deceased.

(10) Patronymic phrase

> mi larθia hulχenas velθurus cles (Vs 1.28)
> 'I (am the tomb) of Larth Hulkhenas, son of Velthur.'

> mi 'I', 1ST PERS PRO, NOM; **larθia** 'Larth', MASC PRAE, 2ND GEN; **hulχenas**
> 'Hulkhenas', MASC NOMEN, 1ST GEN; **velθurus** 'Velthur', MASC PRAE, 1ST GEN;
> **cles** 'son', 1ST GEN

7.5 Etruscan nomenclature changed over time. In funerary inscriptions of the Archaic period, an individual was designated by his/her praenomen and nomen. Patronymics, metronymics, and cognomina were rare. By the end of the fourth century BCE, however, the name of the deceased, as it appeared on funerary inscriptions, regularly included a patronymic and a metronymic.

The number of masculine and feminine praenomina in common use in the Neo-Etruscan period was limited to twenty (for a list, see below, §7.9). A more robust inventory of Etruscan praenomina existed in the seventh and sixth centuries BCE. But the importance of the nomen and the cognomen as a means of distinguishing individuals led to the disappearance of many praenomina that were in use during the Archaic period.

Nomenclature also differed on a regional basis. In northern areas, the cognomen, whether familial or personal (see §7.11 and §7.12), became common toward the end of the third century BCE. In contrast, cognomina rarely appeared in funerary inscriptions from Caere, Tarquinia, Volsinii, and Volcii. In the epitaphs of Etruscan women it was common, though never obligatory, to include a gamonymic.

7.5.1 For the origins of the nomen and its use in the languages of ancient Italy see Rix 1972. Two important papers published in the mid-70s, Cristofani 1974 and 1976, focus on the onomastic structures of the ancient cities of Veii and Volsinii.

Nomen

7.6 The family name or nomen was the most important element in the Etruscan system of names. The nomen referred to the family that an Etruscan belonged to by birth. Etruscan children inherited this name from their fathers. Women who married maintained the nomen of their paternal family; they did not adopt the nomen of the family into which they married. For example, Larthi Spantui, the wife of Arnth Partunus, was known by the nomen Spantui, which was that of her father, Larce Spantus.

(11) larθi : spantui : larces : spantus : seχ : arnθal : partunus : puia :
(Ta 1.13)
'Larthi Spantui, daughter of Larce Spantus, wife of Arnth Partunus'

larθi 'Larthi', FEM PRAE, NOM/ACC; **spantui** 'Spantui', FEM NOMEN, NOM/ACC; larces 'Larce', MASC PRAE, 1ST GEN; **spantus** 'Spantus', MASC NOMEN, 1ST GEN; seχ 'daughter', NOM/ACC; arnθal 'Arnth', MASC PRAE, 2ND GEN; **partunus** 'Partunus', MASC NOMEN, 1ST GEN; puia 'wife', NOM/ACC

7.7 In the onomastic phrase the nomen was either in the same case as the praenomen (see (4)) and therefore in agreement with it, or it was in the genitive case and was syntactically dependent upon the praenomen (see (5)). The construction in (4) was the standard in the northern sectors of Etruria; that in (5) was the rule in the south.

The nomen generally occupied the second position in the onomastic phrase following the praenomen. However, at Tarquinia and environs, and at Vulci as well, the order of the names was often inverted so that the nomen occupied first position, the most prominent position in the phrase (see further §7.23).

(12) vipinanas · velθur · velθurus · avils · XV (AT 1.15)
'Velthur Vipinanas, (son) of Velthur, (dead) at fifteen years of age'

vipinanas 'Vipinanas', MASC NOMEN, 1ST GEN; velθur 'Velthur', MASC PRAE, NOM/ACC; velθurus 'Velthur', MASC PRAE, 1ST GEN; avils 'year', 1ST GEN

7.8 Nomina referring to women were distinguished in form from those of men by having an *i*-suffix in the nominative/accusative case, e.g. spantu- → spantui (Ta 1.13), tarχna- → tarχnai (Cr 1.8), aleθna- → aleθnai > aleθnei (Ta 1.201). They were also distinguished by inflection. Feminine nomina inflected by means of the *l*-endings rather than the *s*-endings, despite the fact that the latter were the rule for names ending in vowels (on which, see §7.21).

Praenomen

7.9 The personal name or praenomen designated the individual within the family. As mentioned earlier, in the Neo-Etruscan period the number of praenomina in general use was limited. These names were: arnθ, larθ, vel, aule (avle), laris, larce, velθur, marce, óeθre (śeθre), cae, tite, and vipe. About half of these names were very common (arnθ, larθ, vel, aule/avle, laris, velθur, and óeθre/śeθre); the rest were rare. The praenomen cae was restricted in large part to Clusium and environs.

The number of praenomina referring to Etruscan women was also limited. The most common names were: ramθa, θanχvil, larθi (larθia), óeθra (śeθra), ravnθu, θana (θania), velia (vela), and fasti (fastia; also hasti, hastia in Clusium). Of these, fasti, larθi, and velia (vela) were not very common in the south, and ravnθu appears but twice in the north, both times in inscriptions from Volaterrae.

7.10 In Neo-Etruscan funerary inscriptions praenomina were abbreviated frequently. Common abbreviations are listed in (13).

(13) Neo-Etruscan praenomina with abbreviations

    (a) men: arnθ (a, ar, aθ); avle, aule (av, au); cae (c, ca); vel (v, ve, vl); velθur (vθ); larce (lc); larθ (l, la, lθ); laris (l, li, lr, ls); marce (m); śeqre (ś, śθ); tite (ti)

    (b) women: fasti, fastia, hasti, hastia (f, fa, h, ha); θana, θania (θ, θa); θanχvil (θχ); larθi (lθ); ramθa (r, ra)

Abbreviations in Etruscan names are not unambiguously attested before the fourth century BCE in the Neo-Etruscan period, and even then they were not common. Roman models may have inspired the use of abbreviations for Etruscan personal names, but this can neither be proven nor disproved.

Cognomen

7.11 The cognomen became a vital member of the Etruscan onomastic system during the course of the third and second centuries BCE. The cognomen had two functions. First, it was employed to distinguish between two branches of the same family (the so-called familial cognomen). Second, it was employed to distinguish individuals who had the same praenomen and nomen (the so-called individual cognomen). Since a cognomen could distinguish a branch of a particular family, a descendant could inherit the familial cognomen. For example, in the third and second centuries BCE the śeianti family of Clusium had several branches: the śeianti hanunia (FEM), the śeianti cumerunia (FEM), the śeianti viliania (FEM), and the śeiante trepu (MASC).

7.12 The cognomen, in its individualizing aspect, gradually usurped the function of the praenomen. At the end of the Neo-Etruscan period funerary inscriptions did not always record the praenomen of the deceased, as in (14).

(14) śeianti · hanunia · tleσnaśa (Cl 1.373)
   'Sheianti Hanunia, the (wife) of Tlesna'

> śeianti 'Sheianti', FEM NOMEN, NOM/ACC; hanunia 'Hanunia', FEM COGN, NOM/ACC; tleσnaśa = tleσnaσ 'Tlesna', MASC NOMEN, 1ST GEN + -śa 'the', DEF ART, NOM

Similarly, in instances where the cognomen became the primary name for identifying the family, the nomen could be omitted from the onomastic phrase.

(15) vel · fastntru · aθ (Cl 1.1006)
   'Vel Fastntru, (son) of Arnth'

> vel 'Vel', MASC PRAE, NOM/ACC; fastntru 'Fastntru', MASC COGN, NOM/ACC; aθ, abbrev. of arnθal 'Arnth', MASC PRAE, 2ND GEN

7.13 Syntactically, the cognomen agreed either with the praenomen (velia śeianti hanunia) or it was inflected in the genitive (veliea titi vetuσ). The position of the cognomen in the onomastic phrase was relatively free. It could appear before or after the patronymic, metronymic, and gamonymic, but it regularly followed the praenomen and nomen.

7.14 Feminine cognomina, just as feminine nomina, were generally derived from masculine stems. For example, the feminine cognomen vetui was formed by addition of -i to the masculine stem vetu. Many other masculine cognomina ending in -u formed their feminine counterparts with the suffix -nia. The feminine cognomina fastntrunia and trepunia were built upon the masculine stems fastntru and trepu. Cognomina ending in -ia inflected with the s-endings, e.g. fastntruniaσ 1ST GEN.

> **7.14.1** Rix 1963 is the classic discussion of Etruscan cognomina.

Patronymic, Metronymic, and Gamonymic

7.15 The remaining pieces of the Etruscan onomastic system, the patronymic, the metronymic, and the gamonymic, made use of the onomastic constituents described in §§7.6–14.

The patronymic was typically expressed by means of the father's prae-nomen, which was inflected in the genitive and was dependent on the words **clan** 'son' or **seχ** 'daughter' (16). In most instances, however, these words were suppressed and omitted from the onomastic phrase (17).

(16) **partunus · vel · velθurus · | óatlnalc · ramθas · clan · avils | XXIIX lupu** (Ta 1.15)
'Vel Partunus, son of Velthur, and Ramtha Shatlnai, dead at twenty-eight years (of age)'

partunus 'Partunus', MASC NOMEN, 1ST GEN; **vel** 'Vel', MASC PRAE, NOM/ACC; **velθurus** 'Velthur', MASC PRAE, 1ST GEN; **óatlnalc** = **óatlnal** FEM NOMEN, 2ND GEN + **-c** 'and', ENCLITIC CONJ; **ramθas** 'Ramtha', FEM PRAE, 1ST GEN; **clan** 'son', NOM/ACC; **avils** 'year', 1ST GEN; **lupu** 'dead', U-PART

(17) **pulenas · velθur · larisal · acnatrualc · avils LXXV** (Ta 1.18)
'Velthur Pulenas, (son) of Laris and Acnatrui, (dead) at seventy-five years (of age)'

pulenas 'Pulenas', MASC NOMEN, 1ST GEN; **velθur** 'Velthur', MASC PRAE, NOM/ACC; **larisal** 'Laris', MASC PRAE, 2ND GEN; **acnatrualc** = **acnatrual** 'Acnatrui', FEM NOMEN, 2ND GEN + **-c** 'and', ENCLITIC CONJ; **avils** 'year', 1ST GEN

On the mother's side, an individual could be designated by means of a metronymic, which was indicated by the nomen of the mother. This was inflected in the genitive and it too was dependent on the word for 'son' or 'daughter'. A married woman was sometimes designated by a gamonymic. This was expressed by the nomen of the husband in the genitive case. It was dependent on the word for 'wife', **puia** (18).

(18) **θanχvil : ruvfi : puia arnθal aleθ{na}s** (AT 1.111)
'Thankhvil Ruvfi, wife of Arnth Alethnas'

θanχvil 'Thankhvil', FEM PRAE, NOM/ACC; **ruvfi** 'Ruvfi', FEM NOMEN, NOM/ACC; **puia** 'wife', NOM/ACC; **arnθal** 'Arnth', MASC PRAE, 2ND GEN; **aleθ{na}s** 'Alethnas', MASC NOMEN, 1ST GEN

The patronymic, metronymic, and gamonymic could also be indicated by means of phrases employing the enclitic article **-(i)óa/-(i)śa**. The article was in agreement with the word for 'son' or 'daughter' and was affixed to the end of the patronymic, metronymic, or gamonymic. Inscription (19) has two patronymic constructions. They have the same underlying structure: genitive + article + noun. In the second patronymic phrase the article -ióla is in agreement with the noun **clens** 'son', 1ST GEN, which is to be supplied from the context.

(19) **ravnθu | velχai̯ | velθuruóa | seχ | larθialióla** (Ta 1.59)
'Ravnthu Velkhai, the daughter of Velthur, (who is) the (son) of Larth'

> **ravnθu** 'Ravnthu', FEM PRAE, NOM/ACC; **velχai̯** 'Velkhai', FEM NOMEN, NOM/ACC; **velθuruóa** = **velθurus** 'Velthur', MASC PRAE, 1ST GEN + **-óa** 'the', DEF ART, NOM; **seχ** 'daughter', NOM/ACC; **larθialióla** = **larθial** 'Larth', MASC PRAE, 2ND GEN + **-ióla** 'the', DEF ART, 2ND GEN

Other Familial Relationships

7.16 Familial relationships other than those described above appear occasionally in funerary inscriptions from Tarquinia and Volsinii. They were expressed through the following words and phrases: **ati** 'mother', **apa** 'father', **ruva** 'brother', **ati nacna** or **teta** 'grandmother', **apa nacna** or **papa** 'grandfather', **tetals** and **papals** 'grandchild', **nefts** 'nephew; grandson', and **prums/prumaθs** 'great grandson (?)'. Inscription (20) from Volsinii illustrates two of these relationships.

(20) Etruscan **ruva** and **prumaθσ**

> **vel le̞i̯nies : larθial : ruva : arnθialum | clan : velusum : prumaθσ : avils : semφσ | lupuce** (Vs 1.178)
> 'Vel Leinies, brother of Larth (and) son of Arnth (and) great-grandson (?) of Vel, died at seven years of age.'

> **vel** 'Vel', MASC PRAE, NOM/ACC; **le̞i̯nies** 'Leinies', MASC NOMEN, 1ST GEN; **larθial** 'Larth', MASC PRAE, 2ND GEN; **ruva** 'brother', NOM/ACC; **arnθialum** = **arnθial** 'Arnth', MASC PRAE, 2ND GEN + **-um** 'and', ENCLITIC CONJ; **clan** 'son', NOM/ACC; **velusum** = **velus** 'Vel', MASC PRAE, 1ST GEN + **-um** 'and', ENCLITIC CONJ; **prumaθσ** 'great grandson (?)', NOM/ACC; **avils** 'year', 1ST GEN; **semφσ** 'seven', NUM, 1ST GEN; **lupuce** 'died', PAST ACT

Slaves and Ex-slaves

7.17 In the Etruscan world slaves were distinguished from free persons by means of their nomenclature. A slave did not have a nomen, only a personal name followed by the nomen or the cognomen of his/her master or mistress, as in inscriptions (21) and (22).

(21) anti{:}pater · cicuσ (Cl 1.1502)
     'Antipater, (slave) of Cicu'

   anti{:}pater 'Antipater', MASC NAME, NOM/ACC; cicuσ 'Cicu', MASC COGN,
   1ST GEN

(22) hasti : petruσ : (Cl 1.970)
     'Hasti, (slave) of Petru'

   hasti 'Hasti', FEM PRAE, NOM/ACC; petruσ 'Petru', MASC PRAE, 1ST GEN

7.18 Slaves who were freed were referred to by the terms **lautni** and
lautniθa. The former referred to men, the latter to women. In spite of
being free, they did not have full rights. This is indicated by the fact that
the nomenclature referring to them was similar to that for slaves. In (23)
for example the freed person was identified by a personal name followed
by the nomen of her patron. In (24) the freed person was designated by a
noun phrase with the names of his patrons.

(23) θana : punp|naσ : lautni|θa (Cl 1.314)
     'Thana, freedwoman of Punpna'

   θana 'Thana', FEM PRAE, NOM/ACC; punpnaσ 'Punpna', MASC NOMEN, 1ST GEN;
   lautniθa 'freedwoman', NOM/ACC

(24) tiφile : lau | velχeσ | puliac (Cl 1.1645)
     'Tiphile, freedman of Velkhe and Pulia'

   tiφile 'Tiphile', MASC PRAE, NOM/ACC; lau, abbrev. of lautni 'freedman', NOM/
   ACC; velχeσ 'Velkhe', MASC NOMEN, 1ST GEN; puliac = pulia 'Pulia', FEM NOMEN,
   NOM/ACC + -c 'and', ENCLITIC CONJ

   7.18.1 A collection of *lautni*-inscriptions and a discussion of the nomenclature pertinent to
   slaves and freed persons in the Etruscan world can be found in Rix 1994:96–116.

7.19 The offspring of freed persons were referred to by nomenclature similar to that used to refer to citizens, with the exception that the
personal name of the father was employed as a nomen. Thus the son of
Tiphile (24) adopted a standard Etruscan praenomen and used his father's
name as his nomen (25). This is the so-called *Vornamengentilicium*, a term
that may be paraphrased as 'the use of a personal name as a family name'.

(25) aθ : tiφile : palpe : pulias (Cl 1.2513)
     'Arnth Tiphile Palpe, (son) of Pulia'

aθ, abbrev. of **arnθ** 'Arnth', MASC PRAE, NOM/ACC; **tiφile** 'Tiphile', MASC NOMEN, NOM/ACC; **palpe** 'Palpe' MASC COGN, NOM/ACC; **pulias** 'Pulia', FEM NOMEN, 1ST GEN

Examples of *Vornamengentilicia* are common with names of Italic origin, e.g. **cae/cai, tite, vipi, trepi, marce,** and **σepie**. Presumably, Italic immigrants who were incorporated into the ranks of citizens took their personal names as nomina.

(26) **vel : tite : aules** (Cl 1.1134)
     'Vel Tite, (son) of Aule'

> **vel** 'Vel', MASC PRAE, NOM/ACC; **tite** 'Tite', MASC NOMEN, NOM/ACC; **aules** 'Aule',
> MASC PRAE, 1ST GEN

7.20 After the passage of the *lex Iulia de civitate* in 90/89 BCE, which gave Roman citizenship to all eligible Italians, the nomenclature of Etruscan freed persons more closely approximated Roman usage. Some Etruscan names followed Roman models. The Latin/Etruscan bilingual cited in (27) is a good example. The Etruscan term **lautni** was used to translate the Latin term *libertus* 'freedman', here abbreviated as L. The nomen of the freed person was taken from the nomen of his patron.

(27) L · SCARPIUS · SCARPIAE · L · POPA (Pe 1.211)
     'Lucius Scarpius, freedman of Scarpia, priest's assistant'
     lar{n}θ · ścarpe · lautṇi
     'Larth Shcarpe, freedman'

> **lar{n}θ** 'Larth', MASC PRAE, NOM/ACC; **ścarpe** 'Shcarpe', MASC NOMEN, NOM/ACC;
> **lautṇi** 'freedman', NOM/ACC

However, even in first century BCE, the Etruscan-style nomenclature for freed slaves was preserved. In (28) the freedman took his father's personal name as nomen.

(28) **l · eucle · φisis · lavtni** (Pe 1.219)
     'Larth Eucle, freedman of Phisi'
     L · PHISIUS · L · L · UCL[ES]
     'Lucius Phisius, freedman of Lucius, Ucles'

> **l**, abbrev. of **larθ** 'Larth', MASC PRAE, NOM/ACC; **eucle** 'Eucle', MASC NOMEN,
> NOM/ACC; **φisis** 'Phisi', MASC NOMEN, 1ST GEN; **lavtni** 'freedman', NOM/ACC

Inflectional Features

7.21 The inflection of names followed the patterns described for nouns in Chapter 4. There we noted that there were fewer irregularities in the inflection of names than in the inflection of nouns. Stems ending in vowels regularly took the 1st genitive, 1st pertinentive, and 1st ablative inflectional suffixes, while stems ending in consonants (-θ, -s, -ś) took 2nd genitive, 2nd pertinentive, and 2nd ablative inflection. Feminine nomina, even though they were vocalic stems, inflected with 2nd genitive, 2nd pertinentive, and 2nd ablative endings. Inflectional paradigms for the Archaic period and for the Neo-Etruscan period are given in (29) and (30).

(29) Archaic Etruscan inflection

    (a) Males

NOM/ACC	larice	larθ	venel	papana
1ST GEN	larices		venelus	papanas
2ND GEN		larθia		
1ST PERT	laricesi		venelusi	papanasi
2ND PERT		larθiale		

    (b) Females

NOM/ACC	ramuθa	θanakvil	hirminai
1ST GEN	ramuθas	θanakvilus	
2ND GEN			hirminaia
1ST PERT	ramuθasi	θanakvilusi	
2ND PERT			hirminala
2ND ABL			hirminalas

(30) Neo-Etruscan inflection

    (a) Males

NOM/ACC	larce	larθ	vel	papna
1ST GEN	larces		velus	papnas
2ND GEN		larθa		
1ST PERT	larcesi		velusi	papnasi
2ND PERT		larθale		
1ST ABL	larceis			papnes
2ND ABL		larθals	veluis	

(b) Females

NOM/ACC	ramθa	θanχvil	hirmnei	hustli
1ST GEN	ramθas	θanχvilus		
2ND GEN			hirmnal	hustlial
1ST PERT	ramθasi	θanχvilusi		
2ND PERT			hirmnale	hustliale
1ST ABL	ramuθes	θanχviluis		
2ND ABL			hirmnals	huslials

Masculine nomina followed vocalic inflection. The genitive, pertinentive, and ablative cases were inflected with endings of the s-type. Feminine nomina, most of which ended in -i, followed the 2nd genitive, 2nd pertinentive, and 2nd ablative patterns of inflection. Inflectional differences distinguished the nomina of males from those of females (see **papana(s)** and **hirminai** in (29), and **papna(s)** and **hirmnei** in (30)).

Archaic feminine nomina had a distinctive pertinentive case ending -la, e.g. **hirminala**. The ending was added directly to the underlying stem, not to the nominative/accusative **hirminai** or to the genitive **hirminaia**. Based on the pattern of inflection, we might have expected an Archaic pertinentive form to have the shape *hirminaiala*.

Patterns of inflection for feminine nomina became more opaque during the Neo-Etruscan period because feminine nomina that originally ended in -**nai** came to end in -**nei** by regular sound change. As a result, a nominative/accusative form ending in -**nei**, e.g. **hirmnei**, corresponded to a 2nd genitive form ending in -*nal*, e.g. **hirmnal**.

Onomastic Phrases

7.22 In the Archaic period, the order of constituents in an onomastic phrase was, almost without exception, praenomen followed by nomen. If a patronymic was present, it was placed in third position. However, patronymic phrases are rarely attested in Archaic inscriptions. Examples of funerary inscriptions recovered from the Crocifisso necropolis near Volsinii are typical of the Archaic period.

(31) Archaic funerary inscriptions from Volsinii

    (a) **mi aranθia ḟlavienas** (Vs 1.55)
        'I (am the tomb) of Aranth Flavienas.'

        mi 'I', 1ST PERS PRO, NOM; **aranθia** 'Aranth', MASC PRAE, 2ND GEN;
        ḟlavienas 'Flavienas', MASC NOMEN, 1ST GEN

(b) mi velelias hirminaia (Vs 1.85)
     'I (am the tomb) of Velelia Hirminai.'

   mi 'I', 1ST PERS PRO, NOM; velelias 'Velelia', FEM PRAE, 1ST GEN; hirminaia
   'Hirminai', FEM NOMEN, 2ND GEN

(c) mi larθia hulχenas velθurus cles (Vs 1.28)
     'I (am the tomb) of Larth Hulkhenas, son of Velthur.'

   mi 'I', 1ST PERS PRO, NOM; larθia 'Larth', MASC PRAE, 2ND GEN; hulχenas
   'Hulkhenas', MASC NOMEN, 1ST GEN; velθurus 'Velthur', MASC PRAE, 1ST
   GEN; cles 'son', 1ST GEN

Some of the earliest examples of the use of the cognomen and the
metronymic were discovered on inscriptions in this necropolis. Examples
of cognomen and metronymic are cited in (32a) and (32b), respectively.

(32) Archaic funerary inscriptions from Volsinii

(a) [mi ma]marces apenas qutus (Vs 1.120)
     'I (am the tomb) of Marce Apenas Qutu.'

   [mi] 'I', 1ST PERS PRO, NOM; [ma]marces 'Mamarce', MASC PRAE, 1ST GEN;
   apenas 'Apenas', MASC NOMEN, 1ST GEN; qutus 'Qutus', MASC COGN,
   1ST GEN

(b) aveles vhulχenas rutelna (Vs 1.45)
     '(The tomb) of Avele Fulkhenas, (son) of Rutelnai'

   aveles 'Avele', MASC PRAE, 1ST GEN; vhulχenas 'Fulkhenas', MASC NOMEN,
   1ST GEN; rutelna 'Rutelnai', FEM NOMEN, 2ND GEN

7.23 The two nuclear constituents of the onomastic phrase, the praenomen and the nomen, generally occupied the first two positions in the
phrase. Most commonly the praenomen stood in front of the nomen, but
even for these constituents there was some flexibility. For example, as
noted earlier, in the funerary inscriptions from Tarquinia and Vulci in the
third century BCE it became fashionable to reverse the order of praenomen
and nomen so as to give more prominence to the family name. In inscriptions (33a) and (33b) the nomina, ceicnas and tutes respectively, occupied
the first position; the praenomina followed.

(33) Neo-Etruscan inscriptions from Tarquinia and Vulci

(a) ceicnas : arnθ : arnθal : avils : XXIX (Ta 1.147)
     'Arnth Ceicnas, (son) of Arnth, (dead) at age twenty-nine'

ceicnas 'Ceicnas', MASC NOMEN, 1ST GEN; aᶦrnθ 'Arnth', MASC PRAE, NOM/
ACC; arnθal 'Arnth', MASC PRAE, 2ND GEN; avils 'year', 1ST GEN

(b) tutes · arnθ · larθal (Vc 1.84)
     'Arnth Tutes, (son) of Larth'

> tutes 'Tutes', MASC NOMEN, 1ST GEN; arnθ 'Arnth', MASC PRAE, NOM/ACC;
> larθal 'Larth', MASC PRAE, 2ND GEN

7.24 The order and arrangement of other constituents in the onomastic phrase was also subject to some degree of variation. The position of
the cognomen was relatively free. It could appear behind the nomen, as
in (34a), or it could be positioned at the very end of the phrase, as in (34b).
When the patronymic and metronymic appeared together in an inscription, the most common order was patronymic first, metronymic second,
as in (34a). Less commonly, the metronymic was positioned before the
patronymic, as in (34c).

(34) Cognomen and metronymic

(a) aule : śeiante : σinu | larθal : tiścuśn|al : clan (Cl 1.2261)
     'Aule Sheiante Sinu, son of Larth and Tishcushnei'

> aule 'Aule', MASC PRAE, NOM/ACC; śeiante 'Sheiante', MASC NOMEN, NOM/
> ACC; σinu 'Sinu', MASC COGN, NOM/ACC; larθal 'Larth', MASC PRAE, 2ND GEN;
> tiścuśnal 'Tishcushnei', FEM NOMEN, 2ND GEN; clan 'son', NOM/ACC

(b) aθ : herine : vipinal : | fufle (Cl 1.1807)
     'Arnth Herine, (son) of Vipinei, Fufle'

> aθ, abbrev. for arnθ 'Arnth', MASC PRAE, NOM/ACC; herine 'Herine', MASC
> NOMEN, NOM/ACC; vipinal 'Vipinei', FEM NOMEN, 2ND GEN; fufle 'Fufle',
> MASC COGN, NOM/ACC

(c) larθ : peθna : śeθrnal : arnθal (Cl 1.2050)
     'Larth Pethna, (son) of Shethrnei and Arnth'

> larθ 'Larth', MASC PRAE, NOM/ACC; peθna 'Pethna', MASC NOMEN, NOM/
> ACC; śeθrnal 'Shethrnei', FEM NOMEN, 2ND GEN; arnθal 'Arnth', MASC
> PRAE, 2ND GEN

The position of the gamonymic, when it was part of the onomastic
phrase, was also relatively free. In example (35) the gamonymic tutnaśa
was placed between the cognomen and the metronymic.

(35) Gamonymic and metronymic

> larθia : latini : ceśunia : tutnaśa | ultimnial : σeχ (Cl 1.1885)
> 'Larthia Latini Ceshunia, the (wife) of Tutna, daughter of Ultimni'

> larθia 'Larthia', FEM PRAE, NOM/ACC; latini 'Latini', FEM NOMEN, NOM/ACC;
> ceśunia 'Ceshunia', FEM COGN, NOM/ACC; tutnaśa = tutnaσ 'Tutna', MASC
> NOMEN, 1ST GEN + -śa 'the', DEF ART, NOM; ultimnial 'Ultimni', FEM NOMEN,
> 2ND GEN; σeχ 'daughter', NOM/ACC

Origin and Formation of Names

7.25 Many praenomina were native Etruscan words (as far as we can tell), e.g. aranθ (arnθ), larθ, venel, vel, avile (aule), laris, velθur, śeθre (śeθre), ramuθa (ramθa), θana, and θanaχvil (θanχvil). Unfortunately, we know very little about the etymological sources of these names and we can construct plausible etymologies in only two cases, namely, avile/aule and uśile.

Avile/aule was derived from the Etruscan word meaning 'year', avil. Uśile was formed from the word for 'sun', uśil. Both words were formed by means of a suffix -e of undetermined meaning. Spurie has also been tapped as a native formation; it may be a derivative from the word for 'community', spura. Unfortunately, this connection is not guaranteed. *Spurius* is a common Italic praenomen, which means that the Etruscan name could be a borrowing. In that case the formal similarity to spura 'community' would be fortuitous.

Other Etruscan praenomina, attested much less frequently, were derived from names cited above. For example, the suffix -θu was used to form masculine praenomina, e.g. aranθu (< *aranθ-θu), velelθu, larθu (< *larθ-θu). The suffix -θur appeared in the following names: aranθur (< *aranθ-θur), velθur, and larθur (< *larθ-θur). The diminutive suffix -za was used to form names of endearment. For example, the son of Larth Cushu, as attested on the *Tabula Cortonensis* (see Chapter 11), is referred to as larza (< *larθ-tsa), that is to say, Larth junior.

The most common praenomina referring to Etruscan women were also native formations. Some names were built by suffixation from existing onomastic stems. For example, ramuθa (ramθa) and θanaχvil (θanχvil) were built from the bases ramu and θana by addition of the suffixes -θa and -χvil. The name θesanθei is a derivative of the theonym θesan 'dawn'. Other names were derived from masculine names by means of the suffixes -a, -i, and -ia, e.g. larθi/larθia from larθ, velia from vel, and śeθra (śeθra) from śeθre (śeθre).

7.26 Etruscan nomina were formed most commonly by means of the adjective-forming suffix -na 'belonging to, of'. (This suffix continued to be productive in the formation of adjectives, e.g. óuθi 'tomb' → óuθina 'of the tomb'.) In prehistoric Etruscan, -na was employed to make patronymic adjectives from personal names, e.g. velθur 'Velthur' → velθur-na- '(son) of Velthur'. After the Etruscans adopted the nomen as the cornerstone of their onomastic system, this suffix was employed to form family names, and patronymics in turned were formed by syntactic means (see §7.4). From the Archaic period, we find examples of family names derived from personal names, e.g. teiθur-na-, velθie-na-, θanarsie-na-, larice-na-, spurie-na-, lauχusie-na-, but we also find a substantial number of nomina built to stems that never appear, at least as far as the inscriptional record is concerned, as personal names, e.g. auka-na-, karka-na-, avhirici-na-.

The suffix -na appears in a high percentage of Etruscan family names, but other native suffixes could be used to form nomina as well. The suffix -ra, which was used to form adjectives from nouns, e.g. caθra 'of Catha', ceizra 'of Ceisie', was employed as early as the seventh century BCE in the formation of nomina, e.g. velvhe-ra, velθura (< *velθur-ra). A handful of nomina ended in the suffix -u, e.g. apiqu, qutu, etc.

Ethnic names were also a source of family names. The oldest examples are kaviate and kaiseriθe, the former built from the stem kavi- (Gabii?), the later built from the stem kaiseri- (Caere). A dispute exists whether the suffix -(a)te/-θe is Etruscan or Italic in origin, but this does not alter the fact that ethnic names could be conscripted for use as nomina.

7.27 A significant segment of the names in the Etruscan system were taken from foreign sources. Most derive from one of the Italic languages spoken in the territories adjacent to Etruria, but names with Celtic, Venetic, and Raetic bases have also been identified, particularly in inscriptions originating from areas settled by Etruscan colonists.

7.28 Sabellic and Latino-Faliscan names were Etruscanized and incorporated into the native system of nomenclature. The following nomina are from Latin or Sabellic sources: apunie, atie, latinie, petrunie, pumpunie, etc. The ending -ie is an Etruscan recasting of the Italic suffix *-iyo-, which appeared as -ios/-ius in Latino-Faliscan, e.g. Latin Latinius, and as -ies/-iís in Sabellic languages, such as South Picene pompúnies. The number of foreign items borrowed into the system was sufficiently large by the seventh century BCE to lead to the detachment of the suffix -ie from its original locus in borrowed names, predominantly nomina, and to its extension to native Etruscan word-forms. For example, the

names <n>uzinaie (cf. nuzina), hermenaie, hirsunaie, palenaie, and paiθi-
naie combine the native Etruscan suffix -na with the (Etruscanized) native Italic suffix -ie.

The most common praenomina of Italic extraction were **luvcie**, **marce**,
puplie, **salvies**, and **cae** (*Lucius, Marcus, Publius, Salvius, Gaius*). Italic was
also a prominent source of cognomina, such as the following, derived
from Latin or Sabellic sources: **catu**, **sceva**, **lusce**, **palpe**, **macre**, and **raufe**
(*Cato, Scaeva, Luscus, Balbus, Macer, Rufus*).

8 SYNTAX

Introduction

8.1 Etruscan may be described as an agglutinating language. Languages with this type of morphological structure tend to share certain features of syntax. For example, the major constituents in sentences are often arrayed in the order S(ubject) O(bject) V(erb). Genitives tend to be positioned before the nouns that they determine, and such languages generally have postpositions rather than prepositions. Etruscan also had these characteristics.

8.1.1 For the typological characteristics of agglutinating languages see the brief discussion in Agostiniani 1993.

Functions of Cases

8.2 In Etruscan the syntactic role or function of a noun or a noun phrase within a sentence was determined by the feature case (see §§4.11–17). Case marked relationships between nouns and verbs, between nouns and other nouns, and between postpositions and nouns.

8.2.1 Compare the synopses of cases and case usage in Rix 1984b:222–9 and 2004:952–3 as well as in Steinbauer 1999:167–80.

8.3 The complements of verbs were marked by the nominative/accusative case for the nominal subjects of transitive and intransitive verbs, and for the direct objects of transitive verbs. Pronominal subjects were in the nominative case; pronominal direct objects were in the accusative.

(1) Nominative/accusative = subject of transitive verb

mini muluvanice vhlakunaie venel (Vt 3.1)
'Venel Vhlakunaie gave me (as a gift).'

mini 'me', 1ST PERS PRO, ACC; **muluvanice** 'gave (as a gift)', PAST ACT; **vhlakunaie** 'Flakunaie', MASC NOMEN, NOM/ACC; **venel** 'Venel', MASC PRAE, NOM/ACC

(2)   Nominative/accusative = subject of intransitive verb

larθia : ateinei : | flereσ : m̥atrnσl : | turce (Co 3.7)
'Larthia Ateinei dedicated (this statue) to the divinity Matrns.'

larθia 'Larthia', FEM PRAE, NOM/ACC; ateinei 'Ateinei', FEM NOMEN, NOM/ACC;
flereσ 'divinity', 1ST GEN; m̥atrnσl 'Matrns', THEO, 2ND GEN; turce 'dedicated', PAST ACT

(3)   Pronominal accusative = direct object of transitive verb

itun turuce vene.l .a.telinas tinas cliniiaras (Ta 3.2)
'Venel Atelinas dedicated this (vase) to the sons of Tinia.'

itun 'this', DEM PRO, ACC; turuce 'dedicated', PAST ACT; vene.l 'Venel', MASC
PRAE, NOM/ACC; .a.telinas 'Atelina', MASC NOMEN, 1ST GEN; tinas 'Tinia', THEO,
1ST GEN; cliniiaras 'sons', ANIM PL, 1ST GEN

The nominative/accusative case was also the citation form of a noun.
For example, the nominative/accusative form tusna (OI S.45), which is
generally interpreted as meaning 'swan', was inscribed beside the figure
of a swan on the reverse of a mirror. The names of the deceased and the
names of mythological and heroic characters painted alongside images in
tombs or incised on mirrors were written in this case, e.g. araθ vinacna
'Ara(n)th Vinacna', NOM/ACC (Ta 7.17), tuχulχa 'Tukhulkha', THEO, NOM/ACC
(Ta 7.73).

8.4 The most frequent function of the genitive case as attested in
inscriptions was to indicate a relationship between one noun or noun
phrase and another. Most commonly the genitive case indicated possession or familial relationships.

(4)   Genitive = possession, familial relationships

(a)   mi faσena tataσ tulaluσ (Sp 2.36)
       'I (am) the libation vessel of Tata Tulalu.'

       mi 'I', 1ST PERS PRO, NOM; faσena 'libation vessel', NOM/ACC; tataσ 'Tata',
       MASC PRAE, 1ST GEN; tulaluσ 'Tulalu', MASC NOMEN, 1ST GEN

(b)   avle · tarχnas · larθal · clan (Cr 1.10)
       'Aule Tarkhnas, son of Larth'

       avle 'Aule', MASC PRAE, NOM/ACC; tarχnas 'Tarkhna', MASC NOMEN, 1ST
       GEN; larθal 'Larth', MASC PRAE, 2ND GEN; clan 'son', NOM/ACC

The genitive case was also used to indicate the person or divinity to whom or for whom a gift or an offering was given; this is the so-called *genitivus donandi* (see also (2) and (3)).

(5)   Genitive = recipient of a votive offering

cn · turce · murila · hercnas : | θuflθas · cver : (Ta 3.6)
'Murila, (slave) of Hercnas, dedicated this (statue) to Thufltha as a votive offering (?).'

cn 'this', DEM PRO, ACC; **turce** 'dedicated', PAST ACT; **murila** 'Murila', NAME, NOM/ACC; **hercnas** 'Hercnas', MASC NOMEN, 1ST GEN; **θuflθas** 'Thufltha', THEO, 1ST GEN; **cver** 'votive offering (?)', NOM/ACC

8.5   The range of usage of the pertinentive case is the subject of debate. It seems reasonably safe to conclude that it had two closely connected functions, namely, indirect object and beneficiary, when in construction with a transitive verb such as **muluvanice** 'gave (as a gift)'.

(6)   Pertinentive = indirect object/beneficiary

(a)   mi<ni> aranθ ramuθaçi veçtiricinala muluvanice (Cr 3.20)
'Aranth gave me to/for Ramutha Vestiricinai.'

mi 'I', 1ST PERS PRO, ACC; **aranθ** 'Aranth', MASC PRAE, NOM/ACC; **ramuθaçi** 'Ramutha', FEM PRAE, 1ST PERT; **veçtiricinala** 'Vestiricinai', FEM NOMEN, 2ND PERT; **muluvanice** 'gave', PAST ACT

(b)   mini muluvanice tetana ve.l.ka.s.na.s. veleliiasi (ETP 269)
'Tetana Velkasnas gave me to/for Veleliia.'

mini 'me', 1ST PERS PRO, ACC; **muluvanice** 'gave', PAST ACT; **tetana** 'Tetana', MASC PRAE, NOM/ACC; **velkasnas** 'Velkasnas', MASC NOMEN, 1ST GEN; **veleliiasi** 'Veleliia', FEM PRAE, 1ST PERT

When in construction with a passive verb, it is possible, and indeed some have so argued, that the pertinentive signaled the agent. However, a benefactive reading in this context is equally plausible, and may actually be preferred for (7a), particularly if one does not want to admit that the design on the mirror was incised or commissioned by a woman.

(7)   Pertinentive + passive

(a)   mi titasi cver menaχe (AH 3.4)
'I was made (= commissioned) as a votive offering (?) by/for Tita.'

mi 'I', 1ST PERS PRO, NOM; titasi 'Tita', FEM PRAE, PERT; cver 'votive
offering (?)', NOM/ACC; menaχe 'was made', PAST PASS

(b) mi araθiale ziχuχe (Fa 6.3)
     'I was decorated/designed by/for Ara(n)th.'

     mi 'I', 1ST PERS PRO, NOM; araθiale 'Ara(n)th', MASC PRAE, PERT; ziχuχe
     'was decorated, designed', PAST PASS

The function of the pertinentive case when in construction with the
u-participle has generated considerable debate. The interpretation of the
pertinentive depends in part on whether or not this sentence type provides the same information as the type represented by **muluvanice** (see
(6a) and (6b)). If sentences of the **muluvanice**-type and sentences of the
mulu-type are interpreted as active and passive counterparts of one another, then one can conclude that the pertinentive had agentive function.
If sentences of the **mulu**-type focused on the recipient of the gift rather
than on the donor, then the pertinentive is best interpreted as having
had a benefactive or indirect object function.

(8) U-participle + pertinentive

     (a) mi mulu larisale velχainasi (Cr 3.10)
          'I (was) given by/for/to Laris Velkhainas.'

          mi 'I', 1ST PERS PRO, NOM; mulu 'given', U-PART; larisale 'Laris', MASC
          PRAE, 2ND PERT; velχainasi 'Velkhainas', MASC NOMEN, 1ST PERT

     (b) mi spurieisi teiθurnasi aliqu (Cr 3.7)
          'I (was) donated by/for/to Spurie Teithurnas.'

          mi 'I', 1ST PERS PRO, NOM; spurieisi 'Spurie', MASC PRAE, PERT; teiθurnasi
          'Teithurnas', MASC NOMEN, 1ST PERT; aliqu 'donated', U-PART

Inscription (9), in which a genitive appears alongside the pertinentive, appears to favor the interpretation that the pertinentive signaled
the agent when in construction with a u-participle. Other interpretations
are possible, but less convincing.

(9) Pertinentive + mulu

     mi mulu araθiale θanaχvilus prasanaia (ETP 269)
     'I (was) given by Aranth to Thankhvil Prasanai.' or 'I (was) given by
     Aranth. (I am the property) of Thankhvil Prasanai.'

mi 'I', 1ST PERS PRO, NOM; mulu 'given', U-PART; araθiale 'Aranth', MASC PRAE, 2ND PERT; θanaχvilus 'Thanakhvil', FEM PRAE, 1ST GEN; prasanaia 'Prasanai', FEM NOMEN, 2ND GEN

There is a further consideration. Ablative noun phrases in construction with passive verbs are considered by virtually all Etruscologists to signal the agent of an action (see §8.7 below). The fact that the ablative has this function could be added to the balance of the evidence against the pertinentive as the case for agent in passive constructions. Unfortunately, all inscriptions with this construction date to the Neo-Etruscan period. It could well be then that the use of the ablative in agent phrases was a Neo-Etruscan innovation or that the agent could be signaled by different constructions in different syntactic contexts.

In summary, it does not seem possible at this time to decide definitively in favor of one or another interpretation for the pertinentive case when in construction with the u-participle.

8.5.1 The function of the pertinentive case has been the focus of several articles published by de Simone (1996b, 1998a, and 2004a). Wylin 2000:142–7 is a concise and informative review of the problems and the difficulties surrounding the interpretation of the functions of this case.

8.6 The pertinentive case had yet another function. A few inscriptions incised on pottery bear names inflected in the pertinentive case. A reasonable proposal is that these names refer to the workshop in which the ceramic in question was produced. For example, serturiesi (Ta 6.14) may mean 'in the (workshop) of Serturie'. The idea is that serturiesi is to be parsed as serturie-s-i, that is to say, as the locative of the genitive. The word for 'workshop' is supplied from the context. According to some Etruscologists, this type of analysis may reflect the historical origins of the pertinentive. It may also explain unusual features of agreement, as attested for example in the absolute construction (for which see §8.14).

8.7 The ablative case was used to denote the source from which something was derived. In the following clause from the *Tabula Cortonensis*, the ablative phrase śparzêσtiσ σazleiσ is best interpreted in this fashion.

(10) Ablative of source

cên · zic · ziχuχe · śparzêσtiσ · σazleiσ · in | θuχti · cuśuθuraσ · śuθiu · ame (ETP 74, 18–19A)
'This document was written (= copied ?) from a tablet of bronze/ wood (?) which is placed in the house/depository (?) of the Cushu.'

cên 'this', DEM PRO, NOM; zic 'document', NOM/ACC; ziχuχe 'was written', PAST PASS; śparzêσtiσ = śparzê 'tablet', 1ST ABL + -tiσ 'this', DEM PRO, 1ST ABL; σazleiσ 'bronze/wood (?)', 1ST ABL; in 'which', INANIM REL PRO, NOM/ACC; θuχti = θuχ 'house, depository', LOC + -ti 'in', POST; cuśuθuraσ 'Cushu family', ANIM PL, 1ST GEN; śuθiu 'placed', U-PART; ame 'is', NON-PAST ACT

The ablative was also used after verbs of birth or origin (11a–b). In (11a) the ablatives are in construction with the passive verb farθnaχe 'was born'. They refer to the father and the mother of the deceased. This same notion was conveyed by the bare ablative in an Archaic text from Caere (11b).

(11) Ablatives of birth

>   (a) larθ tutes anc farθnaχe veluis | tuteis θanχviluisc | turials{c}
>   (Vc 1.64)
>   '(It was) Larth Tutes who was born from Vel Tutes and Than-
>   khvil Turi.'
>
>   larθ 'Larth', MASC PRAE, NOM/ACC; tutes 'Tutes', MASC NOMEN, 1ST GEN;
>   anc 'who', ANIM REL PRO, NOM + -c '?', ENCLITIC PART (?); farθnaχe 'was
>   born', PAST PASS; veluis 'Vel', MASC PRAE, 1ST ABL; tuteis 'Tutes', MASC
>   NOMEN, 1ST ABL; θanχviluisc 'Thankhvil', FEM PRAE, 1ST ABL + -c 'and',
>   ENCLITIC CONJ; turials{c} 'Turi', FEM NOMEN, 1ST ABL (with the enclitic
>   conjunction erroneously repeated)
>
>   (b) mini turuce larθ ⫶ apunaς veleθnalaς (Cr 3.17)
>   'Larth Apunas, (born) from Velethnai, dedicated me.'
>
>   mini 'me', 1ST PERS PRO, ACC; turuce 'dedicated', PAST ACT; larθ 'Larth',
>   MASC PRAE, NOM/ACC; apunaς 'Apunas', MASC NOMEN, 1ST GEN; veleθnalaς
>   'Velethnai', FEM NOMEN, 2ND ABL

The ablative of source may have been the stepping-stone for the extension of the ablative to phrases marking the agent of a passive verb. In (12) the ablative phrase tuθineσ tlenaχeiσ served as the agent of the passive verb menaχe. The meaning of the ablative phrase is a guess, perhaps even a reasonable one, but it is not guaranteed.

(12) Ablative of agent

>   veliaσ · fanacnal · θuflθaσ | alpan · menaχe · clen · ceχa · tuθineσ ·
>   tlenaχeiσ (Co 3.6)

'Thank offering (?) of Velia Fanacnei for (the divinity) Thufltha. It was made (= commissioned) in honor of her son by the city district (?) Tlenakhe (?).'

veliaσ 'Velia', FEM PRAE, 1ST GEN; fanacnal 'Fanacnei', FEM NOMEN, 2ND GEN; θuflθaσ 'Thufltha', THEO, 1ST GEN; alpan 'thank offering (?)', NOM/ACC; menaχe 'was made', PAST PASS; clen 'son', ABL; ceχa 'in honor of', POST; tuθineσ 'city district (?)', 1ST ABL; tlenaχeiσ 'Tlenakhe (?)', PLACE NAME (?), 1ST ABL

8.7.1 See Cristofani 1971:38–42 for the ending -als and the syntactic function of the ablative.

8.8 The locative case indicated place where and time when, as in (13a) and (13b).

(13) Locative case functions

(a) eta : kavθaσ : aχuiaσ : perśie | avle numnaσ turke (Pe 3.1)
'This (vase) is for (the divinity) Kautha Akhuia in Perusia; Aule Numna dedicated (it as an offering).'

eta 'this', DEM PRON, NOM; kavθaσ 'Kautha', THEO, 1ST GEN; aχuiaσ 'Akhuia', THEO EPITHET, 1ST GEN; perśie 'Pershia (Perusia)', CITY NAME, LOC; avle: 'Aule', PRAE, NOM/ACC; numnaσ 'Numna', MASC NOMEN, 1ST GEN; turke 'dedicated', PAST ACT

(b) zaθrumsne · luśaσ · fler · hamφisca · θezeri (LL VI, 9)
'On the twentieth (day) for (the divinity) Lusha the victim, the one from the left (?), must be immolated.'

zaθrumsne 'twentieth', LOC; luśaσ 'Lusha', THEO, 1ST GEN; fler 'sacrificial victim', NOM/ACC; hamφisca 'left (?)', 1ST ABL + -ca 'the', DEM PRO, NOM; θezeri 'must be immolated', NECESS

Evidence indicates that the locative case was also used to indicate instrument and/or means. Unfortunately, the syntactic contexts in which such functions are found and the meanings of the lexical items at issue are not always clear, even if the interpretations, such as the one cited in (14), are plausible.

(14) Instrumental locative

nunθenθ · cletram · σrenχve | tei · faσei (LL II, 10–11)
'(after) anointing (?) the litter with *srenkhvas* (and) with this libation'

nunθenθ '(after) anointing (?)', θ-PART; cletram 'litter', NOM/ACC; σrenχve
'?', INANIM PL, LOC; tei 'this', DEM PRO, LOC; faσei 'libation', LOC

Postpositions

8.9 Etruscan had postpositions rather than prepositions. Postpositional phrases had the structure Noun + Postposition. Some postpositions
were attached directly to the end of the inflected nominal forms that they
governed and so were written as a single orthographic unit, e.g. **spureθi**
'in the community' = **spure** + **-θi**. Others stood as free words. In sentence
(12) above the constituents of the postpositional phrase **clen · ceχa** 'in
honor of (her) son' were separated by punctuation. As a postposition, **ceχa**
governed the ablative case.

The postposition **-θi** 'in' was affixed to nouns inflected for locative case
to form postpositional phrases. In (15) the postposition was attached to
the locative of the noun **óuθi** 'tomb', to the head of the phrase, and to the
pronominal modifier **cl-** 'this'.

(15) Locative + postposition **-θi**

> clθị̣ [: óuθi]θi : ra[m :] ceisatrui | cesu : p[ru]ól̥nas : [p]ụia velus |
> rapi : [– – –]e : ṭe[– – –] (Vc 1.59)
> 'In this tomb (was) buried Ramtha Ceisatrui, the wife of Vel
> Prushlnas, *rapi …*'

> clθị̣ = cl- 'this', DEM PRO, LOC + -θị̣ 'in', POST; [óuθi]θi = óuθi 'tomb', LOC + -θi
> 'in', POST; ra[m], abbrev. for ramθa 'Ramtha', FEM PRAE, NOM/ACC; ceisatrui
> 'Ceisatrui', FEM NOMEN, NOM/ACC; cesu 'buried', U-PART; p[ru]ól̥nas
> 'Prushlnas', MASC NOMEN, 1ST GEN; [p]ụia 'wife', NOM/ACC; velus 'Vel', MASC
> PRAE, 1ST GEN; rapi '?'

The postposition **-θi** could also be attached to nouns in the genitive case,
as for example **tarχnal-θi** in (16). In such cases the locative noun governed
by the postposition is to be supplied from the context: **tarχnal-θi** = 'in the
[city] of Tarkhna'.

(16) [al]ẹθnas : arnθ : larisal : zilaθ : ṭạrχnalθi : aṃce (AT 1.100)
> 'Arnth Alethnas, (son) of Laris, was governor in the [city] of
> Tarkhna.'

> [al]ẹθnas 'Alethnas', MASC NOMEN, 1ST GEN; arnθ 'Arnth', MASC PRAE, NOM/ACC;
> larisal 'Laris', MASC PRAE, 2ND GEN; zilaθ 'governor', NOM/ACC; ṭạrχnalθi =
> ṭạrχnal 'Tarkhna', CITY NAME, 2ND GEN + -θi 'in', POST; aṃce 'was', PAST ACT

In the Neo-Etruscan period this postposition had four forms. In addition to -θi, which was the most common form, -θ (tarχnalθ 'in the (city) of Tarkhna'), -ti (zilcti 'in the governorship'), and -t (θuχt 'in the house') were also attested. The variants came into being as the result of two phonological changes, one eliminating the final vowels of enclitic forms in certain contexts (perhaps before other vowels) and the other causing aspirates to become deaspirated when adjacent to other consonants. The distribution of the variant forms of this postposition suggests that they were extracted from the phonetic context in which they arose and extended to new contexts as stylistic variants. Compare θuχti and θuχt, both of which are found in virtually the same phonetic context (before /k/) in the *Tabula Cortonensis*.

The postposition -te 'on', which was affixed to nouns in the locative case, had functions similar to the postposition discussed in the preceding paragraphs. It seems likely that in the Neo-Etruscan period, particularly in northern Etruria, -te and -θi were converging in form due to the sound changes mentioned above. In terms of meaning the two postpositions had become similar, if not entirely isofunctional, in this part of Etruria. Compare the function of the postpositions in the forms śpanθi and śpante, which appear near the beginning of the *Tabula Cortonensis*. Both forms appear to require the same constituent analysis, that is to say, stem + postposition, and the same translation, namely, 'on the plain' (see §11.6, section I.1).

The postposition -ri 'for, on behalf of' also governed the locative case. In (17) the postposition is affixed to a series of three nouns, σacnicleri, σpureri, and meθlumeri.

(17) Postposition -ri

σacnicleri · ciḷθl · σpureri | meθlumeric · enaσ · raχθ · tur · heχσθ | vinum (LL IX, 5–6)
'On behalf of the sanctuary (?) of the citadel (?), on behalf of the community, and on behalf of the city of Ena (?) place (it) on the *rakh* (after/while) pouring (?) the wine.'

σacnicleri = σacnicle- 'sanctuary (?)', LOC + -ri 'on behalf of', POST; ciḷθl 'citadel (?)', 2ND GEN; σpureri = σpure 'community', LOC + -ri 'on behalf of', POST; meθlumeric = meθlume- 'city', LOC + -ri 'on behalf of', POST + -c 'and', ENCLITIC CONJ; enaσ 'Ena (?)', CITY NAME (?), 1ST GEN; raχθ = raχ '?', LOC + -θ 'on', POST; tur 'put', IMPV; heχσθ 'pour (?)', θ-PART (?); vinum 'wine', NOM/ACC

Another postposition, -tra, which seems to have had a meaning similar to that of the postposition -ri, governed the genitive case. In (18) the postposition was affixed to the 2nd genitive of the feminine name **vipinei**, i.e. **vipinal-tra** 'on the part of Vipinei'.

(18) Postposition -tra

> **fl · śupri manince | vipinaltra ulχniśla | clẓ tetanuσ** (Vt 4.5)
> 'Fl(avia) Shupri offered (?) (this statue) to (the divinity) Cel Tetanu (?) in honor of Vipinei, the wife of Ulkhni.'
>
> **fl**, abbrev. of **flavia** 'Flavia', FEM PRAE, NOM/ACC; **śupri** 'Shupri', FEM NOMEN, NOM/ACC; **manince** 'offered (?)', PAST ACT; **vipinaltra** = **vipinal** 'Vipinei', FEM NOMEN, 2ND GEN + **-tra** 'in honor of', POST; **ulχniśla** = **ulχniσ** 'Ulkhni', MASC NOMEN, 1ST GEN + **-śla** 'the', DEF ART, 2ND GEN; **clẓ** 'Cel' THEO, 1ST GEN; **tetanuσ** 'Tetanu', THEO EPITHET, 1ST GEN

The postposition -tra appears also to have governed nouns inflected for locative and ablative case, e.g. **hilχvetra** (= **hilχve** INAM PL, LOC + **-tra**), **snenaziulastra** (= **snenaziulas** ABL + **-tra**), but it is not possible to be sure of the meaning in these contexts because we do not know the meanings of the inflected forms. Some claim that this postposition was itself capable of receiving inflectional suffixes. This idea is supported, so it is argued, by the forms **spurestres** and **sacnicstres** from the *Liber Linteus* and by the form **unialastres** from Pyrgi Tablet Cr 4.4. The latter has been analyzed as a postpositional phrase with both noun and postposition marked for ablative, i.e. **unialas-tres** (from older *unialas-tra-is*). Under this interpretation **unialas** is the 2nd ablative of the name of the goddess **uni** 'Uni'; **-tres** is analyzed as the postposition -tra inflected with the 1st ablative suffix. This phrase is generally translated as 'in honor of Juno'.

The function of the postposition –tra, its use with multiple cases, and the question of whether it may receive inflectional suffixes is a fascinating topic that calls for additional investigation.

8.9.1 For discussion of the postposition -tra see de Simone 1990a. Facchetti (2002a:75–82) provides short descriptions of the postpositions -θi, -te, -ri, -tra, and -pi.

Absolute Construction

8.10 Funerary inscriptions of aristocratic Etruscans were sometimes dated by reference to the public official that was governing at the time of death. At Tarquinia dating by eponymous official had the form of a construction in which the noun referring to the political office was inflected in the locative case and the name of the magistrate was in the pertinentive or, perhaps more accurately, in the locative of the genitive (see §8.6).

In sentence (19) the pertinentive case forms in the absolute construction behave as if they were locatives of a genitive ('in [the governorship] of Vel Hulkhnies').

(19) Dating by eponymous official

zįlci : vel[u]ṣ[i] : hul|χniẹsi larθ : vel|χas : vel[θur]us : aprθn[al]|c : cl[a]n : sacnióa : θui | [ecl]θ : óuθiθ : acazrce (Ta 5.5)
'In the governorship of Vel Hulkhnies, Larth Velkhas, the son of Velthur and of Aprthnei, the *sacni, acazrce* here in this tomb.'

zįlci 'governorship', LOC; vel[u]ṣ[i] 'Vel', MASC PRAE, 1ST PERT; hulχniẹsi 'Hulkhnies', MASC NOMEN, 1ST PERT; larθ 'Larth', MASC PRAE, NOM/ACC; velχas 'Velkhas', MASC NOMEN, 1ST GEN; vel[θur]us 'Velthur', MASC PRAE, 1ST GEN; aprθn[al]c = aprθn[al] 'Aprthnei', FEM NOMEN, 2ND GEN + -c 'and', ENCLITIC CONJ; cl[a]n 'son', NOM/ACC; sacnióa = sacni '?', NOM/ACC + -óa 'the', NOM; θui 'here', ADV; [ecl]θ = [ecl] 'this', DEM PRO, LOC + -θ 'in', POST; óuθiθ 'tomb', LOC + -θ 'in', POST; acazrce '?', PAST ACT

8.10.1 For the locative absolute construction see Rix 1984b:227 and Steinbauer 1999:176–7. Rix (1968a) compares the Etruscan construction with what appears to be a similar construction attested in Lemnian (for which see §12.8, (9b)).

Noun Phrases with avil *'year'*

8.11 Etruscan funerary inscriptions commonly indicate the age of the deceased at the time of death. The age of the deceased was marked by a phrase in which the word **avil** 'year' and the numbers indicating the age were inflected for genitive case. It is worthy of note that the word for 'year' is not marked for plural number in this construction. In (20) the phrase **ciem zaθrms** 'twenty minus three' is in agreement with the genitive **avils**.

(20) Age of the Deceased

larθ : χurχles : arnθal : χurχles: θanχvilus[c] cracial | clan : avils : ciem zaθrms : lupu (AT 1.172)
'Larth Khurkhles, son of Arnth Khurkhles and Thankhvil Craci, (was) dead at seventeen years of age.'

larθ 'Larth', MASC PRAE, NOM/ACC; χurχles 'Khurkhles', MASC NOMEN, 1ST GEN; arnθal 'Arnth', MASC PRAE, 2ND GEN; χurχles 'Khurkhles', MASC NOMEN, 1ST GEN; θanχvilus[c] = θanχvilus 'Thankhvil', FEM PRAE, 1ST GEN + -c 'and', ENCLITIC CONJ; cracial 'Craci', FEM NOMEN, 2ND GEN; clan 'son', NOM/ACC; avils 'year', 1ST GEN; ciem = ci 'three', NUM, NOM/ACC + -em 'from', POST; zaθrms 'twenty', NUM, 1ST GEN; lupu 'dead', U-PART

The number of years that a person lived was indicated by a phrase in the nominative/accusative case. In this type of phrase the word avil 'year, age' and the numbers indicating the age of the deceased were uninflected.

(21) Age of the Deceased

arnθ · apunas · velus · {ma–} | max · cezpalx · avil | svalce (Ta 1.82)
'Arnth Apunas, (son) of Vel, lived for thirty-five years.'

arnθ 'Arnth', MASC PRAE, NOM/ACC; apunas 'Apunas', MASC NOMEN, 1ST GEN; velus 'Vel', MASC PRAE, 1ST GEN; {ma–} (scribal error); max 'five', NUM, NOM/ACC; cezpalx 'thirty', NUM, NOM/ACC; avil 'year', NOM/ACC; svalce 'lived', PAST ACT

8.11.1   For time constructions with avil 'year' the most useful resource is Cristofani 1973b.

Syntax of the Article

8.12   The enclitic -óa/-śa /ʃa/ functioned as a definite article. It agreed in case and number with the head of its noun phrase. In the corpus of inscriptions at our disposal the article is attested primarily in funerary contexts in phrases where it is in agreement with clan 'son', sex 'daughter', or puia 'wife'. In inscription (22) the pronoun -óa was nominative/accusative because it was in agreement with the noun clan, which was itself in apposition to the noun phrase laris velxas.

(22) Article

laris : velxas | veluóa | clan (Ta 1.62)
'Laris Velkhas, the son of Vel'

laris 'Laris', MASC PRAE, NOM/ACC; velxas 'Velkhas', MASC NOMEN, 1ST GEN; veluóa = velus 'Vel', MASC PRAE, 1ST GEN + -óa 'the', DEF ART, NOM; clan 'son', NOM/ACC

In most noun phrases that included the article -óa/-śa, the head noun was not expressed, but was to be understood from the context of the inscription. So, for example, in the following inscription the word clan does not appear in the patronymic phrase, which was expressed by the praenomen of the father plus the article -óa.

(23) Article

vel · crepus · [lar]θalióa (Cr 1.141)
'Vel Crepus, the (son) of Larth'

vel 'Vel', MASC PRAE, NOM/ACC; crepus 'Crepus', MASC NOMEN, 1ST GEN; [lar]θalióa = [lar]θal 'Larth', MASC PRAE, 2ND GEN + -ióa 'the', DEF ART, NOM

In (24), the pronominal form -ióla /iʃla/ was inflected for genitive case because the noun that it modified, the unexpressed genitive of clan, namely, clens, stood in apposition to the genitive phrase velθurus sta<t>lanes 'Velthur Statlanes'.

(24) Article

>eca : mutna : velθurus : sta<t>lanes | larisalióla (AT 1.34)
>'This (is the) sarcophagus of Velthur Statlanes, the (son) of Laris.'
>
>eca 'this', DEM PRO, NOM; mutna 'sarcophagus', NOM/ACC; velθurus 'Velthur', MASC PRAE, 1ST GEN; sta<t>lanes 'Statlanes', MASC NOMEN, 1ST GEN; larisalióa = laris 'Laris', MASC PRAE, 1ST GEN + -ióla 'the', DEF ART, 2ND GEN

The article -óa/-śa was used almost exclusively as a modifier of animate nouns. Only two inscriptions have been identified in which the referent was an inanimate object (see §8.17).

8.13 The question of whether demonstrative pronouns were inflected for number is *sub judice*. For the article, however, the question has been decided. In (25) the article -iśvle /iʃule/ is in agreement with the pertinentive plural clenaraσi 'sons'. The corresponding singular of this phrase would be larθialiśle clensi.

(25) cehen : śuθi : ... careśri : auleσ : larθial : precuθuraσi : | larθialiśvle : ceσtnal : clenaraσi : ... (Pe 5.2)
'This tomb ... must be *careshri*-ed by/for members of the Precu family, Aule (and) Larth, the sons of Larth and Cestnei.'

>cehen 'this', DEM PRO, NOM; śuθi 'tomb', NOM/ACC; careśri 'must be ?', NECESS; auleσ 'Aule', MASC PRAE, 1ST GEN; larθial 'Larth', MASC PRAE, 2ND GEN; precuθuraσi 'the Precu family', ANIM PL, 1ST PERT; larθialiśvle = larθial 'Larth', MASC PRAE, 2ND GEN + -iśvle 'the', DEF ART, PL, 2ND PERT; ceσtnal 'Cestnei', FEM NOMEN, 2ND GEN; clenaraσi 'sons', ANIM PL, 1ST PERT

8.13.1 For the syntax of the article see Rix 1984b:230. Evidence for the plural endings is discussed in Adiego 2006 and Eichner 2002.

Demonstrative Pronouns

8.14 The Etruscan demonstratives eca/ca (Archaic ika) and eta/ta (Archaic ita) were used with both adjectival and pronominal function. Exactly how these two forms are to be distinguished from one another is not clear at this point. Examples of each usage are given in (26).

(26) Demonstratives with adjectival and pronominal function

    (a) vel ⫶ matunas ⫶ larisalióa | an ⫶ cn ⫶ ҫuθi ⫶ cerixunce (Cr 5.3)
         '(It was) Vel Matunas, the (son) of Laris, who built this tomb.'

         vel 'Vel', MASC PRAE, NOM/ACC; matunas 'Matunas', MASC NOMEN, 1ST;
         GEN; larisalióa = larisal 'Laris', MASC PRAE, 2ND GEN + -ióa 'the', DEF ART,
         NOM; an 'who', ANIM REL PRO, NOM/ACC; cn 'this', DEM PRO, ACC; ҫuθi
         'tomb', NOM/ACC; cerixunce 'built', PAST ACT

    (b) [e]cạ ⫶ óuθi anes | cuclnies (Ta 1.31)
         'This (is) the tomb of Ane Cuclnies.'

         [e]cạ 'this', DEM PRO, NOM; óuθi 'tomb', NOM/ACC; anes MASC PRAE, 1ST
         GEN; cuclnies 'Cuclnies', MASC NOMEN, 1ST GEN

8.15 Demonstratives were also used in phrases having the same structure as those of the article -óa/-śa. In these constructions the demonstratives may have been enclitics. In (27b), for example, the pronoun ta was
likely bound as an enclitic to the genitive of the name cupes. It had an articular function similar to that described for -óa, the only difference being
that ta (and ca) referred to nouns classified as inanimate, here pieces of
ceramic (27a–b) and sacrificial victims (27c), whereas -óa was generally
used with reference to human beings.

(27) Demonstratives with articular function

    (a) mi limu.r.ce.s. ta pruxu.m. (Cm 2.32)
         'I (am) the jug of Limurce.'

         mi 'I', 1ST PERS PRO, NOM; limu.r.ce.s. 'Limurce', MASC PRAE, 1ST GEN; ta
         'the', DEM PRO, NOM; pruxu.m. 'jug', NOM/ACC

    (b) mi cupes ta (Cm 2.65)
         'I (am) the (ceramic) of Cupe.'

         mi 'I', 1ST PERS PRO, NOM; cupes 'Cupe', MASC PRAE, 1ST GEN; ta 'the',
         DEM PRO, NOM

    (c) zaθrumsne · luśaσ · fler · hamφisca · θezeri (LL VI, 9)
         'On the twentieth (day) for (the divinity) Lusha the victim, the
         one from the left (?), must be immolated.'

         zaθrumsne 'twentieth', LOC; luśaσ 'Lusha', THEO, 1ST GEN; fler 'sacri-
         ficial victim', NOM/ACC; hamφisca 'left (?)', 1ST ABL + -ca 'the', DEM PRO,
         NOM/ACC; θezeri 'must be immolated', NECESS

Inscription (28), which is a votive inscription dedicated to the god Selvans, illustrates the second function of the demonstrative pronoun used

as an enclitic. In this case the pronoun -(i)ta was affixed to an adjective stem, sanχuna-, effectively turning it into a substantive, in this instance one serving as an epithet of the god Selvans.

(28) Demonstratives with substantivizing function

> selvans | sanχuneta | cveṛạ (Vs 4.8)
> 'Selvans, the one of *Sankhu*, a votive offering (?)'

> selvans 'Selvans', THEO, NOM/ACC; sanχuneta = sanχuna 'of Sankhu', THEO EPITHET, NOM/ACC + -ita 'the', DEM PRO, NOM; cveṛạ 'votive offering (?)', NOM/ACC

Relative Pronouns

8.16 The pronoun **an** referred back to nouns of the animate class. As sentence (29) demonstrates, personal names counted as animate for the purpose of agreement. The antecedent was the deceased, Larth Camnas.

(29) Animate **an**

> camnas · larθ · larθal · śatnalc · clan · an · ᴼuθi · lavtni · zivas · ceriχụ<nce> ... (Ta 1.182)
> '(It was) Larth Camnas, the son of Larth and Shatnei, who built (this) family tomb while still living.'

> camnas 'Camnas', MASC NOMEN, 1ST GEN; larθ 'Larth', MASC PRAE, NOM/ACC; larθal 'Larth', MASC PRAE, 2ND GEN; śatnalc 'Shatnei', FEM NOMEN, 2ND GEN + -c 'and', ENCLITIC CONJ; clan 'son', NOM/ACC; an 'who', ANIM REL PRO, NOM/ACC; ᴼuθi 'tomb', NOM/ACC; lavtni 'family', NOM/ACC; zivas 'living', AS-PART; ceriχụ<nce> 'built', PAST ACT

In contrast, the pronoun **in** was used with reference to inanimate antecedents. In (10), repeated below as (30), the antecedent of **in** is the ablative phrase śparzêᴼtiᴼ ᴼazleiᴼ, which, in one reasonable interpretation, refers to a bronze or wooden tablet.

(30) Inanimate **in**

> cên · zic · ziχuχe · śparzêᴼtiᴼ · ᴼazleiᴼ · in | θuχti · cuśuθuraᴼ · śuθiu · ame (ETP 74, 18–19A)
> 'This document was written (= copied ?) from a tablet of bronze/ wood (?) which is placed in the house/depository (?) of the Cushu.'

cên 'this', DEM PRON, NOM; zic 'document', NOM/ACC; ziχuχe 'was written',
PAST PASS; śparzêστισ = śparzêσ 'tablet', 1ST ABL + -tiσ 'this', DEM PRO, 1ST
ABL; σazleiσ 'bronze/wood (?)', 1ST ABL; in 'which', INANIM REL PRO, NOM/ACC;
θuχti = θuχ 'house, depository', LOC + -ti 'in', POST; cuśuθuraσ 'Cushu
family', ANIM PL, 1ST GEN; śuθiu 'placed', U-PART; ame 'is', NON-PAST ACT

8.16.1 For the distinction in form and function for the pronouns an/in see Agostiniani and
Nicosia 2000:99–100. The rule of agreement is now known, at least informally, as Agostiniani's
Law.

Agreement

8.17 The syntactic feature of agreement for case is attested in Etruscan noun phrases, although the evidence here is not always easy to interpret. One example is provided by the adjective **mlaχ** 'good, beautiful'
NOM/ACC, **mlakas** 1ST GEN, **mlacasi** 1ST PERT. In (31), the adjective **mlakas**,
which modifies the genitive **squlias**, was separated from its head and
placed in sentence-final position; the adjective **mlaχ** modifies **θina** 'water vessel'.

(31) **mi squḷias θina mlaχ mlakas** (Cr 2.33)
     'I (am) the beautiful water vessel of the beautiful Squlia.'

   mi 'I', 1ST PERS PRO, NOM; **squḷias** 'Squlia', FEM PRAE, 1ST GEN; **θina** 'water
   vessel', NOM/ACC; **mlaχ** 'beautiful', NOM/ACC; **mlakas** 'beautiful', 1ST GEN

Evidence of agreement for number in noun phrases is more difficult to
evaluate. At this point, no indisputable examples have been found of an
adjective agreeing in plural number with its head noun. In sentence (32)
the adjective **sval** 'living' modifies the subject of the sentence, which is a
coordinate noun phrase (the names **laris** and **avle**), but it is not marked
with a plural suffix.

(32) **laris · av|le · laris|al · clenar | sval · cn · ¢uθi | ceriχunce ...** (Cr 5.2)
     'Laris (and) Aule, sons of Laris, (while) living built this tomb.'

   laris 'Laris', MASC PRAE, NOM/ACC; **avle** 'Avle', MASC PRAE, NOM/ACC; **larisal**
   'Laris', MASC PRAE, 2ND GEN; **clenar** 'sons', ANIM PL, NOM/ACC; **sval** 'alive', NOM/
   ACC; **cn** 'this', DEM PRO, ACC; **¢uθi** 'tomb', NOM/ACC; **ceriχunce** 'built', PAST ACT

In a noun phrase specifying the age at which a person died, 1st genitive inflection indicated time when (see (33a)), whereas a noun phrase
with the numerals in the nominative/accusative form indicated duration
(33b). Phrases containing numbers (other than **θu** '1'), whose nouns were
of the inanimate class, did not require that the noun be marked for plural.
Compare the phrase **ci clenar** 'three sons', in which the noun **clenar** has

animate plural inflection, to the phrase **ci avil** 'for three years', in which the noun **avil** is without its inanimate plural suffix.

(33) Phrases indicating age of deceased

    (a) velθur larθal · clan | pumpual clan · larθial | avils · cealχls · lupu (Ta 1.191)
'Velthur, son of Larth and son of Larthi Pumpui, (was) dead at thirty years of age.'

        velθur 'Velthur', MASC PRAE, NOM/ACC; **larθal** 'Larth', MASC PRAE, 2ND GEN; **clan** 'son', NOM/ACC; **pumpual** 'Pumpui', FEM NOMEN, 2ND GEN; **clan** 'son', NOM/ACC; **larθial** 'Larthi', FEM PRAE, 2ND GEN; **avils** 'year', 1ST GEN; **cealχls** 'thirty', NUM, 1ST GEN; **lupu** 'dead', U-PART

    (b) lucer · laθerṇa | svalce avil | XXVI (Ta 1.89)
'Lucer Latherna lived for twenty-six years.'

        lucer 'Lucer', MASC PRAE, NOM/ACC; **laθerṇa** 'Latherna', MASC NOMEN, NOM/ACC; **svalce** 'lived', PAST ACT; **avil** 'year', NOM/ACC

Sentence Types

8.18 Two of the three major sentence types, declaratives and imperatives, are found in Etruscan inscriptions. Interrogative sentences have not yet been identified to the satisfaction of all scholars.

8.18.1 See Rix 1984b:230–1 for the interpretation of **ipa** as an interrogative and for the interpretation of .i.pa.ç. .i.ka.m., the first text of inscription Fa 0.4, as an interrogative sentence (ipaç 'whose', INTERROGATIVE PRO, 1ST GEN; ikam = ika 'this', DEM PRO, NOM + -m 'but', ENCLITIC CONJ = 'But whose is this?'). This interpretation, while plausible, is not yet verifiable.

8.19 Declarative sentences come in two varieties: nominal sentences and verbal sentences. Nominal sentences are those that do not have a verb. Epitaphs and proprietary inscriptions were commonly written with this type of sentence structure. Inscription (34), which is an epitaph from the Crocefisso Necropolis at Orvieto, has predicate nominative structure.

(34) Nominal sentence

    mi larices telaθuras óuθi (Vs 1.86)
'I (am) the tomb of Larice Telathuras.'

    mi 'I', 1ST PERS PRO, NOM; **larices** 'Larice', MASC PRAE, 1ST GEN; **telaθuras** 'Telathuras', MASC NOMEN, 1ST GEN; **óuθi** 'tomb', NOM/ACC

We may assume that nominal sentences without a predicate noun overtly expressed are to be interpreted in the same manner as (34). In (35) it is possible to understand the name of the ceramic object or perhaps a generic term such as 'property' as the predicate noun of the sentence.

(35) **mi lariça velθieç** (Cr 2.15)
  'I (am) the (vase/property) of Laris Velthies.'

  mi 'I', 1ST PERS PRO, NOM; lariça 'Laris', MASC PRAE, 1ST GEN; velθieç 'Velthies',
  MASC NOMEN, 1ST GEN

In the Archaic Etruscan period a commemorative inscription could be expressed in the form of a nominal sentence with a *u*-participle. Sentences of this type did not have the predicate structure typical of sentences (34) and (35). In this type of nominal sentence the *u*-participle was typically in construction with a pertinentive case form (see §8.5).

(36) Nominal sentence with *u*-participle

  mi hirumesi mulu (Cr 3.12)
  'I (was) given by/for/to Hirume.'

  mi 'I', 1ST PERS PRO, NOM; hirumesi 'Hirume', MASC PRAE, 1ST PERT; mulu
  'given', U-PART

Mood

8.20 Verbal sentences can be classified according to the mood of the main verb. Imperative verbs were used to issue commands; jussives were used for activities that were prescribed; and so-called necessitative constructions for activities that were considered to be obligatory. Indicative verbs were employed for all other functions.

  8.20.1 Wylin 2000:121–8 is a short but informative discussion of mood markers in Etruscan.

8.21 Imperative verbs are attested most prominently in the *Liber Linteus* in passages where the priest or priestly attendant is directed to perform ritual acts outlined in the text. In (37) the imperative **trin**, at least according to one interpretation, governs the noun phrase that follows.

(37) **trin · flere · neθunɔl** (LL IX, 7)
  'Invoke the divine spirit of Nethuns.'

  trin 'invoke', IMPV; flere 'divine spirit', NOM/ACC; neθunɔl 'Nethuns', THEO,
  2ND GEN

In (38) the officiant is directed to place (śuθ) some object (a **var**) on the ground (**celi**).

(38) var · celi · śuθ (LL V, 10)
  'Place the *var* on the ground.'

  var '?', NOM/ACC; celi 'earth', LOC; śuθ 'put, place', IMPV

Prohibitions were signaled by the negator **ei/ein/en** and a verb in the imperative mood. The best examples of this type are found in so-called 'anti-theft' inscriptions incised on pottery (39).

(39) mi χuliχna cupe.s. .a.l.θ.r.na.s. .e.i. minipi çapi | mini θanu (Cm 2.13)
  'I (am) the vessel of Cupe Althrnas. Don't take me. *θanu* me.'

  mi 'I', 1ST PERS PRO, NOM; χuliχna 'vessel', NOM/ACC; cupe.s. 'Cupe', MASC
  PRAE, 1ST GEN; .a.l.θ.r.na.s. 'Althrnas', MASC NOMEN, 1ST GEN; e.i. 'not', NEG;
  minipi = mini 'me', 1ST PERS PRO, ACC + -pi '?', ENCLITIC PARTICLE (?); çapi
  'take', IMPV; mini 'me', 1ST PERS PRO, ACC; θanu '?', IMPV (?)

Verbs ending in -**a** occur in the same syntactic contexts as imperatives. It is reasonable to assume, and indeed most scholars do assume, that the verbs ending in -**a** were functionally similar to imperatives. Presumably, then, verb forms ending in -**a** had jussive function. Compare sentences (40a) and (40b).

(40) Imperative vs. jussive

  (a) raχθ · tur · heχσθ · vinum (LL IX, 6–7)
      (to the officiant) 'Put (it) on the *rakh* (after) pouring (?) the wine.'

      raχθ = raχ '?', LOC + -θ 'in, on', POST; tur 'put', IMPV; heχσθ 'pour (?)',
      θ-PART (?); vinum 'wine', NOM/ACC

  (b) raχθ · tura · heχσθ | vinum (LL IV, 9)
      'He (the officiant) shall put (it) on the *rakh* (after) pouring (?) the wine.'

      raχθ = raχ '?', LOC + -θ 'in, on', POST; tura 'put', JUSSIVE; heχσθ
      'pour (?)', θ-PART (?); vinum 'wine', NOM/ACC

In the *Tabula Capuana*, ritually prescribed activities that are to be performed on behalf of certain divinities were signaled by verb phrases headed by a so-called necessitative form. Sentence (41) is typical of this mode of description.

(41) ióve.i.tule ilu.c.ve .a.pirase leθa.m.su.l. ilucu cuie.s.χu pe.r.pri
      (TCa 8)
      'On the Ides, on the *ilucu*, in April, for (the divinity) Lethams *ilucu
      cuieskhu* must be celebrated (?).'

      ióve.i.tule = ióve 'Ides', LOC (?) + -.i.tule 'the', DEM PRO, LOC; ilu.c.ve '?',
      LOC (?); .a.pirase 'April', LOC; leθa.m.su.l 'Lethams', THEO, 2ND GEN; ilucu '?',
      NOM/ACC; cuie.s.χu '?', NOM/ACC; pe.r.pri 'must be celebrated (?)', NECESS

Another type of verb phrase, which is often compared to the Latin
phrase *opus est* 'it is necessary', was also used to refer to activities that
were prescribed. In Etruscan this type of phrase was introduced either by
acilθ ame or by **acil** alone, without any discernible distinction between
the two. The internal structure of the syntax governed by this phrase is
not perfectly clear, but it seems likely that it involved a subordinate verb.
In (42) the verb **ture** appears to be, at least formally, a non-past active, but
other analyses are possible; indeed, in this context some scholars have interpreted it as an infinitive.

(42) luθti · raχ · ture · acil (LL VI, 15)
      '(It is) necessary (that) he (the officiant) put the *rakh* in the sacred
      area (?).'

      luθti = luθ 'sacred area (?)', LOC + -ti 'in', POST; raχ '?', NOM/ACC; ture 'put',
      NON-PAST ACT (?); acil '(is) necessary', NOM/ACC

      8.21.1 For the identification and analysis of prohibitions see Agostiniani 1984.

Coordination and Subordination

8.22 Two conjunctions were used to coordinate the constituents of
sentences. The enclitic conjunction **-c**, which appeared also as **-χ** in Neo-
Etruscan, was used to link together constituents within a sentence. When
two constituents were coordinated, as in (43a–b), **-c** was affixed to the first
word in the second constituent.

(43) Conjunction -c

      (a) ceisu[i] : óeθra | óeθres : sec | calisnia[l]c : ramθ[as] | avils : XV
           (AT 1.46)
           'Shethra Ceisui, daughter of Shethre and Ramtha Calisni, (was
           dead) at fifteen years.'

ceisu[i] 'Ceisui', FEM NOMEN, NOM/ACC; óeθra 'Shethra', FEM PRAE,
NOM/ACC; óeθres 'Shethre', MASC PRAE, 1ST GEN; sec 'daughter', NOM/ACC;
calisnia[l]c = calisnial 'Calisni', FEM NOMEN, 2ND GEN + -c 'and', ENCLITIC
CONJ; raṃθ[as] 'Ramtha', FEM PRAE, 1ST GEN; avils 'year', 1ST GEN

(b) vinum · θic ... (LL XI, 4)
     'wine and water'

     vinum 'wine', NOM/ACC; θic = θi 'water', NOM/ACC + -c 'and', ENCLITIC
     CONJ

If more than two constituents were enumerated, enclitic -c was affixed to
the last item in the series (17), repeated below as (44).

(44) Conjunction -c

     σacnicleri · ciḷθl · σpureri | meθlumeric · enaσ · raχθ · tur · heχσθ |
     vinum (LL IX, 5–6)
     'On behalf of the sanctuary (?) of the citadel (?), on behalf of the
     community, and on behalf of the city of Ena (?) place (it) on the
     rakh (after/while) pouring (?) the wine.'

     σacnicleri = σacnicle 'sanctuary (?)', LOC + -ri 'on behalf of', POST; ciḷθl
     'citadel (?)', 2ND GEN; σpureri = σpure 'community', LOC + -ri 'on behalf of',
     POST; meθlumeric = meθlume 'community', LOC + -ri 'on behalf of', POST +
     -c 'and', ENCLITIC CONJ; enaσ 'Ena (?)', CITY NAME (?), 1ST GEN; raχθ = raχ '?',
     LOC + -θ 'on', POST; tur 'put', IMPV; heχσθ 'pour (?)', θ-PART (?); vinum 'wine',
     NOM/ACC

The enclitic -(u)m was also used to join constituents within a sentence.
In (45a) it links three noun phrases. In this inscription it was placed after
the first word in the second and third constituents. In (45b) -(u)m joins
two sentences; in this context it may have had an adversative meaning.

(45) -(u)m

     (a) vel leịnies : larθial : ruva : arnθialum | clan : velusum : prumaθσ
          : avils : semφσ | lupuce (Vs 1.178)
          'Vel Leinies, brother of Larth and son of Arnth and grandson (?)
          of Vel, died at seven years of age.'

          vel 'Vel', MASC PRAE, NOM/ACC; leịnies 'Leinies', MASC NOMEN, 1ST GEN;
          larθial 'Larth', MASC PRAE, 2ND GEN; ruva 'brother', NOM/ACC; arnθialum

= arnθial 'Arnth', MASC PRAE, 2ND GEN + -um 'and', ENCLITIC CONJ; clan 'son', NOM/ACC; velusum = velus 'Vel', MASC PRAE, 1ST GEN + -um 'and', ENCLITIC CONJ; prumaθσ 'grandson (?)', NOM/ACC; avils 'year', 1ST GEN; semφσ 'seven', NUM, 1ST GEN; lupuce 'died', PAST ACT

(b) mulaχ · huślna · vinum| laiveism · acilθ · ame (LL VIII, 5–6)
'and one should give *hushlna* wine, but it is necessary (to offer it) from the left (?).'

mulaχ = mula 'give', JUSSIVE + -χ 'and', ENCLITIC CONJ; huślna '?', NOM/ACC; vinum 'wine', NOM/ACC; laiveism = laiveis 'left (?)', 1ST ABL + -m 'but', ENCLITIC CONJ; acilθ = acil 'necessary' + -θ '?', ENCLITIC PARTICLE; ame 'is', NON-PAST ACT

Asyndetic constructions are common in Etruscan inscriptions. For example the onomastic phrase **larθal fulnial** in (46) forms a coordinate phrase even though the conjunction is not expressed.

(46) Asyndetic noun phrase

saturinies · arnθ · | larθal · fulnial | avils · XXXVIII (AT 1.47)
'Arnth Saturnies, (son) of Larth (and) Fulni, (dead) at thirty-eight years'

saturinies 'Saturnies', MASC NOMEN, 1ST GEN; arnθ 'Arnth', MASC PRAE, NOM/ACC; larθal 'Larth', MASC PRAE, 2ND GEN; fulnial 'Fulni', FEM NOMEN, 2ND GEN; avils 'year', 1ST GEN

8.23 Few subordinating conjunctions have been identified in Etruscan. Three that are relatively secure are described below.

The subordinator **iχnac** was identified in an inscription incised upon a mirror (Vt S.2). The scene etched on the reverse of the mirror depicted the god Hercle sucking at the teat of the goddess Uni. A tablet held by another figure in the scene displayed the inscription cited below, which served as commentary on the mythological scene.

(47) eca : sren : | tva : iχna|c hercle : | unial cl|an : θra{:}sce (Vt S.2)
'This scene (?) shows (?) how/that Hercle became the son of Uni.'

eca 'this', DEM PRO, NOM; sren 'scene (?)', NOM/ACC; tva 'shows (?)', NON-PAST ACT; iχnac 'how', SUBORD; hercle 'Hercle', THEO, NOM/ACC; unial 'Uni', THEO, 2ND GEN; clan 'son', NOM/ACC; θra{:}sce 'became', PAST ACT

The basic assumption here is that the inscription was composed of two clauses linked by the word iχnac. The function assigned to the subordinator depends to some degree on the meaning assigned to the verb **tva**, which itself is an unusual form because it does not end in the vowel **-e**, as one would expect a non-past verb form to do. Nonetheless, if the meaning of **tva** is in the semantic area of 'to show, demonstrate', then it is reasonable to assume that iχnac meant 'how, that'.

The word iχ is found fourteen times in Etruscan inscriptions. In all instances but one it appears in syntactic contexts that are difficult to interpret or in inscriptions that have been damaged. In the *Cippus Perusinus* (Pe 8.4), however, the word introduces the final clause of the text. In meaning this clause appears comparable to clauses in Latin such as ITA UTEI SUPRAD SCRIPTUM EST 'just as was written above' (*Senatus Consultum de Bacchanalibus*).

(48) iχ · ca | ceχa · ziχuχ|e (Pe 8.4, 20–22)
  'as this was written above (?)'

   iχ 'as', SUBORD; ca 'this', DEM PRO, NOM; ceχa 'above (?)', ADV; ziχuχe 'was written', PAST PASS

If the comparison is valid, Etruscan iχ must mean something along the lines of 'as, like'.

A subordinator **nac** is attested in both gold tablets from Pyrgi (Cr 4.4 and Cr 4.5). In tablet Cr 4.4, **nac** appears in a passage that is too obscure to analyze. And it is not clear what word, if any, **nac** matches up with in the corresponding Punic text. In tablet Cr 4.5 **nac** introduces the first sentence in the inscription. But since we cannot translate this sentence, we cannot delimit the range of meanings for the subordinator. Nevertheless, most commentators assume that the first sentence describes the circumstances under which the main sentence of the inscription took place. Translations such as 'because', 'when', 'as', and so forth are possibilities. The subordinator **nac** also appears in a famous inscription from Volcii, which was described in §1.14.

(49) eca : ersce : nac : aχrum : flerθrce (Vc 7.38)
  'this one *ersce* when/because Acheron *flerthrce*'

   eca 'this', DEM PRO, NOM; ersce '?', PAST ACT; nac 'when, because (?)', SUBORD; aχrum 'Acheron', THEO, NOM/ACC; flerθrce '?', PAST ACT

Unfortunately, and despite the fact that some scholars have published translations of this text, we do not know the meanings of the verbs **ersce** and **flerθrce** and so cannot be sure of the overall meaning of the sentence. As a result, a similarly wide range of meanings is possible for **nac**.

Interestingly, the three words that have been identified as subordinators may be bound to one another in an etymological network: **iχ**, **nac**, and **iχnac**.

The word **ipa**, which some have identified as an interrogative word, may have been used to introduce complement clauses. Unfortunately, in all of the examples the subordinate clause depends on a verb whose meaning is uncertain.

(50) eθ : fanu : lautn : precuσ : ipa : murzua : cerurum : ein : | heczri
(Pe 5.2)
'Thus the family of Precu (has) determined (?) that (?) the ossuaries and the *cerur* (?) must not be *heczri*.'

eθ 'thus', ADV; fanu 'determined (?)', U-PART; lautn 'family', NOM/ACC; precuσ 'Precu', MASC NOMEN, 1ST GEN; ipa 'that (?)', SUBORD (?); murzua 'ossuary', INANIM PL, NOM/ACC; cerurum = cerur '?' NOM/ACC; -um 'and', ENCLITIC CONJ; ein 'not', NEG; heczri 'must be (?)', NECESS

8.23.1 For the use of ipa as a subordinator, see Facchetti 2002a:68 and Rix 2004:964.

8.24 Subordinate ideas are often conveyed by other syntactic means. In Etruscan, many of the complex sentences found in funerary inscriptions make use of a participle to convey ideas that might be expressed by subordinate clauses in a language such as English. Inscription (50) is an example. In this sentence the participle **acnanas**, which governs the noun phrase **huóur ci**, refers to the subject of the sentence, Ramtha Semni, as does the participle **lupu** 'having died'.

(51) ṣemni · ṛ[a]mθa · spitus la̤[rθal] | puia · amce · lupu · avils · xXII | huóur · ci · acnanas (Ta 1.168)
'Ramtha Semni was wife of Larth Spitus, dead at ? years (after) having given birth to three children.'

ṣemni 'Semni', FEM NOMEN, NOM/ACC; ṛ[a]mθa 'Ramtha', FEM PRAE, NOM/ACC; spitus 'Spitus', MASC NOMEN, 1ST GEN; la̤[rθal] 'Larth', MASC PRAE, 2ND GEN; puia 'wife', NOM/ACC; amce 'was', PAST ACT; lupu 'dead', U-PART; avils 'year', 1ST GEN; huóur 'children', ANIM PL, NOM/ACC; ci 'three', NUM, NOM/ACC; acnanas 'having given birth to', NAS-PART

More complex structures exist. In (51) three subordinate ideas are bound to the subject of the sentence by the participles **acnanasa** (2×) and **zilaχnu**. The main verb, **arce**, was placed near the end of the text.

(52) aleθnas · v · v · θelu · zilaθ · parχis · | zilaθ · eterav clenar · ci · acnanasa · | elsói zilaχnu · θeluóa ril · XXVIIII | papalser · acnanasa · VI · manim · arce ril · LXVI (AT 1.105)

'Vel Alethnas, (son of) Vel, (was) *thelu* (?), governor of the *parχ*, (and) governor of the *etera*. Having produced three sons, having served X times as governor, the *thelu* (?) by (?) age twenty-nine, having produced six grandchildren, he constructed a funerary monument (?) at age sixty-six.'

aleθnas 'Alethnas', MASC NOMEN, 1ST GEN; v, abbrev. of **vel**, 'Vel', MASC PRAE, NOM/ACC; v, abbrev. of **velus** 'Vel', MASC PRAE, 1ST GEN; θelu '?', NOM/ACC; zilaθ 'governor', NOM/ACC; **parχis** '?', 1ST GEN; zilaθ 'governor', NOM/ACC; eterav '?', NOM/ACC; clenar 'sons', ANIM PL, NOM/ACC; ci 'three', NUM, NOM/ACC; acnanasa 'having produced', NASA-PART; elsói 'X times', NUM ADV; zilaχnu 'having served as governor', U-PART; θeluóa = θelu '?', NOM/ACC + -óa 'the', DEF ART, NOM; ril 'age', NOM/ACC; papalser 'grandchildren', ANIM PL, NOM/ACC; acnanasa 'having produced', NASA-PART; **manim** 'funerary monument (?)', NOM/ACC; arce 'constructed', PAST ACT; ril 'age', NOM/ACC

8.24.1 For a survey of the syntax of participles and of forms labeled as verbal nouns see Rix 2004:959–61.

Order of Constituents

8.25 It is difficult to make definitive statements about the underlying order of the major constituents (Subject, Direct Object, Verb) in an Etruscan sentence. Nonetheless, it is generally assumed, based on the order of the major constituents in inscriptions of the **turce**-type (e.g. Co 3.3, 3.4, 3.5, 3.7; Vt 3.3) and in inscriptions dealing with the construction of tombs or tomb chambers (e.g. Cr 5.2; Ru 5.1), which date from the Neo-Etruscan period, that the basic arrangement for the these constituents was SOV. Evidence from the order of constituents in relative clauses also supports the primacy of SOV order (Cr 5.3, 5.4). This order is in keeping with what might be expected of an agglutinating language.

8.25.1 Schulze-Thulin (1992) discusses the order of constituents in Etruscan sentences.

8.26 It is worthy of note, however, that some of the most important material from the Archaic period contradicts the assumption of a basic

SOV order. For example, Archaic commemorative inscriptions headed by the verb **muluvanice** rarely have SOV order. In fact, the orders OVS and OSV are statistically more common than SOV in this type of inscription. For inscriptions recovered from Veii, the most common order is OVS (11×). SOV is found in two inscriptions; OSV is not attested. At Caere, on the other hand, OSV is more common (5×) than OVS (2×); SOV is not attested. Nevertheless, it seems reasonable to think that these orders are the result of the movement of the direct object pronoun **mini** 'me' into sentence-initial position, which is a common position for the first person pronoun in inscriptions of this type in all of the languages of ancient Italy. It is quite possible, then, to assume SOV as the basic order for the Archaic period, even though the evidence for this order is not as great as for other arrangements, and to derive the various permutations of this basic order by means of syntactic movement rules, SOV → OVS (by moving the verb phrase to the front of the sentence), SOV → OSV (by moving the direct object out of the verb phrase to the front of the sentence).

(53) Word order in **muluvanice**-inscriptions

  (a) OVS: **mini mu.l.vanice mama.r.ce ⫶ ve.l.χana.ç.** (Cr 3.11)
       'Mamarce Velkhanas gave me (as a gift).'

       mini 'me', 1ST PERS PRO, ACC; **mu.l.vanice** 'gave', PAST ACT; **mama.r.ce** 'Mamarce', MASC PRAE, NOM/ACC; **ve.l.χana.ç.** 'Velkhnas', MASC NOMEN, 1ST GEN

  (b) OSV: **mini kaisie θannursiannaš mulvannice** (Cr 3.14)
       'Kaisie Thannursiannas gave me (as a gift).'

       mini 'me', 1ST PERS PRO, ACC; **kaisie** 'Kaisie', MASC PRAE, NOM/ACC; **θannursiannaš** 'Thannursiannas', MASC NOMEN, 1ST GEN; **mulvannice** 'gave', PAST ACT

  (c) SOV: **velθur tulumneš pesn<a n>uzinaie mene mul[uvanice]** (Ve 3.2)
       'Velthur Tulumnes (and) Pesna Nuzinaie gave me (as a gift).'

       velθur 'Velthur', MASC PRAE, NOM/ACC; **tulumneš** 'Tulumnes', MASC NOMEN, 1ST GEN; **pesn<a>** 'Pesna', MASC PRAE, NOM/ACC; **<n>uzinaie** 'Nuzinaie', MASC NOMEN, 1ST GEN; **mul[uvanice]** 'gave', PAST ACT; **mene** 'me', 1ST PERS PRO, ACC

8.27 The order of the elements within a noun phrase depended on the type of modifier. Genitives were typically positioned before the head noun, e.g. larθal clan 'son of Larth' (Ta 1.191). Pronouns with attributive function were also placed before the noun, e.g. cn · óuθi | ceriχunce 'built this tomb' (Cr 5.2). Adjectives typically followed the noun they modified, e.g. açka eleivana 'an askos for oil' (Fa 2.3). In noun phrases containing numbers, the number usually occupied the position following the noun, e.g. clenar ci 'three sons' (AT 1.105), clenar zal 'two sons' (AT 1.96), but there are also examples of the number in front of the noun that it modified, e.g. ci clenar 'three sons' (Ta 1.167).

8.28 In onomastic phrases the praenomen usually stood before the nomen, e.g. velθur tarχna[s] 'Velthur Tarkhnas' (Cr 1.42), but at Tarquinia and Volcii, particularly during the final centuries of the Neo-Etruscan period, it became fashionable to move the nomen into the first position in the epitaph, e.g. spitus larθ 'Larth Spitus' (Ta 1.164), tarnas vel 'Vel Tarnas' (Vc 1.36), and murai óeθra 'Shethra Murai' (Vc 1.47).

8.29 In proprietary inscriptions of the mlaχ mlakas type, the constituents of the predicate noun phrase referring to the ceramic object and to its owner could be distracted, that is to say, pulled apart or separated from one another. Presumably this was meant to achieve an artistic effect. In (54) the nominative/accusative phrase mlaχ pruχum appears on both sides of the genitive mlakaš.

(54) mi mlaχ mlakaš pruχum (Cr 2.27)
     'I (am) the beautiful vase of a beautiful (person).'

   mi 'I', 1ST PERS PRO, NOM; mlaχ 'beautiful', NOM/ACC; mlakaš 'beautiful', 1ST GEN; pruχum 'vase', NOM/ACC

One can also identify discontinuous constituents in commemorative inscriptions from the Archaic period. So, for example, the constituents of the verb phrase mini muluvanice in (55) were separated, the personal pronoun being placed in first position and the verb muluvanice being placed at the end.

(55) mini σpurie utaš muluvanice (Cr 3.9)
     'Spurie Utas gave me (as a gift).'

   mini 'me', 1ST PERS PRO, ACC; σpurie 'Spurie', MASC PRAE, NOM/ACC; utaš 'Utas', MASC NOMEN, 1ST GEN; muluvanice 'gave', PAST ACT

9 VOCABULARY

Introduction

9.1 Although the total number of Etruscan inscriptions is rather high, somewhere around 10,000, the number of different lexical items recovered from these inscriptions—excluding proper names—is somewhere in the range of 700+. Words whose meanings can be determined, even roughly, constitute at most a quarter of the total. It goes without saying that such a small number of words cannot provide an adequate view of the lexicon of a language. Moreover, Etruscan vocabulary items whose meanings can be identified with the greatest degree of security come primarily from a small set of epigraphic types: epitaphs, proprietary texts, inscribed gifts, and votive dedications. As a result, the slice of Etruscan vocabulary that we possess is narrow and specialized. Many of the words that belonged to the most common layers of vocabulary, words used by Etruscan speakers to express their most immediate and common needs, are unknown to us.

Native Vocabulary

9.2 The core segment of the attested Etruscan lexicon consists of kinship words and words denoting familial relationships: **clan** 'son', **seχ** 'daughter', **huóur** 'children', **puia** 'wife', **ati** 'mother', **apa** 'father', **ati nacna** or **teta** 'grandmother', **apa nacna** or **papa** 'grandfather', **ruva** 'brother', **tetals** and **papals** 'grandchild'. These words were extracted in large part from funerary inscriptions recovered from the cities of Tarquinia and Vulci.

Other vocabulary from funerary contexts includes the verbs **amce** 'was', **farθnaχe** 'was born', **ceriχunce** 'built, constructed', **svalce** 'lived', and **lupuce** 'died', the participles **cesu** 'deposited, buried' and **lupu** 'dead', and a small set of words referring to the resting places of the deceased, namely **óuθi** 'tomb', **mutna** 'sarcophagus', **muró** 'urn', **hupnina** 'sarcophagus, funerary niche (?)', **capra** 'funerary urn', and **tamera** 'funerary chamber'. **Penθna** may be the word for 'funerary cippus'. The forms **man** and **manim** appear to refer to a funerary monument of some sort as well.

9.3 Funerary inscriptions documenting the *cursus honorum* of aristocratic Etruscans yield the titles of important public magistracies and religious offices. We can only hazard guesses as to meanings and functions.

The political official attested most frequently in inscriptions was called zilaθ, which we translate here as 'governor'. The word appears in inscriptions covering a fairly extensive geographical cross-section of Etruria: Caere in the south; Tarquinia, Vulci, and Volsinii in the center; and Vetulonia, Chiusi, and Bologna in the north. Generally, this term is assumed to correspond more or less closely to the Latin term *praetor* (magistrate with juridical functions), but we have no idea how close the functional correspondence actually was.

Modifiers sometimes accompanied the word zilaθ. At Tarquinia for example we know of officials referred to as zilaθ parχis and zilaθ eterav (AT 1.105). We assume that parχis and eterav referred to more specific spheres of authority or somehow limited the range of official duties, but we do not know in what ways. Another phrase, zilaθ meχl rasnal, is even more controversial because of the long-standing discussion surrounding the word rasna. This word recalls the form ῥασεννα, which was cited by Dionysios of Halikarnassos in a discussion on the origins of the Etruscans. Extrapolating from this passage, some scholars argue that rasna is an adjective meaning 'Etruscan' and that the phrase means 'governor of the Etruscan league' or something comparable. Others argue that the word means 'public' or 'people'. The phrase would then be translated as 'governor of the public territory or the commonwealth' and thus roughly equivalent to the Latin phrase *res publica*. Regardless of the meaning of rasnal, the phrase zilaθ meχl rasnal is unlikely to refer to someone with authority over the entire territory of Etruria. Evidence for a centralized political structure does not exist.

The word zilχ/zilc, which is etymologically connected to zilaθ by means of the root zil, referred to the most important public office in the Etruscan political sphere. Etruscans referred to this office and to those who occupied it as the official means of dating documents (compare the Roman practice of citing the names of consuls). It is not clear whether the office of zilχ/zilc was held by a single person or by two colleagues who presumably shared power. Some inscriptions refer to one person (Ta 5.5); other inscriptions refer to two people (Ta 8.1). The verb zilaχnce, which means 'held the office of zilχ/zilc', was derived from this noun stem.

The word maru, as it appears in the phrase maru paχaθuras caθsc (AT 1.32), probably refers to the official head of a religious group. The phrase seems to mean 'chief officer (*vel sim.*) of the Bacchants and of (the divinity) Cath(a)'. Derivatives of this word, which end in the suffix -uc/-uχ, refer to some type of political office, e.g. marunuc spurana (Ta 1.88) and marunuχ spurana (AT 1.171) '*marunuc* of the community'. The plural **marunuχva** must refer to multiple offices, that is to say, '*marunuc*-ships', but it is not clear what these might be.

Other words for public offices also end in the suffix -uc/-uχ. These are **mulauc** (ETP 76), **eprθnevc** (AT 1.1), **eisnevc** (AT 1.1), and **macstrevc** (AT 1.1). The latter may be based on a Latin word *magister* (see §9.9), but that does not provide much insight into its functions (head of a religious organization?).

The phrase **camθi eterau** is found in two inscriptions, both recovered from Tarquinia (Ta 1.96, Ta 1.115). Since **eterau** could be used as a modifier of **zilaθ**, it is assumed that **camθi** referred also to an official position of some sort. This word may be related to the verb **canθce** (Ta 1.170), but this connection provides no insight into meaning because we cannot determine the meaning of the verb.

Cepen is generally translated by the English word 'priest'. It appears frequently in the *Liber Linteus* but in contexts that are of little help for extracting meaning. It is found in funerary inscriptions from Tarquinia (Ta 1.23, 1.34, 1.184, 5.4) and from the *Ager Tarquiniensis* (AT 1.108, 1.171). In these inscriptions **cepen** is in construction with the *u*-participle **tenu** 'having held (?)', which suggests that it refers to an office or an official position of some sort, perhaps a religious one. Interestingly, in four of the five cases just mentioned, **cepen** is preceded by a form of the word **marunuc-**, e.g. **marunuχva cepen** (AT 1.108, Ta 1.23, 1.34), **marunuc [ce-pe]n** (Ta 1.184). Unfortunately, we do not know whether these words are to be taken together as a unit or whether they are part of a coordinate construction.

9.3.1 The names of Etruscan political offices are discussed in Agostiniani 1997a and Maggiani 1996. Both agree that the suffix -uc/-uχ forms words referring to public offices. Wylin (2002b:105–6) analyzes the suffix as originally adjectival (-u-c/-u-χ). He also takes up the issue of the morphological composition of the word zilaθ (2002b:96). Facchetti 2002b is the most recent discussion of eterav/eterau; references to earlier articles on this word may be found there. The best place to begin an investigation of the meaning of rasnal is Rix 1984a. For a defense of the position that rasna- means 'Etruscan' see Facchetti 2000a:29–41.

9.4 Dedications and inscribed gifts have produced a smaller inventory of words, all belonging to the semantic fields of 'giving, dedicating', and so forth. Three important verbs are found in dedicatory texts: **muluvanice** 'give (as a gift)', **turuce/turce** 'dedicate (as an offering)', and **alice** 'give, dedicate'. The verb **turuce** distinguishes itself from **muluvanice** and **alice** by being restricted to use in inscriptions that were votive in nature. **Muluvanice** and **alice** are attested in both secular and sacral contexts. Votive inscriptions also yield words that are likely to mean 'votive offering (?)', **cver**, and 'thank offering (?)', **alpan**.

On occasion the artisan or the craftsman who made, designed, or decorated a vase or mirror signed his name. The verb **menece**, which is found in an inscription from Populonia, **metru menece** 'Metru made (me)' (Po 6.1), matches up nicely with the Greek verb ἐποίησεν, which was used in the "signatures" of Greek artisans. In Archaic Etruscan inscriptions the corresponding verb was **zinace**, which may have meant, at least originally, 'fashioned from clay'. In most contexts derivatives of the verb root **ziχ** refer to the act of writing or to a written document, but when the root appears in inscriptions on decorated ceramic a more likely meaning is 'to decorate' or 'to design'. For the inscription Fa 6.3, **mi araθiale ziχuχe**, which was incised on a decorated bucchero vase, the most likely interpretation is, 'I was decorated/designed for/by Ara(n)th'.

Designations for types of ceramic were in large part loanwords from Greek (§9.7), but a fair number of native Etruscan formations have been identified. The most secure are **θina**, a word derived from the root **θi** 'water', and **faσena**, a word built from the stem **faσe** 'libation'. **θavhna** /tʰafna/ 'bowl', also spelled **θahvna**, **θafna**, **θafina**, can be a derivative of a root **θaf-**, but the root itself is not independently attested. Further, a diminutive form, **θapnza**, appears in the *Liber Linteus*. This word was generated from the stem **θafn(a)-**; it shows a secondary phonological development of /f/ to /p/ before the nasal stop. **Zavena** and its diminutive **zavenuza** refer to a type of jug or beaker. A **spanti** is a type of plate. **Aχapri**, if it is indeed a type of ceramic, may refer to a vase, possibly a wine pitcher. Two diminutive formations referring to ceramic vessels may also be native formations, **putiza** and **çunθeruza** 'pyxis'.

9.5 A substantial portion of the words in the attested Etruscan lexicon is made up of terms associated with the practice of religious ritual procedures as described in the *Liber Linteus* and the *Tabula Capuana*.

Most of the imperative forms in our inventory of verbs come from the *Liber Linteus*. Among the most secure in interpretation are **trin** 'say, invoke', **tur** 'give, put (?)', **nunθen** 'offer (?)', and **śuθ** 'put, place'. Necessitative constructions are common in both texts, but only a handful of forms can be translated, e.g. **θezeri** 'must be immolated', **nunθeri** 'must be offered (?)'. The words for sacrificial offerings, for the instruments and utensils employed, and for the places where offerings were made are the topics of current investigation. The following items are reasonably secure: **fler** 'offering, sacrificial victim' and its derivative **flere** 'divine spirit, divinity', **faσe** 'libation', **huslna vinum** *'huslna* wine', and **zusle** 'type of (animal?) offering'.

In the *Liber Linteus* and the *Tabula Capuana* ritual procedures were organized by date. As a result, we know the names for 'month', **tiur**, and 'day', **tins**. To these we can add the name for 'year', **avil**. We also know the names of several months: **apirase** 'in April', **anpilie** 'in May', **acalve** 'in June', **parχuni** 'in July (?)', and **zalχiri** 'in September (?)'. The first three names are confirmed because ancient literary sources provide them. One of the terms corresponding to Latin *Kalendae, Nonae*, and *Idus*, the cardinal reference points of the month in the Roman calendar, has also been identified, **ióve** 'on the Ides'.

9.6 The publication of the *Tabula Cortonensis* has permitted us to add a few words to the Etruscan lexicon and to confirm the meaning of a few others. For example, we now can be sure that the root **mal-**, which is attested in words generally thought to mean 'mirror', e.g. **malstria, malena**, means 'to see, look'. The word for 'level tract of land' was **span**. The derivative **spanti**, which we have seen as a word for 'plate', must refer to a 'flat piece of ceramic'. The word **nuθanatur** refers to those who were present at the legal transaction stipulated by the two parties in the *Tabula*. The root of this word is attested as a simple verb form **nuθe** in a passage recording the name of the public official who oversaw the transaction. The fact that it forms part of a coordinate phrase with **male** 'see' suggests that the meaning may be 'hear'. Finally, we also learn the word for 'tablet', **σparza**, and the word for 'house' or 'depository', **θuχ**.

9.6.1 For further discussion see Chapter 11.

Borrowings from Greek

9.7 An important segment of the Etruscan lexicon consists of words borrowed from Ancient Greek. Mythological scenes incised on Etruscan mirrors were often based on or inspired by Greek models. The names of mythological and heroic characters were adopted and assimilated into Etruscan together with the stories and legends. The names were incised or painted as captions next to the figures themselves. We cite a few examples from what is an extensive list: **aivas, eivas** = Αἴϝας 'Ajax'; **hercle** = Ἡρακλῆς 'Herakles', **cerca** = Κίρκα 'Circe', **memrun/memnun** = Μέμνων 'Memnon', **θetis/θeθis** = Θέτις 'Thetis'.

In the seventh and sixth centuries BCE Greek craftsmen settled in Etruscan communities, set up workshops, and trained Etruscan workers. Many of the ceramic styles produced in local Etruscan workshops imitated Greek prototypes. Etruscans borrowed the names for the different styles of Greek pottery. A selection of borrowed words follows: **aska** = Greek ἀσκός 'wine bag'; **χuliχna** = κυλίχνα 'small cup'; **qutum** = κῶθον 'drinking vessel'; **larnaó** = λάρναξ 'dolium'; **leχtumuza** = λήκυθον 'oil flask'; **pruχum**

= πρόχουν 'jug'; and **ulpaia** = ὄλπα 'oil flask'. Etruscans also borrowed the Doric Greek word for olive oil, which appears as the base for an adjectival derivative **eleivana** 'for/of olive oil'.

9.7.1 The now classic work on Greek loanwords in Etruscan is de Simone 1970a. For a shorter summary of the issues and the lexical items involved see de Simone 1972:490–521. Extensive bibliography is available in both sources. See Colonna 1973–1974 for a discussion of the names of Greek pottery borrowed by the Etruscans.

Borrowings from Sabellic Languages

9.8 Eastern Sabellic languages were the source for Etruscan vocabulary items belonging to a variety of semantic spheres. The word **nefts** 'nephew, grandson' was borrowed from a Sabellic language in which the medial consonant cluster *-pt- developed to -ft-, *nefts (< *neptis). The words **prums** and **prumaθσ** 'great-grandson' are often cited as loanwords, perhaps from an unattested Sabellic word *pronefts. However, the phonological distance between the proposed Sabellic form and the attested Etruscan word-forms is considerable and not easily traversed. The Etruscan word for 'god', **ais**, may also be a loan from Sabellic, perhaps from Umbrian: *ais- is the stem for several Umbrian words of religious significance, e.g. **esunu** 'ceremony' (< *aiso:no-), and it is attested in other Sabellic languages as well, e.g. Paelignian **aisis** 'gods' DAT PL and Marrucinian **aisos** 'gods' NOM PL. The word **cletram**, which refers to a cult object of some sort, was also borrowed from Umbrian, cf. **cletra** 'cart' ACC SG.

9.8.1 The most informative discussion of Sabellic loans in Etruscan is Steinbauer 1993:287–306.

Borrowings from Latin and Faliscan

9.9 The number of words in Etruscan that can be attributed to Latin and to its sister language, Faliscan, is surprisingly small. As a possible Faliscan borrowing, we can cite the funerary term **cela** 'room, chamber', which may be a synonym of **tamera** 'chamber'. The Neo-Etruscan political term **macstrevc** is likely to be based on the Latin word *magister* 'chief official'. The ending -vc is probably the same as that found on other Etruscan words referring to political offices. **Vinum** 'wine', a word of Mediterranean vintage, may have entered Etruria through an Italic, possibly a Faliscan, contact. The word is attested in a Faliscan inscription dating to the seventh century BCE. A Greek source for Etruscan and Italic **vinum** is in our opinion unlikely on phonological grounds, although such a claim has recently been made. The word **putlumza** 'small drinking cup' has been connected with Latin *poculum* 'drinking vessel', but the connection remains unsubstantiated because there is no evidence for a change *-kl- > -tl- in Etruscan. The claim that the Etruscan word reflects the original Italic form of the word, that is to say *po:tlom, has very little to recommend it.

9.9.1 For Etruscan **macstrevc** see de Simone 2002:430–56. See Agostiniani 1994a for the claim that Etruscan **vinum** was taken from a Greek source.

Etruscan Words in Latin

9.10 Apart from anthroponyms and theonyms, few words in Latin can be shown to be of Etruscan patrimony, at least with any degree of certainty. At most there are twenty to thirty words that may be considered legitimate candidates, and this includes words that entered Latin from Ancient Greek sources via Etruscan intermediation.

9.10.1 Recent treatments of Etruscan loanwords in Latin are Breyer 1993 and Watmough 1997. The latter is a detailed investigation of a small number of loanwords in Latin. Rix (1995b) provides a short list of words that are, according to the author, *bona fide* Etruscan loans in Latin, including words that entered Latin from Greek via Etruscan intermediation.

9.11 Latin words such as *santerna* 'solder for gold', *torus* 'strand, thong, conjugal bed', *satelles* 'armed bodyguard', *tina* 'vessel for water', *mantissa* 'addition (to weight)', *lucumo* 'king', *idus* 'the Ides', *favissae* 'subterranean deposits', *napurae* 'cords, rope of straw', *mundus* 'decoration', *fala* 'framework of wood', and *persona* 'mask' may go back to Etruscan sources, but such connections are never straightforward and so must be evaluated on a case-by-case basis. At the very least they must be treated with caution. In some instances the Etruscan word is not even attested. In other cases the putative Etruscan source word is not attested in a context where it is possible to determine its meaning. In yet other cases the phonology and the morphology of the Etruscan word do not carry over easily into the Latin.

9.12 One of the most notable—and notorious—examples of a putative Etruscan-Latin connection, namely Etruscan φersu : Latin *persona*, is not without its problems. The Etruscan word appears twice; both times the word is painted on the wall of a tomb (*Tomba degli Auguri*) next to masked figures that appear to be holding the leash of an animal (Ta 7.4, 7.11). Scholars who support this Etruscan-Latin connection generally take φersu to be an agent noun in -*u* meaning 'performer', cp. **zicu** 'writer'.

Although the correspondence is attractive, the Latin word *persona* cannot come directly from φersu. In order to establish a connection between the two words, it is necessary to posit an intermediate form, an

Etruscan adjective formation in -na, namely *φersuna 'having to do with a performer'. But even if an adjective of this form existed in Etruscan, it is not clear that it would yield Latin persona /perso:na/. The long vowel in the penultimate syllable of the Latin word is not easy to explain in any convincing way.

9.12.1 Watmough (1997:66-67) describes the difficulties that exist for those who wish to see Latin persona as a loan from Etruscan φersu. Rix (1995b:75) defends the connection.

9.13 A relationship between Etruscan zatlaθ and the Latin word satelles 'armed guard', which the literary tradition mentions in connection with Porsenna, king of Clusium, is both attractive and problematic. Assuming that these forms are to be connected by a borrowing relationship, Latin satelles would seem to point to an Etruscan pre-form *zatilaθ, an agent noun derived from an unattested noun stem *zatil-. It seems reasonable to think that the Latin third declension would be the most accommodating spot for an Etruscan stem ending in a stop consonant, and so it is not surprising to find satelles in the company of other dental-stop stems. That said, it is not at all easy to explain the -ll- cluster in the Latin word; Etruscan zatlaθ has but a single -l.

In terms of meaning, zatlaθ appears in the phrase zatlaθ aitas, which was painted next to the figures of warriors on the back wall of the Tomba Golini at Orvieto (Vs 7.25). The phrase may be plausibly interpreted as 'guard of Aita (Hades)'. Interestingly, zatlaθ belongs to a constellation of words including zati, a noun in the locative case, and zatlχne, a present-tense verb form. The phrase zati zatlχne appears also in a passage from the Liber Linteus (VIII, 13) in which an officiant at a sacrifice is instructed to immolate (θezine) a living victim (zivaσ fler). It is possible that zati zatlχne refers in some way to the means by which the fler was to be dispatched ('shall be struck with a club'). If this interpretation has merit, the form zatlaθ could well be an agent noun derived ultimately from the root/stem zat meaning 'weapon'. The etymological meaning of zatlaθ would then be 'one who brandishes a weapon'.

9.13.1 See Rix 1995b:81 and Watmough 1997:103–23 for arguments that zatlaθ is the source of Latin satelles.

9.14 A second layer of Etruscan words in Latin are those that come ultimately from Greek but via Etruscan intermediation. In some cases there is no evidence in Etruscan for the donor word, e.g. ancora 'anchor', gruma 'surveyor's instrument', lanterna 'lantern', and triumphus 'procession'. In other cases the phonological, morphological, and semantic distance between the donor word and the Latin word is so great that it is difficult to bridge. *Amurca* 'oil dregs', *ancora* 'anchor', *gruma* 'surveyor's instrument', *lanterna* 'lantern', *lucerna* 'oil lamp', *sporta* 'basket', and *triumphus* 'procession' may come ultimately from Greek via Etruscan intermediation. However, the assumption that these loanwords were recast in Etruscan before making their way into Latin is not always easy to support based on the evidence available to us. For example, the Etruscan word **spurta** is widely believed to be a borrowing of Greek σπυρίδα, the accusative singular of σπυρίς 'basket', a development that is acceptable on phonological grounds (Greek δ → Etruscan t; syncope of medial -*i*-). The Etruscan word **spurta** was subsequently borrowed into Latin as *sporta*, which is a form that is acceptable for a loanword from Etruscan (Etruscan *u* → Latin *o*). However, the contexts in which **spurta** occurs in the *Liber Linteus* do not permit us to confirm the meaning of the Etruscan word. The possibility that **spurta** is derivationally related to **spura-**, the word for 'community', cannot be discounted.

An Etruscan Word in Faliscan

9.15 The only possible example of an Etruscan loanword in Faliscan, although ultimately of Greek patrimony, is the word **quton** 'drinking vessel', which appears on an inscription from the seventh century BCE (LF 2). The quality of the penultimate vowel in the Faliscan word, which is **u** rather than **o**, points to an intermediate Etruscan source for the word rather than a Greek one.

Theonyms

9.16 Theonyms in Etruscan inscriptions come from two sources. Some were native formations; others were borrowed.

9.16.1 Rix (1998b:207–29) examines many of the issues covered in this and the following sections. Cristofani (1993b:9–21) addresses the topic of anthropomorphism and Etruscan deities.

9.17 Theonyms borrowed from Greek appear most prominently as captions for figures incised or painted on mirrors and vases; they rarely appear in votive dedications, in the *Liber Linteus*, or in the *Tabula Capuana*. Thus we cannot be sure whether any of the divinities whose names appear only on mirrors and vases were the object of cult worship.

The epithet **paχie**, which sometimes accompanied **fufluns**, a divinity associated with Dionysius and Bacchus, was derived from the Greek adjective Βακχεῖος. We may translate **paχie** as 'of Bacchus' and assume that the Etruscan divinity was attracted into the orbit of Dionysiac rites and

worship. Other words referring to members of a Bacchic cult have also
been identified. The word **paχaθuras** had as its stem the form **paχa-**, also
borrowed from a Greek source, perhaps Doric Βάκχα. Worship of the god
hercle may have made its way to central Italy from Greek cults established
in Campania. Latin and/or Sabellic peoples may have served as intermedi-
aries in the transmission of the worship of this divinity. The name of one
of the demons of the Etruscan underworld, **χaru/χarun**, was borrowed
from Greek, Χάρων. The names of other underworld divinities and mon-
sters had native Etruscan origins, e.g. **vanθ** 'Vanth', **tuχulχa** 'Tukhulkha'.

9.18 The god **neθuns** 'Neptune' is one of the most important deities in
the *Liber Linteus*. The name of this divinity was borrowed from a Sabellic
language, most likely Umbrian. The key piece of evidence is the fact that
the consonant cluster *-pt-* was simplified to *-t-* and the vowel in the final
syllable was lost by syncope. The divinities **selvans** and **klaninσ**, which
have final syllables comparable in form to **neθuns**, appear to have been
borrowed from Sabellic languages as well.

The goddess **menerva** 'Minerva' was the object of worship at the Portonaccio sanctuary in Veii. Inscriptions dedicated to her are found on ceramic vessels dating to the sixth century BCE. A reasonable etymological
proposal connects the root of the word for this goddess with the Indo-
European root **men-* 'to think', which would then make the name of this
divinity a good candidate for a loan from an Italic language, perhaps Latin
given the geographical proximity of Veii to Latin-speaking peoples.

9.19 Deities, in large part native ones, to whom Etruscans dedicated
votive inscriptions are cited here in alphabetical order: **cel, culsu, cavaθa,
culsans, vucina, hercle, θanr, θesan, θuflθa, laran, lurmita, mantrnσ,
maris, menerva, selvans, tinia, turan, turms, uni, fufluns**. Some of names
of these divinities match names inscribed on the Liver from Piacenza (Pa
4.2). Nevertheless, very little is known about the attributes or the spheres
of influence of these gods and goddesses. Some, such as **tinia, fufluns**,
and **culsans**, were identified with major divinities from the Greek and
Roman pantheons, namely Zeus/Jupiter, Dionysius/Bacchus, and Janus
respectively, and so appropriated iconography and attributes from these
sources. We know the epithets of a few divinities, e.g. **selvansl tularias**
(GEN) 'of Selvans Tularia (associated with boundaries)', **unial huinθnaias**
(GEN) 'of Uni Huinthnaia (?)', although we do not always know, as the last
example shows, how the attributes are to be interpreted.

The divinities listed above do not correspond to those mentioned in
the *Liber Linteus* or in the *Tabula Capuana*, except for the gods **laran** and
leθams. Three of the divinities mentioned in the linen book have clear

Italic origins, namely **veive**, **vetis**, and **neθuns**. It is also possible that the divinity **crap-** (**flere in crapsti** 'godhead which [is] in the [sanctuary] of Crap') is to be identified, at least in terms of its stem, with the Umbrian epithet *Grabovius*. Two of the divinities mentioned in the *Tabula Capuanus* have Sabellic sources, namely **seθumsna**, which comes from the Sabellic stem **setums-* 'seventh', and **natinusna**, which is built from the Sabellic stem **natin-* 'birth'. Unfortunately, these divinities do not correspond to any attested in Sabellic inscriptions, although Cicero informs us that the goddess of birth at Ardea was called *Natio* (*De Natura Deorum* 3.47).

Place-names

9.20 The names of the major settlements in Etruria can be pieced together based on information extracted from inscriptions and coins. Not all of the evidence is equally compelling, however, and some of the identifications require further evaluation.

9.20.1 Pallottino's article (1937:342–58) on the names of Etruscan cities remains a very useful resource.

9.21 The names of the cities Tarquinia, Vulci, and Volsinii are attested in postpositional phrases. The locatives, **tarχnalθi** 'in the (city) of Tarkhna', **velclθi** 'in the (city) of Velca' and **velsnalθi** 'in the (city) of Velsna-' permit the reconstruction of the stems **tarχna-**, **velca-**, and **velsna-** for the names of these three cities. The name of the Etruscan city Caere can be reconstructed based on the Punic transliteration *kjšrj*. This consonantal frame matches up perfectly with the stem **kaiseri-**, which appears in the ethnic name **kaiseriθe** attested on a recently published funerary stele (see §10.2, no. 5).

Boundary inscriptions from Faesulae (see §10.10, no. 77) may contain references to a city. The word at issue is **vipσa-**, cf. **vipσl** 2ND GEN. Unfortunately the context in which **vipσl** appears does not delimit in any significant way the interpretative possibilities. We must be satisfied to say that this is at least a reasonable interpretation.

The names for Clusium and Cortona may also be extracted from inscriptions, although the case for these identifications is not clear-cut. The nomen **clevsinas** is attested in several funerary inscriptions from Tarquinia. The usual assumption is that the nomen is in origin an adjective built to the stem of the name of the Etruscan city, that is to say, **clevsi-** + **-na**. The stem **cleusinσ-** (**cleusinσl** 2ND GEN) is attested in a proprietary inscription from Clusium that dates to the fourth century BCE (Co 2.26). The word refers to the proprietor of a vase. But the fact that the stem ends in the cluster -nσ /ns/, which is a common ending for the stems of theonyms, e.g. selvans, óeθlans, klanins, makes it tempting to take this word as a theonym, perhaps referring to the titular deity of the city. Curtun is attested on a votive inscription (Co 4.6) dedicated to the goddess uni 'Uni', but it is not clear how this form, which is uninflected and quite possibly an abbreviation, functions in the text. So, while cleusi- and curtun- may indeed refer to Etruscan cities, we must admit that the identifications are not as secure as we would like them to be.

The names of two cities situated on the northeastern border between Etruria and Umbria are likely to be borrowings, at least to judge from their phonological structure. The first name is aritimi 'in Arretium' LOC (stem aritim-), which has been interpreted as the name of the city Arretium; the second form, persie 'in Perusia' LOC (stem persia-), is the name of the city Perusia. These cities may originally have been Umbrian settlements that only later admitted large numbers of Etruscan settlers.

A few place-names are attested in adjective formations. The first is sveitmaχ 'from Sveitma' (Vc 7.28), which is found as a descriptive adjective modifying a man named pesna arcmsnas 'Pesna Arcmsnas'. Sveitma- has been identified with the southern Etruscan settlement of Sovana, but this claim cannot be corroborated. The adjective rumaχ is derived from the base ruma-, the name for Rome. This word, which appears in a caption from the François Tomb at Vulci, functions as an adjective modifying cneve tarχunies. We translate: 'Cneve Tarkhunies of Rome' (Vc 7.33).

9.22 Two place-names have been identified on Etruscan coins. The first is velaθri, which refers to the city of Volaterrae. The second is pupluna 'Populonia', which is attested also in the variant forms pupfluna and pufluna. These word-forms can be connected etymologically. A Neo-Etruscan sound law changed stops to fricatives before liquid and nasal consonants. It is not clear whether fufluna, which was also incised on a coin recovered at Populonia, belongs here. If it does, it is either by way of a long-distance assimilation of *p...f* to *f...f* or by a folk-etymology associating the city of pupluna with the divinity *Fufluns*.

10 INTERPRETATION OF INSCRIPTIONS

Introduction

10.1 The Etruscan inscriptions presented in this chapter cover the spectrum of shorter texts drawn from the major epigraphic types. The interpretation of the *Tabula Cortonensis*, one of the longer texts in the Etruscan corpus, is discussed in the following chapter.

The inscriptions are organized into subsections according to epigraphic category. Within each subsection the order of inscriptions is chronological, beginning with the oldest. Inscriptions are numbered serially for the entire chapter.

The entry for each inscription has four parts:

(a) Background information. This includes a reference number, either to ET (Rix et al., *Etruskische Texte*) or to ETP (Wallace, Mimno, Patterson, and Shamgochian, *Etruscan Texts Project*), the place of discovery, the date of production, the type of object on which the text was inscribed, and the fabric or material out of which the object was made.

(b) The inscription. The text of the inscription is accompanied by a translation and a word-by-word analysis.

(c) Commentary. This section covers information pertinent to the interpretation of the inscription, most importantly, linguistic commentary on word-forms in the text. Also included are notes on letter-forms and orthography.

(d) Bibliographic references. References to articles containing the most important epigraphic and linguistic information for each inscription, if such exist, are placed at the end of each entry. If the reference includes a photograph, the table or figure in which it appears is cited at the end of the reference.

Funerary Inscriptions

10.2 Etruscan funerary inscriptions at their most elemental recorded the name of the deceased. As discussed in Chapter 7, if the deceased was an Etruscan citizen, then the inscription included praenomen and nomen. To this basic framework it was customary, particularly in the Neo-Etruscan period, to add cognomen, patronymic, and metronymic. Inscriptions referring to married women could also include a gamonymic. Nos. (5), (8), and (13) belong to this basic type. Funerary inscriptions were composed with other, more complex, syntactic patterns as well. For example, nos. (1), (2), and (3) are nominal sentences of the "iscrizione parlante" variety. The tomb of the deceased "speaks" to its visitors. Funerary inscriptions on stelae were more expansive still. They often included the name of the person who dedicated the funerary monument. Inscription (4) is an example of this type. Neo-Etruscan inscriptions from Tarquinia and Volsinii sometimes offered a detailed accounting of familial relationships as well as notification of the political and religious offices held by the deceased. This type is represented by inscription (10).

(1)   Vn 1.1, Vetulonia, ca. 600 BCE
      stele (stone)

      [mi] aveleσ feluśkeσ tuσnutai[– pa]
      panaḷaσ mini mul
      vaneke hirumi[n]a φerśnaχś
      'I (am the stele) of Avile Felushke, *tuσnutai*[–], (son) of Papanai.
      Hirumina, *phershnakhsh*, gave me.'

      [mi] 'I', 1ST PERS PRO, NOM; aveleσ 'Avile', MASC PRAE, 1ST GEN; feluśkeσ 'Felushke', MASC NOMEN, 1ST GEN; tuσnutai[–] '?'; [pa]panaḷaσ 'Papanai', FEM NOMEN, 2ND ABL; mini 'me', 1ST PERS PRO, ACC; mulvaneke 'gave', PAST ACT; hirumi[n]a 'Hirumina', MASC NOMEN, NOM/ACC; φerśnaχś '?'

The text was incised around the border of the stele, within which the figure of a warrior was carved. The text given here incorporates features of the reading offered by Bagnasco Gianni (1996:249–52).

The text consists of two sentences. The usual assumption is that the accusative pronominal form **mini**, which customarily stands in first position in *muluvanice*-texts, begins the second sentence.

The inscription gives the name of the warrior, Avele Felushke, in whose honor the stele was erected, and the name of the person, Hirumina, who was responsible for having the stele made and erected. Damage to the stele makes it difficult to determine the inflectional ending of **tuσnutai**[–]. The function of this word is problematic in any case, even if the restoration **tuσnutal**[a] offered by Rix (ET Vn 1.1) is correct. Given the word placement, situated as it is between the nomen of the deceased and the nomen of the deceased's mother, Papanai, one might treat the word as a patronymic form. One could also think of a descriptive adjective, as suggested by Facchetti (2000b:72). How these possibilities match up with the form of the word is another and more difficult question. Equally problematic is φerśnaχś. Were it not for the final *sigma*, the word would be analyzed as an adjective describing the city in which Hirumina resided. The form resists a convincing morphological analysis. A final noteworthy aspect of this inscription is the metronymic, [pa]panaḷaσ, which is inflected in the ablative case.

Bagnasco Gianni 1996:249–52, no. 237; Bonfante and Bonfante 2002:141, no. 14, fig. 18; Colonna 1977:183–9; Facchetti 2000b:72; Vetter 1955–56:301–10.

(2) ETP 213, Volsinii (Orvieto), 600–500 BCE
     lintel of tomb (stone)

     [mi] aranθia lapanas
     'I (am the tomb) of Aranth Lapanas.'

     [mi] 'I', 1ST PERS PRO, NOM; **aranθia** 'Aranth', MASC PRAE, 2ND GEN; **lapanas** 'Lapanas', MASC NOMEN, 1ST GEN

The inscription was incised on the lintel over the entrance to the tomb. The personal name **aranθia** is inflected with the Archaic genitive ending -a. The nomen **lapanas** may also be attested at Veii in the form **lapinaš** (Ve 3.13), provided the fluctuation in the quality of the medial vowel in these two forms (**a** vs. **i**) reflects different representations of the sound that was the outcome of vowel weakening.

De Simone 1990b:75–9.

(3) ETP 214, Volsinii (Orvieto), 600–500 BCE
     lintel of tomb (stone)

     mi aveles metienas
     'I (am the tomb) of Avele Metienas.'

     mi 'I', 1ST PERS PRO, NOM; **aveles** 'Avele', MASC PRAE, 2ND GEN; **metienas** 'Metienas', MASC NOMEN, 1ST GEN

The inscription was incised on the lintel over the entrance to the tomb. The medial vowel of the praenomen **aveles** is from older /i/, cf. **avile**. This change is due to medial vowel weakening. The family name **metienas** is derived from the stem **metie-**, which is attested without the suffix -na as a family name on five inscriptions from Volsinii (Vs 4.79–83).

De Simone 1990b:75–9.

(4) ETP 43, Ager Chiusinus (Chianciano Terme), 550–500 BCE
     fragment of cippus (travertine)

mi lauχumeśa katilaσ
'I (am) the (cippus/tomb) of Laukhume Katila.'

mi 'I', 1ST PERS PRO, NOM; lauχumeśa = lauχumeσ 'Laukhume', MASC PRAE,
1ST GEN + -śa 'the', DEF ART, NOM; katilaσ 'Katila', MASC NOMEN, 1ST GEN

The surviving portion of the cippus has the shape of a sphere. The
inscription was incised without punctuation in a spiral around the upper
part of the stone.

The pronoun **mi** refers to the cippus or to the tomb of the deceased.
The most straightforward interpretation is that cited above. In Neo-
Etruscan inscriptions the article -śa was used almost exclusively to refer
to human beings (but see ET Cm 2.54). In this inscription, however, there
is no easy way to interpret the text such that the article refers to a person.
The interpretation suggested by Benelli (2004:219–20), namely, 'I (belong
to) Katila, the (servant) of Laukhume', is not sanctioned by the syntax.

Benelli 2001:213–24, tav. XXXVc–f; Paolucci 1999:375–6, REE 9, tav. XXIX.

(5) ETP 333, Saturnia, 525–500 BCE
     stele (stone [travertine])

1   larθ laucies θamequ
     larecesi ka
     iseriθesi celeniarasi
     mịnị ẓịnẹçe γe<l>θur kam
5   arṭeθi
'Larth Laucies (was) *θamequ* by (his) sons, Larece (and) Kaiserithe.
Ve(l)thur made me in Kamarta.'

larθ 'Larth', MASC PRAE, NOM/ACC; laucies 'Laucies', MASC NOMEN, 1ST GEN;
θamequ '?', U-PART; larecesi 'Larece', MASC PRAE, 1ST PERT; kaiseriθesi
'Kaiserithe', MASC PRAE, 1ST PERT; celeniarasi 'son', ANIM PL, 1ST PERT; mịnị
'me', 1ST PERS PRO, ACC; ẓịnẹçe 'made', PAST ACT; γe<l>θur 'Velthur', MASC
PRAE, NOM/ACC; kamarṭeθi = kamarṭe 'Kamarta', PLACE NAME, LOC + -θi 'in',
POST

The inscription was incised on the face of a stone stele, which served
as a funerary monument. The letter **u** of **laucies** was written above the
line. The first sentence, which includes lines 1–3, was incised in the following manner. Line 1 was written in sinistroverse direction starting just

beneath the upper border of the stele on the right-hand side. Line 2 descended along the left border in sinistroverse direction. Near the bottom of the stele the inscription changed its orientation and was written from left to right. The second sentence, lines 4 and 5, was written in bustrophedon style. Line 4 was written in sinistroverse direction below line 5.

This inscription shows the Archaic distribution of the letters, c, k, and q. *Kappa* is found before *alpha*, *qoppa* before *upsilon*, and *gamma* before *epsilon* and *iota*.

The interpretation of the first sentence is uncertain even though the syntactic structure is clear. θamequ is a *u*-participle built upon the past active verbal stem θameq-. Typically *u*-participles are passive in voice, so it is reasonable to think that the phrase **larecesi kaiseriθesi celeniarasi**, which is inflected in the pertinentive, had agentive function. The names are combined asyndetically. The sentence had nominal structure: subject (**larθ laucies**) + *u*-participle **θamequ** + agent phrase (**larecesi kaiseriθesi celeniarasi**).

The stem of the *u*-participle **θamequ** is etymologically related to the stem attested in the past active verbs θamce (Ta 5.2) and θamuce (Cr 4.4). Unfortunately, they do not appear in contexts from which it is possible to recover a meaning confidently. The idea that the verb means 'to build' does not make sense for this inscription unless there is a syntactic break separating the name of the deceased from the participle θamequ. This would yield a translation 'Larth Laucies. (This tomb) was built by (L's) sons L [and] K'. **Celeniarasi** is the pertinentive plural of the noun clan 'son'. The spelling is unusual. The first vowel is either an error, which seems most likely, or an epenthetic vowel. If epenthetic, this form may be compared to the adjective **malak** 'good, beautiful' (AV 2.3), whose first vowel may also be epenthetic since the base form begins with the cluster ml-, mlaχ (Cr 2.27). The -*i* that follows medial -*n* is generally understood to mark palatalization of the preceding nasal, but it seems likely that the original stem of this noun was **klanya-*. The name of the second son, kaiseriθe-, has the form of an ethnic, presumably formed on the stem of the word for the city of Caere, **kaiseri**. For comparable formations cf. **velθrite**, a nomen built from the name of the city velaθri 'Volaterrae', and **mantvate**, a nomen derived from the name of the city **mantva-** 'Mantua'. The name of the deceased, **larθ laucies**, is also worthy of note because the name **laucies**, though formally a praenomen, appears to be used here as a nomen (for **laucies** as a praenomen see the Archaic inscription (32)). This interpretation of **laucies** as a nomen is better than the alternative, which is to treat **laucies** as a patronymic. Patronymic constructions are rare in Archaic Etruscan; moreover, the interpretation of **laucies** as a patronymic would leave us without a family name for the deceased.

The second sentence is a craftsman's signature. The verb ẓịṇẹçe is a past active form. The medial vowel was originally -a, as shown by **zinace**, which is attested in the seventh century BCE. The change to -e reflects vowel weakening. Typically, this verb referred to the production of ceramic pottery. Here however it must refer to the production of the stele. The omission of the letter l in ɣe<l>θur is an error on the part of the stonecutter. **kamarṭeθi** is to be parsed as locative of the stem **kamarta-** followed by the locative postposition **-θi**, i.e. *kamartai-tʰi* > **kamarte** + **-θi**. The word refers to the place where the stele was cut. The stem **kamarta-** recalls the ancient name for the city of Clusium, *Camars* (stem *Camart-*), as recorded by Livy (10.25–6). But a connection with Clusium seems tenuous at best and it is safer to conclude that this site was located in the vicinity of Saturnia, though it is impossible to say where.

Maggiani 1999:51–61, tav. I–II.

(6)   AS 1.40, Ager Sienensis (Montaperti), 500 BCE
      funerary cippus (stone)

      [m]i lariśa fẹḷẹśkẹnaσ aṃ[– – –]
      'I (am the cippus) of Larish Feleshkena…'

      [m]i 'I', 1ST PERS PRO, NOM; **lariśa** 'Larish', MASC PRAE, 2ND GEN; **fẹḷẹśkẹnaσ**
      'Feleshkena', MASC NOMEN, 1ST GEN; **aṃ**[– – –] '?'

The text was incised around the border of the cippus. Due to damage to the stone, the number of letters following **aṃ** cannot be determined.

The genitive of the praenomen, **lariśa**, is of the Archaic variety. There is no final -l. The nomen **fẹḷẹśkẹna-** is to be connected with the nomen **feluśke-** attested in inscription (1) (Vn 1.1). The differences in the quality of the medial vowels before -śk- can be attributed to different outcomes of vowel weakening. **Fẹḷẹśkẹna-** was built by addition of the suffix **-na**, common in the formation of nomina, to the stem **feleśke-**. It is not clear whether the final letters of the inscription belong to a name. Nevertheless, this may be the best interpretation since the word-initial sequence *am-* does not match up with any words for tomb or funerary cippus.

(7)   Li 1.1, Liguria (Busca), 500 BCE
      funerary cippus (stone)

      mi śuθi larθial muθikuσ
      'I (am) the tomb of Larth Muthiku.'

      mi 'I', 1ST PERS PRO, NOM; **śuθi** 'tomb', NOM/ACC; **larθial** 'Larth', MASC PRAE,

2ND GEN; **muθikuσ** 'Muthiku', MASC NOMEN, 2ND GEN

The text was incised in sinistroverse direction without punctuation. The alphabet is a northern variety; *sade* represents the dental sibilant /s/.

The nomen of the deceased, **muθiku**, is not attested in Etruria proper. It may be derived from a local onomastic source.

(8) Vt 1.58, Volaterrae, 500–400 BCE
     cippus (stone)

     mi laruσ ⋮ arianaσ ⋮ anaσnieσ klan
     'I (am the tomb) of Laru Ariana, son of Anasnie.'

     mi 'I', 1ST PERS PRO, NOM; **laruσ** 'Laru', MASC PRAE, 1ST GEN; **arianaσ** 'Ariana',
     MASC NOMEN, 1ST GEN; **anaσnieσ** 'Anasnie', MASC PRAE, 1ST GEN; **klan** 'son',
     NOM/ACC

The inscription was incised on the face of a stone cippus in sinistroverse direction. Interpunction isolates the nomen of the deceased from the praenomen and patronymic. The use of the letter kappa to spell the velar stop /k/ is noteworthy.

The nomen descends from an earlier **ariena-*. The stem appears in Neo-Etruscan as **arina-** (for the change of medial **-ie-* to -i- see §3.20). The name **anaσnieσ** is a *hapax*. Note finally that **klan** should be inflected in the genitive case to agree with the name of the deceased.

(9) Co 1.3, Cortona, 400–300 BCE
     wall of tomb

     tuσθi θui ḥupnineθi
     arnt mefanateσ
     veliak ḥapiśnei
     'Arnt Mefanate and Velia Hapishnei (were interred) in/on the **tuσ**-here in the funerary niche (?).'

     tuσθi = **tuσ**- '?', LOC + -**θi** 'in', POST; **θui** 'here', ADV; **ḥupnineθi** = hupnine
     'funerary niche (?)', LOC + -**θi** 'in', POST; **arnt** 'Arnt', MASC PRAE, NOM/ACC;
     mefanateσ 'Mefanate', MASC NOMEN, 1ST GEN; **veliak** = velia 'Velia', FEM PRAE,
     NOM/ACC + -**k** 'and', ENCLITIC CONJ; **ḥapiśnei** 'Hapishnei', FEM NOMEN, NOM/ACC

The inscription was painted in sinistroverse direction over the entrance to the tomb. As in nos. (6) and (8), the velar stop /k/ was spelled by *kappa*.

The word **tuσθi** is difficult. Formally, it appears to be the locative of a consonant-stem noun **tuσ-**. Some scholars have interpreted the word as meaning 'cushion, couch' and have pointed to Latin *torus* 'conjugal bed' as a possible loan from Etruscan. Within Etruscan, connections to **tuσurθi** (Pe 1.408) and **tusurθir** (Pe 1.410) are tempting to make though not necessarily easy to explain. The claim that these words are to be analyzed as exocentric derivatives from a locative plural ('on the cushions') and that they mean 'those on the cushions' = 'marriage partners' has no support in Etruscan morphology. Additional suffixes cannot be added to the locative postposition **-θi**. Moreover, one would not expect an inanimate noun such as **tuσ-** to inflect with the animate plural ending **-ur**. Steinbauer (1999:250–2, no. G14) avoids these difficulties by taking the stem **tuσ-** to mean 'sarcophagus'. His interpretation eliminates one problem, but creates another. He interprets **hupnineθi** as an adjective derived from the stem **hupni-**, i.e. **hupni-na-**, and then translates the phrase **tuσθi θui ḥupnineθi** as 'in the sarcophagus'. In this analysis it is not clear exactly what meaning is to be attributed to **hupnina-**. If **hupnina-** refers, at least in some contexts, to a sarcophagus or funerary urn of some type or style, as seems to be the case in texts such as AH 1.52, AS 1.236, and AS 1.266, then one has to wonder why two words for sarcophagus would be employed in the same phrase.

Steinbauer 1999:250–2, no. G14.

(10) Ta 1.9, Tarquinia, 350–325 BCE
     sarcophagus (stone)

     1   velθur : partunus : larisaliόa : clan : ramθas : cuclnial : zilχ :
          ceχaneri : tenθas : avil
     2   svalθas : LXXXII
'Velthur Partunus, the son of Laris (and) of Ramtha Cuclni, having held the governorship on behalf of the *Cekhana*, (and) having lived for eighty-two years, (died/was interred here).'

velθur 'Velthur', MASC PRAE, NOM/ACC; partunus 'Partunus', MASC NOMEN, 1ST GEN; larisaliόa = larisal 'Laris', MASC PRAE, 2ND GEN + -iόa 'the', DEF ART, NOM; clan 'son', NOM/ACC; ramθas 'Ramtha', FEM PRAE, 1ST GEN; cuclnial 'Cuclni', FEM NOMEN, 2ND GEN; zilχ 'governorship', NOM/ACC; ceχaneri = ceχane '?', LOC + -ri 'on behalf of', POST; tenθas 'having held', θAS-PART; avil 'year', NOM/ACC; svalθas 'having lived', θAS-PART

The inscription was incised on the cask of a sarcophagus.

The political office held by the deceased is not attested elsewhere. The word **ceχaneri** appears to be a locative + postposition construction. We cannot determine the meaning of **ceχana-**, although some scholars take it to be a derivative of **ceχa**, an adverb meaning 'above', and assume that it refers to a deliberative body that stands over the citizenry. The participles **tenθas** and **svalθas** were built upon verb roots **ten-** and **sval-** by means of the suffix combination **-θ-as**. It is unclear what semantic contribution the suffix **-θ** makes to the verb stem or how this type of participle differs from those ending in the combination **-n-as**, e.g. **acnanas** 'having produced'.

(11) Ta 1.66, Tarquinia, 300 BCE
   wall of tomb

   vel : aties : velθurus :
   lemnióa : celati cẹsu (Ta 1.66)
   'Vel Aties, the (son) of Velthur and Lemni, (was) buried in this chamber.'

   vel 'Vel', MASC PRAE, NOM/ACC; **aties** 'Aties', MASC NOMEN, 1ST GEN; **velθurus** 'Velthur', MASC PRAE, 1ST GEN; **lemnióa** = lemnis 'Lemni', FEM NOMEN, 1ST GEN (?) + **-óa** 'the', DEF ART, NOM; **celati** = cela 'chamber', LOC + **-ti** 'in', POST; **cẹsu** '(was) buried', U-PART

This epitaph was painted on the wall of a tomb chamber.

The metronymic was either formed irregularly by means of the 1st genitive suffix **-s** or the scribe erroneously painted **lemnióa** for expected **lemnialióa**. The word for chamber, **cela-**, is a borrowing from Faliscan (**cela**). The word is uninflected; its locative function being marked only by the postposition **-ti**.

Bonfante and Bonfante 2002:172, no. 56; Cristofani 1991a:130–1, no. 22.

(12) ETP 192, Ager Tarquiniensis (Tuscania), 275–250 BCE
   sarcophagus (stone)

   cleusinas : laris : larisal : clan
   'Laris Cleusinas, son of Laris.'

   cleusinas 'Cleusinas', MASC NOMEN, 1ST GEN; **laris** 'Laris', MASC PRAE, NOM/ACC; **larisal** 'Laris', MASC PRAE, 2ND GEN; **clan** 'son', NOM/ACC

The inscription was incised along the upper border of the chest of the sarcophagus. The same inscription was also incised on one of the short sides.

The order of the major constituents of the name was reversed. The nomen was placed in first position, followed by the praenomen. This order, attested at Tarquinia and environs as early as the fourth century BCE, was particularly common in funerary inscriptions. The family name **cleusina-** is found at Tarquinia (Ta 1.186 **clevsinas**) and Caere (ETP 170). Since the inscription cited here is older than those from Tarquinia and Caere, the family may have originated in Tuscania.

Colonna 1994a:294–5, REE 45.

(13) Ta 1.168, Tarquinia, 300–100 BCE
     wall of tomb

  ṣemni · ṛ[a]mθa · spitus · lạ[rθal]
  puia · amce · lupu · avils · xXII
  huóur · ci · acnanas
  'Ramtha Semni was wife of Larth Spitus, having died at year ?,
  having given birth to three children.'

  ṣemni 'Semni', FEM NOMEN, NOM/ACC; ṛ[a]mθa 'Ramtha', FEM PRAE, NOM/ACC;
  spitus 'Spitus', MASC NOMEN, 1ST GEN; lạ[rθal] 'Larth', MASC PRAE, 2ND GEN;
  puia 'wife', NOM/ACC; amce 'was', PAST ACT; lupu 'having died', U-PART; avils
  'year', 1ST GEN; xXII '?'; huóur 'children', ANIM PL, NOM/ACC; ci 'three', NUM,
  NOM/ACC; acnanas 'bear', NAS-PART

The text was painted on the wall of a tomb.

Lupu and **acnanas** are bound to the subject of the sentence. Numbers were occasionally placed before nouns of the animate class, e.g. **ci clenar**, but here the number **ci** follows the noun that it modifies. The age of the deceased is either **XXII** or **LXII**; unfortunately, the first cipher is illegible.

Vanoni 1965b:511, REE 5.

(14) Ta 1.81, Tarquinia, 200–100 BCE
     wall of tomb

  θui · clθi · mutn{ai}θi[1]
  vel · veluóa · avils
  cis · zaθrmisc
  seiṭiθialióa
  'Here in this sarcophagus (lies) Vel, the (son) of Vel, (dead) at age
  twenty-three, the (son) of Seitithi.'

  θui 'here', ADV; clθi = cl- 'this', DEM PRON, LOC + -θi 'in', POST; mutn{ai}θi =

---
[1] mutn{ai}θi is corrected from mutniaθi.

mutn{ai} 'sarcophagus', LOC + -θi 'in', POST; **vel** 'Vel', MASC PRAE, NOM/ACC; **veluóa** = velus 'Vel', MASC PRAE, 1ST GEN + -óa 'the', DEF ART, NOM; **avils** 'year', 1ST GEN; **cis** 'three', NUM, 1ST GEN; **zaθrmisc** = zaθrmis 'twenty', NUM, 1ST GEN + -c 'and', ENCLITIC CONJ; **seiṭiθialióa** = seiṭiθial 'Seitithi', FEM NOMEN, 2ND GEN + -ióa 'art', DEF ART, NOM

The text was painted on the wall of a tomb. The nomen of the deceased is not mentioned. Other inscriptions in the tomb indicate that he belonged to the **apunas** (Ta 1.82)/**apnas** (Ta 1.83) family.

The pronominal form **clθi** appears to have been formed by adding the postposition directly to the pronominal stem **cl-**. The form should go back to a locative having the shape *kale-t^{h}i*. The locative **mutn{ai}θi**, if it has been properly restored, is also unusual. The stem and the locative suffix **-i** are uncontracted. In an inscription from the second century BCE we expect a locative to have the form **mutneθi**, showing contraction of stem-final **-a** and the locative case ending **-i**. The number indicating the age of the deceased was inflected in the 1st genitive, and the constituents were linked together by the enclitic conjunction **-c**, **cis zaθrmis-c** 'three and twenty'.

(15) Ta 1.107, Tarquinia, 200–100 BCE
    wall of tomb

    felsnas : la : leθes
    svalce : avil : CVI
    murce : capue
    tleχe : hanipaluscle
    'Larth Felsnas, (son) of Lethe, lived for 106 years. He *murce* in Capua. He *tlekhe* in the (army) of Hanipal.'

    felsnas 'Felsnas', MASC NOMEN, 1ST GEN; **la**, abbrev. of larθ 'Larth', MASC PRAE, NOM/ACC; **leθes** 'Lethe', MASC PRAE, 1ST GEN; **svalce** 'lived', PAST ACT; **avil** 'year', NOM/ACC; **murce** '?', PAST ACT; **capue** 'in Capua', LOC; **tleχe** '?', PAST PASS; **hanipaluscle** = hanipalus 'Hanipal', 1ST GEN + -cle 'the', DEM PRO, LOC

The inscription was painted on the wall of a tomb in the necropolis of Villa Tarantola in Tarquinia. It is justly famous for several reasons. First, the deceased had a remarkably long life, 106 years. Second, the final word of the inscription likely refers to Hannibal, the Carthaginian general who conducted campaigns against Rome during the last quarter of the third century BCE. This is one of the few historical references in Etruscan inscriptions that can be corroborated by external sources.

The deceased may have been of servile origin. The name of his father, leθe felsnas, suggests as much. The praenomen leθe was common among members of the lower social orders.

The overall interpretation of the inscription is impeded by lack of understanding of the forms **murce** and **tleχe** in lines 3 and 4. If they are verbs, they can be analyzed morphologically (**mur-ce** past active; **tle-χe** past passive of a verb), but the meanings cannot be determined. The form **murce** is attested in the *Liber Linteus* (XI, 6), where it appears to govern an accusative **tesamitn**, but this does not shed any light on its meaning. The final word of the text, **hanipaluscle**, is made up of two constituents: **hanipalus**, which is the genitive of the stem **hanipal(u)-**, and **-cle**, the locative/pertinentive of the demonstrative pronoun **eca/ca**. The syntactic function of this form is impossible to gauge because the meaning of the verb with which it is in construction is unknown. We speculate: 'He was X-ed in/for the (army?) of Hanipal = Hannibal'. The fact that the verbs in lines 3 and 4 cannot be translated means that the debate about whether or not Larth Felsnas fought with or against Hannibal remains unresolved.

Bonfante and Bonfante 2002:176, no. 63, fig. 53; Cristofani 1991a:163–4, no. 28; Olzscha 1970; Pallottino 1966:355–6, REE 1; Pfiffig 1967a:659–63; 1967b:53–61; Sordi 1991:123–5; Steinbauer 1999:253–4, no. G17; Vanoni 1965a:472–3, REE 1, tav. CIVa.

(16) ETP 287, Volsinii, 200–100 BCE
   funerary cippus (stone)

   ś : cemnil : v
   'Shethras Cemni, (daughter) of Vel.'

   ś, abbrev. of śeθras, 'Shethra', FEM PRAE, 1ST GEN; cemnil 'Cemni', FEM NOMEN, 2ND GEN; v, abbrev. of velus, MASC PRAE, 1ST GEN

The inscription was incised in sinistrograde direction on the face of the cippus.

The abbreviations may be filled out as follows: śeθras cemnil velus. Feminine nomina ending in -l as opposed to -al are rare. The editor suggests two ways to emend **cemnil**: (1) Expunge the final -l, in which case the nomen has zero inflection and the inscription would read śeθra cemni{l} velus 'Shethra Cemni, (daughter) of Vel'. At Volsinii onomastic phrases in funerary texts were typically rendered in the nominative/accusative form, so the genitive would be unusual. (2) The second possibility is to emend the genitive form **cemnil** to cemni<a>l. The inscription would then read: śeθras cemni<a>l velus, '(The grave) of Shethra Cemni, (daughter) of Vel'.

Tamburini 1991:264–5, REE 35, tav. XLVI.

(17) ETP 181, Ager Clusinus, 200 BCE
     funerary urn (stone)

meinei · papasliś
a · vl · titialc · σec
'Meinei Papaslisha, daughter of Vel and Titi.'

meinei 'Meinei', FEM NOMEN, NOM/ACC; papasliśa 'Papaslisha', FEM COGN,
NOM/ACC; vl, abbrev. of veluσ, MASC PRAE, 1ST GEN; titialc = titial 'Titi', FEM
NOMEN, 2ND GEN + -c 'and', ENCLITIC CONJ; σec 'daughter', NOM/ACC

The text was incised in sinistroverse direction on the cover of the urn.
The onomastic phrase of the deceased is worthy of note for several
reasons. First of all, the praenomen was not recorded. The deceased
was referred to by nomen, cognomen, patronymic, and metronymic. The
father's name was abbreviated, v(e)l(uσ). The word for 'daughter' was
spelled σec /sek/. The final consonant of this word was in origin a velar aspirate /kʰ/, σeχ /sekʰ/. The change from aspirated stops to unaspirated stops in word-final position was common in the Neo-Etruscan period, particularly in the settlements along the northern tier of Etruria
(see §3.27).

Hjordt-Vetlesen 1994:254–7, REE 17, tav. XLIV.

(18) Pe 1.948, Perusia, Neo-Etruscan
     cippus (travertine)

śuθiσ : eça
penθuna
cai : velσ : caiọ
θareσ : lautni
'This (is) the cippus of the tomb. Cai, freedman of Vel Cai Thare.'

śuθiσ 'tomb', 1ST GEN; eça 'this', DEM PRO, NOM; penθuna 'cippus', NOM/ACC;
cai 'Cai', MASC NOMEN, NOM/ACC; velσ 'Vel', MASC PRAE, 1ST GEN; caiọ 'Cai',
MASC NOMEN, 1ST GEN; θareσ 'Thare', MASC COGN, 1ST GEN; lautni 'freedman',
NOM/ACC

The text was incised in sinistroverse direction. Lines 1 and 2 form an
independent sentence. The name of the deceased appears in lines 3 and 4.
Interest in this text stems first from the genitive case of the word
'tomb', śuθiσ. This word is generally assumed to have had an *l*-genitive,

óuθil. However, it may be best to treat óuθil as a nominal derivative in -il
and thus the same type of formation as aril and acil. The word penθuna is
attested only at Perusia, where it is generally found in the form penθna.
Medial -u- must be an epenthetic vowel inserted to break up the consonant cluster -nθn-.

The deceased is cited by his nomen and then by the full name of
his master or patron. The praenomen velσ is missing the stem-final
vowel -u, cf. veluσ, either by mistake or by generalization of the nomi-
native/accusative stem vel as the stem for other case forms.

Steinbauer 1999:249–50, no. G13.

(19) ETP 334, Ager Chiusinus, ca. 90 BCE
     cinerary urn (terracotta)

hasti : velθuria : lautniθa
'Hasti Velthuria, freedwoman'

hasti 'Hasti', FEM PRAE, NOM/ACC; velθuria 'Velthuria', FEM NOMEN, NOM/ACC;
lautniθa 'freedwoman', NOM/ACC

The text was painted along the upper border of a funerary urn in sinistroverse direction. The scriptor painted the letters -θa from top to bottom at the lefthand edge of the urn.

The inscription records the name of an Etruscan freedwoman. The
praenomen hasti shows the change of word-initial *f*- to *h*-, cf. fasti. The
locus of this change was Clusium and environs (§3.27). Velθuria is a feminine nomen derived from the masculine praenomen velθur. The structure of the onomastic phrase, which follows the Latin model, points to a
date for the inscription sometime after 90/89 BCE, which was the date of
passage of the *lex Iulia de civitate* granting citizenship to all Italians.

Rix 1995d:242–3, REE 14, tav. XXXVII.

(20) AS 5.1, Ager Sienensis, late Neo-Etruscan period
     ossuary (ceramic)

     (a) ane · cae · vetus · acnaice
          'Ane Cae Vetu made (?) (this urn).'

          ane 'Ane', MASC PRAE, NOM/ACC; cae 'Cae', MASC NOMEN, NOM/ACC; vetus
          'Vetu', MASC COGN, 1ST GEN; acnaice 'made (?)', PAST ACT

     (b) aneσ · caeσ · puil · hu<p>
          ni · ei · itruṭa

'The remains (?) of the wife of Ane Cae. One should not disturb (?) (them = the remains).'

aneσ 'Ane', MASC PRAE, 1ST GEN; caeσ 'Cae', MASC NOMEN, 1ST GEN; puil 'wife', 2ND GEN; hu<p>ni 'remains (?)', NOM/ACC; ei 'not', NEG; itruṭa 'disturb (?)', JUSSIVE

These inscriptions were written in sinistroverse direction on the cover (a) and the body (b) of the ossuary. The letter p of hu<p>ni was written as an i (a single vertical stroke). The scriptor erroneously omitted the oblique bar. Note that the final /s/ of the patronymic vetus is a three-bar *sigma*. We expect /s/ to be written by the letter *sade*, as it was in text (b).

Text (a) refers to the husband of the women referred to in (b). He was responsible for manufacturing the ossuary or for having it manufactured. The verb acnaice is probably to be connected with the root *ac-* 'make, manufacture', but the middle portion of the form (ac-nai-ce) cannot be interpreted. Text (b) has two parts: a funerary text for the wife of the manufacturer and a prohibition.

The genitive of puia 'wife' is puil. This form is unusual. We expect *puial*, but that is not attested. The negator ei is written without the final nasal. The verb itruṭa may be connected with truta, which is found in inscription (53), also in a clause of prohibition, but the prefixal element i-, if this is what it is, is problematic.

(21) ETP 230, Clusium, late Neo-Etruscan period
     cinerary urn (travertine)

θa : titi : parfilunia
melutaśa
'Thana Titi Parfilunia, the (wife) of Meluta.'

θa, abbrev. of θana 'Thana', FEM PRAE, NOM/ACC; titi 'Titi', FEM NOMEN, NOM/ACC; parfilunia 'Parfilunia', FEM COGN, NOM/ACC; melutaśa = melutaσ 'Meluta', MASC NOMEN, 1ST GEN + -śa 'the', DEF ART, NOM

The inscription was incised on the upper front of the chest of the urn.
The onomastic phrase of the deceased includes praenomen (abbreviation of θana), nomen, cognomen, and gamonymic. The nomen titi was common at Clusium and environs. The cognomen, parfilunia, is attested here for the first time. The nomen of the deceased's spouse, meluta, was also not very common. A nomen derived from the stem melut- is also found at Clusium, melutnei (Cl 1.44).

Paolucci 2001:338, REE 9, tav. XXXVIII.

(22) ETP 240, Ager Saenensis (Pienza), first century BCE
slab (sandstone)

VEL · BER
COMSN
A · VELOSA I[2]
'Vel Percomsna, the (son) of Vel.'

VEL 'Vel', MASC PRAE, NOM/ACC; BERCOMSNA 'Percomsna', MASC NOMEN, NOM/
ACC; VELOSA = VELOS 'Vel', MASC PRAE, 1ST GEN + -SA 'the', DEF ART, NOM

The inscription was written in dextroverse direction in Republican
Latin letter-forms. The praenomen VEL was written as a ligature. The o of
VELOSA is very small and appears to have been erroneously omitted and
inserted later.

The northern Etruscan spelling of the nomen BERCOMSNA is **percum-
óna**. In Etruscan script the patronymic VELOSA was spelled **veluóa**. Some
researchers have suggested that the spelling of the Etruscan back vowel
u by Latin o is evidence that this Etruscan vowel occupied mid- to high-
vowel space. The substitution of Latin B for Etruscan **p** is similarly noteworthy because it is the only example found in word-initial position. Examples of Latin B substituting for Etruscan **p** in medial position are more
frequent, e.g. PABASSA, TLEBONIA.

Maggiani 2001c:344-5, REE 19; Vilucchi 2001:342-3, REE 19, tav. XL.

Etruscan-Latin Bilingual Inscriptions

10.3   Twenty-eight Etruscan-Latin bilingual inscriptions have survived. They are funerary texts. In almost all instances a Latin inscription
is accompanied by an Etruscan version that provides ROUGHLY the same
information. The three bilingual inscriptions presented here are typical
of the genre.

The study of Etruscan-Latin bilingual funerary inscriptions provided
scholars with information about the Etruscan system of names (see Chapter 7). These inscriptions were also useful in establishing an inventory
of vocabulary designating core familial relationships, e.g. **clan** 'son', **seχ**
'daughter', **puia** 'wife', etc. In addition, they provided insight into the
form and function of some of the case-suffixes of Etruscan nouns.

---

[2]The status of the letter I or, perhaps more accurately, the vertical bar at the end of line 3 is
unclear. It may simply mark the end of the inscription.

10.3.1 Benelli 1994 is the most recent edition and commentary on Etruscan-Latin bilingual inscriptions.

(23) Pe 1.211, Perusia, 100 BCE
     funerary urn (stone)

L · SCARPIUS · SCARPIAE · L · POPA
'Lucius Scarpius, freedman of Scarpia, priest's assistant'

lar{n}θ · ścarpe · lautṇị
'Larth Shcarpe, freedman'

lar{n}θ 'Larth', MASC PRAE, NOM/ACC; ścarpe 'Shcarpe', MASC NOMEN, NOM/ACC; lautṇị 'freedman', NOM/ACC

The Latin text was inscribed on the cover of the urn. The Etruscan was incised on the body of the cask beneath the head of a Gorgon. The praenomen of the deceased was misspelled in Etruscan. Perhaps the stonemason conflated the praenomina **larθ** and **arnθ**.

The deceased was the freedman of a woman named Scarpia. The Latin also provides additional information. He was POPA, a 'priest's assistant'. The first two words of the Etruscan inscription correspond to the first two Latin words. The Etruscan word **lautni** matches the Latin abbreviation *l(ibertus)*. The Etruscan inscription does not specify the name of the former master/mistress, nor does it indicate the deceased's occupation.

Benelli 1994:29, no. 25, tav. IX; Rix 1957:532, REE; Steinbauer 1999:192–3, B7.

(24) Ar 1.3, Arretium, after ca. 50 BCE
     funerary urn (travertine)

CN · LABERIUS · A · F
POM
'Gnaeus Laberius, son of Aulus, of the voting tribe Pomptina'

a · haprni · a
aχratinaliśa
'Aule Haprni, (son) of Aule, the (son) of Akhratinei'

a, abbrev. of **aule** 'Aule', MASC PRAE, NOM/ACC; **haprni** 'Haprni', MASC NOMEN, NOM/ACC; a, abbrev. of **auleσ** 'Aule', MASC PRAE, 1ST GEN; **aχratinaliśa** = **aχratinal** 'Akhratinei', FEM NOMEN, 2ND GEN + **-iśa** 'the', DEF ART, NOM

The inscriptions were incised on the cask of a funerary urn.

The words in the first line of both inscriptions match up perfectly: praenomen (abbreviated) + nomen + patronymic (abbreviated). The final word of the Latin inscription is an abbreviation of the name of the voting tribe to which the deceased belonged, namely, the tribe *Pomptina*. In contrast, the final word of the Etruscan inscription is the metronymic of the deceased, 'the (son) of Akhratinei'.

Benelli 1994:16–7, no. 3; Cristofani 1991a:128–9, no. 20; Maetzke 1954:352–6; Pallottino 1954:399–403, REE; Steinbauer 1999:190, B4.

(25) Um 1.7, Pisaurum, 100–50 BCE
     funerary monument (stone)

[L · CA]FATIUS · L · F · STE · HARUSPE[X]
FULGURIATOR
'Lucius Cafatius, son of Lucius, of the voting tribe Stellatina, haruspex, interpreter of lightening strikes.'

[c]afates · lr · lr · netóvis · trutnvt · frontac
'Laris Cafates, (son of) Laris, haruspex, interpreter of lightning.'

[c]afates 'Cafates', MASC NOMEN, 1ST GEN; lr, abbrev. of laris 'Laris', MASC PRAE, NOM/ACC; lr, abbrev. of larisal 'Laris', MASC PRAE, 2ND GEN; netóvis 'haruspex', NOM/ACC; trutnvt 'interpreter', NOM/ACC; frontac 'of lightning', NOM/ACC

Um 1.7 is the most famous Etruscan/Latin bilingual. It was discovered at Pisaurum in Umbria. The text was incised on a slab of stone that probably belonged to a funerary monument of some type. The Latin inscription was placed above the Etruscan; it was written in large capital letters in dextroverse direction. The Etruscan inscription, though neat in appearance, was carved with smaller letter-forms in a cursive style. The direction of writing was sinistroverse. The Etruscan letter transcribed as o had an unusual form (𐌈). The quality of the vowel that the sign 𐌈 represented is uncertain. The alphabet follows the southern type; *sigma* stands for the dental sibilant /s/.

In terms of content, this is one of the more substantial bilinguals. Not only does it yield the name of the deceased, but it also provides his job description. He worked as HARUSPEX, inspector of livers, and FULGURIATOR, interpreter of lightning strikes.

This bilingual also poses interesting problems of interpretation. The words of the Etruscan text do not match up with the Latin except for the name of the deceased. The voting tribe of the deceased is mentioned in the Latin text. In the Etruscan text the deceased's job description, **netóvis** · **trutnvt** · **frontac**, is longer by a word than the Latin, which is HARUSPEX FULGURIATOR. The most likely interpretation is that Latin HARUSPEX and

Etruscan **netóvis** form one match and that Latin FULGURIATOR and Etruscan **trutnvt frontac** form the other. Under this interpretation, **trutnvt** may be interpreted as an agent formation in -t < *-(a)tʰ and **frontac** may be taken as an adjectival derivative in -c meaning 'of, concerning, relating to lightning'. The noun-adjective phrase may be translated as 'interpreter of lightning'.

In the Etruscan text the nomen of the deceased is placed before the praenomen. This arrangement is unusual for Etruscan texts in this area. The only parallel that can be cited is Fe 1.2 (**pentlnaσ arnθiạl**), an inscription recovered from Bologna. However, this text is irrelevant as regards the arrangement of words in the bilingual; it dates to ca. 450 BCE. Also worthy of note is the fact that the nomen is inflected with the s-ending. This too is standard for Neo-Etruscan inscriptions written in southern Etruria, but is an uncommon feature in the north.

Benelli 1994:13–5, no. 1, tav. I; Steinbauer 1999:194–6, B6.

Tomb Construction

10.4 This category of inscription is a subtype of the funerary inscription. In its most common form it states that the deceased was responsible for building a tomb or a tomb chamber, or for enlarging an existing tomb.

The verb found most commonly in this type of inscription is **ceriχunce** 'built, constructed'. The suffix on this verb, **-un-**, may be traced back historically to the suffix -vani- found in **muluvanice**, though here it must have had a causative meaning. The verb is always transitive. Interestingly, despite the fact that this type of inscription is parallel in structure to the votive dedication (§10.7) and the commemorative gift inscription (§10.8), the direct object is always specified in full, most often by a noun phrase consisting of a demonstrative followed by its head noun, e.g. **cn tamera** 'this chamber'.

10.4.1 For an investigation of this type of inscription see Pfiffig 1972.

(26) Cr 5.2, Caere, 400–300 BCE
        column in tomb (tufa)

> laris · av
> le · laris
> al · clenar
> sval · cn · ςuθi
> 5   ceriχunce
> apac · atic

sani꜀va θu
i · cesu
clavtieθ
10 urasi

'Laris (and) Aule, sons of Laris, (while) living constructed this tomb.
Both mother and father, the *sani*, (were) buried here. For the
Claudii family.'

laris 'Laris', MASC PRAE, NOM/ACC; avle 'Avle', MASC PRAE, NOM/ACC; larisal
'Laris', MASC PRAE, 2ND GEN; clenar 'sons', ANIM PL, NOM/ACC; sval 'alive',
NOM/ACC; cn 'this', DEM PRO, ACC; ꜀uθi 'tomb', NOM/ACC; ceriχunce
'constructed', PAST ACT; apac = apa 'father', NOM/ACC + -c 'and', ENCLITIC CONJ;
atic = ati 'mother', NOM/ACC + -c 'and', ENCLITIC CONJ; sani꜀va '?', PL, NOM/ACC;
θui 'here', ADV; cesu '(were) buried', U-PART; clavtieθurasi 'Claudii family',
ANIM PL, 1ST PERT

The inscription was incised on one of the columns in the atrium of the
chamber tomb.

The text is divided into three units: (1) Lines 1–5 refer to the construction of the tomb. (2) Lines 6–8 refer to the parents of the builders. (3) Lines
9–10 refer to the family for whom the tomb was constructed. The main
issue in this inscription is the form sani꜀va in line 7. Formally this word
consists of a stem followed by the article inflected in the plural nominative, sani- + -꜀va. Some have suggested that this noun referred to the
bones of the parents of Laris and Aule and that apac and atic were adjectives rather than members of a coordinate noun phrase. They offer
the translation 'the bones of their mother and father (were) buried here'.
While this interpretation is feasible, it seems difficult to separate the stem
sani- from sacni-, which is attested in several funerary inscriptions from
Tarquinia. This word probably refers to some type of public or religious
title or function. If the two forms are to be connected, we are compelled
to assume that sani꜀va is a misspelling for sa<c>ni꜀va.

Agostiniani 1994b:9–20; Carruba 1974:301–13; Holleman 1984:504–8; Pfiffig 1976:697–703;
Steinbauer 1999:243–4, no. G7.

(27) Cr 5.4, Caere, late Neo-Etruscan period
cippus (stone)

laris : a[t]ies : an cn : tamera : φurθce
'(It was) Laris Aties who *φurθce* this tomb chamber.'

laris 'Laris', MASC PRAE, NOM/ACC; a[t]ies 'Aties', MASC NOMEN, 1ST GEN; an
'who', ANIM REL PRO, NOM/ACC; cn 'this', DEM PRO, ACC; tamera 'tomb
chamber', NOM/ACC; φurθce '?', PAST ACT

The inscription was incised in sinistroverse direction on a stone cippus. The feminine form of the nomen of the deceased is well attested at Caere, e.g. atiial 2ND GEN (Cr 2.49, 2.50, and 2.59). The form atiia (2ND GEN) is found on an Archaic inscription from the *Ager Tarquiniensis* (AT 2.3).

The most interesting aspect of this inscription is the verb φurθce, which is attested only here. There can be no doubt that it is a past active form in -ce. The meaning has to be in the semantic sphere of constructing, designing, enlarging, remodeling, etc.

Steinbauer 1999:252, no. G15.

(28) Ru 5.1, Rusellae, 225–200 BCE
stone block (peperino)

vl · afuna · vl · pes
nalióa · cn · óuθi
ceriχunce
'Vel Afuna, (son) of Vel and Pesnei, constructed this tomb.'

vl, abbrev. of vel 'Vel', MASC PRAE, NOM/ACC; afuna 'Afuna', MASC NOMEN, NOM/ACC; vl, abbrev. of velus 'Vel', MASC PRAE, 1ST GEN; pesnalióa = pesnal 'Pesnei', FEM NOMEN, 2ND GEN + -ióa 'the', DEF ART, NOM; cn 'this', DEM PRO, ACC; óuθi 'tomb', NOM/ACC; ceriχunce 'constructed', PAST ACT

The inscription was incised on the face of a stone block forming the cornice of a tomb. The direction of writing is sinistroverse. There is no punctuation separating the demonstrative cn from its noun.

The metronymic base is pesnei; it may be connected with the praenomen pisna found in inscription (65).

Saladino 1971:344–5, REE 14, tav. LXXI.

(29) Ta 1.108, Tarquinia, 200–100 BCE
wall of tomb

palazuị · θạṇa
ạvils · L · enẓa · huóur
acṇạnas · manim
ạṛce
'Thana Palazui (died) at fifty years of age (after) having produced *enza* children. She made (this) funerary monument (?).'

palazuị 'Palazui', FEM NOMEN, NOM/ACC; θạṇa 'Thana', FEM PRAE, NOM/ACC; ạvils 'year', 1ST GEN; enẓa '?'; huóur 'children', ANIM PL, NOM/ACC; acṇạnas 'having produced', NAS-PART; manim 'funerary monument (?)', NOM/ACC; ạṛce 'made', PAST ACT

The inscription was painted in sinistroverse direction on the wall of a tomb in the necropolis of Villa Tarantola in Tarquinia. The deceased may be the wife of Larth Felsnas whose funerary inscription is no. (15).

The word en̦za is a *hapax*. Given its position next to the plural hućur, it is tempting to compare it to the number in phrases such as ci clenar 'three sons'. However, since we know the names for the numbers 1 through 10 and since we know that the number 13 was indicated by means of the phrase ci sar, the possibilities are limited. Giannecchini (1997:190–206) has proposed that the word snuiaφ/snuiuφ be identified as '12'. Could enza be the word for '11'?

A. Morandi 2005:334–5, REE 54.

Proprietary Inscriptions

10.5 Household objects, usually pieces of pottery, were often incised or painted with the names of their owners and then accompanied the deceased to the tomb. This type of epigraphic category is the proprietary inscription. The most expansive structure for this type of text consisted of three constituents: pronoun (NOM) + name of proprietor (GEN) + word for the type of object (NOM/ACC). During the Archaic period the pronoun of choice was 1st person singular and the inscriptions were of the "iscrizione parlante" variety. The constituents were arranged in the order described above, but it was possible for the name of the proprietor and for the word referring to the type of ceramic to be inverted, e.g. inscription (35). The proprietor could be identified by his/her praenomen, which was particularly common for seventh-century inscriptions, or by his/her praenomen and nomen. Scaled-down versions of this type of inscription were also possible in Archaic Etruscan. So, for example, some inscriptions, e.g. nos. (32) and (33), had two constituents: the pronoun mi and the name of the proprietor or, more rarely, as in no. (38), the name of the type of ceramic and the name of the proprietor. Other inscriptions, e.g. no. (37), consisted only of the name of the proprietor.

Toward the end of the Archaic period proprietary inscriptions of this type went out of vogue. A few writers replaced the 1st person pronoun with a demonstrative form. Inscription (40) is an example. A more streamlined version of this type became the norm. It consisted of the name of the proprietor, generally the praenomen, in the genitive case, e.g. ramθas 'of Ramtha' (Ta 2.145). Occasionally, the name of the proprietor was written in the nominative/accusative form, e.g. tite : uplu 'Tite Uplu' (Ta 2.33)

Proprietary inscriptions are interesting as a class because they contain the words for types of ceramic in use in the Etruscan world among the aristocratic classes. These terms, many of which were borrowed from Greek artisans, were discussed in Chapter 9.

A subtype of proprietary inscription included the Etruscan adjective mlaχ 'good, beautiful', which served as a modifier of the word referring to the type of ceramic or as a modifier of both ceramic and proprietor. In the inscriptions of this subtype, the adjectives were often "distracted" or pulled apart from the nouns that they modified. So, for example, in inscription no. (31) the adjective mlakas, which stands in word-final position, refers back to the name of the proprietor titelaς. (It is not clear why the base form of the adjective mlaχ ends in an aspirated consonant and the oblique forms have a plain stop. This type of morphophonemic alternation is found in no other Etruscan word that we are aware of.)

10.5.1 See Agostiniani 1982 for an analysis of "iscrizioni parlanti". Proprietary inscriptions of the mlaχ mlakas type are discussed in Agostiniani 1981.

(30) ETP 289, Caere, 700–670 BCE
fragment of plate (impasto)

ṃi hvlaveς : ςpati
'I (am) the plate of Flave.'

ṃi 'I', 1ST PERS PRO, NOM; hvlaveς 'Flave', MASC PRAE, 1ST GEN; ςpati 'plate', NOM/ACC

The text was incised on the border of the plate in sinistroverse direction. Punctuation separates the predicate noun from its dependent genitive. Both *sigmas* were written with five strokes. The name of the proprietor, hvlave, begins with the sound /f/. As is typically the case at Caere, this sound is spelled by means of the digraph hv. The word for 'plate' is usually spelled spanti. The omission of the nasal before the homorganic stop suggests that the preceding vowel may have been nasalized with subsequent loss of the nasal.

Bagnasco Gianni 1996:113–4, no. 92; Cristofani 1991a:276, tav. L; Heurgon 1989:185–6, no. 3, fig. 6.

(31) Cr 2.9, Caere, 700–675 BCE
fragment of olla (impasto)

mi titelaς θị[na] {mḷa} m[l]ạχ mlakas
'I (am) the beautiful storage vessel of the beautiful Titela.'

mi 'I', 1ST PERS PRO, NOM; titelaς 'Titela', FEM PRAE, 1ST GEN; θị[na] 'storage vessel', NOM/ACC; m[l]ạχ 'beautiful', NOM/ACC; mlakas 'beautiful', 1ST GEN

The letters m̤la in the middle of the text were erroneously inscribed. It is not clear why the scriptor left this sequence unfinished and began anew. The inscription was written in sinistroverse direction along the body of the ceramic.

The name of the proprietor, **titelaç**, was derived from the masculine praenomen **tite-** by means of the suffix **-la**. The corresponding masculine form ends in **-le, titele**. The suffixes **-le/-la** may have had diminutive function. The adjective **mlakas** was separated from its noun; it modifies **titelaç**.

Bagnasco Gianni 1996:49–51, no. 2; Colonna 1972:463, REE 80, tav. LXXXV; Steinbauer 1999:226, no. D23; Vanoni 1962:294, REE 2, tav. XXII, 1.

(32) ETP 344, Caere, 700–675 BCE
    chalice (impasto)

mi laucies mezenṭies
'I (am the chalice) of Laucie Mezenzies.'

mi 'I', 1ST PERS PRO, NOM; **laucies** 'Laucie', MASC PRAE, 1ST GEN; **mezenṭies** 'Mezenzies', MASC NOMEN, 1ST GEN

The inscription was incised in dextroverse direction around the lower portion of the body of the chalice. Briquel (1991:355) reads the nomen as **mezenṭies**. Bagnasco Gianni (1996:108) reads it as **mezenẓies**.

The text is interesting because it calls to mind the legend of Mezentius, king of Caere, whose story is told by Cato (*Origines* 1.9–12) and Vergil (*Aeneid* 7–10). Unfortunately, the inscription does not lend any support to the historical veracity of the Mezentius character as the king of Caere.

Bagnasco Gianni 1996:108, no. 84; Briquel 1989:78–92; Gaultier and Briquel 1989:99–115; Gaultier, Gran-Aymerich, and Briquel 1991:350–6, REE 73, tav. LXIV.

(33) ETP 209, origin unknown, 650–600 BCE
    askos in shape of a ring (ceramic)

mi veneluç óiθurnaç
'I (am the askos) of Venel Shithurnas.'

mi 'I', 1ST PERS PRO, NOM; **veneluç** 'Venel', MASC PRAE, 1ST GEN; **óiθurnaç** 'Shithurnas', MASC NOMEN, NOM/ACC

The inscription was incised in sinistroverse direction without punctuation. The sound /s/ was represented by five-bar *sigmas*. The inscription was written in an alphabet belonging to the southern style.

The nomen óiθurnaç is not attested in any other inscription. The editor offers the nomen śitrinas (Cm 2.62), which is attested on an inscription from the city of Nola in Campania, as a possible comparandum, but he also points out—and rightly so—that this nomen has among other phonological differences an unaspirated dental.

Naso 1996:336–7, REE 16.

(34) OA 2.2, origin unknown, 650–600 BCE
    small oil-flask (bucchero)

mi larθaia telicles leχtumuza
'I (am) the oil-flask of Larthai, of the (family) Telicles.'

mi 'I', 1ST PERS PRO, NOM; larθaia 'Larthai', FEM PRAE, 2ND GEN; telicles
'Telicles', MASC NOMEN, 1ST GEN; leχtumuza 'oil-flask', NOM/ACC

The inscription was incised in sinistroverse direction without punctuation. The sound /s/ was represented by *sigma*.

The owner of the flask was of Greek heritage. She was most likely the daughter of a Greek immigrant who employed his name as a nomen. Another possibility is that **telicles** is a patronymic. This would yield the interpretation 'Larthai, (daughter) of Telicles'. The nomen **larθaia** is distinctively feminine; the masculine genitive form is **larθia**, cp. inscription (41).

Leχtumuza is a diminutive formation in -**uza**. For the suffix see the following inscription.

Bagnasco Gianni 1996:315, no. 313; Bonfante and Bonfante 2002:138–40, no. 11, fig. 11; Hammarström 1930:261–6.

(35) ETP 28, origin unknown, 625–600 BCE
    pyxis (bucchero)

mi çunθeruza çpuriaç mlakaç
'I (am) the pyxis of the beautiful Spuria.'

mi 'I', 1ST PERS PRO, NOM; çunθeruza 'pyxis', NOM/ACC; çpuriaç 'Spuria', FEM
PRAE, 1ST GEN; mlakaç 'beautiful', 1ST GEN

The inscription was incised in sinistroverse direction around the lip of the body of the pyxis before it was fired. The form of the alphabet points to Caere as a likely source.

The adjective **mlakaç** is in agreement with the name of the owner, **çpuriaç**. The placement of the constituents of the genitive noun phrase after the head, çunθeruza, is not very common in this type of inscription, cp. no. (31). The name for the type of ceramic is a *hapax*. çunθeruza is a diminutive formation in -(u)za made from a stem çunθer- or çunθeru-. The word may be a native formation, but one cannot rule out a borrowing, perhaps from a Greek source, though exactly what that might be is not clear.

Bonfante and Bonfante 2002:137–8, no. 10, fig. 16; Bonfante and Wallace 2001:201–12, tav. XXXIII–XXXIV.

(36) ETP 118, Veii, 700–600 BCE
    fragment of olla (impasto)

mi : raq[u]nθia : tipeia : θina : malaχ [: malaka]ṣị : ita : menạ[q]u
'I (am) the olla of Raqunthi Tipei. This beautiful (vessel) was made for a beautiful (woman).'

mi 'I', 1ST PERS PRO, NOM; raq[u]nθia 'Raqunthi', FEM PRAE, 2ND GEN; tipeia 'Tipei', FEM NOMEN, 2ND GEN; θina 'storage vessel', NOM/ACC; malaχ 'beautiful', NOM/ACC; [malaka]ṣị 'beautiful', 1ST PERT; ita 'this', DEM PRO, NOM; menạ[q]u '(was) made', U-PART

The inscription was incised in dextroverse direction on the perimeter of the bottom portion of the olla. The final section of the inscription spiraled inward so that it was written beneath the beginning.

The inscription consists of two sentences. The first has the proprietary format; it mentions the name of the ceramic and its owner. Both members of the name are attested here for the first time. Raq[u]nθia is derived from a masculine stem *raqunthʰ-; tipei is derived from a stem *tipe, which the editor (Colonna) suggests has its origins in a Greek name Τίβειος/Τίβιος, common for slaves. The second sentence is a dedication. Interestingly, the subject changes from first to third person. The pronoun ita 'this' refers back to the ceramic. The u-participle was derived from the past active stem menaq- of the verb menece 'made'. The construction is passive in voice. The position of the adjectives makes their syntactic allegiance ambiguous. They could be interpreted as belonging to the first or the second sentence. It is also possible to split the difference and take malaχ with θina in the first sentence, 'beautiful vessel', and take the pertinentive [malaka]ṣị with the second sentence, 'this (vessel) was made for a beautiful (woman).' The form of the adjective malaχ is possibly the result of anaptyxis. See the discussion following inscription (5).

Colonna 2002a:351–2, 353–7, REE 71; Di Napoli 2002:352–3, REE 71, tav. XXXIII.

(37) Cr 2.42, Caere, ca. 600 BCE
   fragment of palette (?) (bucchero)

   (a) θanakviluš sucisnaia
       '(the palette) of Thanakvil Sucisnai'

   (b) .a.šu

θanakviluš 'Thanakvil', FEM PRAE, 1ST GEN; sucisnaia 'Sucisnai', FEM NOMEN, 2ND GEN. .a.šu '?', NOM/ACC

Inscription (a) was incised in sinistroverse direction within a car-touche on one side of the fragment. Inscription (b) was written on the other side of the fragment near the back of the head of the figure of a sphinx. It was also written in sinistroverse direction.

The dental sibilant /s/ is spelled with the sign of the cross, X, in θanakviluš and in .a.šu. The letter *alpha* of .a.šu appears to be marked with punctuation; there is a dot beneath the medial bar. Also notewor-thy here is the fact that the *upsilons* of inscription (a) are distinct in form from the *upsilon* in inscription (b). In (a) *upsilon* has the form Y with an oblique shooting off from a vertical stroke. In (b) *upsilon* has the form Y.

Bonfante 2004:357–9 corrects the reading of inscription (a), which is cited in Rix, ET Cr 2.42 as beginning with the 1st personal pronoun **mi**. The spelling of θanakviluš is somewhat unusual in that it has *kappa* in place of *khi*. **Sucisnaia** has the Archaic genitive ending -a. Since inscription (a) gives the name of the owner of the palette, the word **ašu**, which was writ-ten in its base form, is unlikely to be a name. Fiesel (1935:80) thought that it might be the Etruscan word for the sphinx.

Bagnasco Gianni 1996:310–1, no. 303; Bonfante 2004:357–9, REE 92a, 92b, tav. LIX; MacIntosh Turfa 2005:137–8, tav. 100:MS 1628; Steinbauer 1999:216, no. D6.

(38) ETP 323, Aemilia (Marzabotto), 520–500 BCE
   handle of amphora (impasto)

   θina rakaluσ
   'storage vessel of Rakalu'

θina 'storage vessel', NOM/ACC; rakaluσ 'Rakalu', MASC NOMEN, 1ST GEN

The inscription was incised in destroverse direction on the handle of an amphora. The letter θ has the form of a cross, X. This letter-form, which was common at Clusium in the sixth century BCE, points to north-ern Etruria as the ultimate source of the alphabet that was used in this part of Aemilia.

The name of the proprietor, **rakalu-**, has the suffix -alu. This suffix was very common in the formation of Etruscan nomina in the Po Valley.

Sassatelli 1993:284–6, tav. LXIII.

(39) ETP 325, Blera, 500 BCE
   fragment of bowl (bucchero)

mi ramaθas treseles
'I (am the bowl) of Ramatha, (family) of Treseles.'

mi 'I', 1ST PERS PRO, NOM; **ramaθas** 'Ramatha', FEM PRAE, 1ST GEN; **treseles** 'Treseles', MASC NOMEN, 1ST GEN

The inscription was incised in a circle on the bottom of the vase. Although the proprietor is female, the nomen, **treseles**, is masculine in form.

Ricciardi 1993:290–1, REE 21, tav. LXV.

(40) OA 2.20, origin unknown (South), 500 BCE
   bowl (ceramic)

ica{i} patara vinumaia
'This (is) the bowl of Vinumai.'

ica{i} 'this', DEM PRO, NOM; **patara** 'shallow bowl', NOM/ACC; **vinumaia** 'Vinumai', FEM NOMEN, 2ND GEN

The text was incised in sinistroverse direction without punctuation. We take **ica{i}** to be a misspelling for **ica**. As written, **icai** would be difficult, if not impossible, to interpret.

The word **patara** may be a borrowing from Latin *patera* 'shallow bowl'. The nomen of the owner, **vinumaia**, shows the Archaic genitive ending -**a** (vinumai-a).

(41) ETP 335, origin unknown (South), 475–450 BCE
   mirror (bronze)

mi malana larθiia cavis spuriies
'I (am) the mirror of Larth Cavis, (son) of Spurie.'

mi 'I', 1ST PERS PRO, NOM; **malana** 'mirror', NOM/ACC; **larθiia** 'Larth', MASC NOMEN, 2ND GEN; **cavis** 'Cavis', MASC NOMEN, 1ST GEN; **spuriies** 'Spuries', MASC NOMEN, 1ST GEN

The inscription was incised in sinistroverse direction inside the decorative border that encircles the rim of the mirror. There was no punctuation.

The word-form **malana** is a variant of **malena**. The difference in the spelling of the medial vowel is due to vowel weakening. The original quality of the vowel cannot be determined. The word appears to be a substantive derived from an adjective ending in the suffix -**na**. The stem is **male-/mala-**. Interestingly, **malana/malena** is found only in proprietary inscriptions with masculine names.

The onomastic phrase refers to a male, 'Larth Cavi, (son) of Spurie'. The praenomen **larθiia** has the Archaic genitive case ending -**a**. The double spelling of iota in **larθiia** and in **spuriies** is unusual.

De Grummond 2000:69–77; Pandolfini Angeletti 2000:224.

(42) ETP 83, origin unknown, 450–400 BCE
      wine pitcher (metal)

mi arnθial tetnies σuθiθi velclθi
'I (am the wine pitcher) of Arnth Tetnies in the tomb in Velca.'

mi 'I', 1ST PERS PRO, NOM; **arnθial** 'Arnth', MASC PRAE, 2ND GEN; **tetnies**
'Tetnies', MASC NOMEN, 1ST GEN; **σuθiθi** = σuθi 'tomb', LOC + -θi 'in', POST;
velclθi = velcl 'Velca', PLACE NAME, 2ND GEN + -θi 'in', POST

Although the find spot of this inscription is unknown, there can be little doubt that the point of origin is Vulci. The final word in the text is the locative form of the name of that city, **velclθi** = 'in (the city) of Vulci'. That the inscription originated in Vulci is also supported by the fact that other members of the Tetnies family appear in funerary inscriptions from this area.

The spelling of the genitive singular **velcl** in **velclθi** as -l rather than -**al** is unusual for this period, but one can perhaps point to medial vowel weakening in a postpositional phrase as the culprit.

Briquel 2003:7, 10; Briquel and Landes 2005:7–25; Colonna 2005b:357, REE 89.

(43) ETP 331, Venetia (Spina), 350 BCE
      small plate (ceramic)

mi venuσ platunaluσ
'I (am the plate) of Venu Platunalu.'

mi 'I', 1ST PERS PRO, NOM; **venus** 'Venu', MASC PRAE, 1ST GEN; **platunalus**
'Platunalu', MASC NOMEN, 1ST GEN

The inscription was incised in a circle on the inner portion of the top of the plate. The direction of writing is sinistroverse.

The nomen was built by adding the suffix -*alu* to the Greek name Πλάτων, which was borrowed into Etruscan as **platun-**. For the suffix see no. (38).

Pandolfini 1993:275–6, REE 1, tav. LXIII.

Prohibitions

10.6 Prohibitions were incised on pieces of pottery as warnings against theft, usually in tandem with a proprietary inscription. This type of text has close parallels in other Italic languages and in Greek, so identification of the type for Etruscan is secure.

The interpretation and analysis of the word-forms in the prohibition proper is not controversial, but a few problems remain unresolved. No one is quite sure what to do with the element -**pi**/-**pe**, which is regularly affixed to the object pronoun **mini**. It may be an emphatic particle, though some interpret it as a postposition. The form of the negator appears as **ei**, **ein**, and **en** without any clear principle governing the distribution. Indeed, the syntactic contexts in which the variants are found appear to be the same.

In several inscriptions prohibitions are followed by the words **mi nunar** or **mi nunai**. Mi can be identified as the 1st personal pronoun, but a persuasive interpretation of or a convincing analysis for the words **nunar**, **nunai**, and the phrase as a whole has yet to be offered. Anti-theft texts in Latin, while providing parallels for the prohibition and the proprietary statement, do not provide a key to the meaning of this section of the Etruscan.

Also included here is a recently published text, no. (47), ETP 285, discovered in a tomb near Clusium. The inscription forbids the making or constructing of objects in a certain area of a tomb. It differs from prohibitions incised on pieces of ceramic in terms of sentence type; the verb is a jussive form rather than an imperative.

10.6.1 For negation and negative commands see Agostiniani 1984.

(44) Ve 3.13, Veii, 600–500 BCE
  fragment of vase (ceramic)

  ṃ[i]ni mulvaṇice venali.a. .š.lapina.š. .e.n. mi<ni>pi capi ṃ[i] ṇ[u]ṇa.i.
  'Venalia, (family) of Slapinas, gave me (as a gift). Don't steal me. I (am) *nunai*.'

ṃ[i]ni 'me', 1ST PERS PRO, ACC; mulvaṇice 'gave', PAST ACT; venali.a. 'Venalia', FEM PRAE, NOM/ACC; .š.lapina.š. 'Slapinas', MASC NOMEN, 1ST GEN; .e.n. 'not', NEG; mi<ni>pi = mi<ni> 'me', 1ST PERS PRO, ACC + -pi '?', ENCLITIC PARTICLE (?); capi 'take', IMPV; ṃ[i] 'I', 1ST PERS PRO, NOM; ṇ[u]ṇa.i. '?'

The inscription was written in sinistroverse direction without punctuation between words. Mi<ni>pi was written as mipi. We assume that the pronominal form is the object of the imperative capi and so restore the accusative form. Syllabic punctuation marks the final letter of the negator .e.n.

The text has two constituents: a dedication and a prohibition. Rix divides the sequence venali.a..š.lapina.š. as venali .a..š.lapina.š. This is possible but Latin-style endings in -ia are not to be dismissed out of hand since there is evidence for borrowings from Latin already in the earliest inscriptions from Veii, e.g. latineç 'Latines', 1ST GEN (Ve 2.4). The spelling of the negator as .e.n. is unusual. The spellings ein and ei are more common in Archaic-period texts. For en in a Neo-Etruscan inscription, see no. (53).

Maras 2002a:267–8; Pallottino 1939:464–5, REE I-Veio, 12.

(45) ETP 110, Pisa, 500–450 BCE
    bowl (ceramic)

ei menepi χape mi · mi : karkus
· venelus
'Don't take me. I (am the bowl) of Venel Karku.'

ei 'not', NEG; menepi = mene 'me', 1ST PERS PRO, ACC + -pi '?', ENCLITIC PARTICLE (?); χape 'take', IMPV; mi 'I', 1ST PERS PRO, NOM; karkus 'Karku', MASC NOMEN, 1ST GEN; venelus 'Venel', MASC PRAE, 1ST GEN

The inscription was incised, except for the praenomen venelus, around the rim of the foot of the bowl. The praenomen was incised inside the rim on the flat portion of the foot.

The first part of the text is a warning against theft. The final portion is proprietary, but it is not clear how it is organized syntactically. The editor suggests a division into three constituents: ei menepi χape. mi venelus. mi karkus. Following this analysis, one of the names refers to the owner of the bowl; the other refers to the person who gave it.

χape is most likely an error for kape. The spelling of the pronoun mene is difficult to explain, as is the spelling of the final vowel of the imperative χape. For some discussion of the change of i to e see §§3.11–12.

Maggiani 2002b:315–8, REE 15, tav. XXXI.

(46) ETP 15, Pyrgi, 500–450 BCE
     Attic skyphos (ceramic)

[cav]aθas mi seχis ein men[p]e kape mi nunax
'I (am the skyphos) of Cavatha, the daughter. Don't take me. I am
nunax.'

[cav]aθas 'Cavatha', THEO, 1ST GEN; mi 'I', 1ST PERS PRO, NOM; seχis 'daughter',
1ST GEN; ein 'not', NEG; men[p]e = men- 'me', 1ST PERS PRON, ACC + -[p]e '?',
ENCLITIC PARTICLE; kape 'take', IMPV; mi 'I', 1ST PERS PRO, NOM; nunax '?'

The inscription was incised in sinistroverse direction on the body of
the vase, just above the foot. The final letter of **nunax** cannot be determined; both -i and -r are possible. Compare **nunar** and **nunai** in other texts
with prohibitions.

The inscription is composed of three independent sentences: (1) proprietary text in a religious context; (2) prohibition; (3) **mi nunax**. The
skyphos was the 'property' of the goddess Cavatha (Neo-Etruscan Cautha, Catha). The genitive of the word 'daughter', **seχis**, is an epithet of the
goddess. The second clause is a prohibition against theft of the object. In
contrast to inscription (45), the prohibitive particle has a final nasal, **ein**.
The final clause is predicative: **mi nunax**.

The loss of the medial vowel in **men[p]e** may be explained by vowel
syncope (< *minipi*). However, the change in the quality of the *i*-vowel in
this word-form and in **kape** (cf. **kapi**) are difficult (see above, inscription
(45)).

Maras 2003:316–8, REE 26, tav. XXVI.

(47) ETP 285, Clusium, 500–450 BCE
     wall of tomb

ein θui ara enan
'(One) shall not make anything here.'

ein 'not', NEG; θui 'here', ADV; ara 'make', JUSSIVE; enan 'anything', INDEF
PRO, ACC

The inscription was incised in sinistroverse direction on the rear wall
of the tomb. It was written in scriptio continua. The inscription is most
reasonably dated to near the end of the Archaic period.

The verb **ara** is a jussive form built to the root **ar-**. Benelli (1998) suggests the meaning of the verb in this context is 'put, place', but one can
probably make some sense of the construction without going beyond the

semantic sphere generally acknowledged for formations associated with this root. Perhaps the most notable aspect of this inscription is **enan**, which has been interpreted as an indefinite pronominal form (stem **ena-**). It is tempting to connect **enan** with **enaσ**, which is found in the *Liber Linteus*, but it is difficult to see how this connection works semantically.

Benelli 1998:107–11 and 2001:213–24, tav. XXXVc–f.

Votive Dedications

10.7 Inscriptions offered to or on behalf of Etruscan deities generally adopted one of two syntactic patterns. The more interesting pattern had **turuce** 'dedicated (as an offering)' as its verb (Neo-Etruscan **turce**). Votive inscriptions of this type span the history of the language from the Archaic period to the demise of Etruscan as a spoken language. In Archaic Etruscan inscriptions the direct object of **turuce** was **mini**, the accusative of the first person pronoun, and the inscriptions were of the "speaking text" variety. At the end of the Archaic period the personal pronoun **mini** was replaced as direct object by one of the demonstratives, e.g. **itun**. In Neo-Etruscan inscriptions the demonstrative **ecn/cn** was much more common as the direct object than **etan/tn**; the latter refers to the votive object in only three inscriptions from the entire Neo-Etruscan period. The object pronouns in votive inscriptions refer to the object dedicated to the divinity. The object itself is never mentioned by name, although it is on occasion identified as **cver** 'votive offering (?)', **cvera** 'votive offering (?)' (a substantivized adjective < *cver-ra-), or **alpan** 'thank offering (?)'. A handful of inscriptions (see nos. (50), (53), (57)) had no direct object pronoun and so reference to the votive object was to be understood from the context. The name of the deity to whom or on behalf of whom the object was offered was inflected in the genitive case. The order of the major constituents in sentences of this type, particularly in the Neo-Etruscan period, fluctuated between Object-Verb-Subject and Object-Subject-Verb. The divinity to whom the object was dedicated usually occupied sentence-final position.

Votive dedications could also follow the proprietary syntactic pattern: **mi** + name of divinity inflected in the genitive. The "iscrizione parlante" format was common in the Archaic period; in the Neo-Etruscan period it was replaced by the name of the divinity in the genitive or in the nominative/accusative case.

Inscription (61), which was incised on a lead weight, stands apart from other dedications in its complexity. The phrase **hercles alpan** 'thank offering (?) to Herakles' is a good indicator that the object was a votive

offering, but there is much about this inscription that remains uninterpretable.

The inscriptions in this section deviate from chronological order because all **turuce/turce** inscriptions are grouped together as a unit. Votive
dedications with other syntactic structures follow.

10.7.1 Colonna (1989–90) presents a good overview of the structural features of votive inscriptions.

(48) Ve 3.29, Veii, 600–500 BCE
fragment of kylix (ceramic)

[mini avi]le zuqu {me̦} ṭuṛaçe̦ me̦n[er]ạvas
'Avile Zuqu dedicated me to Minerva.'

[mini] 'me', 1ST PERS PRO, ACC; [avi]le 'Avile', MASC PRAE, NOM/ACC; zuqu
'Zuqu', MASC NOMEN, NOM/ACC; ṭuṛaçe̦ 'dedicated', PAST ACT; me̦n[er]ạvas
'Minerva', THEO, 1ST GEN

The inscription was incised in sinistroverse direction around the inner
surface of the kylix. The letters **me̦** were inscribed by error. The scribe
may have lost his place and started incising the word **meneravas** before
realizing his mistake, at which point he returned to inscribe the verb.

The nomen **zuqu** is a *hapax*, but it must be counted among the relatively small number of nomina ending in **-u**, e.g. **camu, zuχu**. The verb
ṭuṛaçe̦ shows the impact of vowel weakening. The original form of the
past active is **turuce**. The oldest form of the theonym 'Minerva' is **menerva** (see ETP 251, inscription (1f) in Ch. 1), so the vowel intruding between the **r** and **v** is anaptyctic. For another example of anaptyxis in this
theonym, compare **meneruva** (OI S.11).

Colonna 1987:421–3, fig. 1a, 1b; Nogara 1930:318, no. 4.

(49) Ve 3.30, Veii, 600–500 BCE
fragment of vase (ceramic)

(a) mini θanirširie turice hvuluveš
'Thanirsiie Fuluves dedicated me.'

(b) mi mla[χ] mlakaš
'I (am) the beautiful (vase) of a good (person).'

mini 'me', 1ST PERS PRO, ACC; θanirširie 'Thanirsiie', MASC PRAE, NOM/ACC;
turice 'dedicated', PAST ACT; hvuluveš 'Fuluves', MASC NOMEN, 1ST GEN; mi 'I',
1ST PERS PRO, NOM; mla[χ] 'good', nom/acc; mlakaš 'good', 1ST GEN

Inscription (a) was incised in sinistroverse direction on the edge of the handle of the vase; (b) was written in dextroverse direction. The dental sibilant /s/ was written with the sign of the cross X in both inscriptions.

The nomen **hvuluve** is a borrowing from an Italic language, cp. the Latin name *Fulvus*. The praenomen **θaniršire** is attested at Tarquinia, but with medial -a, **θanarsiie**. A nomen built from this praenomen by addition of the suffix -na appears on an inscription from Volsinii, **θanarsienas**. The spelling of the verb **turice**, like the spelling of **turace** in no. (48), shows the impact of vowel weakening.

Nogara 1930:332, no. 39, fig. 40, pg. 317; Steinbauer 1999:224, D21.

(50) ETP 339, Perusia, 500–450 BCE
greaves (bronze)

arnθ savpunias turce menrvas
'Arnth Saupunias dedicated (these greaves) to Minerva.'

arnθ 'Arnth', MASC PRAE, NOM/ACC; **savpunias** 'Saupunias', MASC NOMEN, 1ST GEN; **turce** 'dedicated', PAST ACT; **menrvas** 'Minerva', THEO, 1ST GEN

The inscription was written *scriptio continua* along the central portion of the greaves. According to Colonna the greaves were found in the grave of the Acsi family of Perusia. However, since the inscription was written in an alphabet of the southern type, he suggests that the greaves were manufactured elsewhere, perhaps at Volsinii, and were later brought to Perusia. If the place of manufacture was indeed Volsinii, then one might imagine that they were spirited away after Volsinii was destroyed by Rome in 264 BCE.

Menrvas is a *genitivus donandi*. Notice the syncope of the medial vowel and the syllabification of -r (see §3.23).

Bonfante and Bonfante 2002:144–5, no. 22, fig. 23; Colonna 1999:95–103.

(51) ETP 29, origin unknown (South), 500–400 BCE
Attic kylix (ceramic)

(a) it[u]n turuc[e – – –]s
'? dedicated this (kylix) to ?.'

(b) [ecn · tur]ce · cavi · cr[ai]culi · hercle.s.
'Cavi Craiculi dedicated (this kylix) to Herakles.'

it[u]n 'this', DEM PRO, ACC; **turuc[e]** 'dedicated', PAST ACT; [– – –]s '?'; [ecn] 'this', DEM PRO, ACC; [**tur]ce** 'dedicated', PAST ACT; **cavi** 'Cavi', MASC PRAE, NOM/ACC; **cr[ai]culi** 'Craiculi', MASC NOMEN, NOM/ACC; **hercle.s.** 'Herakles', THEO, 1ST GEN

Inscription (a) was incised on the bottom of the foot of the kylix along the outer portion of the rim. This inscription belongs to the Archaic period and so was incised sometime shortly after production of the kylix. Inscription (b), which is chronologically later and dates to the Neo-Etruscan period, was incised inside of and parallel to the first inscription. This inscription was added after the kylix was repaired because of damage to the foot of the vessel. Both inscriptions were incised in sinistroverse direction.

It is difficult to determine how many letters are missing in inscription (a). Twenty is a reasonable guess. If this is even close to being correct, there may be enough space for the praenomen and nomen of the dedicator as well as the theonym Herakles. It could well be that the final letter of this inscription is the 1st genitive ending of the god's name. If inscription (b) is also a votive dedication, as seems likely, then our restoration yields a complete text.

The kylix was signed by the Attic vase-maker Euphronios. In the late 1990s the kylix was the subject of a dispute between the Getty Museum and Italian authorities. The vase was returned to Italy in 1999 and is now on display in the Museo di Villa Giulia in Rome.

Bonfante and Bonfante 2002:143–4, no. 21, fig. 22; Colonna 1989–90:902–3; Cristofani 1996:55–60; Heurgon 1989:181–5, fig. 1–4; Martelli 1991:613–21; Wallace 1996:291–4, tav. IX.

(52) ETP 189, origin unknown, 400–200 BCE
    weight (?) (bronze)

ecn : turce : laris : θefries : espial : atial : caθas
'Laris Thefries dedicated this (bronze weight) to Espi, mother of Catha.'

ecn 'this', DEM PRO, ACC; turce 'dedicated', PAST ACT; laris 'Laris', MASC PRAE, NOM/ACC; θefries 'Thefries', MASC NOMEN, 1ST GEN; espial 'Espi', THEO, 2ND GEN; atial 'mother', 2ND GEN; caθas 'Catha', THEO, 1ST GEN

The inscription was incised in sinistroverse direction around the cone-shaped body of a bronze weight. We do not know where the bronze was produced, but it was probably made in a workshop in the south because of the style of alphabet.

Laris θefries is the name of the person who dedicated the object. The family is Sabellic in origin. This name appears as the praenomen of the king of Caere in the Pyrgi Tablets, θefarie. The three genitives at the end of this inscription are the primary source of interpretative difficulties. Espial (stem espi-) is a *hapax*. It could be a personal or divine name. Atial is either the genitive of the word **ati** 'mother' or the genitive of a feminine nomen. **Caθas** is the genitive of the divinity **caθa** (Archaic **cavaθa**). The difficulty lies in determining the constituent structure of the three genitives. The possibilities are:

(a) **Espial** is the metronymic of **laris θefries**. This leaves **atial caθas** as the indirect object phrase: 'Laris Thefries, (son) of Espi, ... to Mother Catha'. This is the view advocated by Bonfante (1994).

(b) **Espial atial** is a metronymic. There are two possibilities: (b1) **Atial** means 'mother' and is in apposition to **espial**, so '(son) of Espi, his mother'. (b2) **Atial** is a nomen, so '(son) of Espi Ati'. In both cases **caθas** is the recipient of the votive. Cristofani (1994) considers these interpretations more likely than (a) given that there are votive inscriptions in which the epithet of **caθa** is the noun **seχ** 'daughter' (see no. (46)).

(c) **Espial** is the head of the indirect object phrase; **atial** is in apposition to **espial**, and **caθas** is a dependent of **atial**: 'to Espi, mother of Catha'.

At this point it is not possible to decide what the person who dedicated the statue actually intended.

Bonfante 1994:269–70, REE 26, tav. XLVII–XLVIII; Bonfante and Bonfante 2002:145, no. 23, fig. 24; Cristofani 1994:270–1, REE 26.

(53) OA 3.9, origin unknown, 350–300 BCE
statue base (bronze)

1   cae siprisnies {i} tur
    ce hercles clen ce
    χa munis en cae lur
    χve : truta : ala : alp
5   nina luθs inpa lxχn/a

'Cae Siprisnies dedicated (this statue) to Herakles on behalf of his son as a *munis* (?). Cae shall not in/with/by means of the *lurkhva*(pl.) disturb (?) (it), donate (it), (or) *alpnina* (it) to the sacred area (?) *inpa likhna*.'

cae 'Cae', MASC PRAE, NOM/ACC; siprisnies 'Siprisnies', MASC NOMEN, 1ST GEN; turce 'dedicated', PAST ACT; hercles 'Herakles', THEO, 1ST GEN; clen 'son', ABL; ceχa 'on behalf of', POST; munis '?', NOM/ACC; en 'not', NEG; cae 'Cae', MASC PRAE, NOM/ACC; lurχve '?', INANIM PL, LOC; truta 'disturb (?)', JUSSIVE; ala 'donate', JUSSIVE; alpnina '?'; luθs 'sacred area (?)', 1ST GEN; inpa '?'; lxχn/a '?', NOM/ACC (?)

The text was inscribed on the front of the statue base in sinistroverse direction. The final letter in line 5 was inscribed on the back of the bronze.

The last word of the text (line 5, end) may be read as liχn/a. The reading adopted here, which is in large part that of Maras (2002), is different in many respects from the one published by Rix in ET (OA 3.9).

The division into word-forms in line 1 is based on that of Colonna 1987–88. Maras (2002:217–9) argues for a substantially different division, namely, **caesi prisniesi**, in which the names are inflected in the pertinentive case. The problem with this analysis is that it leaves **munis**, which appears to be the final word in the first sentence, as the subject of the verb **turce**. If this interpretation is accepted, it yields the only **turuce/turce**-text in the entire corpus in which the name of the person making the offering was not expressed. The choices are the following: (a) Divide the first line as per Colonna and assume the vertical stroke after **siprisnies** is an error, or (b) divide as per the proposal of Maras and admit that the text has unusual syntactic structure.

The meaning of **munis** cannot be determined, but if it is nominative/accusative in form it probably refers in some way to the object dedicated to Herakles. The second sentence begins with **en**, which is best taken as the negator 'not'. This part of the text refers to two (**truta, ala**) or possibly three (**alpnina**) activities (depending on whether or not **alpnina** is treated as a jussive verb) that Cae is prohibited from performing in or with the **lurχva**. The genitive **luθs** does not fit easily into the syntax of this sentence, particularly if **alpnina** is interpreted as a verb.

The final words of the text cannot be interpreted. It is tempting to think that **inpa** introduces subordinate syntax and is somehow connected to the relative word **in**, but exactly how is unclear.

Bonfante and Bonfante 2002:175, no. 61, fig. 52; Colonna 1987–88:345, REE 126; MacIntosh 1982:183, no. 72; Maras 2002a:213–38; Pallottino 1982:193–5.

(54) ETP 332, Volsinii (Bolsena), ca. 300 BCE
    statue (bronze)

   ecn : turce : avle : havrnas : tuθina : apana
   selvansl tularias
   'Aule Havrnas (and) his paternal community (?) dedicated this (statue) to Selvans Tularia.'

   ecn 'this', DEM PRO, ACC; **turce** 'dedicated', PAST ACT; **avle** 'Aule', MASC PRAE,
   NOM/ACC; **havrnas** 'Havrnas', MASC NOMEN, 1ST GEN; **tuθina** 'community (?)',
   NOM/ACC; **apana** 'paternal', NOM/ACC; **selvansl** 'Selvans', THEO, 2ND GEN;
   tularias 'of the boundary', THEO EPITHET, 1ST GEN

The inscription was incised in two lines. The first line runs from the chest of the bronze figure down along the right side of the torso and ends just above the knee. Line 2 was incised on the torso to the left of line 1. Both lines were written in sinistroverse direction. Line 1 has punctuation; line 2 does not.

The nomen of the dedicator was built upon the stem **havre-**, which is found also in the nomen **havrenies**, itself attested four times at Volsinii. The general structure of the text is clear, but the word **tuθina** is not. There are two possible syntactic analyses: (1) **Avle havrnas** and **tuθina apana** are the subjects of the verb **turce**. (2) **Tuθina apana** stands in apposition to the pronominal object **ecn** 'this (statue)'. **Tuθina** is found in two other inscriptions: Pe 3.3 and Co 3.6. In both, it is inflected in the ablative case and it functions as the agent of the verb. The meaning 'district, community' has been suggested as a possibility. An alternative semantic approach, in which **tuθina** refers to a votive gift of some type, works for this inscription but it does not make much sense in Pe 3.3 or Co 3.6.

Selvansl shows syncope of the syllable-final vowel -a- in the ending -al. The liquid serves as the nucleus of the final syllable. The adjective **tularias** was derived from the stem **tular-** 'boundary' or 'boundary-stone'.

Bonfante and Bonfante 2002:167, no. 50, fig. 46; Cristofani 1991a:148, no. 36; de Simone 1989b:346–51, REE 128; M. Morandi 1990:85–6, no. 29; Rendeli 1994:163–6; Steinbauer 1999:291–2, no. S52.

(55) ETP 238, Volcii, 300–250 BCE
   statue (bronze)

   ecn turce : pivi
   patrus : unial
   huinθnaias
   'Pivi Patrus dedicated this (statue) to Uni Huinthnaia.'

   ecn 'this', DEM PRO, ACC; turce 'dedicated', PAST ACT; pivi 'Pivi', MASC PRAE, NOM/ACC; patrus 'Patrus', MASC NOMEN, 1ST GEN; unial 'Uni', THEO, 2ND GEN; huinθnaias 'Huinthnaia', THEO EPITHET, 1ST GEN

The text begins at the lower portion of the tunic of the statue and runs vertically in three lines.

The praenomen **pivi** appears only in this inscription. **Patrus** is also a *hapax*, but it may be the base for the nomen **patruni**, which is attested on an inscription recovered from Perusia (Pe 1.407). The statue was dedicated to **uni huinθnaia**. The meaning of the modifier **huinθnaia** is unknown. Formally, it appears to be an adjective ending in -**ia**. For the formation compare **tular-ia-** in (54).

Cristofani 1991b:348–9, REE 69, tav. LVIII; Steinbauer 1999:292–3, S53.

(56) ETP 340, Volcii (?), 250–200 BCE
   club (bronze)

   1   cn · turce
        tite · uta
        ves · v · l ·
        hercles
   5   alpan ·
        'Tite Utaves, freedman of Vel, dedicated this (bronze statue)
        to Herakles as a thank offering (?).'

   cn 'this', DEM PRO, ACC; turce 'dedicated', PAST ACT; tite 'Tite', MASC PRAE,
   NOM/ACC; utaves 'Utave', MASC NOMEN, 1ST GEN; v, abbrev. of velus 'Vel', MASC
   PRAE, 1ST GEN; l, abbrev. of lautni 'freedman', NOM/ACC; hercles 'Herakles',
   THEO, 1ST GEN; alpan 'thank offering (?)', NOM/ACC

The inscription was incised in five lines on the grip of the club.
   The masculine nomen **utaves** is an Etruscan makeover of the Sabellic
name **uhtavis** (Oscan). The corresponding form in Latin is *Octavius*. For
the god Herakles as the object of votive dedications, see inscriptions (51)
and (53).

   Colonna 1989–90:894–8.

(57) ETP 279, origin unknown, 200–100 BCE
   statue (bronze)

   au · ceisina · la eiser
   aσ · θuflθas ·
   turce
   'Aule Ceisina, (son) of Larth, dedicated (this bronze statue) to the
   gods of Thufltha.'

   au, abbrev. of aule 'Aule', MASC PRAE, NOM/ACC; ceisina 'Ceisina', MASC NOMEN,
   NOM/ACC; la, abbrev. of larθal 'Larth', MASC PRAE, 2ND GEN; eiseraσ 'gods',
   ANIM PL, 1ST GEN; θuflθas 'Thufltha', THEO, 1ST GEN; turce 'dedicated', PAST
   ACT

The inscription was incised on the toga of the statue. It runs vertically
from the hem of the bottom of the toga in three lines. The final /s/ of
eiseraσ was written with the letter *sade*, but the final /s/ of **θuflθas** was
written with three-bar *sigma*.
   Eiseraσ is the plural genitive of the stem **ais-/eis-** 'god'. The syntactic
relationship between **eiseraσ** and **θuflθas** is problematic: are these two
words in a coordinate relationship or is **θuflθas** a dependent of **eiseraσ**?

If the latter, it is not clear what the 'gods of Thufltha' actually refers to. Are these divinities that are in some way associated with or subordinate to Thufltha? A similar phrase **aiseras θuflθicla** appears in another inscription (OA 3.5), but **θuflθicla** is even more difficult to interpret and so sheds little if any light on the interpetation of our phrase.

Wylin 2001:447–9, REE 115, tav. LIII, and 2002a:97.

(58) ETP 239, Volcii, 300 BCE
   small altar or base (bronze)

   truφu/n · peθu/nus · v · l/av
   lurmic/la · turc/e · XXX / cver
   'Truphun, freedman of Vel Pethunus, dedicated thirty (statues) to Lurmica as a votive offering (?).'

   truφun 'Truphun', MASC NAME, NOM/ACC; peθunus 'Pethunus', MASC NOMEN, 1ST GEN; v, abbrev. of **velus** 'Vel', MASC PRAE, 1ST GEN; lav, abbrev. of **lavtni** 'freedman', NOM/ACC; lurmicla 'the *lurmi* one', = lurmi '?', NOM/ACC + -cla 'the', DEM PRO, 2ND GEN; turce 'dedicated',PAST ACT; cver 'votive offering (?)', NOM/ACC

The inscription was incised on the four sides of the altar/base. Each side was divided into two registers. Line 1 was inscribed in the top register, line 2 in the bottom. The oblique line / is used to mark the sides of the base.

Truφun is the Etruscanized version of the Greek name Τρύφων. This name was transcribed in Latin as *Tryphon*, which was a common name for freedpersons of Greek descent. **lav** is an abbreviation of **lav(tni)**. **Lurmica** (appearing above as 2ND GEN **lurmicla**) is in origin a substantive consisting of two constituents: a stem **lurmi** of unknown meaning and a demonstrative pronoun -**ca**. A similarly formed theonym **lurmitla** (2ND GEN), derived by means of the demonstrative -**ta** rather than -**ca**, is also attested (OA 3.6). Presumably these formations refer to the same divinity, 'the *lurmi* one'. The cipher **XXX** may refer to the number of votive gifts offered to the god.

Benelli 1991:364–6, REE 82, tav. LVIII; Steinbauer 1999:286–7, S45.

(59) ETP 253, Pyrgi, 480–470 BCE
   Attic krater (ceramic)

   mi fuflunusra
   'I (am) of Fufluns.'

   mi 'I', 1ST PERS PRO, NOM; fuflunusra 'of Fufluns', NOM/ACC

The inscription was incised on the bottom of the foot of the krater. The direction of writing is sinistroverse. There is no punctuation.

Fuflunusra is an adjective derived from the base of the theonym **fufluns-**. The vowel -u is anaptyctic. The stem **fuflunus-** cannot be a genitive because s-stems, including theonyms, take *l*-inflection, cp. **selvansl** 'Selvans', 2ND GEN. The adjective suffix -ra, which had a meaning and a function similar to the suffix -na, was also used to produce the theonymic adjective **caθra** 'belonging to Catha, of Catha' from the stem **caθa-**.

Colonna (1997:95–6) suggests that the adjective should be seen as an epithet of the god Shuri, who is the target of many votive offerings at Pyrgi. The translation would be: 'I (am Shuri) Fuflunusra'. Maras (2001:377) follows this same approach.

Colonna 1997:94–8; Maras 2001:376–7, REE 37, tav. XLIV.

(60) ETP 329, origin unknown (South), 400 BCE
       incense burner (bronze)

   mi · selvansl · canlas
   'I (belong) to Selvans Canla.'

   mi 'I', 1ST PERS PRO, NOM; **selvansl** 'Selvans', THEO, 2ND GEN; **canlas** 'Canla'
   THEO EPITHET, 1ST GEN

The inscription was incised on the base of an incense burner.

The genitive ending of **selvansl** has been syncopated; -l serves as the vocalic element of the final syllable. The meaning of **canlas** cannot be determined, but it no doubt refers to a function or sphere of activity of the divinity Selvans, cp. **selvansl tularias** (54).

Cristofani 1993a:306–7, REE 32; Steinbauer 1999:265, S17.

(61) ETP 352, Caere, 350 BCE
       weight (bronze with lead nucleus)

           raθs · turmsal
           veluṣ ḷuvχmsal
           θusti · θui meθlmθ
           mu[n]sl[e]c [·] ims · epl
     5   macuni · hercles
           alpan tece IIC
           ei · ụtta θesca
           ac · penθa · [- (-)] · hu
           lave · zilci· la<r>θ
    10   ale · nulaθes ·

'To Rath (and) Turms. The *thusti* of Vel, (son) of Luvkhmes, here in the city and in the *munsla-*...as a thank-offering (?) in the *macun* of Herakles. *IIC*. One shall not...(?) Hulave *pentha* in the governorship of La(r)th Nulathe.'

raθs 'Rath', THEO, 1ST GEN; turmsal 'Turms', THEO, 2ND GEN; veluṣ 'Vel', MASC PRAE, 1ST GEN; ḷuvχmsal 'Luvkhmes', MASC PRAE, 2ND GEN; θusti '?', NOM/ACC; θui 'here', ADV; meθlmθ = meθlm 'city', LOC + -θ 'in', POST; mu[n]sl[e]c = mu[n]sl[e] '?', LOC + -c 'and', ENCLITIC CONJ; ims '?', 1ST GEN; epl '?', 2ND GEN; macuni '?', LOC; hercles 'Herakles', THEO, 1ST GEN; alpan 'thank offering (?)', NOM/ACC; tece '?'; IIC '?'; ei 'not', NEG; ụtta '?'; θesca '?'; ac '?'; penθa '?'; hulave 'Hulave', MASC NOMEN, NOM/ACC; zilci 'governorship', LOC; la<r>θale 'Larth', MASC PRAE, 2ND PERT; nulaθes 'Nulathe', MASC NOMEN, 1ST GEN

The text printed here is that of Facchetti and Wylin 2004. The inscription was incised in ten lines running horizontally around the body of the weight, which has the shape of an oval. The weight was found in an area known to be associated with a cult of Herakles.

Much about this inscription is impenetrable. However, some sections can be elucidated and in other sections word-forms can be identified. Line 1 gives the names of two divinities that are linked together asyndetically, Rath (and) Turms. Lines 2–6 refer to the act of dedicating the object on the part of Vel, son of Lavkhmes. Exactly how or why the divinities Herakles, Rath, and Turms are to be associated is not clear. The end of line 6 specifies the weight of the object. This seems a reasonable way to understand the ciphers IIC. Lines 7 and 8, which are introduced by the negator ei, form a prohibition, but it is impossible to say against what. The name of the magistrate who was responsible for insuring the accuracy of weights and measures is inscribed in lines 8–9, but his praenomen is illegible. The final phrase, lines 9–10, dates the votive by means of the name of official who served as governor (zilc). The head of the phrase is the locative form zilci. This is followed by the name of the official, la<r>θale nulaθes ('in the governorship of La(r)th Nulathe'). Since the two names do not agree in case, it is likely that the final -i of nulaθes<i> was omitted by the scribe.

Cristofani 1996:39–54, fig. 19–28; Facchetti and Wylin 2001:143–62 and 2004:389–96; Maggiani 1996:136, no. 69, 2001b:153 (with photo and facsimile), 2001d:67, 72, n. II.3, fig. 35, and 2002a:163–99.

(62) Co 4.1–4.5, Castiglione del Lago, late Neo-Etruscan period
   votive statue (bronze)

   mi celσ atial celθi
   'I (belong to) mother Cel in this (sanctuary).'

mi 'I', 1ST PERS PRO, NOM; celσ 'Cel', THEO, 1ST GEN; atial 'mother', 2ND GEN;
celθi 'this', LOC

The same text appears on five bronze statues recovered from a votive
waste site. The inscription was incised running in sinistroverse direction
down the front of the garment of the statue. There was no punctuation.

The final word of the inscription may be understood as the locative
of the demonstrative pronoun eca/ca. Celθi is an unusual form, however,
because the locative of this word does not otherwise have the vowel e as
part of its inflectional ending, cf. clθi, eclθi, calti. Steinbauer (1999:267)
prefers to see this form as a locative of the noun cel 'earth' (celθi < *celi-
tʰi 'on the earth'). Under this analysis the reference would be to the cult
site of the god.

Bonfante and Bonfante 2002:166, no. 49; Colonna 1976–77:45–62; Steinbauer 1999:266–7, S20.

Inscriptions on Commemorative Gifts

10.8 A particularly important category of inscription and one found
only in the Archaic period is the so-called commemorative gift inscription. Inscriptions of this type are known informally as *muluvanice*-
inscriptions after the form of the verb found in a majority of them. They
were incised on pieces of pottery, some quite fancy, that were exchanged
as gifts by members of the aristocratic classes. For the most part the gifts
and the inscriptions incised on them served a secular function. However,
as the vases recovered from the Portonaccio sanctuary at Veii show (see,
for example, (44)), they could also be used for votive purposes.

Two common syntactic structures are found in commemorative gift
inscriptions. The first uses the transitive verb **muluvanice** together with
mini, the accusative of the first personal pronoun, as direct object. Occasionally the recipient of the gift was indicated, always by a noun phrase
in the pertinentive case. In an alternative construction, the u-participle
mulu was used, a form built from the same verb root found in **muluvanice**.
In this construction the participle was passive in voice. The subject was
the nominative form of the first person pronoun, **mi**, and the name of the
donor or the recipient, depending on one's interpretation, appeared in
the pertinentive case. Examples of this type of inscription are very common at Caere and Veii, and are attested sporadically at other sites as well.

The most common order of the major constituents in the **muluvanice** inscriptions was Object-Verb-Subject, but Object-Subject Verb had a
fair number of representatives also. The violation of the canonical order,

Subject-Object-Verb, is best explained, as noted in §8.26, as due to movement of the object phrase or the entire verb phrase to the front of the sentence for focus or emphasis.

The lifespan of texts incised on commemorative gifts did not last much beyond the end of the sixth century BCE. This suggests that the social circumstances in which gift exchanges occurred had been altered or had disappeared entirely.

10.8.1 For discussion of this type of inscription as well as the votive dedication see Cristofani 1975b. Schirmer (1993) investigates the semantics of the verbs **muluvanice** and **turuce**.

(63) ETP 353, Ager Saenensis (Murlo), 650–625 BCE
fragment of kyathos (bucchero)

mi[ni velθ]ụr paiθịnaiẹ[(s) mu]lụ[vani]çe
'Velthur Paithinaies gave me (as a gift).'

mi[ni] 'me', 1ST PERS PRO, ACC; **[velθ]ụr** 'Velthur', MASC PRAE, NOM/ACC; **paiθịnaiẹ[(s)]** 'Paithinaie(s)', MASC NOMEN, NOM/ACC or 1ST GEN; **[mu]lụ[vani]çe** 'gave (as a gift)', PAST ACT

The inscription was inscribed in a spiral around the conical base of the kyathos. The direction of the writing was sinistroverse; there was no punctuation.

Restoration of the praenomen as **velθur** is relatively safe but not absolutely certain. However, the number of Etruscan praenomina ending in -ur is small and **velθur** is the most common name ending in these letters. The nomen **paiθịnaiẹ** was built by addition of the suffix -ie to an earlier patronymic formation ending in -na, *paithena- + -ie. It is impossible to determine whether the family name was inflected with a final -s or not. Both **paiθịnaiẹ** and **paiθịnaiẹ[s]** are possible restorations. The nomen **paiθịnaiẹ** may also be attested in inscription (64).

Colonna 2005a:331–2, REE 51; Wallace 2007.

(64) ETP 196, Caere, 650 BCE
kyathos (bucchero)

[mi]ni venel paiθina[s mu]luv<a>nice
'Venel Paithinas gave me (as a gift).'

[mi]ni 'me', 1ST PERS PRO, ACC; **venel** 'Venel', MASC PRAE, NOM/ACC; **paiθina[s]** 'Paithinas', MASC NOMEN, NOM/ACC or 1ST GEN; **[mu]luv<a>nice** 'gave (as a gift)', PAST ACT

The verb was spelled [mu]luvnice; the vowel in the antepenultimate syllable was omitted by the scribe. The inscription was incised in sinistro-verse direction in a spiral around the conical base of the cup. There is no punctuation.

The amount of space for letters in the damaged area following the nomen **paiθina[** is not made clear in the discussion by the editors Rizzo and Cristofani. It may be possible to restore the name as **paiθina[ie(s)]**, in which case one might speculate that this inscription and (63) above were commissioned by different members of the same family.

Rizzo and Cristofani 1993:1–10; Rizzo 2001:166–7; Wallace 2006.

(65) ETP 284, Colle di Val D'Elsa, ca. 600 BCE
double vase (bucchero)

mini m̥u̥l̥uvu̥nike pisna perkena
'Pisna Perkena gave me (as a gift).'

mini 'me', 1ST PERS PRO, ACC; m̥u̥l̥uvu̥nike 'gave (as a gift)', PAST ACT; pisna 'Pisna', MASC PRAE, NOM/ACC; perkena 'Perkena', MASC NOMEN, NOM/ACC

The inscription was written *scriptio continua* around the belly of one of the vessels. The writing was in sinistroverse direction.

The verb m̥u̥l̥uvu̥nike has medial u by vowel weakening. **Pisna** belongs to the category—a small one—of praenomina that ended in the suffix -*na*. The name **pesn(a)** is attested at Veii in an inscription from the late seventh century BCE (Ve 3.2); it is possible that this form is to be connected to **pisna** since the change of *i* to *e* seems to have taken place by the sixth century at Veii. The name is also attested in Neo-Etruscan texts as **peśna** (/s/ → /ʃ/ before /n/). The nomen is not common, though it is attested a few times in Neo-Etruscan inscriptions: **perkna** (Co 1.4), **percnal** (AS 1.125), **percnei** (Cl 1.720). It is also found in inscriptions recovered in areas outside of Etruria, including Liguria and Aemilia: **percnaz** (Li 2.9), **perknas** (Sp 2.45).

Martelli 1993:173–6.

(66) ETP 106, Veii, 600 BCE
aryballos (bucchero)

(a) mi θana.c.vilu.s. kanzina<ia>
venel muluva<ni>ce
.s.etiu
'I (am the aryballos) of Thanakhvil Kanzinai. Venel Setiu gave (me as a gift).'

(b) uθuzteθs vuvze
    'Vuvze, son of Odysseus'

mi 'I', 1ST PERS PRO, NOM; θana.c.vilu.s. 'Thanacvil', FEM PRAE, 1ST GEN;
kanzina<ia> 'Kanzinai', FEM NOMEN, 2ND GEN; venel 'Venel', MASC PRAE, NOM/
ACC; muluva<ni>ce 'gave (as a gift)', PAST ACT; .s.etiu 'Setiu', MASC NOMEN,
NOM/ACC; uθuzteθs 'of Uthuzteths (?)', NOM/ACC or 1ST GEN; vuvze 'Vuvze',
MASC PRAE, NOM/ACC

Inscription (a) was incised in three lines around the top portion of
the body of the aryballos. The direction of writing was sinistroverse. Inscription (b) was incised in dextroverse direction below inscription (a).
Differences in the forms of the letters point to different writers for (a)
and (b).

Inscription (a) has two utterances: a proprietary text (line 1) followed
by a commemorative dedication (lines 2–3). The nomen, kanzina, was
written in the nominative/accusative form. It should be a feminine genitive singular, *kanzinaia, in agreement with θana.c.vilu.s. The onomastic
phrase, venel setiu, is separated by the verb. The verb in text (a) was misspelled as muluvace; the form should be restored as muluva<ni>ce.

Maras (2002c) suggests that text (b) is the name of the artisan. Vuvze is a Sabellic loan, perhaps from Umbrian, cf. Umbrian vuvçis 'Lucius'.
Uθuzteθs may be a loan from Greek. Maras proposes Ὀδυσσείδης 'descendant of Odysseus', advancing the hypothesis that the artist bolsters his
reputation by claiming a heroic lineage. This is an interesting hypothesis, but by no means certain. As it stands, the inflectional form is unclear.
NOM/ACC and 1ST GEN are both possibilities. The style of the letter-forms
indicates that inscription (a) was inscribed by a different hand from inscription (b).

Colonna 1991:326–7, REE 42, tav. LXII; Di Gennaro 1991:325–6, REE 42, tav. LXII; Maras
2002b:237–9.

(67) ETP 128, Campania (Pontecagnano), 650–600 BCE
    cup (impasto)

mi mulu venelasi velχaesi rasuniesi
'I (was) given by/to/for Venel and Velkhae Rasunies.'

mi 'I', 1ST PERS PRO, NOM; mulu 'given', U-PART; venelasi 'Venel', MASC PRAE,
1ST PERT; velχaesi 'Velkhae', MASC PRAE, 1ST PERT; rasuniesi 'Rasunies', MASC
NOMEN, 1ST PERT

The inscription was inscribed around the foot of the cup in sinistroverse direction.

The most interesting aspect is the nomen **rasuniesi.** De Simone (2004a) argues for a connection with the Etruscan nominal stem **rasna-.** Underlying the attested stem **rasunie-** is an old adjective form **rasuna-* built to a stem **rasu-.** If **rasu-** was the original form of the word for 'people', then an adjectival derivative **rasuna-* would mean 'belonging to the people', of which **rasna-** would be a syncopated form.

Colonna 2002c:385–8, REE 84, tav. XXXIV; de Simone 2004a:73–96.

(68) ETP 186, Ager Faliscus (Mazzano Romano), 600–550 BCE
     fragment of handle kantharos or kyathos (ceramic)

leθaie mulvanice mi.ne vhulve.s.
'Lethaie Fulves gave me (as a gift).'

leθaie 'Lethaie', MASC PRAE, NOM/ACC; **mulvanice** 'gave (as a gift)', PAST ACT; **mi.ne** 'me', 1ST PERS PRO, ACC; **vhulve.s.** 'Vhulve', MASC NOMEN, 1ST GEN

The inscription was incised on the handle of a ceramic vase.

The name of the dedicator was **leθaie vhulves.** The constituents of the name have been pulled apart and placed at the beginning and the end of the sentence. Although the order of the constituents in this type of text varies, this arrangement, with the object pronoun positioned after the verb, is not common. The nomen, **vhulves,** was borrowed from Latin or, perhaps more likely given the findspot, from Faliscan. The praenomen **leθaie** ends in the Etruscan version of the Italic suffix **-io(s)*. The spelling of the 1st person pronoun **mi.ne** with final **e** is unusual (see §5.3).

Naso 1994:263–4, REE 22, tav. XLV.

Artisans' Inscriptions

10.9 Ancient Greek vase painters sometimes signed their work, typically by a short sentence of the type 'so and so made me' (μ' ἐποίησεν). Local artisans working in Italy (in Etruria, Latium, and Sabellic-speaking territories) produced native versions of this type of sentence.

In the Archaic period artisans' inscriptions adhered to the format of their Greek models. The inscriptions were of the "iscrizione parlante" type and the word order followed the pattern of other inscriptions of this variety: Object-Verb-Subject (name). The Etruscan verb that matched up with Greek ἐποίησεν was **zinace,** and it seems to have been used, at least originally, to refer to the production of ceramic. However, as inscription (5) shows, this verb could refer also to the work of a stonemason. Interestingly, **zinace** may have become moribund. It does not appear in Neo-

Etruscan texts, at least not with reference to the production or decoration of pottery (AT 1.121). Two artisans' inscriptions from the Neo-Etruscan period employ a different verb, namely **menece** (for which see §9.4).

Neo-Etruscan texts of this category sometimes bear only the name of the artisan, either in the nominative/accusative, e.g. **larθ** 'Larth' (Ru 6.3, 6.4, 6.5), **atrane** 'Atrane' (AV 6.4, 6.5), or in the genitive, e.g. **atraneσ** 'of Atrane' (Vc 6.7), **serturies** 'of Serturie' (Pe 6.7). A particularly interesting type, exemplified by (74), attests a construction in which the name of the artisan has the form of a derived adjective modifying the noun **acil** 'work, product'. Finally, the name of the artisan could appear in the pertinentive case. In these inscriptions the assumption is that the name is to be understood as the locative of a genitive, e.g. **atraneσi** 'in the (workshop) of Atrane' (Vt 6.2).

10.9.1 See Colonna 1975 for discussion.

(69) ETP 120, Veii, 600–500 BCE
     fragment of phiale (ceramic)

   mi<ni> ziṇace vel[θur a]ncinie.š.
   'Velthur Ancinies fashioned me.'

   mi<ni> 'me', 1ST PERS PRO, ACC; ziṇace 'fashioned', PAST ACT; vel[θur]
   'Velthur', MASC PRAE, NOM/ACC; [a]ncinie.š. 'Ancinies', MASC NOMEN, 1ST GEN

This inscription is the companion to a votive dedication (Rix, ET Ve 3.44). It was incised within the silhouette of the figure of an animal, and follows roughly the outline of the animal's torso. The final /s/ of the nomen has the form of a cross and it is punctuated with a single dot.

The nomen of the artisan, [a]ncinieš, is related to the feminine nomen **ancnei** found in a Neo-Etruscan inscription from the *Ager Tarquiniensis* (AT 1.27). The suggestion that this nomen was built to the praenomen **anχe** (Cr 3.16, Vs 1.91) does not take into account the differences in the quality of the medial stop consonant (unaspirated vs. aspirated).

Colonna 2002b:359–63, REE 73, tav. XXXIII.

(70) AV 6.1, Ager Vulcentanus, 600–575 BCE
     plate (bucchero)

   [θ]ụçer iṭane zinace ṭitenas
   'Thucer Titenas made this (vase).'

   [θ]ụçer 'Thucer', MASC PRAE, NOM/ACC; iṭane 'this', DEM PRO, ACC; zinace
   'made', PAST ACT; ṭitenas 'Titenas', MASC NOMEN, 1SG GEN

The inscription was incised in dextroverse direction.

The order of the constituents is unusual. The name of the artisan is distracted, one constituent standing at the beginning of the inscription, the other at the end. The form of the demonstrative, iṭane, is also unusual. It is not clear how to explain the final -e, though it has been suggested that this reflects the final -i of the original accusative ending -ni as attested in the accusative of the 1st person pronoun **mini**.

Colonna 1975:184, n. 19.

(71) ETP 304, origin unknown, 350–250 BCE
strigil (bronze)

men tite
'Tite made (this).'

men, abbrev. of **menece** 'made', PAST ACT; **tite** 'Tite', MASC PRAE, NOM/ACC

The text was stamped on the handle of a bath scraper (strigil). The letters are in dextroverse direction.

It seems likely that **men** is an abbreviation for **menece** 'made' and that the inscription is to be interpreted as 'Tite made (this)'. An alternative interpretation that takes **men** as an abbreviation of the object pronoun **mene**, 'Tite (made) me', is possible, though less attractive given the date of the inscription.

Rix 1995e:250–1, REE 20, tav. XXXIX; Stutzinger 1995:249, REE 20, tav. XXXIX.

(72) ETP 195, origin unknown, 300 BCE
strigil (bronze)

ae vipie cultces
'Aule Vipie Cultces'

ae, abbrev. of **aule** 'Aule', MASC PRAE, NOM/ACC; **vipie** 'Vipie', MASC NOM, NOM/ACC; **cultces** 'Cultces', MASC COGN, 1ST GEN

The text was stamped on the handle of the scraper. The direction of writing is sinistroverse.

The abbreviation **ae** stands for the praenomen **aule**. The cognomen **cultces** was inflected in the genitive.

Colonna 1994b:300–2, REE 51, tav. LIV.

(73) Vc 6.6, Vulci, 300–200 BCE
   lamp (ceramic)

ruvfies : acil
'the work of Ruvfie'

ruvfies 'Ruvfie', MASC NOMEN, 1ST GEN; **acil** 'work', NOM/ACC

The inscription was incised on the body of a ceramic lamp. The name of the artisan is Italic in origin, most likely coming from a Sabellic source.

(74) ETP 112, Vulci, 250–200 BCE
   fragment of small flask (ceramic)

putina ⋮ ceizra ⋮ acil
'a flask, the work of Ceise'

putina 'flask', NOM/ACC; **ceizra** 'of Ceisie', NOM/ACC; **acil** 'work', NOM/ACC

The inscription was stamped on the inside of the neck of the flask. The direction of writing is sinistroverse. Punctuation is in the form of four dots aligned vertically.

According to the most common interpretation, **ceizra** is an adjective formed from the name of the city Caere by means of the suffix **-ra**. Another interpretation, which we find more intriguing, takes **ceizra** as an adjective derived from the praenomen of the craftsman, *ceisie-ra-*.

Briquel 2002:324, REE 19, tav. XXXI.

(75) AV 6.9, Ager Vulcentanus, 150 BCE
   vase (ceramic)

pultuceσi
'in the (workshop) of Pultuce'

pultuceσi 'Pultuce', MASC NAME, 1ST PERT

The inscription was stamped in sinistroverse direction on the handle of the vase.

The name **pultuce** is of Greek origin. The workshop was under the direction of a Greek slave or freedperson.

Pfister 1964:274.

Boundary Markers

10.10 Boundary stones served two functions in the ancient world: to establish the boundaries of private or public property and to delimit the boundaries of sacred space. The word for 'boundary' or 'boundary stone' was **tular**. This word is often interpreted as a plural of a stem **tul-**, but that is morphologically unlikely because inanimate plurals should have the ending -χva. A better interpretation is to take **tular** as a derived form in -**ar** from a base **tul** (attested as **tvl** in several inscriptions from Africa, Af 8.1–8.8), which may mean 'boundary'. **Tular** would then refer specifically to a boundary stone, other boundary marker, or cippus.

Fourteen Etruscan inscriptions are headed by the term **tular**, all recovered from sites located in northeastern Etruria (Arretium, Clusium, Cortona, Faesulae, Perusia) or Aemilia (Spina) and all dating to the Neo-Etruscan period.

The word **luθ**, which appears in inscriptions (78) and (79), seems to mean 'sacred area (?)'. In religious contexts it refers to the boundaries of the *templum*.

10.10.1 See Lambrechts 1970 for a discussion of the word **tular** and of the Etruscan inscriptions that have this word.

(76) Pa 4.1, Padana (Feltre), 500 BCE
cippus (stone)

ki · aiser · tinia · ti[– – –] · sil<v>anẓ
'three gods: Tinia, Ti[?], Silvans'

ki 'three', NUM, NOM/ACC; aiser 'gods', ANIM PL, NOM/ACC; tinia 'Tinia', THEO, NOM/ACC; ti[– – –] '?'; sil<v>anẓ 'Silvans', THEO, NOM/ACC

The letter **v** in the word sil<v>anẓ was written as an **n**. The text was incised in sinistroverse direction.

The interpretation of this stone as a boundary marker is uncertain. However, it is tempting to think that it may have marked a precinct sacred to the three divinities mentioned in the text.

Tinia is the Etruscan divinity that is equivalent, roughly, to Greek Zeus/Latin Jupiter. The spelling sil<v>anẓ 'Silvans' is interesting for two reasons. First, the vowel in the first syllable is **i** rather than **e**, which is the vowel found in all other attestations of this name. If this is the original vowel, then the **e** in the other forms may be derived by vowel lowering since the vowel of the ultimate syllable is **a**. Secondly, the spelling of the final cluster as -**nz** suggests that an epenthetic -**t** was inserted between -**n** and -**s**, cp. English *sense* /sents/.

(77) Fs 8.3, Faesulae, Neo-Etruscan
cippus (stone)

tular · σpur
al · hil · pura
pum · vipśl
vχ · papr

'Boundary stone (?) of the community. *Hil* (and) *purapum* of Vipsha. Velkhe Paprsina.'

tular 'boundary', NOM/ACC; σpural 'community', 2ND GEN; hil '?', NOM/ACC; purapum '?', NOM/ACC or possibly = purapu '?', NOM/ACC + -m 'and', ENCLITIC CONJ; vipśl 'Vipsa', CITY NAME, 2ND GEN; vχ, abbrev. of velχe 'Velkhae', MASC PRAE, NOM/ACC; papr, abbrev. of paprσina 'Paprsina', MASC NOM, NOM/ACC

This inscription was written in sinistroverse direction on the face of the stone cippus.

According to most interpretations, the phrase **tular spural** refers to the 'boundaries (pl.) of the community'; but this view is unlikely, as discussed above in §10.10. Lines 2 and 3 are not particularly clear, but one might suppose that hil and **purapum** were conjoined, either by the final -m of **purapum** or asyndetically, and that vipśl depended on these two items. Line 4 is an abbreviation of the name of the magistrate under whose aegis the boundary stone was erected. This does not, unfortunately, bring us any closer to an interpretation for hil or **purapum**. Some have plausibly interpreted vipśl as the genitive of the name of the Etruscan city Faesulae. The name of the administrator responsible for erecting the cippus can be expanded as **velχe paprσina** or as **velχe paprnie**. The nomina are not attested in other incriptions from Faesulae or in other inscriptions from this area. However, the nomen **paparσina** is found in several inscriptions from Tarquinia, and the nomen **paparnie** is attested once at Vulci.

Cristofani 1991a:146–8, no. 35.

(78) ETP 286, Cortona, 200–150 BCE
cippus (stone)

luθcval
canθiśa
l

'(boundary) of the sacred areas (?) of the canthish'

luθcval 'sacred areas (?)', INANIM PL, 2ND GEN; canθiśal '?', 2ND GEN

The text was inscribed in three lines running from the bottom of the cippus toward the top. The direction of writing is sinistroverse. The final -*l* of the genitive **canθiśal** was written on a separate line (line 3).

The syntactic structure of the inscription is clear: plural genitive of the inanimate stem **luθ** + genitive of the stem **canθiś**. If the stem **canθ**- is to be connected with the verb form **canθce**, then it is conceivable at least that this form is an agent noun, as proposed by Wylin (2004:113–5). Unfortunately, there is no way of determining what the base **canθ**- means.

Agostiniani and Torelli 2001:129–39; Wylin 2004:113–5.

(79) Ar 4.3, Arretium, Neo-Etruscan
   cippus (stone)

    tinσ
    lut
    'sacred area (?) of Tinia'

    tinσ 'Tinia', 1ST GEN; lut 'sacred area (?)', NOM/ACC

The inscription was incised in sinistroverse direction on the face of the stone.

Rix (ET Ar 4.3) thinks that line 2 was written in dextroverse direction and for this reason reads **tul**. Steinbauer (1999:272) follows Rix's reading and understands the text to mean 'the boundaries (of the sanctuary) of Tinia'. However, since **lut** is an Etruscan word-form (here with deaspiration of the word-final aspirate), as inscriptions (53) and (78) show, there seems to be little reason to follow the reading of Rix. The meaning of **lut** is difficult to determine, but we may assume, as was assumed above, that it has some sort of geographical reference. Given that the dependent genitive is the name of a divinity, **tinσ**, it seems reasonable to interpet **lut** as 'sacred area' *vel sim.*

Steinbauer 1999:272, no. S28.

Tesserae hospitales

10.11 A *tessera hospitalis* was an object that served as a formal recognition of hospitable relations between inhabitants of different cities. Possession of a *tessera hospitalis* entitled the bearer to protection and assistance from his host.

Etruscan tesserae were generally incised on small pieces of ivory. The inscriptions were in the form of an "iscrizione parlante", in which the tessera declared who its owner was. Inscription (81) may also yield the name of the bearer's host. Inscription (82) belonged to a Carthaginian.

One could imagine that in cases where the bearer did not speak the language of his host the tessera was presented as a form of identification.

(80) AS 2.1, Ager Saenensis (Murlo), 600 BCE
  fragment of tessera (ivory)

  mi avil[eσ – – –] or mi avil[e – – –]
  'I (belong to) Avile…' or 'I (am) Avile…'

  mi 'I', 1ST PERS PRO, NOM; avil[eσ] 'Avile', MASC PRAE, 1ST GEN or avil[e] 'Avile',
  MASC PRAE, NOM/ACC

The ivory is in the form of head of a lion. The inscription was incised on the back of the tessera in sinistroverse direction without punctuation.

All discussions of this text assume that the praenomen is to be restored in the genitive. However, as (82) shows, the text could have simple predicative structure. We assume that the nomen was incised on the portion of the tessera that has been lost.

Cristofani 1975a:9–19, 1977:193–204; Cristofani and Phillips 1970:288–292, REE 1 (Poggio Civitate, Murlo, Siena); de Simone 1989c:25–38; Wallace to appear.

(81) La 2.3, Rome, 600–500 BCE
  plaque (ivory)

  araz silqetenas spurianas
  '(I am) Araz Silqetenas Spurianas.'

  araz 'Araz', MASC PRAE, NOM/ACC; silqetenas 'Silqetenas', MASC NOMEN,
  1ST GEN; spurianas 'Spurianas', MASC NOMEN, 1ST GEN

The ivory plaque is in the form of a crouching lion. The inscription was incised in sinistoverse direction on the back of the plaque. The spelling of the velar /k/ in **silqetenas** by means of *qoppa* rather than *gamma* is worthy of note. *Gamma* is the letter that typically precedes the letters i and e in Archaic Etruscan inscriptions produced in southern Etruria.

The praenomen **araz** is a regional variant—primarily in southern Etruria and Rome—of **aranθ**. Phonologically **araz** is /arat^s/. The final affricate seems to have arisen in oblique case forms, e.g. genitive **aranθia** /aran^{h}ja/, due to the assibilation of the dental stop by the following /j/. This form was then extended to all forms in the paradigm, including the nominative/accusative.

The major issue in this inscription is the function of the word **spurianas**. Since the second word, **silqetenas**, was formed by means of the suffix -na, which was used most commonly to form nomina, it must be the

nomen of the bearer of the tessera. But **spurianas** also has the form of a
nomen. One possibility offered in the literature (Pallottino 1979:324; de
Simone 1981:97) is that this is an adjective form serving as a patronymic.
Comparable forms may be cited from Faliscan, where adjectives derived
from praenomina by means of the suffix -*io*- served to form patronymics,
e.g. **Titos : Titio** 'son of Titus'. However, if **spurianas** has this function in
Etruscan, that is, if it means '(son) of Spurie', then this is the only inscription in which this usage has survived into the historical period. And if the
explanation advocated by Pallottino and de Simone is accepted, then one
must note that **spurianas**, which has s-genitive inflection, does not agree
with the head of the onomastic phrase, but with the nomen. A second
possibility, this one suggested by Messineo (1983:4), is that **spurianas** is
the nomen of the host of Araz Silqetenas. This idea is an interesting one,
but it is difficult to accept because there are no other examples in Etruscan where the name of the host was incised on a tessera. Still, one could
imagine that this tessera was produced for a specific occasion, when Araz
Silqetenas was at Rome and was hosted by a member of the Spurii.

The stem of the nomen **silqetenas** is a personal name *silqete. This appears to be an ethnic formation built with the suffix -**te/-θe**, cp. the em-
ployment of the ethnonym **velaθrite** 'person from **velaθri** (Volaterrae)' as
a nomen.

De Simone 1981:93–103; Messineo 1983:3–4; Pallottino 1979:319–25, REE 29.

(82) Af 3.1, Carthage, 600–500 BCE
plaque (ivory)

mi puinel kartazie ⫶ eḷṣ φ[- - - -]na
'I (am) Poenel Kartazie…'

mi 'I', 1ST PERS PRO, NOM; **puinel** 'Poenel', MASC PRAE, NOM/ACC; **kartazie**
'Kartazie', MASC NOMEN, NOM/ACC; **eḷṣ** '?'; **φ[- - - -]na** '?', NOM/ACC

The inscription was incised in sinistroverse direction on the back of
the tessera. The form of a wild boar was incised in relief on the front. The
text was divided into two segments by means of punctuation. Unfortunately, damage to the ivory precludes restoration and thus interpretation
of the second half of the text.

The ivory plaque was found in a tomb at Carthage. Presumably the
bearer carried the tessera from Italy back to Africa and it was buried with
him as part of his funerary cache. The name is of great interest because it
appears to be an Italic (Latin?) name attributed to or taken by the Punic
traveler. The personal name **puinel** may have been borrowed from a Latin

diminutive formation *poynelos*, for which one may cite Plautus' *Poenulus*. The stem *poyn-* could itself be of Punic origin. The lack of a final *-e* is somewhat surprising if borrowed from a Latin base. However, it is possible that **puinel** was remodeled on Etruscan names ending in *-l* such as **venel**. There is another possibility, namely a borrowing from a Sabellic language. In Sabellic word-final *-ls* developed regularly to *-l*. **Kartazie** is an ethnic name built from the stem for the city *Kartatsa* 'Carthage' by addition of the suffix **-ie**, possibly from a preform *kartats(a)-ie*.

Benveniste 1933:245–9; Rix 1995c:122–3.

(83) ETP 343, Gouraya (ancient Gunugu), Algeria, Neo-Etruscan
    disk (bronze)

    pumpun
    larθal
    '(tessera) of Pumpuna, (son) of Larth'

    pumpun, abbrev. of **pumpun(a)** 'Pumpuna', MASC NOMEN, NOM/ACC; **larθal** 'Larth', MASC PRAE, 2ND GEN

The text is in dextroverse direction, which is explained by the fact that the disk was made from a mold, on which the inscription was incised.

The inscription's main point of interest is its place of discovery. It was found in a necropolis of the city of Gouraya, Algeria. This tessera together with (82) attests to the persistent connections between Etruscans and Punic settlements in Africa. We assume that the bearer of the tessera was an Etruscan traveler or trader who died while abroad.

Briquel 2004:22–60, 2006a:5.

Tabulae defixionis

10.12 The curse inscription is an epigraphic type well attested throughout the ancient Mediterranean. Hundreds of examples exist in Greek and Latin; a few written in the Sabellic language Oscan have survived as well. It is not surprising then that this category of inscription should appear in Etruscan, although thus far the total number of examples is rather low, perhaps surprisingly so. Most of the Etruscan curse inscriptions were recovered from tombs in the environs of Volaterrae and Populonia. Three inscriptions, Vt 4.1, 4.4, and 4.6, consist of the names of those to be cursed. Vt 4.2 and Po 4.1 provide a few lines of text in addition to the names. Unfortunately, parallel texts in Latin, Greek, and Oscan provide little or no valuable insight into the meaning of the Etruscan.

(84) ETP 27, Latium (Ardea), Neo-Etruscan
lamina (lead)

vel uθraσ |
mlaχ
'Vel Uthra, (a) good (man)'

vel 'Vel', MASC PRAE, NOM/ACC; uθraσ 'Uthra', MASC NOMEN, 1ST GEN; mlaχ
'good', NOM/ACC

The inscription was incised on a sheet of lead in sinistroverse direction. The vertical stroke following the nomen in line 1 is either an error or it serves to set the name off from the adjective mlaχ in line 2.

The inscription was discovered at Ardea in the territory of Latium. It was buried in a waste dump adjacent to a temple. The spelling of the final /s/ of the nomen by means of *sade* indicates that the scribe was following the northern style of writing. The editor notes that the nomen uθraσ may be attested in a proprietary inscription from environs of Tarquinia (AT 2.4), utres, but this connection does not account for the phonological distinction between -θ and -t (neutralization of stops before sonorants?).

The function of this curse tablet is also unclear. Presumably we have the name of the person to be cursed, but we do not know why this person is described as mlaχ 'good'.

Colonna 2003:342–7, REE 55, tav. XXXI.

(85) Po 4.4, Populonia, 200–100 BCE
lamina (lead)

śθ · velσu · lθ · c · lθ . ve[lσu ·] inpa · θapicun
θapintaσ · aθ · velσu / lθ c / lθ · velσu
lθ · c · lś · velσu / lθ c / lθ · σuplu
aθ · σuplụ · lś · haśmuni au
5   śθ · clueśtẹ · ạθ · clueśte · vl · pḷunσ
θancvil · velσui · cẹọ · zeriσ · imσ · śe
mutin · aprenσaiσ · inpa · θapicun ·
θapintaiσ . ceuσn . ịnpa · θapicun · i
luu · θapicun · ceσ · zeriσ
10   titi · śetria · lautnita
'Shethre Velsu, son of Larth; Larth Velsu; *inpa θapicun θapintaσ*;
Arnth Velsu, son of Larth; Larth Velsu, son of Larth; Larish
Velsu, son of Larth; Larth Suplu; Arnth Suplu; Larish Hashmuni,
(son) of Aule; Shetre Clueshte; Arnth Clueshte; Vel Pluns[;
Thancvil Velsui; from/by this *zeri*…from/by this *zeri*. Shetria
Titi, freedwoman.'

Repeated names and abbreviations are glossed only once. śθ, abbrev. of śeθre, MASC PRAE, NOM/ACC; velσu 'Velsu', MASC NOMEN, NOM/ACC; lθ, abbrev. of larθal 'Larth', MASC PRAE, 2ND GEN; c, abbrev. of clan 'son', NOM/ACC; inpa '?'; θapicun '?'; θapintaσ '?'; aθ, abbrev. of arnθal 'Arnth', MASC PRAE, 2ND GEN; lś, abbrev. of lariś 'Larish', MASC PRAE, NOM/ACC; σuplụ 'Suplu', MASC NOMEN, NOM/ACC; haśmuni 'Hashmuni', MASC NOMEN, NOM/ACC; au, abbrev. of auleσ 'Aule', MASC PRAE, 1ST GEN; clueśtẹ 'Clueshte', MASC NOMEN, NOM/ACC; vl, abbrev. of vel 'Vel', MASC PRAE, NOM/ACC; pḷunσ abbrev. of 'Pluns[(?)', MASC NOMEN, NOM/ACC; θancvil 'Thancvil', FEM PRAE, NOM/ACC; velσui 'Velsui', FEM NOMEN, NOM/ACC; cẹσ 'this', DEM PRO, 1ST ABL; zeriσ '?', 1ST ABL; imσ... iluu θapicun '?'; ceσ 'this', DEM PRO, 1ST ABL; titi 'Titi', FEM NOMEN, NOM/ACC; śetria 'Shetria', FEM PRAE, NOM/ACC; lautnita 'freedwoman', NOM/ACC

The text was incised in sinistroverse direction on a semicircular sheet of lead. Although the circumstances surrounding the recovery of the lamina are not particularly clear, it seems that the lead sheet was found in a tomb.

An interpretation of the text as a whole is not possible. Almost all of the words, aside from the names, are unknown. The words that are attested in other texts, e.g. inpa and zeri, are uninterpretable. In terms of structure the text seems to have three parts: (1) a list of names (lines 1–5); (2) the content of the curse (lines 5–9); and (3) the name of person who contracted to have the curse composed.

A freedwoman by the name of Shetria Titi had the curse composed against members of the Velsu, Suplu, Hashmui, and Clueshte families. Most of the targets are from the family of Larth Velsu, namely, him, his sons Larth, Larish, Arnth and Larth, and his daughter Thancvil. The remaining targets come from four families: the brothers Arnth and Larth Suplu; the brothers Shethre and Arnth Clueshte; Larish Hashmuni; and Vel Pluns[(?). All of the targets of the curse are male, except for Thancvil Velsui.

Three sections of text are introduced by the word inpa, which has long been suspected of being an element of subordination. Two sections (lines 1–2, 7–8) repeat the same formula: inpa θapicun θapinta(i)σ. The third section echoes the beginning of the first two: inpa θapicun iluu θapicun ceσ zeriσ. The fact that θapicun and θapicun θapinta(i)σ are repeated elements brings to mind the repetitive phrases found in curse tablets in the Graeco-Roman world, e.g. 'bind with this binding spell'. Nevertheless, it is difficult to accept the idea that inpa θapicun θapinta(i)σ should be translated 'whom I curse by/after cursing (them)' because, among other reasons, the morphological structure of θapicun and θapinta(i)σ cannot be determined with any degree of security.

Steinbauer 1999:310–1, S68.

(86) Vt 4.2, Volaterrae, Neo-Etruscan
    lamina (lead)

θuσuθur
σelaśva
θlu θupit
aisece tati
'O *Thusu* gods (?), the *sela* ones, *thlu* (?) in the *thup* (?). Tati *aisece* (this).'

θuσuθur 'Thusu gods (?)', ANIM PL, NOM/ACC; σelaśva = σela- '?', NOM/ACC (?)
+ -śva 'the', DEF ART, NOM PL; θlu '?', IMPV; θupit = θupi '?', LOC (?) + -t 'in, on',
POST; aisece '?', PAST ACT; tati 'Tati', MASC or FEM NOMEN, NOM/ACC

This inscription was found at the entrance of the same tomb in which the curse inscriptions Vt 4.1 and Vt 4.2 were found. Vt 4.2 and Vt 4.3 were folded and enclosed within Vt 4.1. The ensemble was then bound with a strip of lead. The writing in this inscription appears to have been done by two scribes.

θuσuθur is an animate plural noun formed with the collective suffix -θur. σelaśva agrees in case and number with θuσuθur. It is a nominative plural of a substantive built by affixing the pronominal clitic article -śva to a nominal stem. Line 3 probably begins with an imperative form θlu. The next word, θupit, is difficult, but it looks to be a locative formation to a stem θupi plus the enclitic postposition -t. If θlu is an imperative form, it is possible that the first two words of the inscription are to be interpreted as vocatives. The text would be an invocation to a group of divinities (θuσuθur) having the attribute *sela*-.

Tati is a name, either masculine or feminine. Based on form it is impossible to tell. The verb in the last line is a *hapax*. It is tempting to see it as a denominal formation built ultimately from the stem aise- 'god'.

Captions

10.13 Inscriptions that served as captions or as labels to paintings or engravings on mirrors, vases, and the walls of tombs consisted for the most part of names referring to men and women, divinities, or mythological and heroic figures. On a few occasions longer inscriptions accompanied the paintings or engravings and served as commentary on the scene depicted on the object in question (see §1.14). The scenes themselves provide a general framework for the interpretation of the text.

(87) Vs 7.25, Volsinii, 325–300 BCE
   wall of tomb

   zatlaθ : aiθas
   'guard of Aitha (Hades)'

   zatlaθ 'guard', NOM/ACC; aiθas 'Aitha', 1ST GEN

The text was painted on the wall of a tomb near the heads of two armed figures. They are only partially visible. The rest of the scene has faded from view.

The meaning of **zatlaθ** depends on whether or not one accepts an etymological connection with the Latin word *satelles* (see §9.13).

(88) Ta S.8, Tarquinia, 300 BCE
   mirror (bronze)

   óeθlans   uni   trepu
   'Shethlans, Uni, Trepu (worker ?)'

   óeθlans 'Shethlans', NOM/ACC; uni 'Uni', NOM/ACC; trepu 'Trepu', NOM/ACC

The scene incised on the reverse of the mirror depicts the liberation of Hera by Shethlans (Hephaistos). The central figure is the goddess Uni, who sits upon a throne. The god Shethlans attends her. On the right side of the mirror is a crouching figure that has a hammer and chisel in hand. The caption above the head of this figure is **trepu**, which Steinbauer (1993:294-6) has interpreted as a loan from Umbrian *trebo:n-*, possibly meaning 'worker, blacksmith'.

   Steinbauer 1993:294–6.

11 TABULA CORTONENSIS

Introduction

11.1 The inscribed bronze tablet known as the *Tabula Cortonensis* (TCo; ETP 74) is arguably the most significant find for Etruscan language studies in the past quarter-century. The archaeological context in which the TCo was recovered is unknown and the circumstances surrounding its discovery are unclear. According to the workman who brought the artifact to the attention of the authorities, it was recovered in the area of Camucia to the southwest of the city of Cortona, but this report cannot be confirmed. The tablet was turned over to authorities in 1992. However, the official unveiling did not take place until June 30, 1999, and the text was not officially published until February of 2000, when Luciano Agostiniani and Francesco Nicosia released their authoritative edition. Since the publication of the *editio princeps* there has been a steady stream of scholarly articles focusing on the readings of the damaged portions of the inscription, on individual word-forms found in the text, and on linguistic analyses of sections of the text. So much important work has been published by now that an overall comparative review of analyses and interpretations is no longer possible in a single chapter. Nevertheless, we think it is worthwhile to take stock of where we stand in terms of the analysis of words and the overall interpretation of this important inscription.

11.1.1 For discussion of the circumstances surrounding the discovery of the inscription and its delivery to authorities see Nicosia 2002.

The Inscription

11.2 The bronze tablet was recovered in reasonably good shape even though it was broken into eight pieces in antiquity. Seven of the pieces survived. Only the bottommost portion of the tablet on the left side (facing side A) is missing. This portion of the text, which amounts to seven half-lines, is a list of names, so the loss of this piece has little significant impact on the interpretation of the text. We do not know why the text was broken into pieces. We speculate that the bronze was destroyed and buried once the agreement or contract stipulated in the text ceased to be binding.

A handle was affixed to the top of the tablet by means of two bronze nails. The first two lines of text were incised around the spot where the handle was attached, suggesting that it was in place or that space was allotted for it before the text was cut. The tablet was probably suspended by means of a cord so that both sides could be read. The material on which the text was incised was expensive. We conclude that the text must have been important enough to require that it be housed in a repository for safekeeping.

11.3 The inscription was incised on both sides of the bronze plaque. Two scribes were responsible. Side A holds thirty-two lines of text; side B holds eight. The letter-forms on the inscription are characteristic of those found on other inscriptions from Cortona. They point to a date of incision toward the end of the third century BCE. Word-forms were separated from one another by a single point set at mid-line level. A special sign, roughly in the form of a Z, was used to divide the major sections of the text into subsections (see §11.5).

A rough count yields a total of 202 word-forms (excluding enclitics and postpositions). A large percentage of these are names. If these are eliminated from the count, the total number is eighty-two. If the different inflectional forms of the same word are counted as single items and if words that are repeated are counted once, the total number of words (= dictionary entries) is fifty-eight. The length of the text puts the TCo in third place after the *Liber Linteus* and the *Tabula Capuanus*.

11.3.1 Background information on the inscription is discussed in Agostiniani and Nicosia 2000:12–30. The text of the TCo cited here is the one provided by Maggiani 2001a:95–6. It does not differ dramatically from the text of the *editio princeps* (Agostiniani and Nicosia 2000:31–8), but it does include improvements in the reading of some sections, especially as regards punctuation.

11.4 The most interesting paleographic feature, and the one that links this inscription with others found in Cortona and environs, is retrograde *epsilon*, which is transcribed as ê. This letter represents a vowel sound that was distinct from the sound represented by a "normal" *epsilon*, that is to say, by an *epsilon* facing in the direction of writing. In the TCo, the sounds represented by retrograde *epsilon* come from different historical sources. They include the following:

(1)   Sources of ê in the TCo

    (a) the diphthong *ay found in locative case constructions, e.g. śparzê-te < *ʃparzay-

    (b) the diphthong *ey found in ablative case constructions, e.g. śparzêσ-tis < *ʃparzeys-

    (c) the diphthong /ay/ in words borrowed from Sabellic languages or from Latin, e.g. ścêvaσ borrowed from /skaywa-/

    (d) the contraction of sequences of /e/, e.g. cên < *keen < *kehen;

    (e) the vowel /e/ in the initial syllable of words, including native words, e.g. vêl, êliunts, êprus, as well as in loanwords from Sabellic languages and/or Latin, e.g. pêtru, pêtruni, sêtmnal.

Epsilon and retrograde *epsilon* are found in roughly the same phonetic environments, e.g. in word-initial syllables, **cenu** vs. **cên**. Since this is so, the mid-vowel sounds represented by the two *epsilons* were virtually certain to be distinct sounds in the variety of Etruscan spoken at Cortona.

11.4.1 See Agostiniani and Nicosia 2000:46–52 for discussion of the phonological features of the two sounds.

Points of Agreement

11.5 Scholars agree that the TCo is a private legal document and that it involves a transaction between two parties, namely, Pêtru Shcêvas and two members of the Cushu family, Vêlkhe and Larish. Most investigators also believe that the nature of the transaction concerned the purchase or the sale of property or plots of land, measurements of which were specified in the text. Other aspects of the text about which there is general agreement are listed in (2).

(2)   Points of agreement concerning the TCo

    (a) The text is organized into three sections by means of spacing. Sections II and III begin at lines 18A and 2B respectively, in each instance following a list of names that come to a conclusion before the end of the line (lines 17A and 1B). A new section starts at the beginning of the next line. Within sections of the text subsections are set off by means of a special sign in the form of a Z (lines 7A, 8A, 14A, and 23A). By this reckoning the inscription has three major sections. Section I has four subsections, I.1–4; section II has two subsections, II.1–2; and section III has one subsection.

(b) Section I refers to the content of the agreement. This section of the text is the most obscure because it contains new vocabulary items for which we cannot securely determine meanings. As a result there are major disagreements about its interpretation. Section II refers to the copying or the registration of the agreement on a tablet. Section III gives the official date of the deposition of the document.

(c) The inscription has three lists of names. List 1 follows the word **nuθanatur** and most likely designates those who served as guarantors of the agreement. List 2, which follows the introductory phrase **êprus ame**, refers to the two parties involved in the agreement, the Cushu brothers and Pêtru Shcêvas. List 3 begins with the words **cnl nuθe malec**. The names of the luminaries that follow include the public official (**zilaθ meχl raσnal**), **lart cucrina lauśiśa**.

(d) Lines 18–19, beginning with **cên zic ziχuχe** 'this document was written', refer to the copying or to the recording of the agreement. The concluding section, which begins at line 2, side B, with the phrase **zilci larθal cuśus titḷnal lariśalc śaliniσ auleśla** 'in the governorship of Larth Cushu, son of Titlnai, and Larish Shalini, the (son) of Aule' marks the official date of the deposition of the/a tablet. A fourth set of names brings the document to a conclusion.

(e) There is general agreement about the meanings of the following vocabulary in the text: **zic** 'document, text', **ziχuχe** 'was written', **cên** 'this', **clan** 'son', **in** 'which' (inanimate relative pronoun), **zilaθ meχl rasnal** 'governor of the public territory', **zilci** 'governorship', **ame** 'is', **cesu** 'lies', **θui** 'here', **puia** 'wife', **śa** 'four', **σar** 'ten', **zal** 'two'. It also seems clear that the meanings attributed to the following new words are relatively secure, although it must be noted that they are not accepted by all investigators: **śparza** 'tablet', **θuχ** 'house, depository', **śuθiu** '(was) placed', **male** 'observes', **nuθe** 'listens to', **nuθanatur** 'auditors'.

11.5.1 For the division of the text into subsections see Facchetti 2000a:59 and 2002c:88, and Maggiani 2001a:96.

Analysis and Interpretation

11.6 Analysis and interpretation of the text are by subsections (see §11.5). The format is roughly the same as the one employed in Chapter 10.

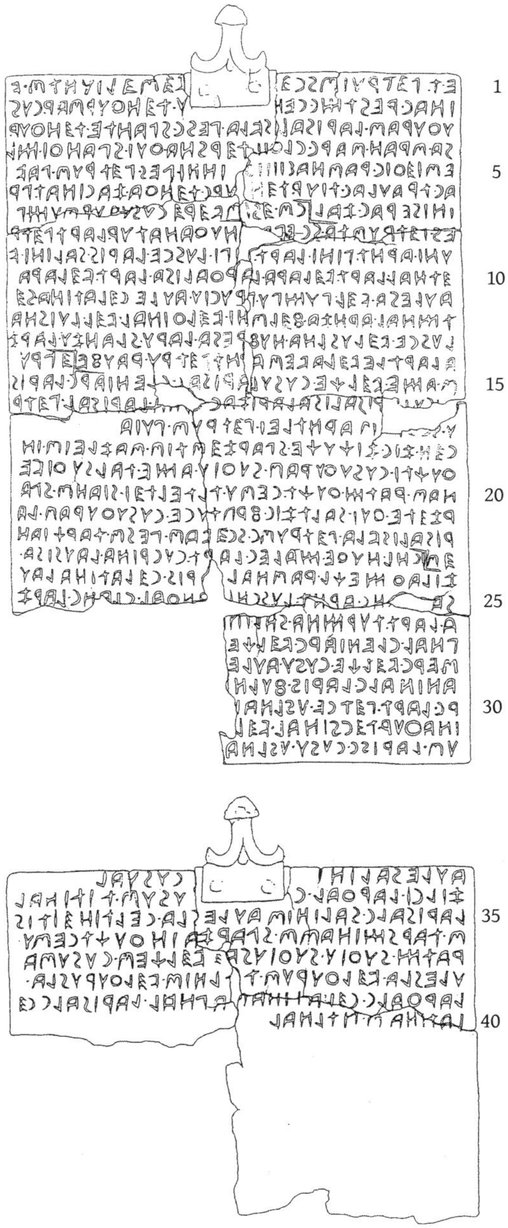

Fig. 11.1. Tabula Cortonensis. Bonfante and Bonfante 2002:179.

The text is given first; word-by-word analysis, commentary, and notes
follow. A provisional translation for the entire tablet is provided in §11.7.

11.6.1 The most thoughtful interpretations of the TCo, both global and partial, are the following: Adiego 2005; Agostiniani and Nicosia 2000:81–114; Facchetti 2000a:59–88 and 2002c:87–92;
Maggiani 2001a:94–114 and 2002c:65–75; Rix 2000:11–31 and 2002a:77–86; Scarano Ussani and
Torelli 2002; and Wylin 2002a and 2006. These interpretations all begin with the assumption that
the TCo is a legal document regarding a transaction or an agreement about the transfer or sale
of property. For an entirely different interpretation, which has garnered little scholarly support,
see de Simone 1998b and 2001–02.

Section I.1

e{}t · pêtruiσ ścê [*vacat*] vêσ êliuntσ · v
inac · restmc · cen [*vacat*] u · tênθur σar · cuś
uθuraσ · lariśaliśvla · peśc · śpante · tênθur ·
śa · σran · σarc · clθil · têrśna · θui · śpanθi · ml
5   eσiêθic · raσna SIIII> [*vacat*] inni · peś · pêtruσ · pav
ac · traulac · tiur · tênθurc · tênθa · zacinat · pr
iniśerac · zal

Line 1: **e · t** was written for **et**.

e{}t 'thus, so', ADV; **pêtruiσ** 'Pêtru', MASC PRAE, 1ST ABL; **ścêvêσ** 'Shcêvas',
MASC NOMEN, 1ST ABL; **êliuntσ** '?', 1ST ABL; **vinac** = **vina** '?', NOM/ACC + -c 'and',
ENCLITIC CONJ; **restmc** = **restm** '?', NOM/ACC + -c 'and', ENCLITIC CONJ; **cenu**
'sold, ceded (?)', U-PART; **tênθur** '?' (unit of measurement?), NOM/ACC; **σar**
'ten', NUM, NOM/ACC; **cuśuθuraσ** 'Cushu family', ANIM PL, 1ST GEN; **lariśaliśvla**
= **lariśal** 'Laris', MASC PRAE, 2ND GEN + -**iśvla** 'the', DEF ART, PL, 2ND GEN; **peśc** =
peś '?', NOM/ACC + -c 'and', ENCLITIC CONJ; **śpante** = **śpan-** 'plain', LOC + -**te** 'on',
POST + LOC; **śa** 'four', NUM, NOM/ACC; **σran** '?', NOM/ACC (unit of measurement); **σarc** = **σar** 'ten', NUM, NOM/ACC + -c 'and', ENCLITIC CONJ; **clθil** '?';
têrśna '?', NOM/ACC; **θui** 'here', ADV; **śpanθi** = **span-** 'plain', LOC + -**θi** 'on',
POST; **mlesiêθic** = **mlesiê-** '?', LOC + -**θi** 'on', POST + -c 'and', ENCLITIC CONJ;
raσna 'public', NOM/ACC; **SIIII>** '14.5'; **inni** 'which', INANIMATE REL PRO, ACC (?);
peś '?', NOM/ACC; **pêtruσ** 'Pêtru', MASC PRAE, 1ST GEN; **pavac** '?', NOM/ACC + -c
'and', ENCLITIC CONJ; **traulac** = **traula** '?', NOM/ACC + -c 'and', ENCLITIC CONJ; **tiur**
'?', NOM/ACC; **tênθurc** = **tênθur** '?' (unit of measurement?), NOM/ACC + -c
'and', ENCLITIC CONJ; **tênθa** 'measures (?)', JUSSIVE; **zacinat** '?', NOM/ACC;
priniśerac '?', NOM/ACC; **zal** 'two', NUM, NOM/ACC

Section I.1 is difficult for all of the usual reasons: unfamiliar vocabulary, uncertainty about divisions into phrases and clauses, and uncertainty about the syntactic function of word-forms. We favor a division
into four syntactic units: (1) lines 1–3, from **e{}t** to **lariśaliśvla**; (2) lines

3–4, from **peśc** to **clθil**; (3) lines 4–5, from **têrśna** to **SIIII>**; and (4) lines 5–7, from **inni** to **zal**.

The basic structure of clause 1 seems clear: ablative + subject phrase + the u-participle **cenu** + nominative/accusative of extent + genitive phrase. The ablative is best taken as an agent phrase in construction with **cenu**, which must then be given a passive reading. Two rather different meanings have been offered for this word: 'to cede, sell' and 'to acquire, obtain, buy'. The meaning selected for this word colors the interpretation of the entire section and thus the agreement as a whole.

(3) Translation of **cenu**

   (a) 'Subject (was) **ceded** by Pêtru Shcêvas to the Cushu.'
   (b) 'Subject (was) **obtained** by Pêtru Shcêvas from the Cushu.'

Note that the meaning attributed to **cenu** delimits the syntactic function of the genitive phrase **cuśuθurao lariśaliśvla** (clause one). In (a), the genitive has indirect object function; in (b), the genitive indicates separation. We prefer analysis (a), because there is not sufficient evidence that the Etruscan genitive could indicate source or separation, a function reserved for the ablative.

The subject phrase in clause one is **vinac restmc**. Most commentators believe that these words refer to property or to land of a certain type. The claim that **vina** means 'vineyard' is based on a formal connection to **vinum** 'wine'. This view, grounded as it is in a formal similarity to a borrowed lexical item (see §9.9), must be regarded with the utmost caution.

The word **tênθur**, which is modified by the number **oar** 'ten', refers to something that is countable. If the object of the transaction is land, which can be counted if organized into units of measurement, the phrase could refer to ten units (= acres *vel sim.*) of property. At this point it is worth emphasizing the fact that **tênθur** cannot be an animate plural because it does not refer to humans or animate beings. It is nominative/accusative in form and functions syntactically to signal a phrase indicating the extent of the property being ceded or obtained.

The word **peś**, which opens clause two, may also be a word for a particular type of property. It has been suggested that the word meant 'farm, country estate', and this seems to fit most of the contexts in which the word is found. Like **vina** and **restm**, **peś** too refers to something that can be divided into units. The **peś** at issue has an extent of **tênθur śa** and **oran oar**, that is to say, four acres and ten **oran**. If the interpretation of the cipher **SIIII>** as 14.5 is correct, then it is possible that ten **oran** were equal to half of an acre. The phrase at issue would then mean roughly '4.5 acres'.

The meaning of **clθil** is unclear, but it appears to be a 2nd genitive formed to the stem **clθ-**.

Clause three is a nominal sentence. The subject is **têrśna**, which is a *hapax*. The predicate adjective is **raσna** 'public'. **Têrśna** may also refer to a piece of land. The cipher SIIII>, which appears in sentence-final position, would then refer to the size of the **têrśna**. It is the same in extent as the acreage acquired by/from the Cushu.

Clause four is introduced by the word **inni**, which appears to be a form of the inanimate relative pronoun **in**. **Inni** is usually interpreted as an accusative ending in -ni (cf. **mini**, 1ST PERS PRO, ACC), but there is reason to be suspicious of this interpretation. There is no evidence that the relative pronouns inflected for case. Nor is there any evidence for archaic morphological features in this text. Moreover, even assuming that the identification of **inni** is correct, its usage as a relative is not obvious. The fact that it appears after what is likely to be a syntactic break suggests that it begins a new clause. In clause-initial position **inni** is not likely to have prototypical relative function. Indeed, most commentators assume that it introduces an adverbial phrase of some sort and that it governs the word **peś**, and perhaps also **pava** and **traula**, particularly if the word-final -c of these words is taken to be the coordinating conjunction and not the adjective suffix -(a)c. A translation along the lines of 'as for (with respect to) the *pesh* of Pêtru, and the pava and the *traula* ...' covers the ideas that are offered by most commentators.

The interpretation of **inni** dictates the organization of the rest of this clause. The main verb is **tênθa**. It is formed on the same base as the nominal form **tênθur**; it has the form of a jussive. If **tênθur** refers to a unit of measurement, then the verb **tênθa** must have something to do with making or checking measurements. The subject phrase is **zacinat priniśerac zal**, whose interpretation is problematic. **Zacinat** ends in the suffix -*at*, which is the local form of the well-known agent noun suffix -*aθ*, cf. **zilaθ**. **Zacinat** refers to a person, perhaps a public official, who is responsible for checking or verifying the extent of the land involved in the agreement. The difficulty concerns the interpretation of **priniśerac**. (**Zal** is the number two.) There are three possibilities: (1) it is an adjective built by means of the suffix -*(a)c*; (2) it is an animate plural noun followed by an enclitic conjunction -**c**; (3) it is an inanimate plural noun followed by an enclitic conjunction -**c**.

Of the three possibilities, (1) is least problematic. However, if **priniśerac** is an adjective form in -*(a)c* modifying **zacinat**, the number **zal** cannot belong to the noun phrase because the head, which is animate, is unmarked for plural. It must instead be treated as an adverb even though it has no formal adverbial marking. Fortunately, there are other examples of numbers without adverbial suffixation functioning as adverbs, e.g. **ci** 'three times'. (Adverbs derived from numbers end in the suffix -*z(i)*, e.g. **ciz** 'three times'.) Perhaps the **zacinat** performed the act of **tênθa** two times as a way of verifying the accuracy of his work.

Assuming that **peś, pava**, and **traula** form part of an adverbial construction, the phrase **tiur tênθurc** is free to serve as the object of the verb. Exactly how this verb phrase is to be translated and what it means is not clear, particularly since **tiur** is generally thought to mean 'month'. We may suppose that the **zacinat** had a finite amount of time within which to verify the measurements of the lands in question.

The general thrust of this section, which is agreed upon by most commentators, concerns the purchase or acquisition of land on the part of the Cushu.

Section I.1.1 For the debate about the meaning of **cenu** see Facchetti 2000a:62–70 and 2003: 202–7, Maggiani 2001a:97–8 and 2002c:69–70, and Wylin 2002a:93 and 2006. Agostiniani and Nicosia (2000:98–9) mention the claim of Giannecchini that the word **vina** may mean 'vineyard'. Facchetti (2000a:61 n. 342) speculates that **vinac restmc** may refer to a 'vineyard' and a 'meadow' respectively. The interpretation of **peś** as 'farm, country estate' is due to Maggiani (2001a:99). Wylin (2002a:93) takes **inni** as a resumptive relative in agreement with **peś**, the phrase serving as the object of the verb **tênθa**.

Section I.2

7   // cσ · êśiσ vêrê cuśuθurσum · p
8   eś · pêtruσta · ścevạ[σ] //

cσ 'this', DEM PRO, 1ST ABL; êśiσ '?', 1ST ABL; vêrê '?', LOC; cuśuθurσum = cuśuθurσ 'Cushu family', ANIM PL, 1ST GEN + -um 'and', ENCLITIC CONJ; peś '?', NOM/ACC; pêtruσta = pêtruσ 'Pêtru', MASC NOMEN, 1ST GEN + -ta 'this', DEM PRO, NOM; ścevạ[σ] 'Shcêvas', MASC COGN, 1ST GEN

This short section does not have a verb; the sentence must be nominal in form. The problem is that the enclitic connective -**um** points to two phrases, but it is not clear what the two phrases might be. It does not seem possible to coordinate **cσ êśiσ vêrê** with the rest of the sentence. An attractive proposal takes the ablative **cσ êśiσ** as a temporal phrase, 'from this point in time' *vel sim*. The basic idea of the sentence would be: 'From this point on, in/on/by means of the *vêra* the *pesh* of Pêtru (belongs) to the Cushu.' Note that this interpretation does not take into account the function of the enclitic -**um**.

Section I.2.1 The interpretation of the ablative **cσ êśiσ** as a temporal phrase is due to Adiego (2005:6).

Section I.3

> nuθanatur · lart · pêtr
> uni · arnt · pini · lart · vịpi · luśce · lariś · śalini · v
> 10   êtnal · lart · vêlara · larθaliśa · lart · vêlara ·
> auleśa · vêl · pumpu · pruciu · aule · cêlatina · śê
> tmnal · arnza · fêlσni · vêlθinal · vêl · luiśna
> luśce · vêl · uślna · nufṛeśa · laru · ślanzu · larz
> a lartle vêl aveσ aṛnt · pêtru · raufe //

nuθanatur 'auditors', ANIM PL, NOM/ACC; lart 'Lart', MASC PRAE, NOM/ACC;
pêtruni 'Pêtruni', MASC NOMEN, NOM/ACC; arnt 'Arnt', MASC PRAE, NOM/ACC;
pini 'Pini', MASC NOMEN, NOM/ACC; vipi 'Vipi', MASC NOMEN, NOM/ACC; luśce
'Lushce', MASC COGN, NOM/ACC; lariś 'Larish', MASC PRAE, NOM/ACC; śalini
'Shalini', MASC NOMEN, NOM/ACC; vêtnal 'Vêtnei', FEM NOMEN, 2ND GEN; vêlara
'Vêlara', MASC NOMEN, NOM/ACC; larθaliśa = larθal 'Larth', MASC PRAE, NOM/ACC
+ -iśa 'the', DEF ART, NOM; auleśa = auleσ 'Aule', MASC PRAE, NOM/ACC + -śa
'the', DEF ART, NOM; vel 'Vel', MASC PRAE, NOM/ACC; pumpu 'Pumpu', MASC
NOMEN, NOM/ACC; pruciu 'Pruciu', MASC COGN, NOM/ACC; aule 'Aule', MASC
PRAE, NOM/ACC; cêlatina 'Cêlatina', MASC NOMEN, NOM/ACC; śêtmnal 'Shêtm-
nei', FEM NOMEN, 2ND GEN; arnza 'Arnza', MASC PRAE, NOM/ACC; fêlσni 'Fêlsni',
MASC NOMEN, NOM/ACC; vêlθinal 'Vêlthinei', FEM NOMEN, 2ND GEN; luiśna
'Luishna', MASC NOMEN, NOM/ACC; luśce 'Lushce', MASC COGN, NOM/ACC; uślna
'Ushlna', MASC NOMEN, NOM/ACC; nufṛeśa 'Nufresha', MASC COGN, NOM/ACC;
laru 'Laru', MASC PRAE, NOM/ACC; ślanzu 'Shlanzu', MASC NOMEN, NOM/ACC;
larza 'Larza', MASC PRAE, NOM/ACC; lartle 'Lartle', MASC NOMEN, NOM/ACC; aveσ
'Aves', MASC NOMEN, 1ST GEN; pêtru 'Pêtru', MASC NOMEN, NOM/ACC; raufe
'Raufe', MASC COGN, NOM/ACC

Section I.3 is introduced by the noun **nuθanatur**, which was formed
from the verb **nuθe** attested in section II.2 (line 23). The internal structure of **nuθanatur** is opaque, but we can identify a root **nuθ-**, a suffix
-tu- (= -θu-), which formed collective nouns referring to a group of family members or a group of people, and an animate plural ending -r. For
the meaning of the root and the probable meaning of this word, see II.2.
Nuθanatur is followed by a list of names referring to the people who were
present when the agreement was officially approved.

Section I.3.1 For the interpretation of **nuθe** and its derived noun **nuθanatur** see Maggiani
2001a:101. Wylin (2002a:217) offers an analysis of the internal structure of this word.

Section I.4

êpru

15   σ · ame · vêlχe · cuśu lariśal · cleniarc · lariś
cu̬śu̬ · la̬riśaliśa larizac · c̬la̬n · lariśal · pêtr
u · ścêva̬σ · arntlei · pêtruσ · puia

êpruσ '?', 1ST GEN; ame 'is', NON-PAST ACT; vêlχe 'Vêlkhe', MASC PRAE, NOM/
ACC; cuśu 'Cushu', MASC NOMEN, NOM/ACC; lariśal 'Larish', MASC PRAE, 2ND GEN;
cleniarc = cleniar 'sons', ANIM PL, NOM/ACC + -c 'and', ENCLITIC CONJ; lariś
'Larish', MASC PRAE, NOM/ACC; cu̬śu̬ 'Cushu', MASC NOMEN, NOM/ACC; la̬riśaliśa
= lariśal 'Larish', MASC PRAE, 2ND GEN + -iśa 'the', DEF ART, NOM; larizac = lariza
'Lariza', MASC PRAE, NOM/ACC; clan 'son', NOM/ACC; lariśal 'Larish', MASC PRAE,
2ND GEN; pêtruσ 'Pêtru', MASC NOMEN, 1ST GEN; ścêva̬σ 'Shcêvas', MASC COGN,
1ST GEN; arntlei 'Arntlei', FEM NOMEN, NOM/ACC; pêtruσ 'Pêtru', MASC NOMEN,
1ST GEN; puia, 'wife', NOM/ACC

Section I.4 begins with the verb phrase êpruσ ame. It is followed by the
names of members of the Cushu family, Vêlkhe and his sons Larish and
Lariza, and by the name of Pêtru Shcêvas and his wife, Arntlei. These are
the legal participants in the agreement.

The word êpruσ is either a u-stem 1st genitive or an s-stem nomina-
tive/accusative. The former is more likely since we might expect a nom-
inative/accusative form in apposition to the names of the two families
to be marked for plural. Translating êpruσ as 'participants' seems to cap-
ture the idea of the passage, but it is difficult to see how the singular form
êpruσ can refer grammatically to the list of names unless it bears a collective sense.

Section I.4.1 Facchetti (2000a:76) is responsible for the interpretation of êpruσ as 'participants'.

Section II.1

cên · zic · ziχuχe · śparzêσtiσ · σazleiσ · in
θuχti · cuśuθuraσ · śuθiu · ame · tal · śuθive
20   naσ · ratm · θuχt · ceσu · tltel · têi · śianσ · śpa
rzête · θui · śalt · zic · fratuce · cuśuθuraσ · la
riśaliśvla · pêtruσc · ścêvaσ · peśσ · tarχian
eσ //

Line 19: The interpunct before the last word in the line, śuθive-, cannot be securely read.

cên 'this', DEM PRO, NOM; zic 'document', NOM/ACC; ziχuχe 'was written',
PAST PASS; śparzêσtiσ = śparzêσ 'tablet', 1ST ABL + -tiσ 'the', DEM PRON, 1ST

ABL; σazleiσ 'of bronze/wood (?)', 1ST ABL; in 'which', INANIMATE REL PRO, NOM/ACC; θuχti = θuχ- 'house', LOC + -ti 'in', POST; cuśuθuraσ 'Cushu family', ANIM PL, 1ST GEN; śuθiu 'placed', U-PART; ame 'is', NON-PAST ACT; tal = ta 'this', DEM PRON, NOM + -l, ENCLITIC PARTICLE (?); śuθivenaσ '?', NAS-PART; ratm '?', ADV; θuχt = θuχ- 'house', LOC + -t 'in', POST; ceσu 'resided', U-PART; tltel '?'; têi '?'; śianσ '?', NOM/ACC; śparzête = śparzê 'tablet', LOC + -te 'on', POST; θui 'here', ADV; śalt '?'; zic 'document', NOM/ACC; fratuce 'incised (?)', PAST ACT; cuśuθuraσ 'Cushu family', ANIM PL, 1ST GEN; lariśaliśvla = lariśal 'Larish', MASC PRAE, 2ND GEN + -iśvla 'the', DEF ART, PL, 2ND GEN; pêtruσ 'Pêtru', MASC NOMEN, 1ST GEN; ścêva[σ] 'Shcêvas', MASC COGN, 1ST GEN; peśσ '?', 1ST ABL; tarχianeσ '?', 1ST ABL

Section I.4 concluded the agreement proper. The most intriguing analysis of Section II of the text starts from the hypothesis that the original agreement was set forth in section I, and that sections II and III were added later when a COPY of the original document was incised on more permanent material (the bronze tablet).

This section has three clauses. Clause one concludes with the verb ame 'to be' in line 19. Clause two probably ends with the phrase tltel têi, but the fact that we cannot provide a secure interpretation means that clause two could just as easily end after the u-participle ceσu.

The only serious grammatical dispute in clause one concerns the case of the phrase śparzêσtiσ σazleiσ. Some commentators take these words to be locatives or, to put it more accurately, as locatives re-characterized by ablative endings. These analyses are guided more by interpretative assumptions than by morphology. Formally these words can only be interpreted as ablatives. The meaning of σazleiσ is uncertain, but the fact that śparza refers to a 'tablet' delimits the possibilities, particularly if σazleiσ is an adjective. A material adjective meaning 'of wood' or 'of bronze' is likely to be correct.

The nucleus of sentence two must be: 'This (document) (was) placed in the house.' ratm would seem—because the sentence is passive—to have adverbial function. It could modify either śuθivenaσ or ceσu. Its position points to the first alternative. Unfortunately, we do not have an airtight analysis of śuθivenaσ, although we know that it is a derivative of śuθiv- 'deposited, placed', the u-participle attested in line 19.

The final clause poses several problems, apart from the issue of determining the end of the sentence. First of all, we do not know the meaning of the major constituents, neither the subject śianσ nor the verb fratuce. We do not know the meaning of śalt; it is generally taken as a locative with postposition -t. The suggestion that the stem is the same as the article /-ʃa/ could well be correct. For the formation one can compare the locatives of demonstratives **calθi, clθi,** etc.

It is not clear how the genitives **cuśuθuraσ** and following (lines 21–2) are to be construed syntactically, nor is it clear how to deal with the ablative phrase **peśσ tarχianeσ**, even if we assume that the preceding genitives are in some way dependent on it. What we do know is that the clause is transitive. The direct object of **fratuce** is the noun **zic** 'document'. Since the general sense of the passage is concerned with the writing or the copying of a document, **fratuce** should have something to do with writing, perhaps 'incised'. This then would make the **śianσ** the person responsible for copying the document, or at least for having it copied onto the tablet.

Section II.1.1 See Adiego (2005:7-14) for arguments that Sections II and III were added when the original agreement was copied. Adiego discusses the interpretation of the form **śalt** on p. 13. See also his interpretation of **tal** as a pronominal genitive (2005:11).

Section II.2

```
     cnl · nuθe · malec · lart · cucrina · lauśiśa ·
     zilaθ · meχl · raσnal · ḷ[a]riś · cêlatina lau
25   śa [cl]ạnc · arnt · luścni · [a]rnθal · clanc · larz
     a · lart · turmna · śalina[l – – – ]
     pnal · cleniarc · vêlχe [ – – – palpa]
     σerc · vêlχe · cuśu · aule [ – – – ]
     aninalc · lariś · fuln[ – – – clenia]
30   rc · lart · pêtce · uślnạḷ [ – – – vip]
     inaθur · têcśinal · vêl [ – – – ]
     uσ · lariśc · cuśu · uślna[l – – – ]
```

Side B

aule śalini [*vacat*] **cuśual**

cnl 'this', DEM PRO, ACC + -l '?', ENCLITIC PARTICLE; **nuθe** 'listens to', NON-PAST ACT; **malec** = **male** 'watch over', NON-PAST ACT + -c 'and', ENCLITIC CONJ; **lart** 'Lart', MASC PRAE, NOM/ACC; **cucrina** 'Cucrina', MASC NOMEN, NOM/ACC; **lauśiśa** 'Laushisha', MASC COGN, NOM/ACC; **zilaθ** 'governor', NOM/ACC; **meχl** 'territory (?)', 2ND GEN; **raσnal** 'public', 2ND GEN; **ḷ[a]riś** 'Larish', MASC PRAE, NOM/ACC; **cêlatina** 'Cêlatina', MASC NOMEN, NOM/ACC; **lauśa** 'Lausha', MASC COGN, NOM/ACC; **[cl]anc** = **clan** 'son', NOM/ACC + -c 'and', ENCLITIC CONJ; **arnt** 'Arnt', MASC PRAE, NOM/ACC; **luścni** 'Lushcni', MASC NOMEN, NOM/ACC; **[a]rnθal** 'Arnth', MASC PRAE, 2ND GEN; **clanc** = **clan** 'son', NOM/ACC + -c 'and', ENCLITIC CONJ; **larza** 'Larza', MASC PRAE, NOM/ACC; **lart** 'Lart', MASC PRAE, NOM/ACC; **turmna** 'Turmna', MASC NOMEN, NOM/ACC; **śalina[l]** 'Shalinei', FEM NOMEN, 2ND GEN; [ ]**pnal**

'?', FEM NOMEN, 2ND GEN; cleniarc = cleniar 'son', ANIM PL, NOM/ACC + -c 'and', ENCLITIC CONJ; vêlχe 'Velkhe', MASC PRAE, NOM/ACC; [palpa]σerc 'children', ANIM PL, NOM/ACC + -c 'and', ENCLITIC CONJ; cuśu 'Cushu', MASC NOMEN, NOM/ACC; aule 'Aule', MASC PRAE, NOM/ACC; [ ]aninalc = [ ]aninal '?', FEM NOMEN, 2ND GEN + -c 'and', ENCLITIC CONJ; lariś 'Larish', MASC PRAE, NOM/ACC; fuln[ ] 'Fuln[ ]', MASC NOMEN, NOM/ACC; [clenia]rc = cleniar 'son', ANIM PL, NOM/ACC + -c 'and', ENCLITIC CONJ; lart 'Lar(n)t', MASC PRAE, NOM/ACC; pêtce 'Pêtce', MASC NOMEN, NOM/ACC; uślnaḷ 'Ushlnei', FEM NOMEN, 2ND GEN; [vip]inaθur 'Vipi family', ANIM PL, NOM/ACC; têcśinal 'Têcshinei', FEM NOMEN, 2ND GEN; vêl 'Vêl', MASC PRAE, NOM/ACC; [ ]uσ '?', 1ST GEN; lariśc = lariś 'Larish', MASC PRAE, NOM/ACC + -c 'and', ENCLITIC CONJ; cuśu 'Cushu', MASC NOMEN, NOM/ACC; uślna[l] 'Ushlnei', FEM NOMEN, 2ND GEN; aule 'Aule', MASC PRAE, NOM/ACC; śalini 'Shalini', MASC NOMEN, NOM/ACC; cuśual 'Cushui', FEM NOMEN, 2ND GEN

Section II.2 begins with the verb phrase cnl nuθe malec. The best interpretation is to treat nuθe malec as a coordinate verb phrase and to take cnl as direct object referring to the copying of the document. The verb male has been connected with the word malena 'mirror'; the most likely meaning is 'sees'. The verb nuθe, given that it is in a coordinate construction with male, should belong in the same semantic territory. A most appropriate suggestion is 'hears'. This meaning also neatly fits the requirements of the derived noun nuθanatur, which can mean 'auditors', that is to say, 'witnesses'. The verb phrase translates then as 'hears and sees this'. Following are the names of the individuals who performed the activities specified by the verbs. This list differs from the first two in that it begins with the name of a public official, the zilaθ meχl rasnal. Included in this list of names are the members of the Cushu family, Vêlkhe and Larish.

Section II.2.1 For discussion of the verb phrase cnl nuθe malec see Agostiniani and Nicosia 2000:105–7, Maggiani 2001a:101, and Rix 2002a:78.

Section III.1

2   zilci · larθal · c [vacat] uśuσ · tit{l}nal
       lariśalc · śaliniσ · aulesla · celtinêi tiś
       σ · tarśminaσσ · śparza · in · θuχt ceσu
5   ratm · śuθiu · śuθiuśvê · vêlχeσ · cuśuσ a
       ulesla · vêlθuruσ · titlniσ · vêlθuruśla ·
       larθalc · cêlatinaσ apnaḷ · lariśalc cê
       latinaσ · ṭitlnal

Line 2: tit{l}nal was written titinal.

zilci 'governorship', LOC; larθal 'Larth', MASC PRAE, 2ND GEN; cuśuσ 'Cushu', MASC NOMEN, 1ST GEN; tit{l}nal 'Titlnei', FEM NOMEN, 2ND GEN; lariśalc = lariśal 'Laris', MASC PRAE, 2ND GEN + -c 'and', ENCLITIC CONJ; śaliniσ 'Shalini', MASC PRAE, 1ST GEN; auleśla = auleσ 'Aule', MASC PRAE, 1ST GEN + -śla 'the', DEF ART, 2ND GEN; celtinêi 'district (?)', LOC (?); tiśσ 'lake (?)', 1ST GEN; tarśminaσσ 'Trasimene', 1ST GEN (?); śparza 'tablet', NOM/ACC; in 'which', INANIMATE REL PRO, NOM/ACC; θuχt = θuχ- 'house', LOC + -t 'in', POST; ceσu 'resided', U-PART; ratm '?', ADV (?); śuθiu 'placed', U-PART; śuθiuśvê = śuθiu- 'storehouse' + -śvê 'the', DEF ART, PL LOC; vêlχeσ 'Vêlkhe', MASC PRAE, 1ST GEN; cuśuσ 'Cushu', MASC NOMEN, 1ST GEN; auleśla = auleσ 'Aule', MASC PRAE, 1ST GEN + -śla 'the', DEF ART, 2ND GEN; vêlθuruσ 'Vêlthur', MASC PRAE, 1ST GEN; titlniσ 'Titlni', MASC NOMEN, 1ST GEN; vêlθuruśla = vêlθuruσ 'Vêlthur', MASC PRAE, 1ST GEN + -śla 'the', DEF ART, 2ND GEN; larθalc = larθal 'Larth', MASC PRAE, 2ND GEN + -c 'and', ENCLITIC CONJ; cêlatinaσ 'Cêlatina', MASC NOMEN, 1ST GEN; apnạl 'Apnei', FEM NOMEN, 2ND GEN; ṭitlnal 'Titlnei', FEM NOMEN, 2ND GEN

The final section of the inscription provides the date of the recording of the document by means of the eponymous official. We note that this phrase differs in syntactic structure from those found in other inscriptions: the names of the officials are not in agreement with the locative noun zilci but are dependent on it and inflected in the genitive case.

The primary difficulty in this passage lies in the division and interpretation of the words celtinêitiśσ, tarśminaσσ, and in the analysis and interpretation of śuθiuśvê.

For celtinêitiśσ three divisions are possible: (1) celti nêi tiśσ, (2) celti nêitiśσ, and (3) celtinêi tiśσ. Although (1) and (2) cannot be ruled out, (3) is safest because it yields a locative ending in -êi, which is attested elsewhere in the TCo. Celtinêi may be a derivative of the root cel- 'earth'. We may start with a nominal derivative cel-ti-, which could mean something along the lines of 'small piece of earth, district', from which an adjectival derivative in -na was built. In this context, however, celtinêi must function as a substantive. The key to the meaning of tiśσ is tarśminaσσ, which is now universally accepted as the word 'Trasimene'. Tiśσ may be the genitive of the word for 'lake' or 'region'. It is very tempting to connect the root of the word tiś etymologically to θi 'water', but there is a phonological impediment to such a connection. There is no evidence that aspirated stops in word-initial position are spelled as plain stops in the TCo.

Section III.1.1 For arguments that the noun phrase tiśσ tarśminaσσ refers to Lake Trasimene see Agostiniani and Nicosia 2000:112–14.

Translation

11.7 The supposition that the TCo is a copy of an agreement between the Cushu brothers and Pêtru Shcêvas has considerable merit. The interpretation may be sketched out as follows: The TCo is a COPY of the original agreement, which is written on a tablet and stored in the home of the Cushu. Copies (?) were made in the presence of witnesses who are listed in Section II.2. Section III summarizes information about the original document. Copies were placed in the storehouses of important witnesses for safekeeping.

This explanation goes a long way toward making sense out of Sections II and III of the text and of their relationship with Section I. Plausible analyses and translations can be provided for considerable portions of sections II and III of the TCo. However, the details of the agreement proper as set forth in Section I remain virtually impenetrable. Satisfactory analysis and translation of these sections, particularly I.1, which is crucial to any understanding of the agreement as a whole, is as yet unattainable.

Section I.1 'Thus both the *vina* and the *restm* were sold/ceded (?) by Pêtru Shcêvas, the *êliun*, to the Cushu, sons of Larish, (in the amount of) ten *tênthur*. And the *pesh* (?) on the plain (was sold/ceded by Pêtru Shcêvas), (in the amount of) four *tênthur* and ten *sran*, to the *clth*. The *têrshna* here on the plain and in/on the *mlesia* (is) public (in the amount of) 14.5 (measures). With respect to (?) the *pesh* of Pêtru, and the *pava* and the *traula*, the *zacinat prinisher* shall measure two times (?) the *tiur* and the *tênthur* (?).'

Section I.2 'From this point in time (*êshi*) in/on/by means of the *vêra* the *pesh* (?), that of Pêtru Shcêvas, (belongs) to the Cushu.'

Section I.3 'The auditors (= witnesses?) (are): Lart Pêtruni, Arnt Pini, Lart Vipi Lushce, Laris Shalini, (son) of Vêtnei, Lart Vêlara, the (son) of Larth, Lart Vêlara, the (son) of Aule, Vêl Pumpu Pruciu, Aule Cêlatina, (son) of Shêtmnei, Arnza Fêlshni, (son) of Vêlthinei, Vêl Luishna Lushce, Vêl Ushlna Nufresha, Laru Shlanzu, Larza Lartle, Vêl Aves, Arnt Pêtru Raufe.'

Section I.4 'Vêlkhe Cushu, (son) of Larish, and his sons, Larish Cushu, the (son) of Larish, and Lariza, son of Larish, (and) Pêtru Shcêvas (and) Arntlei, wife of Pêtru are (the parties) of the *êpru* (transaction?).'

Section II.1 'This document was written (= copied) from the tablet of bronze/wood (?) which is placed (= stored) in the house of the Cushu family. That (document), having been placed in the repository *ratm*, resides in that place (?). The *shians* incised (?) the document on the tablet, this one here, from the *pesh tarkhiane* (?) of the Cushu, the (sons) of Larish, and of Pêtru Shcêvas.'

Section II.2 'Lart Cucrina Laushisha, governor of public territory, Larish Cêlatina Lausha and (his) son, Arnt Lushcni, (son) of Arnth, and his son Larza, Lart Turmna, (son) of Shalinei, [– – –] and his sons, Vêlkhe [– – –] and his children, Vêlkhe Cushu, Aule [– – –], (son) of [– – –]aninei, Larish Fuln[– – –] and his sons, Ar(n)t Pêtce, (son) of Ushlnei, the Vipina family, (sons) of Têcshinei, Vêl [– – –] and Larish Cushu, (son) of Ushlnei, Aule Shalini, (son) of Cushui listen to and watch over this (act).'

Section III.1 'During the governorship of Larth Cushu, (son) of Titlnei, and Larish Shalini, the (son) of Aule, in the district of Lake (?) Trasimene, the tablet, which was stored in the house (of the Cushu), was placed *ratm* in the storehouses (?) of Vêlkhe Cushu, the (son) of Aule, of Vêlthur Titlni, the (son) of Vêlthur, and of Larth Cêlatina, the (son) of Apnei, and of Larish Cêlatina, the (son) of Titlnei.'

11.7.1 For translations, including translations of selected sections of the text, see the references in §11.6.1. The interpretation and translation given here is based on that advanced in Adiego (2005).

12 LANGUAGE RELATIONSHIPS, LEMNIAN, AND RAETIC

Introduction

12.1 The linguistic affiliation of Etruscan with the languages of ancient Italy and the Mediterranean basin has occupied investigators since the late nineteenth century. These issues are alive today and are nowhere near being settled. Nonetheless, we gain some perspective on the situation by clearing away misunderstandings and mistaken notions about how linguistic relationships are determined.

Linguistic Relationships

12.2 It is misguided to think that resemblances between languages necessarily point to a genetic relationship. Languages can resemble one another for all sorts of reasons, including chance. A notorious example of a chance resemblance is Greek θεός 'god' and Latin *deus* 'god'. These two words are similar in form and have the same meaning, but no etymological connection. The root θε- /tʰe-/ in Greek θεός is related to the root *fa:-* /fa:-/ in the Latin word *fa:num* 'holy shrine'. These two forms do not resemble one another in terms of their initial consonants or in terms of the quantity and quality of their vowels, and yet they both descend from a common prehistoric root *dhh_1s- 'religious' (full grade *$dheh_1s$- in Latin *fe:riae* 'holidays'). Another source of linguistic similarity is borrowing. Anyone who is an aficionado of food can think of many words that have been borrowed into English referring to tasty dishes and drinks, e.g. *spaghetti* (from Italian), *punch* (from Hindi), *enchilada* (from American Spanish), *margarita* (from Spanish). Finally, all languages incorporate nursery words or baby-talk words into their vocabulary, for example, *ma*, *mama*, *dada*, and *papa*. These words tell us much about the sounds and syllables that children the world over master in the early stages of language acquisition, but they do not inform us about language relationships. Chance, borrowing, and baby-talk words are reasons why languages resemble one another, but they cannot be offered in support of the claim that two or more languages have descended from a common ancestor.

In order to prove that two or more languages are genetically related, it is necessary to demonstrate that similarities in vocabulary, phonology, and morphology are so pervasive and so systematic that they cannot have risen by chance. For example, we know that Latin, Ancient Greek, and Sanskrit have descended from the same prehistoric language because we can point to systematic phonological relationships in words that are similar in meaning and because we can show that the morphological systems of these languages are similar.

The singular present active paradigm of the verb meaning 'to bear' is cited in (1) for the languages mentioned in the preceding paragraph.

(1) Partial paradigm of verb 'to bear'

    Latin *fero:*   Greek φέρω   Sanskrit *bhara:mi*
    Latin *fers*   Greek φέρεις   Sanskrit *bharasi*
    Latin *fert*   Greek φέρει   Sanskrit *bharati*

The initial sounds of these words, Latin /f-/, Greek /pʰ-/, and Sanskrit /bʰ-/, though different phonologically, form a set of regular sound correspondences for these languages. Latin /f-/ regularly matches up with Greek /pʰ-/ and with Sanskrit /bʰ-/ in word-initial position. The fact that these sounds are phonologically distinct is trivial. What is crucial is that they form a regular set of correspondences. This match-up cannot be ascribed to chance because it is found in other vocabulary items in these languages. The correspondences in the words cited in (2) match up perfectly with the pattern illustrated in (1).

(2) Phonological correspondences φ – f – bh

GREEK	LATIN	SANSKRIT
φύεται 'becomes'	*fuit* 'was'	*bhávati* 'becomes'
φείδεται 'spares'	*findit* 'splits'	*bhinátti* 'splits'
φράτηρ 'member'	*fra:ter* 'brother'	*bhrá:tar-* 'brother'

It is precisely this type of systematic correspondence in large numbers of vocabulary that points to a linguistic relationship for Latin, Greek, and Sanskrit.

The point of our discussion is simple: in order to show that Etruscan is linguistically related to another language it is necessary to be able to construct regular sound correspondences for it and its putative relative(s) across a large segment of vocabulary. It should be possible to show that similarities extend into the system of nominal and verbal morphology. This is a strict and demanding set of requirements, and we can say at the outset that it will be extremely difficult for us to meet them in the case of Etruscan because we possess a very small portion of the language's vocabulary and we know the meanings of relatively few items. A large number of lexical correspondences are required in order to rule out chance resemblances.

12.3 If we investigate a segment of the Etruscan vocabulary for which we are reasonably well informed, the numbers from 1 to 10 for example, we find that there are few resemblances to Latin, Greek, and Sanskrit, and those that do exist cannot be shown to be systematic. Consider the numbers cited in (3).

(3) Comparanda for numbers 1–10

	LATIN	GREEK	SANSKRIT	ETRUSCAN
1	u:nus	εἷς	ékas	θu
2	duo	δύω	dvá:u	zal
3	tre:s	τρεῖς	tráyas	ci
4	quattuor	τέτταρες	catvá:ras	ɓa
5	qui:nque	πέντε	páñca	maχ
6	sex	ἕξ	ṣáṭ	huθ
7	septem	ἑπτά	saptá	cezp
8	octo:	ὄκτω	aṣṭá:u	semφ
9	novem	ἐννέα	náva	nurφ
10	decem	δέκα	dáśa	ɕar

Comparison of the numbers in Latin, Greek, and Sanskrit reveals similarities in form that are not shared by Etruscan. Even in those instances where Latin, Greek, and Sanskrit do not appear to match up, as for example with the initial consonants of the word for 'four', regular sound correspondences are in fact attested. Latin qu- /kʷ/ systematically matches up with Greek τ- and with Sanskrit c- /tʃ/ in the environment before original front vowels. Compare the initial sound in the enclitic conjunction 'and': Latin -que vs. Greek τε vs. Sanskrit ca. In contrast, it is impossible to establish systematic correspondences for the sounds in the Etruscan words and the sounds in the Latin, Greek, and Sanskrit words.

12.3.1 For discussion of methods for determining linguistic relationships see Campbell 2003: 262–82.

12.4 The vocabulary items that are shared by Etruscan, Ancient Greek, and the Italic languages are best attributed to borrowing. For example, the word 'wine' has the same form in Etruscan, Latin, and the Sabellic language Umbrian, i.e. Etruscan **vinum**, Latin *vinum*, and Umbrian **vinum**, but this correspondence tells us nothing about a genetic relationship for these languages. The word *vinum* made its way to Italy from an eastern Mediterranean source. If we remove from our vocabulary lists words such as *vinum*, which are suspected of being borrowed, then few, if any, lexical items remain in Etruscan that are similar in form and meaning to words in Latin, Umbrian, and Ancient Greek.

12.5 The paucity of our knowledge about Etruscan hampers our ability to make judgments about language relationships, but the situation is not entirely hopeless. Evidence suggests that Etruscan MAY be linguistically related to the languages commonly referred to as Lemnian and Raetic.

12.5.1 Some relatively recent papers on the linguistic affiliation of Etruscan, such as Adrados 1989 and 1994 and Woudhuizen 1991, lack methodological rigor. Adrados and Woudhuizen argue that Etruscan is an Indo-European language of the Anatolian branch, and closely related to Luwian. Neu 1991 is a well-reasoned response to Adrados 1989. Facchetti (2002a:111–50) attempts to connect Etruscan and Minoan Linear A. The results are not convincing, again for methodological reasons.

Lemnian

12.6 The Greek historian Herodotos (1.94) relates a fascinating story about the origins of the Etruscans. He writes that they were Lydian colonists who migrated westward from southwestern Anatolia (ancient Lydia), eventually settling in Italy in the land of the Ombricans. Aside from the fact that Etruscans cannot be Lydians—Lydians were Indo-European speakers—this story would remain an interesting piece of pseudo-history were it not for the fact that a small number of pre-Greek inscriptions discovered on the island of Lemnos, located off the coast of Asia Minor, have linguistic features similar to those found in Etruscan. The two most important inscriptions in the Lemnian corpus were incised on a stone stele dating to the end of the sixth century BCE. The first was incised on the front of the stele around the figure of a warrior holding a spear and a round shield; the second was incised in three lines on the right side of the stele. The stele was recovered from Kaminia, an area located on the eastern side of the island.

12.7 A transliteration of the two inscriptions (A: front; B: side) is provided in (4).

Fig. 12.1. Stele from Kaminia, Lemnos. Bonfante and Bonfante 2002:60.

(4)   Transliteration of the Stele of Lemnos

   A   holaies : naφoθ
       siasi :
       maras ː mav
       óialχveiːs ː aviːs
       evióθo ː seronaiθ
       sivai
       aker : tavarsio
       vanalaóial ː seronai ː morinail

   B   holaiesi ː φokiaóiale ː seronaiθ : evióθo ː toverona[
       ]rom : haralio : sivai : eptesio : arai : tis ː φoke
       sivai : avis : óialχvis : marasm : avis : aomai :

The arrangement of the words given above for inscription A is the one that is generally accepted. However, this inscription occupies the space around the engraving of the warrior in such a way that other collocations are possible. Only a few phrases of the text can be translated (see §12.8), so the exact arrangement of the lines in A cannot be determined.

12.7.1 The most important articles on Lemnian are Rix 1968a, de Simone 1986, and Agostini-ani 1986. For the Lemnian alphabet see de Simone 1995 and Malzahn 1999.

12.8 What is most striking about the stele of Lemnos is the fact that we can identify morphemes, words, and syntactic structures that correspond to similar structures in Etruscan. The correspondences are listed in (5–9).

	Lemnian	Etruscan

(5)   Lexical correspondences

   (a) óialχveiːs, óialχvis 'forty'   śealχls 'forty'
   (b) aviːs, avis 'year'   avils 'year'
   (c) sivai 'lived'   zivas 'having lived'
   (d) mav 'five'   maχ 'five'
   (e) -m 'and'   -m/-um 'and, but'

(6)   Derivational pattern (formation of the decades)

   (a) number + -alχveiː-s/-alχvi-s   number + -alχl-s/-alχu-s

(7) Case endings

(a) **holaie-s** 1ST GEN   **mamarce-s** 1ST GEN
(b) **holaie-si** 1ST PERT   **larice-si** 1ST PERT
(c) **vanalaśi-al** 2ND GEN   **larθi-al** 2ND GEN
(d) **ϕokiasi-ale** 2ND PERT   **larθi-ale** 2ND PERT
(e) **seronai-θ** LOC + -θ POST   **hamai-θi** LOC + -θi POST

(8) Verb ending

(a) **sivai** 'lived', **arai, aomai**   **akarai** 'composed (?)'

(9) Phrases

(a) Genitive of duration of time
     avis óialχvis 'for forty years'   **avils maχs śealχls** 'for forty-five
                                            years'
(b) Absolute construction
     holaiesi ϕokiaóiale seronaiθ   **zilci vel[u]s[i] hulχniesi**
     'when Holaie Phokiash (was)   'during the governorship of Vel
     serona'   Hulkhnie'
(c) Nomenclature
     aker tarvasio vanalaóial   **vel rufres larisal**
     'Aker Tarvasio, (son) of   'Vel Rufres, (son) of Laris'
     Vanalash'

The sign in the form of a colon that appears before the final *sigma* of
óialχvei:s and avi:s in (5) and (6) above is generally interpreted as syllabic
punctuation (see §2.21 for Etruscan). This is a possible interpretation, but
there are no other examples, including **avis** on side B. It may not be important, but it is interesting to note that this sign appears in just the place
where one would expect an -l on etymological grounds, e.g. **avi:s** < *awils.
Could this be an attempt to indicate phonological information?

12.9 Let us now address the question of how to account for the similarities in (5–9). Borrowing does not seem likely in this case because Etruscan
and Lemnian were not spoken in geographically contiguous speech areas. Chance also seems remote since the linguistic correspondences listed
in (5) through (9) cover the spectrum of grammatical structure ranging
from phonology to syntax. The best answer, although we may not have
the quantity of evidence to prove it (by being able to establish sound correspondences across a large segment of the two languages' vocabulary), is

that Etruscan and Lemnian are linguistically related. The question of how they are related is another and more difficult matter. Scholars have provided three scenarios to account for the linguistic similarities between the two languages.

(a) Lemnian and Etruscan were geographically diverse descendants of a common proto-language, which some scholars have labeled Proto-Tyrrhenian.

(b) Lemnian was the eastern residue of a language whose speakers moved from an original homeland located somewhere in the northeastern Mediterranean and settled in Etruria. The fact that Etruscan was spoken in Etruria was the result of migrations from this eastern homeland.

(c) Lemnian was a colonial form of Etruscan carried by commercial adventurers to the eastern Mediterranean. A few of these entrepreneurs took up residence on the isle of Lemnos.

Evaluating these scenarios is difficult. Scholars often appeal to evidence gathered from ancient literary sources in order to construct arguments for or against one or another of these competing positions. But the fact of the matter is that there is too little evidence to make a determination one way or another, regardless of the information provided by the ancient literary record. At this point it does not seem possible to establish how the historical situation actually arose. The important point is that the comparative evidence, slender though it may be, points to a possible linguistic relationship.

12.9.1 The "theory" of the eastern origins is plotted in detail in Rix 1995c. See Beekes 1993 for the notion of Proto-Tyrrhenian. De Simone (1996a) argues that Lemnian is a dialect of Etruscan.

Raetic

12.10 The Raetic language is known from approximately 100 inscriptions recovered at sites located in what was to become the Roman province of Raetia. The inscriptions were written in two pre-Roman alphabets, both of which were based on the alphabetic tradition of the Veneti.

The Roman historian Livy (*Ab Urbe Condita* 5.53.11) informs us that the Raeti had Etruscan origins. A linguistic connection between the two languages has long been suspected based on a handful of lexical similarities, e.g. Raetic **zinake** and Etruscan **zinace**. Recent investigations of Raetic inscriptions have led to more intriguing and more substantive results.

12.10.1 The corpus of Raetic inscriptions was published in Schumacher 1992. Subsequent finds were published in *Studi Etruschi*. Schumacher 1998 is a superb introduction to the analysis of Raetic texts, the methodological problems, and the possible linguistic connection to Etruscan. Rix (1998a) covers much the same information.

12.11 The archaeological contexts in which Raetic inscriptions were recovered were not always accurately recorded. Nonetheless, the type of material on which the inscriptions were written provides clues to their epigraphic classification. The working assumption is that texts incised on bone and horn, and on bronze implements and statues, were votive in nature.

12.12 Raetic inscriptions had very simple structures, consisting of names, either a single personal name, e.g. **remina** (SZ-31), **katiave** (SZ-8), or a bipartite name consisting of a personal name and a second name, e.g. **pitamne helanu** (MA-1), **knuse susinu** (MA-18), **laste φutiχinu** (MA-19), **lavisie lavisealu** (VN-1). The second name probably functioned as a patronymic, e.g. **φutiχinu** 'of Phutikhi', but the possibility that it was a family name cannot be excluded.

12.13 Recent investigations have attempted to analyze more complex Raetic inscriptions from an Etruscan perspective. The results have been encouraging. For example, Raetic inscriptions ending in the verb form **zinake** may be compared to Etruscan votive dedications of the **turuce** type.

(10) Etruscan (a) and Raetic (b) votive dedications

(a) **turns turce ramθa venatres** (Ta 3.4)
'Ramtha, of the (family) Venatres, dedicated (this) to Turan.'

turns 'Turan', THEO, 1ST GEN; **turce** 'dedicated', PAST ACT; **ramθa** 'Ramtha', FEM PRAE, NOM/ACC; **venatres** 'Venatres', MASC NOMEN, 1ST GEN

(b) **piθale lemais zinake** (MA-9)
'Pithale dedicated (this) to Lemai.'

piθale 'Pithale', NAME, NOM/ACC; **lemais** 'Lemai', THEO (?), 1ST GEN; **zinake** 'dedicated', PAST ACT

The assumption here is that both texts have the same syntactic structure: dedicator + verb of dedication + genitive of the name of the divinity. Comparisons of this type yield a Raetic past active verb form **zinake** and a divine name inflected in the 1st genitive case -s. The Raetic verb **zinake** 'dedicated' appears to be cognate with Etruscan **zinace** 'fashioned', although such a connection presupposes that the ancestral meaning of the verb has changed in one language or even in both.

12.14 More intriguing examples of parallel Etruscan-Raetic texts are cited in (7). In these inscriptions it is possible to isolate a Raetic word-form ending in *-u*, which is in construction with names ending in *-si* or *-(a)le*, forms that are familiar as Etruscan 1st and 2nd pertinentive endings.

(11) Etruscan (a, b) and Raetic (c, d, e) dedications

    (a) mi spurieisi teiθurnasi aliqu (Cr 3.7)
        'I (was) donated for/by Spurie Teithurnas.'

        mi 'I', 1ST PERS PRO, NOM; spurieisi 'Spurie', MASC PRAE, 1ST PERT; teiθurnasi 'Teithurnas', MASC NOMEN, 1ST PERT; aliqu 'donated', U-PART

    (b) mi larθale melacinasi mulu (Vc 3.2)
        'I (was) given for/by Larth Melacinas.'

        mi 'I', 1ST PERS PRO, NOM; larθale 'Larth', MASC PRAE, 2ND PERT; melacinasi 'Melacinas', MASC NOMEN, 1ST PERT; mulu 'given', U-PART

    (c1) φelipuriesi eluku slepile [back of statue]
    (c2) karapaśna [front of statue] (SZ-14)
        '(This statue) (was) offered (?) for/by Phelipurie Slepi. Karapashna.'

        φelipuriesi 'Phelipurie', NAME, 1ST PERT; eluku 'offered (?)', U-PART; slepile 'Slepile', NAME, 2ND PERT; karapaśna 'Karapashna', NAME, NOM/ACC

    (d) utiku | φeluriesi ∶ φelvinuale (NO-3)
        '(This statue) (was) given (?) by/for Phelurie Phelvinu.'

        utiku 'given (?)', U-PART; φeluriesi 'Phelurie', NAME, 1ST PERT; φelvinuale 'Phelvinu', NAME, 2ND PERT

    (e) laspasi eluku ii[ir] [side 1]
        pitamnux[- ?] r (WE-3)
        '(This statue) (was) offered (?) by/for Laspa. Pitamnu (?).'

        laspasi 'Laspa', NAME, 1ST PERT; eluku 'offered (?)', U-PART; ii[ir] (?); pitamnux[- 'Pitamnu' (?)

Apart from the fact that the first person pronoun does not appear in the Raetic inscriptions, there is a good match with Etruscan in terms of syntactic structure. The Raetic forms **eluku** and **utiku** may be interpreted as *u*-participles corresponding to the Etruscan forms **aliqu** and **mulu**. Etruscan *u*-participles built to transitive verb roots or stems were generally passive in voice, and they were regularly in construction with nouns inflected for the pertinentive case. Indeed, the case endings of the names in this type of Raetic inscription match the Etruscan perfectly. The distribution of the endings may differ (-*si* for first names, -*(a)le* for second?), but formally, and presumably functionally, they were the same. As a result, the Raetic sentences may be translated in much the same manner as the Etruscan, that is to say, by adhering to the formula '(this votive gift) was given/dedicated/offered by/for X'. It seems plausible then to think that Raetic had a class of *u*-participles as part of its inventory of verbal derivatives, and that nouns—personal names in this case—had the case endings -*si* and -*(a)le*, which were similar to those found in Etruscan in both form and function.

12.15 Raetic and Etruscan share few lexical correspondences (but see §12.13). This is not surprising. The corpus of Raetic inscriptions is tiny, and proper names make up a large part of the word-forms that are attested. Even so, it is possible to point to striking correspondences in both nominal and verbal morphology.

(a) Both languages had past active verb forms in /-ke/, e.g. Etruscan **zinace** 'fashioned', Raetic **zinake** 'dedicated'.

(b) Both languages built participles in -*u* to the past active stem, e.g. Etruscan **aliqu** 'donated', Raetic **eluku** 'offered (?)'.

(c) Both languages had case suffixes of the form -*si*, -*(a)le*, marking the agent or the benefactive in a passive construction.

(d) Both languages had a case suffix with the form -*s*. This suffix marked the *genitivus donandi* in votive inscriptions.

Concluding Remarks

12.16 Etruscan shares with Lemnian and with Raetic correspondences in nominal and verbal morphology. The evidence supports the idea that Lemnian and Raetic bear a genetic linguistic relationship to Etruscan. Whether it is sufficient to PROVE such a relationship conclusively is another matter. What type of linguistic relationship these languages had is also unclear. Is Lemnian a dialect of Etruscan or a different language? Are Raetic and Etruscan different languages? Even though it is not possible to provide definitive answers to these questions, the possibility of a three-way linguistic connection suggests that speculation about the prehistory of the Etruscans be viewed in a different light. Any response to the question of the origin of the Etruscans must be prepared to describe how Lemnian and Raetic fit into the prehistoric linguistic picture.

BIBLIOGRAPHY

This bibliography includes the citations given in each chapter as well as complete references to the volumes in the *Corpus Inscriptionum Etruscarum* (CIE). The volumes of CIE are listed in chronological order. If an entry includes photographs of an inscription, a reference is given in square brackets at the end. For example, [tav. XLVII–XLVIII] refers to tables 47–48. In a few instances references to an inscription are embedded in a longer article. In these cases the relevant pages and the citation number of the inscription, if included, are cited in square brackets at the end of the article. For a comprehensive bibliography covering Etruscan language studies and Etruscan inscriptions, see Wallace to appear.

Corpus Inscriptionum Etruscarum

Pauli, Carl, and Olof August Danielsson, eds. 1893. *Corpus Inscriptionum Etruscarum I, 1: Tituli 1–4917*. Leipzig: Barth.

Danielsson, Olof August, ed. 1907. *Corpus Inscriptionum Etruscarum II, 1, 1: Tituli 4918–5210*. Leipzig: Barth.

Herbig, Gustav, ed. 1912. *Corpus Inscriptionum Etruscarum II, 2, 1: Tituli 8001–8600*. Leipzig: Barth.

Herbig, Gustav, ed. 1919/1921. *Corpus Inscriptionum Etruscarum II, 1: Libri lintei Etruschi fragmenta Zagrabiensia*. Leipzig: Barth.

Danielsson, Olof August, ed. 1923. *Corpus Inscriptionum Etruscarum II, 1, 2: Tituli 5211–5326*. Leipzig: Barth.

Sittig, Ernst, ed. 1936. *Corpus Inscriptionum Etruscarum II, 1, 3: Tituli 5327–5606*. Leipzig: Barth.

Cristofani, Mauro, ed. 1970. *Corpus Inscriptionum Etruscarum II, 1, 4: Tituli 5607–6324. I. Tituli; II. Tabulae et indices*. Florence: Centro di Studio per l'Archeologia Etrusco-Italica del Consiglio Nazionale delle Ricerche.

Pandolfini Angeletti, Maristella, ed. 1982. *Corpus Inscriptionum Etruscarum III, 1. (Tituli 10001–10520: Inscriptiones in instrumento et Tarquiniis et in agro Tarquiniensi repertae)*. Rome: Centro di Studio per l'Archeologia Etrusco-Italica.

Magini Carella Prada, Juliana, and Maristella Pandolfini Angeletti, eds. 1987. *Corpus Inscriptionum Etruscarum III, 2. (Tituli 10521–10950: Inscriptiones in instrumento et Volsiniis et in agro Volsiniensi repertae)*. Rome: Centro di Studio per l'Archeologia Etrusco-Italica.

Pandolfini Angeletti, Maristella, ed. 1994. *Corpus Inscriptionum Etruscarum III, 3. (Tituli 10951-11538: Inscriptiones in instrumento et Volciis et in agro volcentano repertae).* Rome: Centro di Studio per l'Archeologia Etrusco-Italica.

Cristofani, Mauro, Maristella Pandolfini Angeletti, and Josepho Coppola, eds. 1996. *Corpus Inscriptionum Etruscarum II, 5. (Tituli 8601-8880: Inscriptiones et in Latio et in Campania repertae).* Rome: Centro di Studio per l'Archeologia Etrusco-Italica.

Maggiani, Adriano, and Serena Zambelli, eds. 2004. *Corpus Inscriptionum Etruscarum III, 4: Tituli 11539-12113 (Inscriptiones in instrumento et Rusellis et Vetuloniae et in earum agris repertae).* Rome: Centro di Studio per l'Archeologia Etrusco-Italica.

Colonna, Giovanni, and Federico Maras, eds. 2006. *Corpus Inscriptionum Etruscarum II, 1, 5 (Tituli 6325-6723), et addit. vol. II, 2, 1 (Tituli 8881-8927) (Inscriptiones Veiis et in agro veientano, nepesino sutrinoque repertae, additis illis in agro capenate et falisco inventis, quae in fasciculo CIE II, 2, 1 desunt, nec non illis perpaucis in finitimis sabinis repertis).* Rome: Centro di Studio per l'Archeologia Etrusco-Italica.

References

Adams, J. N. 2003. *Bilingualism and the Latin Language.* Cambridge: Cambridge University Press.

Adiego, Ignasi-Xavier. 2005. "The Etruscan *Tabula Cortonensis*: A tale of two tablets?" *Die Sprache* 45:3–25.

———. 2006. "Observaciones sobre la formación del plural en etrusco." In Gregorio del Olmo Lete, Lluis Feliu, and Adelina Millet Albà (eds.), *Ša-pal tibnim mû illakû: Studies Presented to Joaquín Sanmartín on the Occasion of His 65th Birthday (Aula Orientalis,* Supplementa 22), 1–13. Barcelona: Ausa.

Adrados, Francisco R. 1989. "Etruscan as an IE Anatolian (but not Hittite) language." *JIES* 17:363–83.

———. 1994. "More on Etruscan as an IE-Anatolian language." *HS* 107:54–76.

Agostiniani, Luciano. 1981. "*Duenom duenas* : καλος καλο : *mlaχ mlakas.*" *SE* 49:95–111.

———. 1982. *Le "iscrizioni parlanti" dell'Italia antica.* Florence: Olschki.

———. 1983. "Aspirate etrusche e gorgia toscana: Valenza delle condizioni fonologiche etrusche." In Luciano Agostiniani and Luciano Giannelli (eds.), *Fonologia etrusca, fonetica toscana: Il problema del sostrato. Atti della giornata di studi organizzata dal Gruppo archeologico colligiano (Colle di Val d'Elsa, 4 aprile, 1982),* 25–59. Florence: Olschki.

———. 1984. "La sequenza *eiminipicapi* e la negazione in etrusco." *AGI* 69:84–117.

———. 1986. "Sull'etrusco della Stele di Lemno e su alcuni aspetti del consonantismo etrusco." *AGI* 71:15–46.

———. 1992. "Contribution à l'étude de l'épigraphie et de la linguistique étrusques." *Lalies* 11:37–64.

———. 1993. "La considerazione tipologica nello studio dell'etrusco." *InL* 16:23–44.

———. 1994a. "La denominazione del 'vino' in etrusco e nelle altre lingue dell'Italia antica." In Luciano Agostiniani, Maria Giovanna Arcamone, Onofrio Carruba, Fiorella Imparati, and Riccardo Rizza (eds.), *Do-ra-qe pe-re: Studi in memoria di Adriana Quattordio Moreschini*, 1–13. Pisa: Istituti Editoriali e Poligrafici.

———. 1994b. "Per una riconsiderazione dell'iscrizione etrusca della tomba dei Claudii a Caere." In Gabriella Del Lungo Camiciotti, Fiorenza Granucci, Maria Pia Marchese Bastianni, and Rossana Stefanelli (eds.), *Studi in onore di Carlo Alberto Mastrelli: Scritti di allievi e amici fiorentini*, 9–20. Padua: Unipress.

———. 1995. "Sui numerali etruschi e la loro rappresentazione grafica." *AION* 17:21–65.

———. 1997a. "Considerazioni linguistiche su alcuni aspetti della terminologia magistratuale etrusche." In Riccardo Ambrosini, Maria Patrizia Bologna, Filippo Motta, and Chatia Orlandi (eds.), *Scríbthair a ainm n-ogaim: Scritti in memoria di Enrico Campanile*, vol. 1, 1–16. Pisa: Pacini.

———. 1997b. "Sul valore semantico delle formule etrusche *tamera zelarvenas e tamera sarvenas*." In [Amalia Catagnoti et al.] (eds.), *Studi linguistici offerti a Gabriella Giacomelli dagli amici e dagli allievi*, 1–18. Padua: Unipress.

———. 2003. "Aspetti formali e semantici del suffisso di diminutivo *-za* in etrusco." *SE* 69:183–93.

Agostiniani, Luciano, and Francesco Nicosia. 2000. *Tabula Cortonensis*. Rome: Bretschneider.

Agostiniani, Luciano, and Mario Torelli. 2001. "Un cippo confinario etrusco da Cortona." *Archaeologia Perusina* 15:129–39.

Bagnasco Gianni, Giovanna. 1996. *Oggetti iscritti di epoca orientalizzante in Etruria*. Florence: Olschki.

Beekes, R. S. P. 1993. "The position of Etruscan." In Gerhard Meiser (ed.), *Indogermanica et Italica: Festschrift für Helmut Rix zum 65. Geburtstag*, 46–60. Innsbruck: Institut für Sprachwissenschaft der Universität Innsbruck.

Belfiore, Valentina. 2001. "Alcune osservazioni sul verbo etrusco." *AGI* 86:2226–45.

Benelli, Enrico. 1991. "REE 82." *SE* 56:364–6 [tav. LVIII].

——. 1994. *Le iscrizioni bilingui etrusco-latine*. Florence: Olschki.

——. 1998. "L'iscrizione della tomba di Poggio Renzo." *Annali dell'Istituto Universitario Orientale di Napoli*, Sezione filologico-letteraria 5:107–11.

——. 2001. "Quattro nuove iscrizioni arcaiche dall'agro chiusino." *SE* 64: 213–24 [tav. XXXVc–f].

Benveniste, Emile. 1933. "Notes étrusques, I: La tablette d'ivoire de Carthage." *SE* 7:245–9.

Boisson, Claude. 1991. "Note typologique sur le systeme des occlusives en étrusque." *SE* 56:175–81.

Bonfante, Giulio, and Larissa Bonfante. 2002. *The Etruscan Language: An Introduction*. 2nd ed. Manchester: Manchester University Press.

Bonfante, Larissa. 1994. "REE 26." *SE* 59:269–70 [tav. XLVII–XLVIII].

——. 2004. "REE 92a, b: Inscriptions in the University of Pennsylvania Museum." *SE* 70:357–9 [tav. LIX].

Bonfante, Larissa, and Rex Wallace. 2001. "An Etruscan pyxis named *sunθeruza*." *SE* 64:201–12.

Borelli, Federica, and Maria Cristina Targia. 2004. *The Etruscans: Art, Architecture, and History*. Los Angeles: The J. Paul Getty Museum.

Breyer, Gertraud. 1993. *Etruskisches Sprachgut im Lateinischen unter Ausschluss des spezifisch onomastischen Bereiches*. Leuven: Peeters.

Briquel, Dominique. 1989. "A propos d'une inscription redécouverte au Louvre: Remarques sur la tradition relative a Mézence." *REL* 67:78–92.

——. 2002. "REE 19." *SE* 65–68:324 [tav. XXXI].

——. 2003. "An inscribed Etruscan Schnabelkanne in the Museum of Montpellier (France)." *ENews* 3:7, 10.

——. 2004. "L'inscription étrusque de Gouraya (Algerie)." *Annales du Musée National des Antiquités* 14:22–60.

——. 2006a. "A neglected Etruscan inscription." *ENews* 5:5.

——. 2006b. "Etruscan Glosses." *ENews* 6:4–5.

——. 2006c. "Les gloses étrusques." *Res Antiquae* 3:301–18.

Briquel, Dominique, and Christian Landes. 2005. "Une inscription étrusque retrouvée dans les collections de la Société Archéologique de Montpellier." *CRAI* 2005:7–25.

Campbell, Lyle. 2003. "How to show languages are related: Methods for distant genetic relationship." In Brian D. Joseph and Richard D. Janda (eds.), *The Handbook of Historical Linguistics*, 262–82. Oxford: Blackwell.

Carruba, Onofrio. 1974. "Sull'iscrizione etrusca della Tomba dei Claudii." *Athenaeum* 62:301–13.

Colonna, Giovanni. 1972. "REE 80." *SE* 40:463 [tav. LXXXV].

——. 1973–74. "Nomi etruschi di vasi." *ArchClass* 25–26:132–50.

——. 1975. "Firme arcaiche di artefici nell'Italia centrale." *MDAI(R)* 82:181–92.

——. 1976. "Il sistema alfabetico." In *Atti del colloquio sul tema "L'etrusco arcaico" (Firenze, 4-5 ottobre 1974)*, 7–24. Florence: Olschki.

——. 1976–77. "La dea etrusca Cel e i santuari del Trasimeno." *Rivista Storica dell'Antichità* 67:45–62.

——. 1977. "Nome gentilizio e società." *SE* 45:183–9.

——. 1982. "Un'iscrizione da Talamone e l'opposizione presente/passato nel verbo etrusco." *PP* 37:5–11.

——. 1985. "Dalla chimera all'Arringatore." *AMAP* 47:167–86.

——. 1987. "Note preliminari sui culti del santuario di Portonaccio a Veio." *SciAnt* 1:419–46.

——. 1987–88. "REE 126." *SE* 55:345.

——. 1989–90. "Le iscrizioni votive etrusche." *SciAnt* 3-4:875–903.

——. 1991. "REE 42." *SE* 56:326–7 [tav. LXII].

——. 1994a. "REE 45." *SE* 59:294–5.

——. 1994b. "REE 51." *SE* 59:300–302 [tav. LIV].

——. 1997. "L'iscrizione del cratere di Pyrgi con Eracle bevitore." In Adriano Maggiani (ed.), *Vasi Attici Figurati*, 94–98. Rome: Bretschneider.

——. 1999. "L'offerta di armi a Minerva e un probabile cimelio della spedizione di Aristodemo nel Lazio." In Marco Nocca, Tiziana Ceccarini, and Andreina Palombi (eds.), *Dalla vigna al Louvre: Pallade di Velletri. Bicentenario del ritrovamento della Pallade di Velletri 1797-1997*, 95–103. Rome: Palombi.

——. 2002a. "REE 71." *SE* 65-68:351–2, 353–7.

——. 2002b. "REE 73." *SE* 65-68:359–63 [tav. XXXIII].

——. 2002c. "REE 84." *SE* 65-68:385–8 [tav. XXXIV].

——. 2003. "REE 55." *SE* 69:342–7 [tav. XXXI].

——. 2005a. "REE 51." *SE* 70:331–2.

——. 2005b. "REE 89." *SE* 70:357.

Corssen, Wilhelm Paul. 1874–75. *Über die Sprache der Etrusker*. Leipzig: Teubner.

Cristofani, Mauro. 1971. "Sul morfema etrusco -als." *AGI* 56:38–42.

——. 1972a. Review of Rix 1971. *SE* 40:585–9.

——. 1972b. "Sull'origine e la diffusione dell'alfabeto etrusco." *ANRW* I,2: 466–89.

——. 1973a. "Ancora sui morfemi etruschi -ke/-khe." *SE* 41:181–92.

——. 1973b. "L'indicazione dell' 'età' in etrusco." *AGI* 58:157–64.

——. 1974. "Diffusione dell'alfabeto e onomastica arcaica nell'Etruria interna settentrionale." In Paolo Enrico Arias and Massimo Pallottino (eds.), *Aspetti e problemi dell'Etruria interna (Orvieto, 27-30 giugno 1972)*.

VIII Convegno nazionale di studi etruschi e italici, sotto l'alto patrocinio del Presidente della Repubblica, 307–24. Florence: Olschki.

——. 1975a. "Considerazioni su Poggio Civitate (Murlo, Siena)." *Prospettiva* 1:9–19.

——. 1975b. "Il 'dono' nell'Etruria arcaica." *PP* 30:132–52.

——. 1976. "Il sistema onomastico." *Atti del colloquio sul tema "L'etrusco arcaico" (Firenze, 4-5 ottobre 1975)*, 92–109. Florence: Olschki.

——. 1977. "Appunti di epigrafia etrusca arcaica, III: Le iscrizioni di Chiusi." *SE* 45:193–204.

——. 1978a. "L'alfabeto etrusco." In Aldo L. Prosdocimi (ed.), *Popoli e civiltà dell'Italia antica: Lingue e dialetti dell'Italia antica*, vol. 6, 401–28. Rome: Bretscheider.

——. 1978b. "Rapporto sulla diffusione della scrittura nell'Italia antica." *S&C* 2:5–33.

——. 1991a. *Introduzione allo studio dell'etrusco*. 2nd ed. Florence: Olschki.

——. 1991b. "REE 69." *SE* 56:348–9 [tav. LVIII].

——. 1993a. "REE 32." *SE* 58:306–7.

——. 1993b. "Sul processo di antropomorfizzazione nel pantheon etrusco." *Miscellanea Etrusco-Latina* 1:9–21.

——. 1994. "REE 26." *SE* 59:270–1.

——. 1995. *Tabula Capuana: Un calendario festivo di età arcaica*. Florence: Olschki.

——. 1996. *Due testi dell'Italia preromana. 1. Per regna Maricae. 2. Aequipodium Etruscum*. Rome: Consiglio Nazionale delle Ricerche.

Cristofani, Mauro, and Kyle M. Phillips. 1970. "REE (Poggio Civitate, Murlo, Siena) 1–6." *SE* 38:288–92.

Deecke, W. 1875. *Corssen und die Sprache der Etrusker: Eine Kritik*. Stuttgart: Heitz.

De Grummond, Nancy. 2000. "An Etruscan mirror in Tokyo." In M. D. Gentili (ed.), *Aspetti e problemi della produzione degli specchi etruschi figurati: Atti dell'incontro internazionale di studio (Roma, 2-4 maggio 1997)*, 69–77. Rome: Aracne.

de Simone, Carlo. 1970a. *Die griechischen Entlehnungen im Etruskischen*, vol. 2: *Untersuchung*. Wiesbaden: Harrassowitz.

——. 1970b. "I morfemi etruschi -*ce* (-*ke*) e -*χe*." *SE* 38:115–39.

——. 1972. "Per la storia degli imprestiti greci in etrusco." *ANRW* I,2:490–521.

——. 1981. "Gli Etruschi a Roma: Evidenza linguistica e problemi metodologici." In *Gli Etruschi e Roma: Atti dell'incontro di studio in onore di Massimo Pallottino (Roma, 11-13 dicembre 1979)*, 93–103. Rome: Bretschneider.

——. 1985. "L'ermeneutica testuale etrusca oggi: Prospettive e problemi." *AION* 7:23–36.

———. 1986. "La Stele di Lemnos." In Giovanni Pugliese Carratelli (ed.), *Rasenna: Storia e civiltà degli etruschi*, 723–5. Milan: Scheiwiller.

———. 1989a. "L'ermeneutica etrusca oggi." *Atti del Secondo Congresso Nazionale Etrusco (Firenze, 26 maggio–2 giugno 1985)*, 1307–20. Rome: Bretschneider.

———. 1989b. "REE 128." *SE* 55:346–51.

———. 1989c. "Le iscrizioni chiusine arcaiche." In *La civiltà di Chiusi e del suo territorio: Atti del XVII Convegno di studi etruschi e italici, Chianciano Terme, 28 maggio–primo giugno, 1989*, 25–38. Florence: Olschki.

———. 1990a. "Il deittico etrusco *-tra* 'da parte di' (von x her)." *AION* 12:261–70.

———. 1990b. "L'epigrafia etrusca arcaica di Orvieto." *AnnMuseoFaina* 4:75–9.

———. 1991. "REE 45." *SE* 57:276 [tav. L].

———. 1995. "I Tirreni a Lemnos: L'alfabeto." *SE* 60.145–63.

———. 1996a. *I Tirreni a Lemnos: Evidenza linguistica e tradizioni storiche*. Florence: Olschki.

———. 1996b. "Il morpho etrusco *-si*: 'dativo' o 'agentivo'? Questioni di principio." *PP* 51:401–21.

———. 1998a. "Etrusco *mi mulu araθiale θanaχvilus prasanaia*: Due 'attanti'." *SE* 62:311–3.

———. 1998b. "La Tabula Cortonensis: Tra linguistica e storia." *ANSP* 3: 1–122.

———. 2001–02. "Il testo etrusco della Tabula Cortonensis: Un primo bilancio critico." *Ocnus* 9–10:69–11.

———. 2002. "Latino *magister* ('capo') - Etrusco *mastarna - macstrna*: Che ordine di relazione." *RFIC* 130:430–56.

———. 2004a. "La nuova iscrizione etrusca di Pontecagnano: Quali 'attanti dei dono', ed in che senso la più antica menzione (*Rasunie*) del nome degli Etruschi?" *Incidenza dell'Antico* 2:73–96.

———. 2004b. Review of Facchetti 2002a. *Gnomon* 76:496–500.

Devine, Andrew M. 1974. "Etruscan language studies and modern phonology: The problem of the aspirates." *SE* 42.123–51.

Di Gennaro, Francesco. 1991. "REE 42." *SE* 56:325–6 [tav. LXII].

Di Napoli, Andrea. 2002. "REE 71." *SE* 65–68:352–3 [tav. XXXIII].

Eichner, Heiner. 2002. "Etruskisch *-svla* auf der Bronze von Cortona." In Fabrice Cavoto (ed.), *The Linguist's Linguist: A Collection of Papers in Honour of Alexis Manaster Ramer*, 141–52. Munich: LINCOM Europa.

Etruscan Texts Project On-line. Ed. Rex Wallace, David Mimno, James Patterson, and Michael Shamgochian. 2004– . University of Massachusetts Amherst. <http://etp.classics.umass.edu>.

Facchetti, Giulio M. 2000a. *Frammenti di diritto privato etrusco*. Florence: Olschki.

——. 2000b. *L'enigma svelato della lingua etrusca.* Rome: Newton & Compton.

——. 2002a. *Appunti di morfologia etrusca con un'appendice sulla questione della affinità genetiche dell'etrusco.* Florence: Olschki.

——. 2002b. "L'appellativo etrusco *etera.*" *SE* 65–68:225–35.

——. 2002c. "La *Tabula Cortonensis* come documento giuridico." In Maristella Pandolfini and Adriano Maggiani (eds.), *La Tabula Cortonensis e il suo contesto storico-archeologico: Atti dell'incontro di studio, 22 giugno 2001,* 87–92. Rome: Consiglio Nazionale delle Ricerche.

——. 2003. "Note etrusche." *AGI* 88:203–19.

——. 2005. "The interpretation of Etruscan texts and its limits." *JIES* 33: 359–88.

Facchetti, Giulio M., and Koen Wylin. 2001. "Note preliminari sull'aequipondium di Cere." *AION* 23:143–62.

——. 2004. "Nuove letture sull'aequipondium di Caere." *PP* 338:389–96.

Gaultier, Françoise, and Dominique Briquel. 1989. "Réexamen d'une inscription des collections du Musée du Louvre: Un Mézence à Caeré au VIIe siècle av. J.-C." *CRAI* 1989:99–115.

Gaultier, Françoise, J. Gran-Aymerich, and Dominique Briquel. 1991. "REE 73." *SE* 66:350–6 [tav. LXIV].

Giacomelli, Gabriella. 1963. *La lingua falisca.* Florence: Olschki.

Giannecchini, Giulio. 1997. "Un ipotesi sul numerale etrusco per 'dodici'." *PP* 294:190–206.

Guarducci, Margherita. 1967. *Epigrafia Greca,* vol. 1. Rome: Libreria dello Stato.

Hammarström, Magnus. 1930. "Eine archaische etruskische Vaseninschrift." *SE* 4:261–6.

Hartmann, Markus. 2006. *Die frühlateinischen Inschriften und ihre Datierung: Eine linguistisch-archäologisch-paläographische Untersuchung.* Bremen: Hempen.

Heurgon, Jacques. 1957. "Influences grecques sur la religion étrusque: L'inscription de *laris pulenas.*" *REL* 35:106–26.

——. 1989. "Graffite étrusques au J. Paul Getty Museum." *Occasional Papers on Antiquities* 5:181–6 [185–6, no. 3 (fig. 6)].

Hjordt-Vetlesen, Ole. 1994. "REE 17." *SE* 59:254–7 [tav. XLIV].

Holleman, A. W. J. 1984. "Considerations about the Tomb of the Claudians at Cerveteri." *Historia* 33:504–8.

Kaimio, Jorma. 1975. "The ousting of Etruscan by Latin in Etruria." In Patrick Bruun, Paavo Hohti, Jorma Kaimio, Eva Michelsen, Marjatta Nielsen, and Eeva Ruoff-Väänänen, *Studies in the Romanization of Etruria,* 85–245. Rome: Bardi.

Lambrechts, Roger. 1970. *Les inscriptions avec le mot 'tular' et les bornages étrusques.* Florence: Olschki.

Lejeune, Michel. 1966. "Notes sur la ponctuation syllabique du Vénète et de l'étrusque meridionale." *REL* 44:141–64.

———. 1981. "Procédures soustractives dans les numérations étrusque et latine." *BSL* 76:241–8.

MacIntosh [Turfa], Jane. 1982. "The Etruscan and Italic collections in the Manchester Museum." *PBSR* 50:166–93 [p. 183, no. 72].

———. 2005. *Catalogue of the Etruscan Gallery of the University of Pennsylvania Museum of Archaeology and Anthropology.* Philadelphia: University of Pennsylvania Museum of Archaeology and Anthropology.

Maetzke, Guglielmo. 1954. "Tomba con urnetta iscritta trovata in Arezzo." *SE* 23:352–6.

Maggiani, Adriano. 1982. "Qualche osservazione sul fegato di Piacenza." *SE* 50:53–88.

———. 1983. "Le iscrizioni di Asciano e il problema del cosidetto 'm cortonese'." *SE* 50:147–75.

———. 1984. "Iscrizioni iguvine e usi grafici nell'Etruria settentrionale." In Aldo L. Prosdocimi, *Le Tavole Iguvine*, vol. 1, 217–37. Florence: Olschki.

———. 1988. "Il segno *h* a cerchiello: Una riforma grafica in Etruria." *SCO* 38.447–67.

———. 1990. "Alfabeti etruschi di età ellenistica." In *La scrittura nell'Italia antica: Relazioni e comunicazioni nel Convegno del 1985 (Orvieto). AnnMuseo-Faina* 4:177–217.

———. 1996. "Appunti sulle magistrature etrusche." *SE* 62.95–138 [n. 69, p. 136].

———. 1999. "Nuovi etnici e toponimi etruschi." In *Incontro di studi in memoria di Massimo Pallottino*, 51–61. Pisa: Istituto Editoriali e Poligrafici Internazionali [tav. I–II].

———. 2001a. "Dagli archivi dei Cusu: Considerazioni sulla tavola bronzea di Cortona." *Rivista di Archeologia* 25:94–114.

———. 2001b. "Pesi e bilance in Etruria." In C. Corti and N. Giordani (eds.), *Pondera: Pesi e Misure nell'Antichità*, 67–74 [p. 67, 72, n. II.3, fig. 35]. Campogalliano: Museo della Bilancia.

———. 2001c. "REE 19." *SE* 64:344–5.

———. 2001d. "II.B.5.2. Peso." In Anna Maria Moretti Sgubini (ed.), *Veio, Cerveteri, Vulci: Città d'Etruria a confronto. Catalogo della Mostra*, 153 [with photo and facsimile]. Rome: Bretschneider.

———. 2002a. "La libbra etrusca: Sistemi ponderali e monetazione." *SE* 65–68:163–99.

———. 2002b. "REE 15." *SE* 65–68:315–8 [tav. XXXI].

———. 2002c. "Riflessioni sulla Tavola di Cortona." In Maristella Pandolfini and Adriano Maggiani (eds.), *La Tabula Cortonensis e il suo contesto storico-archeologico: Atti dell'incontro di studio, 22 giugno 2001*, 65–75. Rome: Consiglio Nazionale delle Ricerche.

Malzahn, Melanie. 1999. "Das lemnische Alphabet: Eine eigenständige Entwicklung." *SE* 63:283–303.

Maras, Daniele. 2001. "REE 37." *SE* 64:376–7 [tav. XLIV].

———. 2002a. "Appendice II: Le iscrizioni." In Giovanni Colonna (ed.), *Il Santuario di Portonaccio a Veio*, 261–73. Rome: Bretschneider.

———. 2002b. "*Munis turce*: Novità sulla basetta di Manchester." *Atti della Pontificia Accademia Romana di Archeologia* 73:213–38.

———. 2002c. "Note sull'arrivo del nome di Ulisse in Etruria." *SE* 65–68: 237–9.

———. 2003. "REE 26." *SE* 69:316–8 [tav. XXVI].

Martelli, Marina. 1991. "Dedica Ceretana a Hercle." *ArchClass* 42:613–21.

———. 1993. "Un nuovo testo etrusco di dono." *SE* 58:173–6.

Meiser, Gerhard. 1996. "Accessi alla protostoria delle lingue sabelliche." In Loretta Del Tutto Palma (ed.), *La Tavola di Agnone nel contesto italico*, 187–209. Florence: Olschki.

Messineo, Gaetano. 1983. "Tesserae hospitales?" *Xenia* 5:3–4.

Morandi, Alessandro. 2005. "REE 54." *SE* 70:334–5.

Morandi, Massimo. 1990. *Epigrafia di Bolsena etrusca*. Rome: Bretschneider.

Naso, Alessandro. 1994. "REE 22." *SE* 59:263–4 [tav. XLV].

———. 1996. "REE 16." *SE* 61:336–7.

Neppi Modona, Aldo, and Friedhelm Prayon, eds. 1981. *Akten des Kolloquiums zum Thema Die Göttin von Pyrgi: Archäologische, linguistische und religionsgeschichtliche Aspekte (Tübingen, 16-17 Januar 1979)*. Florence: Olschki.

Neu, Erich. 1991. "Etruskisch—eine indogermanische Sprache Altanatoliens?" *HS* 104:9–28.

Nicosia, Francesco. 2002. "Il 'contesto' archeologico della Tavola di Cortona." In Maristella Pandolfini and Adriano Maggiani (eds.), *La Tabula Cortonensis e il suo contesto storico-archeologico: Atti dell'incontro di studio, 22 giugno 2001*, 17–25. Rome: Consiglio Nazionale delle Ricerche.

Nogara, Bartholomeo. 1930. "XVI. Veio—Rivenimento di alcune iscrizioni etrusche durante lo scavo del tempio scoperto in contrada Portonaccio, presso Isola Farnese." *Notizie di Scavi* 302–44 [p. 318, no. 4].

Olzscha, Karl. 1939. *Interpretation der Agramer Mumienbinde*. Leipzig: Dieterich.

———. 1954. "Umbrische Monatsdaten." *Glotta* 33:161–79.

———. 1955. "Götterformeln und Monatsdaten in der großen etruskischen Inschrift von Capua." *Glotta* 34:71–93.

———. 1959. "Die Kalenderdaten der Agramer Mumienbinden." *Aegyptus* 39:340–55.

———. 1970. "Die etruskische Hannibal-Inschrift." *Gymnasium* 77:461–6.

Pallottino, Massimo. 1937. "Nomi etruschi di città." *Scritti in onore di Bartolomeo Nogara raccolti in occasione del suo LXX anno*, 341–58. Rome: Città del Vaticano.

——. 1939. "REE I–Veio, 12." *SE* 13:464–5.

——. 1954. "REE." *SE* 23:399–403.

——. 1966. "REE 1." *SE* 34:355–6.

——. 1968. *Testimonia Linguae Etruscae*. 2nd ed. Florence: Nuova Italia.

——. 1979. "REE 29." *SE* 47:319–25.

——. 1982. "Addendum on inscription no. 72: The Etruscan and Italic collections in the Manchester Museum." *PBSR* 50:193–5.

——. 1986. "I documenti scritti e la lingua." In Massimo Pallottino et al. (eds.), *Rasenna: Storia e civiltà degli Etruschi*, 309–67. Milan: Scheiwiller.

Pandolfini, Maristella. 1993. "REE 1." *SE* 58:275–6 [tav. LXIII].

Pandolfini Angeletti, Maristella. 2000. "Iscrizioni e didascalie degli specchi etruschi: Alcune reflessioni." In M. D. Gentili (ed.), *Aspetti e problemi della produzione degli specchi etruschi figurati: Atti dell'incontro internazionale di studio (Roma, 2–4 maggio 1997)*, 209–24. Rome: Aracne.

Pandolfini, Maristella, and Aldo L. Prosdocimi. 1990. *Alfabetari e insegnamento della scrittura in Etruria e nell'Italia antica*. Florence: Olschki.

Paolucci, Giulio. 1999. "REE 9." *SE* 63:375–6.

——. 2001. "REE 9." *SE* 64:338 [tav. XXXVIII].

Pfiffig, Ambros J. 1967a. "Eine Nennung Hannibals in einer Inschrift des 2. Jahrhunderts v. Ch. aus Tarquinia." *SE* 35:659–63.

——. 1967b. "Hannibal in einer etruskischen Grabinschrift in Tarquinia." *AÖAW* 104.53–61.

——. 1969. *Die etruskische Sprache: Versuch einer Gesamtdarstellung*. Graz: Akademische Druck- und Verlagsanstalt.

——. 1972. *Etruskische Bauinschriften*. Wien: Böhlau.

——. 1974. "Zum Methodenproblem in der etruskischen Sprachwissenschaft." *Kadmos* 13:137–45.

——. 1976. "Einige Bermerkungen zu CIE 6213." In G. Devoto, A. Pagliari, and V. Pisani (eds.), *Scritti in onore di Giuliano Bonfante*, vol. 2, 697–703. Brescia: Paideia.

Pfister, Raimund. 1964. "Etruskische Töpferstempel." *SE* 23:263–74.

Rendeli, Marco. 1994. "Selvans tularia." *SE* 64:163–6.

Ricciardi, Laura. 1993. "REE 21." *SE* 58:290–1 [tav. LXV].

Rix, Helmut. 1957. "REE." *SE* 25:532.

——. 1962. "Ein lokal begrenzter Lautwandel im Etruskischen." *Die Sprache* 8:29–45.

——. 1963. *Das etruskische Cognomen: Untersuchungen zu System, Morphologie und Verwendung der Personennamen auf den jüngeren Inschriften Nordetruriens*. Wiesbaden: Harrassowitz.

——. 1968a. "Eine morphosyntaktische Übereinstimmung zwischen Etruskisch und Lemnisch: Die Datierungsformel." In Manfred Mayrhofer, Fritz Lochner-Hüttenbach, and Hans Schmeia (eds.), *Studien zur Sprachwissenschaft und Kulturkunde: Gedenkschrift für Wilhelm Brandenstein*, 213–22. Innsbruck: Amoe.

——. 1968b. "Zur Ursprung der etruskischen Silbenpunktierung." *MSS* 23: 85–105.

——. 1969. "Buchstabe, Zahlwort und Ziffern im alten Mittelitalien." *Studi linguistici in onore di Vittore Pisani*, vol. 2, 845–56. Brescia: Paideia.

——. 1971. "Die moderne Linguistik und die Beschreibung des Etruskischen." *Kadmos* 10:150–70.

——. 1972. "Zum Ursprung des römisch-mittelitalischen Gentilnamensystems." *ANRW* I,2:702–58.

——. 1976. Review of Carlo De Simone, *Die griechischen Entlehnungen im Etruskischen*, vol. 2 (Wiesbaden: Harrassowitz, 1970). *Kratylos* 21:175–83.

——. 1983. "Norme e variazioni nell'ortografia etrusca." *Atti del Convegno su "I problemi della scrittura e delle normative alfabetiche nel mondo mediterraneo antico" (Napoli, 16–17 febbraio 1983)*. *AION* 5:127–40.

——. 1984a. "Etr. *mex rasnal* = lat. *res publica*." *Studi di antichità in onore di Guglielmo Maetzke*, vol. 2, 455–68. Rome: Bretschneider.

——. 1984b. "La scrittura e la lingua." In Mauro Cristofani (ed.), *Gli Etruschi: Una nuova immagine*, 210–38. Florence: Martello.

——. 1985. "Descrizioni di rituali in etrusco e in italico." In Adriana Quattordio Moreschini (ed.), *L'etrusco e le lingue dell'Italia antica: Atti del Convegno della Società Italiana di Glottologia (Pisa, 8–9 dicembre 1984)*, 21–37. Pisa: Giardini.

——. 1989a. "Per una grammatica storica dell'Etrusco." In *Atti del Secondo congresso internazionale etrusco (Firenze, 26 maggio–2 giugno 1985)*, vol. 3, 1293–1306. Rome: Bretschneider.

——. 1989b. "Zur Morphostruktur des etr. *s*-Genetivs." *SE* 55:169–93.

——. 1991a. "Etrusco *un, une, unu* 'te, tibi, vos' e le preghiere dei rituali paralleli nel Liber linteus." *ArchClass* 43:665–91.

——, ed. 1991b. *Etruskische Texte*. Editio minor. Tübingen: Narr.

——. 1994. *Die Termini der Unfreiheit in den Sprachen Alt-Italiens*. Stuttgart: Steiner.

——. 1995a. "Etruskische Personennamen." In Ernst Eichler, Gerold Hilty, Heinrich Löffler, Hugo Steger, and Ladislav Zgusta (eds.), *Namenforschung: Ein internationales Handbuch zur Onomastik*, vol. 1, 719–24. Berlin: de Gruyter.

——. 1995b. "Il latino e l'etrusco." *Eutopia* 4:73–88.

———. 1995c. "L'etrusco tra l'Italia e il mondo mediterraneo." In Addolorata Landi (ed.), *L'Italia e il Mediterraneo antico: Atti del Convegno della Società Italiana di Glottologia (4-6 novembre 1993)*, 119–38. Pisa: Giardini.

———. 1995d. "REE 14." *SE* 60:242–3 [tav. XXXVII].

———. 1995e. "REE 20." *SE* 60:250–1 [tav. XXXIX].

———. 1997. "Les prières du liber linteus de Zagreb." In Françoise Gaultier and Dominique Briquel (eds.), *Les étrusques: Les plus religieux des hommes. État de la recherche sur la religion étusque. Actes du colloque international (Galeries nationals du Grand Palais, 17-18-19 novembre 1992)*, 391–8. Paris: La Documentation Française.

———. 1998a. *Rätisch und Etruskisch*. Innsbruck: Institut für Sprachwissenschaft der Universität Innsbruck.

———. 1998b. "Teonimi etruschi e teonimi italici." *AnnMuseoFaina* 5:207–29.

———. 2000. "Osservazioni preliminari ad una interpretazione dell'aes cortonense." *InL* 23:11–31.

———. 2002a. "La seconda metà del nuovo testo di Cortona." In Maristella Pandolfini and Adriano Maggiani (eds.), *La Tabula Cortonensis e il suo contesto storico-archeologico: Atti dell'incontro di studio, 22 giugno 2001*, 77–86. Rome: Consiglio Nazionale delle Ricerche.

———. 2002b. *Sabellische Texte: Die Texte des Oskischen, Umbrischen und Südpikenischen*. Heidelberg: Winter.

———. 2004. "Etruscan." In Roger Woodard (ed.), *The Cambridge Encyclopedia of the World's Ancient Languages*, 943–66. Cambridge: Cambridge University Press.

Rizzo, M. A. 2001. "II.D.1.1." In Anna Maria Moretti Sgubini (ed.), *Veio, Cerveteri, Vulci: Città d'Etruria a confronto. Catalogo della Mostra*, 166–7. Rome: Bretschneider.

Rizzo, M. A., and Mauro Cristofani. 1993. "Un kyathos e altri vasi iscritti dalle tombe orientalizzanti di San Paolo a Cerveteri." *BdA* 82:1–10.

Roncalli, Francesco. 1985. "Il liber linteus di Zagabria: Il testo." *Scrivere etrusco*, 24–49. Milan: Electra.

———. 1987. "Sul testo del 'cippo di Perugia'." *SE* 53:161–70.

———. 1990. "La pietra come *instrumentum scriptorium* e il 'cippo di Perugia'." *La scrittura nell'Italia antica: Relazioni e comunicazioni nel convegno del 1985 (Orvieto). AnnMuseoFaina* 4:11–20.

Saladino, Vicenzo. 1971. "REE 14." *SE* 39:344–5 [tav. LXXI].

Sassatelli, Giuseppe. 1993. "REE 8." *SE* 58:284–6 [tav. LXIII].

Scarano Ussani, V., and Mario Torelli. 2002. *La Tabula Cortonensis: Un documento giuridico, storico e sociale*. Napoli: Loffredo.

Schirmer, Brigitte. 1993. "I verbi etruschi *mul(u)vanice* e *tur(u)ce*: Prolegomena per una determinazione di semantica ed impiego." *PP* 48:38–56.

Schulze-Thulin, Britta. 1992. "Zur Wortstellung im Etruskischen." *SE* 58: 177–95.

Schumacher, Stefan. 1992. *Die rätischen Inschriften: Geschichte und heutiger Stand der Forschung.* Innsbruck: Institut für Sprachwissenschaft der Universität Innsbruck.

———. 1998. "Sprachliche Gemeinsamkeiten zwischen Rätisch und Etruskisch." *Der Schlern* 72:90–114.

Sordi, Marta. 1991. "Laris Felsnas e la resistenza di Casilino." *SE* 56:123–5.

Steinbauer, Dieter. 1993. "Etruskisch-ostitalische Lehnbeziehungen." In Helmut Rix (ed.), *Oskisch-Umbrisch: Texte und Grammatik. Arbeitstagung der Indogermanischen Gesellschaft und der Società Italiana di Glottologia vom 25. bis 28. September 1991 in Freiburg,* 287–306. Wiesbaden: Reichert.

———. 1999. *Neues Handbuch des Etruskischen.* St. Katherinen: Scripta Mercaturae.

Stutzinger, Dagmar. 1995. "REE 20." *SE* 60:249 [tav. XXXIX].

Tamburini, Pietro. 1991. "REE 35." *SE* 57:264–5 [tav. XLVI].

Vanoni, Lucia Cavagnaro. 1962. "REE 2." *SE* 30:294 [tav. XXII, 1].

———. 1965a. "REE 1." *SE* 33:472–3 [tav. CIVa].

———. 1965b. "REE 5." *SE* 33:511.

Vetter, Emil. 1955–56. "Zu der Kriegerstele von Vetulonia." *SE* 24:301–10.

Vilucchi, Silvia. 2001. "REE 19." *SE* 64:342–3 [tav. XL].

Wachter, Rudolf. 1986. "Die etruskische und venetische Silbenpunktierung." *MH* 43:111–26.

Wallace, Rex. 1991. "The transcription of sibilants in Etruscan: A new proposal." *Glotta* 69:77–83.

———. 1996. "Etruscan inscriptions on an Attic kylix in the J. Paul Getty Museum: Addenda et Corrigenda." ZPE 111:291–4 [tav. IX].

———. 2006. "Notes on an inscribed *kyathos* from Cerveteri." *ENews* 6:4.

———. 2007. "Etruscan inscriptions on fragments of bucchero *kyathoi* recovered at Poggio Civitate." *SE* 72:189–97.

———. To appear. "Etruscan inscriptions on ivory objects recovered from the orientalizing period residence at Poggio Civitate (Murlo)." *Etruscan Studies* 11.

Watmough, Margaret. 1997. *Studies in Etruscan Loanwords in Latin.* Florence: Olschki.

Wylin, Koen. 2000. *Il verbo etrusco: Ricerca morfosintattica delle forme usate in funzione verbale.* Rome: Bretschneider.

———. 2001. "REE 115." *SE* 64:447–9 [tav. LIII].

———. 2002a. "Forme verbali nella Tabula Cortonensis." *SE* 65–68:215–23.

———. 2002b. "I morphemi -(a)θ e -(u)c/χ nei termini delle magistrature etrusche." *AGI* 87:88–108.

———. 2004. "Un morfema agentivo etrusco." *AGI* 89:111–27.

——. 2005. "Un terzo pronome/aggettivo dimostrativo: Etrusco *sa*." *SE* 70: 213–25.

——. 2006. "The first chapter of the Cortona inscription." *ENews* 5:6–7.

Woudhuizen, Fred C. 1991. "Etruscan and Luwian." *JIES* 19:133–50.

Zavaroni, Adolfo. 2002. "Sulla presunta sibilante palatale in etrusco." *InL* 25:87–102.

ETRUSCAN TEXT INDEX

This index lists all the Etruscan texts that are reproduced or cited. Texts referred to by their ETP number are given first, followed by those referred to by their number in ET. References are to chapter number followed by section number (separated by a dot) or inscription/example number (in parentheses). A "T" after an inscription number in chapter 10 refers to the commentary accompanying the inscription. Thus 10.2 means chapter 10, section 2; 10(2) means chapter 10, inscription (2); and 10(2)T means the commentary following inscription (2). Some references are to figure numbers.

WORD INDEX

This index is a list of all word-forms, personal names, place-names, and theonyms found in the inscriptions cited in the text. Words are listed following the order of letters in the Etruscan alphabet. Words whose initial letters are missing and cannot be restored are cited at the end of the alphabet. Except for the *Tabula Cortonensis*, words are cited by chapter and example number. Thus the reference 1.1a refers to Chapter 1, example 1a. For the *Tabula Cortonensis*, which is an opisthograph, we follow the chapter (Chapter 11) with the line number and the side of the bronze on which the word-form appears, e.g. 11.16B = Chapter 11, line 16, side B. Reference information is located at the end of each entry. If a word-form appears more than once within the same inscription, then the number of occurrences is indicated in parentheses at the end of the reference. Enclitic forms are listed as separate entries. If the reading of a word-form is conjectural in any way or has been restored by an editor, then that word-form is cited after the reference number in the index, e.g. amce 'was', PAST ACT (6.8, 8.16 aṃce, 8.5, 10.13). Languages included in the index are: Etruscan, Faliscan, Greek, Latin, Lemnian, Oscan, and Raetic.

Etruscan

ac '?' 10.61

acazrce '?', PAST ACT 8.19

acil '(is) necessary', NOM/ACC 8.42

acil 'work, product (?)', NOM/ACC 10.73, 10.74

acilθ = acil '(is) necessary', NOM/ACC + -θ '?', ENCLITIC PARTICLE 8.45b

acnaice 'made (?)', PAST ACT 10.20a

acnanas 'having given birth to', NAS-PART 8.51, 10.13, 10.29

acnanasa 'having produced', NASA-PART 6.11c, 8.52 (2×)

avil 'year', NOM/ACC 6.11a, 8.21, 8.33b, 10.10, 10.15

avils 'year', 1ST GEN 6.8, 6.11b, 7.12, 7.16, 7.17, 7.20, 7.33a, 8.20, 8.33a, 8.43a, 8.45a, 8.46, 8.51, 10.13, 10.14, 10.29

aisece '?', PAST ACT 10.86

aiser 'gods', ANIM PL, NOM/ACC 10.76

ala 'donate', JUSSIVE 10.53

aliqu 'donated, presented', U-PART 6.7b, 8.8b, 12.11a

alpan 'thank offering (?)', NOM/ACC 8.12, 10.56, 10.61

alpnina '?' 10.53

amce 'was', PAST ACT 6.8, 8.16 aṃce, 8.51, 10.13

ame 'is', NON-PAST ACT 5.3, 8.10, 8.30, 8.45b, 11.15A, 11.19A

an 'who', ANIM REL PRON, NOM/ACC 6.4a, 8.26a, 8.29, 10.27

anc = an 'who', REL PRO, NOM + -c '?', ENCLITIC CONJ (?) 8.11a

apac = apa 'father', NOM/ACC + -c 'and', ENCLITIC CONJ 10.26

apana 'paternal', NOM/ACC 10.54

apasi 'father', 1ST PERT 6.10

.a.pirase 'April', LOC 8.41

aprenσaiσ '?' 10.85

ara 'put, place; make', JUSSIVE 5.12, 10.47

arce 'constructed, made', PAST ACT 5.8, 6.11c, 8.52, 10.29

atic = ati 'mother', NOM/ACC + -c 'and', ENCLITIC CONJ 10.26

atial 'mother', 2ND GEN 10.52, 10.62

.a.ṡu '?', NOM/ACC 10.37b

c, abbrev. of clan 'son', NOM/ACC 7.7, 10.85 (4×)

247

-um 'and', ENCLITIC CONJ 7.20 (2×), 8.45a
    (2×), 8.50, 11.7A
une 'for you (?)', 2ND PERS PRO, PERT (?)
    or 'for him (?)', 3RD PERS PRO, PERT (?)
    5.2
une 'for you (?)', 2ND PERS PRO, PERT (?)
    5.3
ųtta '?' 10.61

φerśnaχś '?' 10.1
φurθce '?', PAST ACT 10.27
φ[- - - -]na '?', NOM/ACC 10.82

-χ 'and', ENCLITIC CONJ 8.45b
χape 'take', IMPV 10.45
χuliχna 'vessel', NOM/ACC 8.39

fanu 'determined (?)', U-PART 8.50
faσei 'libation', LOC 6.12b, 8.14
faσena 'libation vessel', NOM/ACC 8.4.a
farθnaχe 'was born', PAST PASS 8.11a
fler 'victim, sacrificial victim', NOM/ACC
    5.2, 6.6, 8.13b, 8.27c
flere 'divine spirit, divinity', NOM/ACC
    5.2, 8.37
flereσ 'divine spirit, divinity', 1ST GEN
    6.3, 8.2
flerθrce '?', PAST ACT 1.5, 8.49
fratuce 'incised (?)', PAST ACT 11.21A
frontac 'of lightning', NOM/ACC 10.25

[- - -]e '?' 8.15

Personal Names

a, abbrev. of aule 'Aule', MASC PRAE,
    NOM/ACC 10.24
a, abbrev. of auleσ 'Aule', MASC PRAE, GEN
    10.24
acnatrualc = acnatrual 'Acnatrui', FEM
    NOMEN, 2ND GEN + -c 'and', ENCLITIC
    CONJ 7.17
ae, abbrev. of avle 'Aule', MASC PRAE,
    NOM/ACC 10.72
av, abbrev. of avle 'Aule', MASC PRAE,
    NOM/ACC 7.7
av, abbrev. of avles 'Aule', MASC PRAE,
    1ST GEN 7.7
aveleσ 'Avile', MASC PRAE, 1ST GEN 10.1
aveles 'Avele', MASC PRAE, 1ST GEN 7.32b,
    10.3
avenalc = avenal 'Avenai', FEM NOMEN,
    2ND GEN + -c 'and', ENCLITIC CONJ 5.8
aveσ 'Aves', MASC NOMEN, 1ST GEN 11.14A
[avi]le 'Avile', MASC PRAE, NOM/ACC 10.48
avil[eσ] 'Avile', MASC PRAE, 1ST GEN or
    avil[e] 'Avile', MASC PRAE, NOM/ACC
    10.80
avle 'Aule', MASC PRAE, NOM/ACC 6.4b,
    6.10 av[le], 7.5, 8.4b, 8.13a, 8.32,
    10.26, 10.54
aθ, abbrev. of arnθ 'Arnth', MASC PRAE,
    NOM/ACC 7.25, 7.34b, 10.85 (3×)
aθ, abbrev. of arnθal 'Arnth', MASC PRAE,
    2ND GEN 7.2, 7.3, 7.15

aleθnas 'Alethnas', MASC NOMEN, 1ST GEN
    6.10 [al]eθnas, 6.11c, 7.18 aleθnas,
    8.16 [al]ęθnas, 8.52
.a.l.θ.r.na.s. 'Althrnas', MASC NOMEN, 1ST
    GEN 8.39
aṃ[- - -] '?' 10.6
anaσnieσ 'Anasnie', MASC PRAE, 1ST GEN
    10.8
[a]ncinie.š. 'Ancinies', MASC NOMEN, 1ST
    GEN 10.69
ane 'Ane', MASC PRAE, NOM/ACC 10.20a
aneσ 'Ane', MASC PRAE, 1ST GEN 10.20b
anes MASC PRAE, 1ST GEN 8.26b
anti{:}pater 'Antipater', MASC NAME,
    NOM/ACC 7.21
apatrual 'Apatrui', FEM NOMEN, 2ND GEN
    6.11b
apenas 'Apenas', MASC NOMEN, 1ST GEN
    7.32a
apnal 'Apnei', FEM NOMEN, 2ND GEN 11.7B
aprθn[al]c = aprθn[al] 'Aprthnei', FEM
    NOMEN, 2ND GEN + -c 'and', ENCLITIC
    CONJ 8.19
ạpunas 'Apunas', MASC NOMEN, 1ST GEN
    8.21
apunaς 'Apunas', MASC NOMEN, 1ST GEN
    8.11b
araz 'Araz', MASC PRAE, NOM/ACC 10.81
araθiale 'Ara(n)th', MASC PRAE, 2ND PERT
    6.5a, 8.7b, 8.9

larθialiśvle = larθial 'Larth', MASC PRAE,
2ND GEN + -iśvle 'the', DEF ART, PL, 2ND
PERT 8.25

larθiia 'Larth', MASC NOMEN, 2ND GEN
10.41

larices 'Larice', MASC PRAE, 1ST GEN 1.3b,
8.34, 8.21

larizac = lariza 'Lariza', MASC PRAE,
NOM/ACC + -c 'and', ENCLITIC CONJ
11.16A

laris 'Laris', MASC PRAE, NOM/ACC 1.1a,
6.4b, 8.22, 8.32, 10.12, 10.26, 10.27,
10.52

lariś 'Larish', MASC PRAE, NOM/ACC 11.9A,
11.15A, 11.24A ḷ[a]riś, 11.29A

lariśa 'Larish', MASC PRAE, 2ND GEN 10.6

lariça 'Laris', MASC PRAE, 1ST GEN 8.35

larisal 'Laris', MASC PRAE, 2ND GEN 1.1a,
6.4a, 6.4b, 7.17, 8.16, 8.32, 10.12,
10.26

lariśal 'Larish', MASC PRAE, 2ND GEN
11.15A, 11.16A

lariśalc = lariśal 'Laris', MASC PRAE, 2ND
GEN + -c 'and', ENCLITIC CONJ 11.3B,
11.7B

larisale 'Laris', MASC PRAE, 2ND PERT 8.8a

larisalióa 'Laris', MASC PRAE, 2ND GEN +
-ióa 'the', DEF ART, NOM 6.11a, 8.26a,
10.10

larisalióla = laris 'Laris', MASC PRAE, 2ND
GEN + -ióla 'the', DEF ART, 2ND GEN 8.24

ḷariśaliśa = ḷariśal 'Larish', MASC PRAE,
2ND GEN + -iśa 'the', DEF ART, NOM
11.16A

lariśaliśvla = lariśal 'Larish', MASC PRAE,
2ND GEN + -iśvla 'the', DEF ART, 2ND
GEN 5.10, 11.3A, 11.21–22A

lariśc = lariś 'Larish', MASC PRAE, NOM/ACC
+ -c 'and', ENCLITIC CONJ 11.32A

lar{n}θ 'Larth', MASC PRAE, NOM/ACC 7.27,
10.23

lart 'Lart', MASC PRAE, NOM/ACC 5.6, 11.8A,
11.9A, 11.10A (2×), 11.23A, 11.26A,
11.30A

lartiu 'Lartiu', MASC PRAE, NOM/ACC 7.1

lartle 'Lartle', MASC NOMEN, NOM/ACC
11.14A

laru 'Laru', MASC PRAE, NOM/ACC 11.13A

laruσ 'Laru', MASC PRAE, 1ST GEN 10.8

latini 'Latini', FEM NOMEN, NOM/ACC 7.35

laucies 'Laucies', MASC NOMEN, 1ST GEN
10.5

laucies 'Laucies', MASC PRAE, 1ST GEN
10.32

lauśa 'Lausha', MASC COGN, NOM/ACC
11.24–25A

lauśiśa 'Laushisha' MASC COGN, NOM/ACC
11.23A

lauχumeśa = lauχumeσ 'Laukhume',
MASC PRAE, 1ST GEN + -śa 'the', DEF
ART, NOM 10.4

leθaie 'Lethaie', MASC PRAE, NOM/ACC
10.68

leθes 'Lethe', MASC PRAE, 1ST GEN 10.15

leịnies 'Leinies', MASC NOMEN, 1ST GEN
7.20, 8.45a

lemnióa = lemni 'Lemni', FEM NOMEN, 1ST
GEN (?) + -óa 'the', DEF ART, NOM 10.11

lθ, abbrev. of larθ 'Larth', MASC PRAE,
NOM/ACC 7.2, 10.85 (3×)

lθ, abbrev. of larθal 'Larth', MASC PRAE,
2ND GEN 10.85 (4×)

ḷi, abbrev. of laris 'Laris', MASC PRAE,
NOM/ACC 7.6

liceneśi 'Licene', MASC PRAE, 1ST PERT
6.7a

limu.r.ce.s. 'Limurce', MASC PRAE, 1ST GEN
8.27a

lr, abbrev. of laris 'Laris', MASC PRAE,
NOM/ACC 10.25

lr, abbrev. of larisal 'Laris', MASC PRAE,
2ND GEN 10.25

lś, abbrev. of lariś 'Larish', MASC PRAE,
NOM/ACC 10.85 (2×)

lucer 'Lucer', MASC PRAE, NOM/ACC 8.33b

ḷuvχmsal 'Luvkhmes', MASC NOMEN, 2ND
GEN 10.61

luiśna 'Luishna', MASC NOMEN, NOM/ACC
11.12A

luśce 'Lushce', MASC COGN, NOM/ACC
11.9A, 11.13A

luścni 'Luscni', MASC NOMEN, NOM/ACC
11.25A

maclae 'Maclae', MASC NOMEN, NOM/ACC
7.4

mamarce 'Mamarce', MASC PRAE,
NOM/ACC 1.1h

turials{c} 'Turi', FEM NOMEN, 1ST ABL
8.11a

turis 'Turis', NOM/ACC 5.3

turmna 'Turmna', MASC NOMEN, NOM/ACC
11.26A

tutes 'Tutes', MASC NOMEN, 1ST GEN 7.33b,
8.11a

tuteis 'Tutes', MASC NOMEN, 1ST ABL 8.11a

tutnaśa = tutnaσ 'Tutna', MASC NOMEN,
1ST GEN + -śa 'the', DEF ART, NOM 7.35

uθraσ 'Uthra', MASC NOMEN, 1ST GEN
10.84

uθuzteθs 'of Odysseus', NOM/ACC 10.66b

ultimnial 'Ultimni', FEM NOMEN, 2ND GEN
7.35

ulχniśla = ulχniσ- 'Ulkhni', MASC NOMEN,
1ST GEN + -śla 'the', DEF ART, 2ND GEN
8.18

unatn, abbrev. of unatnal 'Unatnei',
FEM NOMEN, 2ND GEN 7.3

uślna 'Ushlna', MASC NOMEN, NOM/ACC
11.13A

uślnal 'Ushlnei', FEM NOMEN, 2ND GEN
11.30A, 11.32A uślna[l]

utaves 'Utave', MASC NOMEN, 1ST GEN
10.56

utaš 'Utas', MASC NOMEN, 1ST GEN 8.55

.ś.lapina.ś. 'Slapinas', MASC NOMEN, 1ST
GEN 10.44

φisis 'Phisi', MASC NOMEN, 1ST GEN 7.28

χurcles 'Khurcles', MASC NOMEN, 1ST GEN
6.8

χurχles 'Khurkhles', MASC NOMEN, 1ST
GEN 8.20 (2×)

fanacnal 'Fanacnei', FEM NOMEN, 2ND GEN
8.12

fastntru 'Fastntru', MASC COGN, NOM/ACC
7.15

feḷeśkẹnaσ 'Feleshkena', MASC NOMEN,
1ST GEN 10.6

fêlσni 'Fêlsni', MASC NOMEN, NOM/ACC
11.12A

felsnas 'Felsnas', MASC NOMEN, 1ST GEN
10.15

feluśkeσ 'Felushke', MASC NOMEN, 1ST GEN
10.1

fl, abbrev. of flavia 'Flavia', FEM PRAE,
NOM/ACC 8.18

flavienas 'Flavienas', MASC NOMEN, 1ST
GEN 7.31a

fuln[- - -] 'Fuln[- - -]', MASC NOMEN,
NOM/ACC 11.29A

fulnial 'Fulni', FEM NOMEN, 2ND GEN 8.46

fulu.ó.la = fulus 'Fulu', MASC PRAE, 1ST
GEN + -.ó.la 'the', DEF ART, 2ND GEN
1.1c

fufle 'Fufle', MASC COGN, NOM/ACC 7.34b

[- - -]aninalc = [- - -]aninal '?', FEM
NOMEN, 2ND GEN + -c 'and', ENCLITIC
CONJ 11.29A

[- - -]pnal '?', FEM NOMEN, 2ND GEN
11.27A

[- - -]uσ '?', 1ST GEN 11.31–32A

City and Place Names

capue 'in Capua', CITY NAME, LOC 10.15

enaσ 'Ena (?)', CITY NAME (?), 1ST GEN
6.12a, 8.17, 8.44

velclθi = velcl 'Velca', CITY NAME, 2ND GEN
+ -θi 'in', POST 10.42

vipśl 'Vipsa', CITY NAME, 2ND GEN 10.77

kamarṭeθi = kamarṭe 'Kamarta', CITY
NAME, LOC + -θi 'in', POST 10.5

perśie 'Pershia (Perusia)', CITY NAME, LOC
8.13a

tarśminaσσ 'Trasimene', PLACE NAME, 1ST
GEN (?) 11.4B

ṭarχnalθi = ṭarχnal 'Tarkhna', CITY NAME,
2ND GEN + -θi 'in', POST 8.16

tlenaχeiσ 'Tlenakhe', PLACE NAME (?), 1ST
ABL 8.12

χiśulicσ 'Khishuli', PLACE NAME (?), 1ST
ABL 6.3

Theonyms and Theonymic Epithets

aiθas 'Aitha', THEO, 1ST GEN 10.87
aχrum 'Acheron', THEO, NOM/ACC 1.5, 8.49
aχuiaσ 'Akhuia', THEO EPITHET, 1ST GEN 8.13a

[cav]aθas 'Cavatha', THEO, 1ST GEN 10.46
caθas 'Catha', THEO, 1ST GEN 10.52
canlas 'Canla', THEO EPITHET, 1ST GEN 10.60
celσ 'Cel', THEO, 1ST GEN 10.62
clẓ 'Cel', THEO, 1ST GEN 8.18

espial 'Espi', THEO, 2ND GEN 10.52

hercle 'Hercle', THEO, NOM/ACC 8.47
hercles 'Hercle', THEO, 1ST GEN 10.53, 10.56, 10.61
hercle.s. 'Hercle', THEO, 1ST GEN 10.51b
huinθnaias '?', THEO EPITHET, 1ST GEN 10.55

θuflθaσ 'Thufltha', THEO, 1ST GEN 8.12
θuflθas 'Thufltha', THEO, 1ST GEN 8.5, 10.57
θuσuθur 'Thusu gods (?)', THEO, ANIM PL, NOM/ACC 10.86

kavθaσ 'Kautha', THEO, 1ST GEN 8.13a

leθa.m.su.l 'Lethams', THEO, 2ND GEN 8.41
lurmicla = lurmi '?', NOM/ACC + -cla 'the', DEM PRO, 2ND GEN 10.58
luśaσ 'Lusha', THEO, 1ST GEN 6.6, 8.13b, 8.27c

matrnσl 'Matrns', THEO, 2ND GEN 8.2

men[er]avas 'Minerva', THEO, 1ST GEN 10.48
menervas 'Menerva', THEO, 1ST GEN 1.1f
menrvas 'Minerva', THEO, 1ST GEN 10.50

neθunσl 'Nethuns', THEO, 2ND GEN 8.37
neθunsl 'Nethuns', THEO, 2ND GEN 5.2

óeθlans 'Shethlans', THEO, NOM/ACC 10.88
raθs 'Rath', THEO, 1ST GEN 10.61

sanχuneta = sanχuna 'of Sankhu', THEO EPITHET, NOM/ACC + -ita 'the', DEM PRO, NOM/ACC 8.28
selvans 'Selvans', THEO, NOM/ACC 8.28
selvansl 'Selvans', THEO, 2ND GEN 10.54, 10.60
sil<v>anẓ 'Selvans', THEO, NOM/ACC 10.76

tece śanσl 'Tece Shans', THEO, 2ND GEN 6.3
tetanuσ 'Tetanu', THEO EPITHET, 1ST GEN 8.18
ti[- - -] '?', THEO (?) 10.76
tinas 'Tinia', THEO, 1ST GEN 1.1e, 8.3
tinia 'Tinia', THEO, NOM/ACC 10.76
tinσ 'Tinia', 1ST GEN 10.79
trepu 'Trepu', NOM/ACC 10.88
turmsal 'Turms', THEO, 2ND GEN 10.61
turns 'Turan', THEO, 1ST GEN 12.10a

uni 'Uni', THEO, NOM/ACC 10.88
unial 'Uni', THEO, 2ND GEN 8.47, 10.55

fuflunusra 'of Fufluns', NOM/ACC 10.59

[- - -]s '?' 10.51a

Faliscan

eqo 'I', 1ST PERS PRO, NOM SG 1.3a

quton{e} 'wine pitcher', NOM SG 1.3a

Personal Names

uo<l>tenosio 'Voltenos', MASC PRAE, GEN SG 1.3a

Greek

εἰμι 'I am', 1ST SG PRES ACT 1.4b

ποτεριον 'cup', NEUT NOM SG 1.4b

Personal Names

θαριο 'Tharios', MASC NAME, GEN SG 1.4b

Latin

ECO 'I', 1ST PERS PRO, NOM SG 1.3a

F, abbrev. of FILIUS 'son', MASC NOM SG
    10.24, 10.25

L, abbrev. of LIBERTUS 'freedman', MASC
    NOM SG 7.20 (2×), 10.23

FULGURIATOR 'interpreter', MASC NOM SG
    10.25

HARUSPE[X] 'haruspex', MASC NOM SG

10.25

POM, abbrev. of POMPTINA 'Pomptina',
    FEM ABL SG 10.24

POPA 'priest's assistant', MASC NOM SG
    10.23

STE, abbrev. for STELLATINA 'Stellatina',
    FEM ABL SG 10.25

URNA 'urn', FEM NOM SG 1.3a

Personal Names

A, abbrev. of AULI 'Aulus', MASC PRAE, GEN
    SG 10.24

[CA]FATIUS 'Cafatius', MASC NOMEN, NOM SG
    10.25

CN, abbrev. of CNAEUS, 'Gnaeus', MASC
    PRAE, NOM SG 10.24

L, abbrev. of LUCIUS 'Lucius', MASC PRAE,
    NOM SG 7.27, 7.28, 10.23, 10.25 [L]

L, abbrev. of LUCI 'Lucius', MASC PRAE,
    GEN SG 7.28, 10.25

LABERIUS 'Laberius', MASC NOMEN,

NOM SG 10.24

PHISIUS 'Phisius', MASC NOMEN, NOM SG
    7.28

SCARPIAE 'Scarpia', FEM NOMEN, GEN SG
    7.27, 10.23

SCARPIUS 'Scarpius', MASC NOMEN, NOM SG
    7.27, 10.23

TITA<S> 'Tita', FEM PRAE, GEN SG 1.3a

UCL[ES] 'Ucles', MASC NOMEN, NOM SG 7.28

VENDIAS 'Vendia', FEM NOMEN, GEN SG 1.3a

Lemnian

avis 'year', 1ST GEN 12.4A/B

avi:s 'year', 1ST GEN 12.4A

aomai '?', PAST ACT (?) 12.4B

arai '?', PAST ACT (?) 12.4B

eviόθo '?' 12.4A/B

-θ 'in', POST 12.4A/B

-m 'and, but', ENCLITIC CONJ 12.4B

mav 'five', NUM, NOM/ACC 12.4A

maras '?' 12.4A

marasm = maras '?' + -m 'and/but', EN-
    CLITIC CONJ 12.4B

morinail '?', 2ND GEN 12.4A

ναφoθ '?' 12.1A

όialχvei:s 'forty', NUM, 1ST GEN 12.4A

όialχvis 'forty', NUM, 1ST GEN 12.4B

seronai '?', LOC 12.4A

seronaiθ '?', LOC + -θ 'in', POST 12.4A/B

siasi '?' 12.4A

sivai 'lived (?)', PAST ACT (?) 12.4A/B

tis '?' 12.4B

toverona['?' 12.4B

Personal Names

aker 'Aker', NOM/ACC 12.4A
vanalaóial 'Vanalash', 2ND GEN 12.4A
eptesio 'Eptesio', NOM/ACC 12.4B
haralio 'Haralio', NOM/ACC 12.4B
holaies 'Holaie', 1ST GEN 12.4A

holaiesi 'Holaie', 1ST PERT 12.4B
tavarsio 'Tarvasio', NOM/ACC 12.4A
φoke 'Phoke', NOM/ACC 12.4B
φokiaóiale 'Phokiash', 2ND PERT 12.4B

Oscan

culchna 'drinking cup', FEM NOM SG 1.4a

sim 'I am', 1ST SG PRES ACT 1.4a

Personal Names

vipiieis 'Vibis', MASC PRAE, GEN SG 1.4a

veliieis 'Veliis', MASC NOMEN, GEN SG 1.4a

Raetic

eluku 'offered (?)', U-PART 12.11c1,
    12.11e
zinake 'dedicated', PAST ACT 12.10b

ii[ir] '?' 12.11e
utiku 'given (?)', U-PART 12.11d

Personal Names

karapaśna 'Karapashna', NOM/ACC
    12.11c2
laspasi 'Laspa', 1ST PERT 12.11e
piθale 'Pithale', NOM/ACC 12.10b
pitamnux[- 'Pitamnu' (?), 12.11e

slepile 'Slepile', 2ND PERT 12.11c1
φelipuriesi 'Phelipurie', 1ST PERT
    12.11c1
φeluriesi 'Phelurie', 1ST PERT 12.11d
φelvinuale 'Phelvinu', 2ND PERT 12.11d

Theonyms

lemais 'Lemai', THEO (?), 1ST GEN 12.10b

GENERAL INDEX

This index lists subjects, authors, and words discussed. Items are cited by chapter number and section number separated by a period. Items from Chapter 10 that appear in the commentaries to inscriptions are cited with the inscription number in parentheses. Thus the reference 10.4 refers to Chapter 10, section 4, whereas 10(4) refers to the commentary to inscription (4) in Chapter 10. Items from Chapter 11, section 6 include references to subsections in parentheses. The reference 11.6 (III.1.1) is to Chapter 11, section 6, subsection III.1.1.

Olzscha, Karl, 1.8.1, 1.13.1, 10(15)
Oscan, 1.13, 7.4

palatalization, 3.5
Pallottino, Massimo, 1.10.1, 1.11.1,
    9.20.1, 10(15), 10(24), 10(44), 10(53),
    10(81)
Pandolfini (Angeletti), Maristella, 2.1.1,
    2.5.1, 10(41), 10(43)
Paolucci, Giulio, 10(4)
participles, 6.12, 8.24; u-formation,
    6.13; as-formation, 6.14; θ-
    formation, 6.15
patronymic, 7.1, 7.4–7.5, 7.15
paχie, 9.17
persona, 9.12
pertinentive case, 4.11, 4.13, 7.21,
    8.5–8.6; 1st pertinentive, 4.13; 2nd
    pertinentive, 4.13
Perusia, 3.5, 3.17, 3.25
Pfiffig, Ambros J., 1.11.1, 5.7.1, 10(15),
    10.4.1, 10(26)
Pfister, Raimund, 10(75)
φersu, 9.12
Phillips, Kyle M., 10(80)
picture bilingual, 1.14
Piombo di Magliano, 1.8.c, 1.8.1
place-names, 9.20–9.22
plural, nouns 4.18–4.21
postpositions, 4.14, 8.9
praenomen, 7.1, 7.3–7.4, 7.9–7.10
Prayon, Friedhelm, 1.8.1
prohibitions, 1.7, 8.21, 10.6
pronouns, distinctive characteristics,
    5.1; personal, 5.3–5.4; demonstra-
    tive, 5.5–5.8, 8.14–8.15, indefinite ,
    5.11; interrogative , 5.11
proprietary inscriptions, 1.7, 1.13, 10.5
Prosdocimi, Aldo L., 2.1.1, 2.5.1
puinel, 10(82)
punctuation, 2.20–2.22
pupluna, pupfluna, pufluna, 9.22
putlumza, 9.9
Pyrgi Tablets, 1.8.h, 1.8.1

quton, 9.15

Raetic, 1.15, 12.9–12.15
rasna, 9.3

regional alphabets, 2.6
regional differences in writing,
    2.10–2.19, 3.5, 3.10, 3.14, 11.4
relative pronoun, 5.11, 8.16
Rendeli, Marco, 10(54)
retrograde epsilon, 2.19, 3.10, 11.4
Ricciardi, Laura, 10(39)
Rix, Helmut, 1.7.1, 1.8.1, 1.11.1, 1.13.1,
    2.8.1, 2.17.1, 2.21.1, 3.3.1, 3.5.1, 3.6.1,
    3.9.1, 3.20.1, 3.27.1, 4.3.1, 4.29.1,
    4.32.1, 5.2.1, 5.4.1, 5.9.1, 5.11.1, 6.1.1,
    6.4.1, 7.1.1, 7.5.1, 7.14.1, 7.18.1, 8.1.1,
    8.10.1, 8.13.1, 8.18.1, 8.23.1, 8.24.1,
    9.3.1, 9.10.1, 9.12.1, 9.13.1, 9.16.1,
    10(19), 10(23), 10(71), 10(82), 11.6.1,
    11.6 (II.2.1), 12.7.1, 12.9.1, 12.10.1
Rizzo, M. A., 10(64)
Roncalli, Francesco, 1.8.1
root(s) of words, 4.4, 6.3–6.4

Sabellic languages, 7.28; borrowings
    from, 3.17, 7.28, 9.8, 9.17, 9.18, 9.19
Saladino, Vicenzo, 10(28)
Sanskrit, 12.3
Sassatelli, Giuseppe, 10(38)
satelles, 9.13
Scarano Ussani, V., 11.6.1
Schirmer, Brigitte, 10.8.1
Schulze-Thulin, Britta, 8.25.1
Schumacher, Stefan, 12.10.1
sibilants, 2.12–2.13, 3.6
Siena, 3.27
snuiaφ, snuiuφ, 4.28
Sordi, Marta, 10(15)
sound correspondences, 12.2
South Picene, 7.4, 7.28
sporta, 9.14
spurianas, 10(81)
spurina, 3.20
spurta, 9.14
Steinbauer, Dieter, 1.8.1, 3.3.1, 3.5.1,
    4.3.1, 5.2.1, 6.1.1, 8.1.1, 8.10.1, 9.8.1,
    10(9), 10(15), 10(18), 10(23), 10(24),
    10(25), 10(26), 10(27), 10(31), 10(37),
    10(49), 10(54), 10(55), 10(58), 10(60),
    10(62), 10(79), 10(85), 10(88)
stem(s) of words, 4.3–4.6, 4.9, 6.3–6.4
Stutzinger, Dagmar, 10(71)
subordination, syntax of, 8.23